Bound to Please

Dress, Body, Culture

Series Editor **Joanne B. Eicher,** *Regents' Professor, University of Minnesota*

Books in this provocative series seek to articulate the connections between culture and dress which is defined here in its broadest possible sense as any modification or supplement to the body. Interdisciplinary in approach, the series highlights the dialogue between identity and dress, cosmetics, coiffure, and body alterations as manifested in practices as varied as plastic surgery, tattooing, and ritual scarification. The series aims, in particular, to analyse the meaning of dress in relation to popular culture and gender issues and will include works grounded in anthropology, sociology, history, art history, literature, and folklore.

ISSN: 1360-466X

Previously published titles in the Series

Bound to Please

A History of the Victorian Corset

Leigh Summers

Oxford • New York

First published in 2001 by
Berg
Editorial offices:
150 Cowley Road, Oxford, OX4 1JJ, UK
838 Broadway, Third Floor, New York, NY 10003-4812, USA

Berg is an imprint of Oxford International Publishers Ltd.

Library of Congress Cataloging-in-Publication Data
Summers, Leigh.
    Bound to please : a history of the Victorian corset / Leigh Summers.
        p. cm. -- (Dress, body, culture, ISSN 1360-466x)
Includes bibliographical references and index.
    ISBN 1-85973-530-4 (cloth) -- ISBN 1-85973-530-4 (pbk.)
    1. Corsets.   2. Body, Human--Social aspects.   3. Costume--History--19th century.   I. Title.
II. Series.
    GT2075 .S85 2001
    391.4'2--dc21
                                                                        2001004390

British Library Cataloguing-in-Publication Data
A catalogue record for this book is available from the British Library.

ISBN   1 85973 530 4 (Cloth)
       1 85973 510 X (Paper)

Typeset by JS Typesetting, Wellingborough, Northants.
Printed in the United Kingdom by Biddles Ltd, Guildford and King's Lynn.

Contents

Acknowledgements

This book would not have been published without enormous help from many people. Dr Joy Damousi and Dr Vera Mackie supervised this project in its doctoral incarnation. Both offered unstinting intellectual support and practical advice tempered by extraordinary patience. Friends (many of them colleagues at the University of Melbourne) provided me with enduring encouragement. Mandy Treagus was instrumental in the completion of this work. Both Rose Kitching and Renate Turrini insisted during bleak moments of insecurity, that Victorian corsetry *was* a legitimate subject of research. Kathryn Earle of Berg Publishers agreed. I am very grateful for her enthusiasm and advice. Rosie Boehm, friend and talented photographer, was critical in reproducing nineteenth-century photographs under exceptionally trying circumstances. I am indebted too, to Bob Track, whom I know only via email, who located and generously supplied me with the exceptional Worcestor Corset images, including photographs of the Worcesteor Factory and its staff, used in this book.

My children, Justine, Rowan, Lockie and David believed I would complete this project, one day. *Bound to Please* is for them, and is dedicated to the memory of my Mother.

Introduction

The private, lived, female experience of corsetry was (and still is) rarely documented. Henry Handel Richardson offers the historian a rare and realistic description of the 'post'-corset body in her splendid short story, titled 'The Bathe; A Grotesque'. The story reveals the terror of a small child whose aunts abandon their knitting to swim naked with her at a secluded beach.

> The tide was out. [wrote Richardson] Dare we risk it? Lets. [said the aunts.] Tight high bodices of countless buttons went first, baring massy arms and fat creased necks of maturity. Thereafter bunchy skirts were slid over hips and stepped out of. Several petticoats followed, the undermost of red flannel, with scalloped edges. Tight stiff corsets were next squeezed from their moorings and cast aside: the linen beneath lay hot and damply crushed. Long white drawers were unbound and leg by leg disengaged, voluminous calico chemises appeared, draped in which the pair sat down to remove their boots – button boots and stockings, their feet emerging red and tired looking . . . Erect again they yet coyly hesitated before casting off the last veil, once more sweeping the distance for a

possible spy ... [then] inch by inch, calves, thighs, trunks and breasts were bared to view ... Above their knees garters had cut fierce red lines in their skin; their bodies were criss-crossed with red furrows, from the variety of strings and bones that had lashed them in. The calves of one showed purple knotted with veins; across the other's abdomen ran a deep longitudinal scar.[1]

Susan Brownmiller noted that 'no discussion of the feminine body in the western world can make real sense without getting a grip on the corset' for it has played a 'starring role in the [female] body's history'.[2] Little has been written to redress this situation since Brownmiller's observation. Despite the cruel reality of fierce red lines and deep furrows carved into women's bodies by 'strings and bones that lashed them in', the contemporary corset discourse continues to reflect the 'public' face of corsetry drawn from quaint advertisements and pornography. While a deluge of material exists that trivializes or sensationalizes the corset in simplistic sexual terms, there has been no sustained feminist criticism of the corset's role in constructing and enforcing the private realm of womanhood. The corset remains profoundly under-theorized, though it is potentially the most illuminating icon of the Victorian era, heavily pregnant with feminine metaphors and associations, unavoidably steeped in and expressive of Victorian female sexuality and its subordination.

The object of the corset was, as British sexologist Havelock Ellis observed, to 'furnish woman with a method of heightening at once her two chief secondary sexual characteristics, the bosom above and the hips and buttocks below'.[3] However, the process of levering the breasts to an appropriate angle and directing the gaze to the accentuated waist and hips exacted on the female body a severe toll not acknowledged by Ellis. The corset's morphic mandate was actually twofold. The accentuation of the secondary sexual characteristics necessitated the obliteration of any evidence of the ribcage, which, by the prevailing aesthetic standards of Victorian femininity, spoiled the illusion of a perfectly tapering torso. The corset was also commissioned to reduce the waist's 'clumsy' somewhat kidney-shaped form and constrict it (ideally) to a tiny symmetrical circle. These ideals were attempted, and often achieved, by corsets of a cage-and-harness-like construction. Most corsets consisted of either a metal or a whalebone and metal framework, encased in sturdy cloth (figure 1). Strong laces, threaded through metal eyelets, were used to tighten the corset over the ribcage and waist (figure 2). Busks added to the torment. Busks were removable panels of steel or bone, usually found in front-fastening corsets. Busks were originally made of wood.[4] They sat directly behind the opening of the corset and ran its whole length. Occasionally two busks were worn to effect real 'firmness and stability'.[5] (see figures 3 and 4).

Not surprisingly the corset attracted considerable attention from the medical profession, but it was also the site of heated public debates that

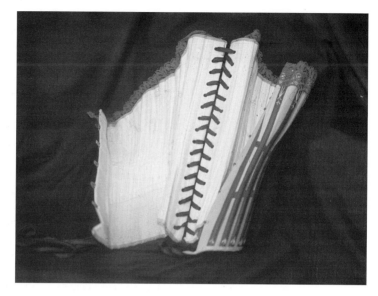

Figure 1
Corset (c 1890) opened to show construction. Note vertical boning and horizontal cording over the abdomen for extra reinforcement. (Courtesy of Mrs Beth Catford, Costume Gallery, Oraroo.)

spoke in veiled terms of cultural anxieties surrounding female sexuality. The corset operated as a multi-functional discursive device, simultaneously offering masculine critics a safe platform to discuss dangerous sexual issues, while ingeniously providing a vehicle to shape and control female sexuality. This book will explore the ways in which the corset operated to construct, define and reinforce women's understanding of themselves as women, as sexual beings, and as women in relationship to men and wider society. It will also examine the role of the corset in

Figure 2
Detail of metal eyelets. The inclusion of metal rather than hand or machine sewn eyelets prevented tearing of the garment when tightly laced. (Courtesy of Migration Museum, Adelaide.)

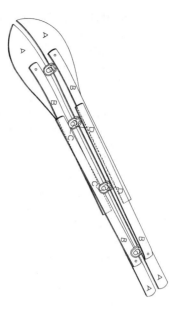

Figure 3
Busk patent lodged by William
Cooper and George Gather in
1898. The designers claimed
that their invention comprised
of 'comparatively thin blades
riveted near each end' made
the busk both 'strong and
unbreakable.' The busk
measured about 18" in length
and was 4" at its widest point.

constructing an appropriate Victorian middle-class femininity. Victorian
femininity was a complex aesthetic, characterized (in large part) by the
successful development of a subjectivity that obeyed a rigid code of moral
as well as sartorial maxims which mutually and intimately inflected each
other. Corsetry was a critical tool in this process. Few garments other
than the corset could claim such an intimate, influential and popular place
in the material culture of Victorian womanhood. The corset was (for many
women) a lifetime companion, fitted in early childhood and worn until

Figure 4
Detail of busk c 1890. Width of
the busk is 4"

death. It was, of course, altered somewhat in puberty, frequently adapted and maintained through maternity, and worn into old age. Its constancy was perhaps eclipsed only by the multiplicity of its physical, social and moral functions. It acted, as one (unnamed) nineteenth-century commentator observed, as 'evidence of a well disciplined mind and well regulated feelings'.[6] Stays were, as their name suggests, designed to make unruly female flesh 'stay put'[7] and in doing so were also thought to arrest the potentially unruly and recalcitrant female mind.

Bound to Please explores the ways corsetry influenced and (to a greater or lesser extent) controlled the bodies and minds of Victorian middle-class women. It demonstrates the crucial role of corsetry in the processes of constructing, as well as articulating, an appropriate Victorian femininity. Unlike previous research involving the corset, my work problematizes the garment, but also offers a sustained examination of corsetry's role in women's lives, to unveil why it remained so popular, despite its discomforts and at times, its dangers. These objectives have been achieved by providing a historical context for the garment, using (where possible) the language of women's experience to describe the way corsetry was implemented and the effects of its implementation. A range of sources has been used to substantiate my claims. Mid- to late-nineteenth-century magazines, medical journals, dress reform and feminist texts, along with corset-related ephemera, have been fundamental to my research. The close examination of hundreds of corsets in British museums has been crucial in realizing the formidable role of material culture in constructing Victorian womanhood. Although this text draws from American as well as British sources, it is predominantly set in a British context. American material has been used to point to similarities rather than differences in the corset-wearing behaviours of women in each country. That is, American material has been used chiefly to *flag*, rather than *compare*, overarching sartorial trends and corporeal issues common to many middle-class Victorian women, regardless of their geographic location.

The intention of this book is, further, to identify and tease out the ways that corsetry oppressed women, physically and emotionally. This is not to imply that Victorian women were hapless, passive victims of corsetry, unaware of its significance in patriarchal constructions of sexuality. As Susan Mendus, Jane Rendell[8] Martha Vicinus[9] and more recently Carol Smart and Lucy Bland[10] have pointed out, Victorian women were not 'quintessential cultural dupes of patriarchy', but were agents in the construction of their own (sexual) subjectivity. Evidence of this exists in the historical record. Nineteenth-century feminists in both America and England enthusiastically and successfully challenged issues surrounding sexuality, principally age of consent and contagious disease legislation. Similarly in both the private and the public spheres, women who understood the sexual politics of corsetry resisted it specifically because of its role in female objectification.

More frequent, however, were the objections to corsetry on 'rational' grounds, these being that corsetry was uncomfortable, restrictive and dangerous to bodily well-being. Nevertheless many Victorian women wore corsets, despite the personal experience of their discomfort and knowledge of the garment's role in sexual objectification. While such compliance appears to confound the notion of Victorian female agency, the popularity of corsetry suggests that it held a range of important meanings for women that have not yet been acknowledged or understood by twentieth-century historians. The garment's ubiquity might indicate that it provided women with a culturally sanctioned eroticism in an era of competing sexual discourses that denoted female sexuality as either negligible[11] or demonic.[12]

There is some disagreement regarding how many women and from what social class actually wore corsets. Historian Edward Shorter, author of *A History of Women's Bodies*, claims that the 'endless attention' paid to the corset by historians is misplaced because 'very few' women wore them.[13] Fashion historians overwhelmingly disagree, though none has discussed the importance of corsetry to working-class women at any length. My work teases out some of the issues that made a 'good tornure' indispensable to women across the class divide and outlines the considerable role working-class women had in the construction and sale of the garment. Standard costume texts support my claim that corsetry was in popular use by working class as well as middle-class women.

Chapter Two examines the dual role of corsetry (of both maternal and standard design) in supporting, as well as disguising, the pregnant Victorian body. Madam Caplin's 'self regulating gestation corset' with elastic dilatable support promised to 'answer all phases of pregnancy' at mid-century.[14] By the 1870s the use of less sympathetic maternity corsetry was commonplace. Both the tightly laced 'standard' and specially designed maternal corset exerted tremendous pressure on the abdomen and pelvic basin, and were, according to numerous primary sources, responsible for miscarriage and high infant-mortality rates. Despite the existence of stringent pregnancy taboos, many Victorian women were aware of the dangers corsetry presented to the foetus, and on occasion capitalized on the corset's ability to produce abortions without recourse to 'physic'.

In the early decades of the nineteenth century the corset was (ostensibly at least) employed to 'support the frame and protect the body from the weight of the under-clothes',[15] a notion which did not entirely decline over the course of the nineteenth century. However the corset's function expanded significantly between 1850 and 1900 to encompass a wide range of physical and moral parameters. To the corset devolved the manifold and complex tasks of developing gender-specific attributes while denying and/ or repressing sexual desire in the women and girls who wore it. The corset's role in gender maintenance and its use in the regulation of juvenile female sexuality are discussed in Chapter Three.

Chapter Four investigates the prevalence of, and attitudes toward, acute and long-term illnesses caused by corsetry. Victorian 'female complaints' have on occasion been thought to have arisen from psychological, rather than physiological, origins. This chapter argues that many female complaints were (to a greater or lesser extent) caused by corsetry. Nineteenth-century medical discourses, as well as feminist and popular writings, have been used to establish the corset's relationship to a plethora of ailments, labelled loosely by the medical profession and women themselves as 'female complaints'.

Paradoxically, corsetry operated as a powerful and multi-faceted signifier of both transgressive and normative femininity. This contradiction worked to secure, rather than diminish, the garment's appeal. The corset was instrumental in achieving the 'socially desirable morbidity of nineteenth-century tastes in female beauty' which, Barbara Ehrenreich and Dierdre English argue, always lies close to the surface of sexual romanticism.[16] Chapter Five establishes the importance of tightly fitted corsetry in the cultivation of 'morbid' female beauty. Tightly laced corsetry allowed women to provoke or enact physical symptoms that betokened female ill health and even death, events that were frequently celebrated in Victorian art, music and literature.

Chapter Six discusses the serious threat to the corset industry posed by Victorian and Edwardian women's escalating interest in sport, and more particularly, the rising female involvement in gymnastics from mid-to late century. Feminists, dress reformers, and enlightened doctors who urged women to abandon corsetry while playing sport, clearly had a serious impact on corset sales. Market forces were quick to respond to plummeting profits. Corset manufacturers promptly produced a range of garments ostensibly designed for women who engaged in all kinds of sporting and even gymnastic activities. This chapter also discusses the emergence of the strengthened female body as a feminine ideal, and the hostility this engendered from critics who claimed it was unnatural, masculine and freakish.

The sheer number of corsetry advertisements published between 1860 and 1900 indicates that corsetry was a vigorous and thriving industry, despite occasional challenges. A close reading of corsetry advertisements yields much more than useful empirical information. Chapter Seven examines the ways in which corsetry advertising made women's bodies accessible to Victorian society, and the ways in which these advertisements ill-served their subjects. It also suggests that lesbians may have appropriated and undermined the dominant readings in corset illustrations.

As the nineteenth century unfolded, the corset and female sexuality became inextricably entwined, a process which reached its apogee in the 1890s with the emergence of a specific pornographic genre concerned with sadomasochistic tight lacing. The increased sexualization of the occupant, the garment, and the erotic conflation of both object and woman, was a slow and irregular process that took decades to complete, but was successful none the less. By the 1880s the pubescent child, the maid, the young woman, the matron, the grandmother, the prostitute, and the subject of the pornographer alike were marked as sexual by the garment, for it simultaneously evoked the entire continuum of sexual stereotypes from chaste innocence to erotic perversion. In other words, corsetry operated at all ages and all stages of women's lives, to create a body that was appropriately modest and virginal, yet sexually alluring. While *Bound to Please* acknowledges that some Victorian women consciously resisted the enormous societal impetus to corset their bodies, it maintains that most women complied with societal dictates to corset themselves and their female children. Further to this it argues that corsetry was a powerful coercive apparatus in the control of Victorian women, and that it was subsequently instrumental, indeed crucial, in the maintenance of Victorian hetero-patriachal dominance.

1

'Elegance, Comfort, Durability!' Class, Contours, and Corsetry

While *Bound to Please* primarily examines the ways in which corsetry operated to construct, maintain and police *middle-class* femininity, it is important in an exercise of this kind to redress three widely held gender- and class-associated misconceptions. The first of these is that nineteenth-century working-class women went uncorseted. The second is that middle-class women had corsetry imposed upon them by a fashion system in which they were cultural dupes, and thirdly, that the design and manufacture of corsetry was entirely the province of men. All charges, I would suggest, need to be challenged.

Women from working and middle classes wore corsetry, both classes were implicated in its production and both groups resisted and manipulated the societal compulsion to corset. Corsetry was essential, not just in constructing femininity, but in constructing a class-based identity and subjectivity. Corsetry was prized by fashion-conscious, middle-class women because it crafted the flesh into class-appropriate contours. That is, corsetry operated to hide any 'coarse' abdominal bulges from view, while it smoothed the hips and created the small, circular (rather than oval shaped) waistline that supposedly denoted good breeding. The well-corseted body, in tandem with suitable clothing, gave an immediate first impression of gentility. It operated, to the distress of many middle-class women, in exactly the same way for their working-class sisters. When successfully corseted and carefully clothed, the working-class woman 'improved' her physical appearance and consequently her chances of securing an 'upwardly mobile' marriage. However, while both groups used corsets for class-specific reasons, the use of the garment by working-class and middle-class women was subtly different. These differences resulted in tensions that were propelled and underpinned by a kind of feminine 'competition'. Middle-class women, as we shall see, used corsetry to strengthen and protect their class hegemony, while working-class women corseted (in part) to obfuscate or escape their working-class origins with the hope of entering the world of their 'betters'.

It has often been suggested that working-class women eschewed corsetry altogether, or alternately donned the garments just on Sundays and special occasions.[1] This may have been true for some women; however, the extant material culture along with numerous primary source textual references indicates that many working-class women wore corsetry as frequently as middle-class women. Working-class women bought, were given, or made corsets, believing as their middle-class sisters did, that corsetry supported the body and made the figure trim. By 1847 Mayhew's *The Greatest Plague Of Life; Or The Adventures Of A Lady in Search of a Good Servant by 'One Who Has Almost Been Worried to Death'* made clear that corsetry was an established and disconcerting item of British working-class feminine attire. The text's chief protagonist who had 'almost been worried to death' in search of a good servant, despaired that

> an excellent *tournure* [could] be had for so little money, that even one's maid-servants [could] walk into any corsetmakers and buy a figure, fit for a lady of the highest respectability, for a mere trifle.[2]

By 1849, texts such as *The Family Economist*, a penny magazine that proclaimed its devotion to 'the moral, physical and domestic improvement of the industrious classes', warned its female readers against the common practice of tight lacing, insisting as many other magazines did, that the practice would indubitably result in a 'red nose'.[3] Stays, corsets, or jumps as they were variously known, were an important part of the wardrobe of women across the social classes. Jumps were the popular choice of working-class women in the early part of the century. Jumps were designed to fit more loosely than standard corsets, which allowed the occupant enough mobility to work. The oft-cited lines regarding their use, being 'Now a shape in neat stays, now a slattern in jumps' drew its censure from the way women wore the garments.[4] When worn loosely, as they generally were, they indicated working-class activities involving menial labour. A tightly laced appearance created by more constrictive corsetry signified that unlike the 'slattern in jumps' the occupant was above physical work. As complaints by the mistress in *The Greatest Plague of Life* demonstrate, the availability of affordable, tightly fitting, professionally made stays in the early part of the century blurred, or at least threatened, corporeal class distinctions based on tightly bound, corseted, respectability.

Working-class women who could not afford even the cheapest of professionally made corsets did not necessarily have to go without them. They could make their own. The plethora of dressmaking and millinery texts published in the 1830s and 1840s, which provided detailed advice on how to make stays, can be seen to indicate the importance the garment held for working-class women. Materials required to make the garments, including whalebone pre-cut into suitable lengths, the sturdy base fabric called buckram, and the required corsetry thread called staysilk, were all commonly available from haberdashers. So too were the strong, specially designed needles used to stitch the garments together, called *between* needles. Numerous basic household texts patiently explained the processes of the corset's construction. While the 1838 edition of *The Workwoman's Guide* did not include actual patterns for corsetry, it suggested that women 'purchase a pair [ready made] from an experienced staymaker that fit[ted] perfectly well' along with an extra pair that had not been sewn up. These, explained *The Workwoman's Guide*, provided a 'good pattern for the home made stays'.[5] Other texts, such as *The Young Woman's Guide Containing Correct Rules for the Pursuit of Millinery, Dress and Corset Making*, included very detailed instructions along with 'Illustrated . . . Lithographic Plans With Many Useful Remarks to Young Women and Servants' who chose to make their own stays.[6]

The industrialization of the corset industry later in the century meant that working-class women had even more opportunities to purchase rather than make their corsetry. However, despite the economic democratization of corsetry, a few women from both the working and middle classes still preferred to make their own garments. The home pattern service published in *The Young English Woman*, a magazine concerned with romance, fashion and to a lesser degree, female employment, occasionally published descriptions and drawings of corsetry which could be made at home for children and 'young' ladies (Figures 5 and 6). These appear to have been far less constrictive than commercially manufactured garments of the time.[7] *Harper's Bazaar* routinely published both detailed illustrations and instructions for making both juvenile and adult corsetry throughout the century[8]. Despite the ease potentially afforded by home-made corsets, the popularity of manufactured garments increased dramatically in the latter half of the century.[9] This process was undoubtedly assisted by the use of advertising. However, while advertising must have been a significant aspect in the demise of the self-made corset, its decreasing popularity was probably due to the superior strength of the manufactured variety and the promises such strength held for women

561.—GIRL'S CHEMISE.

562.—CORSET FOR YOUNG LADY.

563.—DRAWERS FOR YOUNG LADY.

564.—CORSET FOR CHILDREN.

566.—BOY'S NIGHT SHIRT.——*Paper Pattern*, 1s.

567.—UNDER BODICE.

565.—CORSET FOR YOUNG LADY.

568.—UNDER BODICE.

569.—DRAWERS FOR LITTLE GIRL.

570.—CORSET FOR YOUNG LADY.

571.—DRAWERS FOR LITTLE GIRL.

anxious to improve their body shape. The invention of metal eyelets in 1823 was, conceivably, a turning point in corset manufacture, for their inclusion meant that corsets could be laced very tightly without the eyelets tearing open. As a consequence, the mid-century 'store-bought' heavily reinforced corset, complete with metal eyelets riveted into the fabric, furnished a tighter fit and would therefore have more successfully created the sought-after sculpted figure for both working- and middle-class women.

Several major firms whose corset advertisements were actually directed to a middle-class clientele also disclosed that they produced garments for working-class women. On occasion, advertising for these corsets encouraged the idea that their purchase could transform the lives of working-class women to that which approximated the lives of their better-off sisters. Advertisements placed by the William Pretty and Sons corset company claimed that when their garments were worn the occupant would 'look a better woman, [would] feel a better woman [and would] be a better woman'.[10] Advertisements placed by the British corsetry firm R & W. H. Symington were a little subtler though they made similar promises. Symington made a corset called 'The Pretty Housemaid' that was obviously destined for use by the socially aspiring working-class

Figure 5
The *Young Englishwoman* published pattern pages that on occasion promoted corsetry for children as well as young ladies and adult women. See *The Young Englishwoman*, 1875, p.583.

Figure 6
Pattern Service offered to readers of *Queen*, occasionally offered patterns for corsetry. The garments in this illustration were described as 'black satin sewn with black silk.' The garment at left features lacing 'below the waist.' Both garments required considerable needlework skills. See *Queen*, 1880.

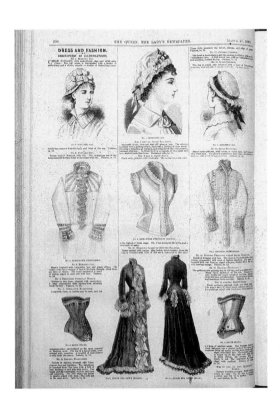

woman. The Pretty Housemaid corset was, according to the packaging, the 'strongest and cheapest [corset] ever made'.[11] The box that contained the garment was decorated with a coloured lithograph of a cheerful, shapely, uniformed domestic servant, admiring her figure in her mistress's mirror. Implicit in this diagram was the notion that the garment moulded the body of the servant into a shape that replicated, mirrored or even excelled the comeliness of her middle-class employer.

Standard corsets such as the Pretty Housemaid were extremely affordable.[12] The price ranges advertised in corset leaflets and handbills indicate that corsetry began at very modest prices.[13] The cost of corsets rose steeply when luxurious fabrics and trims were employed. The use of fleece to line the top and bottom of garments to reduce chafing added to their cost, as did the addition of fine ribbons and rich lace.[14] More prosaic designs destined to encompass the working-class body, such as Brown's Patent Dermathistic corset, were less glamorous. The Dermathistic featured 'bones, busks and steels protected by leather' and ranged from a mere five shillings and eleven pence to ten shillings and sixpence. The utilitarian leather infrastructure of the garment was aesthetically modified and improved by a trim of dainty but inexpensive lace.[15] Similar price ranges designed to accommodate working-class incomes operated in the United States. The American-based Duplex corset company produced a range of garments at various prices. Their one-dollar corsets were, no doubt, produced to contain the working-class torso, while those at six dollars were designed for better-off clients.[16] Despite the disparity in price between the expensive and inexpensive garments, the latter were also trimmed with finery of a lesser quality, which furnished an attractive 'feminine' look that in some cases compared favourably with that of more costly garments (Figures 7 and 8).

Figure 7
Detail of machine lace trim threaded with brown silk ribbon. The decorative flossing is of brown and cream silk.

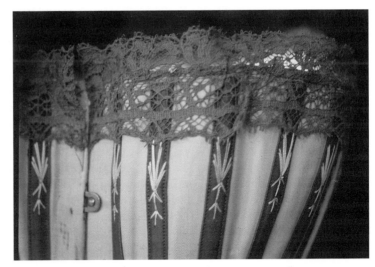

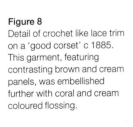

Figure 8
Detail of crochet like lace trim
on a 'good corset' c 1885.
This garment, featuring
contrasting brown and cream
panels, was embellished
further with coral and cream
coloured flossing.

On occasion, working-class women had access to the extravagant corsetry of their betters. Vigorous corset sales in both England and America indicate that middle-class women probably renewed their corsets as newer models were introduced onto the market, rather than waiting for the old garments to wear out. Instead of throwing these garments away, their owners sometimes handed them on to employees. Indeed, claims that the 'dress of the master of one generation may survive as that of the servant in the next' are borne out when discussing the corset-wearing habits of domestic servants.[17] Paradoxically, domestic servants who were in receipt of these garments were often scolded for attempting to dress above their station. The hostile reaction from middle-class women regarding the corseted state of working-class women, reveals the challenges to class that resulted from the accessibility and popularity of the ready-made corset. Conservative women's magazines in the late nineteenth century that defended corsetry for middle-class women, often dwelled on its supposed misuse by working-class employees. *Woman* magazine, which consistently defended corsetry for middle-class readers, claimed that opponents of corsetry could give

> no malady or death rate statistics directly connected with the wearing of corsets pure and simple, [that were not based on] some silly anaemic maidservant or stage struck barmaid with heart disease [who tried] to reduce her podgy frame to an unbearable girth.[18]

So great was the purview and popularity of corsetry that unfortunate working-class women incarcerated in prisons or asylums could not escape its reach, even if they had wanted to. Whether in the social isolation of the prison, the workhouse, or the asylum, few women could divorce themselves from the class hierarchy that was associated with, and surrounded, the corset. According to F.B. Smith's text, *The People's Health 1830–1910*, corsetry, in places where guardians permitted it, was usually bought by contract and then inmates were made to fit the small range of sizes ordered by the institutions.[19] George Roberts, who operated a successful stay warehouse in London, noted in his catalogue produced for distribution at England's Great Exhibition of 1851, that 'contracts for schools and charitable institutions' would be promptly filled at wholesale prices.[20] Several firms in America produced corsetry designed specifically for women and girls in institutions. Corsets displayed at the Great International Trade Exhibition in Philadelphia in 1876 were described in a catalogue as 'among the articles most in use among the working classes, penal establishments and the establishments of beneficiaries'.[21]

Institutional corsets worn by female inmates of prisons, asylums and poorhouses were, even in comparison with the cheapest ready-made garments, uncompromisingly ugly. They had little in common with corsets produced for aspiring working-class and established middle-class women. The Symington museum in Leicestershire has a fine example of institutional corsetry.[22] Though constructed on stalwart principles similar to those of most manufactured garments, Symington's institutional corsetry differed markedly from those garments in that it was made of a hard-wearing, unattractive fabric in a colour known as drab, which is a kind of dull khaki. Institutional corsets were devoid of any trims whatsoever, and were laced at the back and buckled down the front, closing much like an old-fashioned school satchel. While as heavily boned as standard corsets, they do not appear to have been designed to allow tight lacing. This would have allowed the occupant enough mobility to work. Paradoxically, while this design was intrinsically better from a health standpoint, it meant that incarcerated women would have found it impossible to lace their bodies into a shape that enhanced their self-esteem. Indeed, incarcerated corseted working-class women experienced a demeaning double-bind while contained in these garments. Many inmates probably wore these corsets under trying physical conditions, believing that the garments assisted their bodies. However such rudimentary corsets would also have operated to remind these women of their reduced or expunged femininity and their seemingly inescapable criminal-class status. They may have operated, psychologically at least, as an extension of their incarceration.

Corsetry also worked to mark and reinforce class parameters for middle-class women in a similar, but far more positive way. Middle-class women, especially those in 'foreign' lands, may have either consciously or unconsciously considered corsetry to be an ideological ally. Corsetry is a significant, if under-researched, aspect of the (respectable) working- and middle-class colonial project. Women who left England and America, either to settle or temporarily evangelize in India, Africa, Japan, Australia and the Pacific, took corsetry with them. In some cases this corsetry was specially designed to lessen the effect of tropical heat on the body.[23] The Perforated Gossamer Corset was specifically designed for those women who, for whatever reasons, were in tropical climates at mid-century.[24] The English corset company Dickens and Jones (a subsidiary of the department store that bore that name) increased its fortunes by manufacturing corsetry for the colonies. The beautifully illustrated Specialite corset advertisements published by that company claimed that the Specialite led 'the way all the world over, to woman's greatest ambition – a good figure'. The advertisement featured a corseted sylph with crown, wings and petticoats, hovering beside and above planet earth. From her munificent hands fell a bunch of ribbons whose ends lay across the empire. At the end of each ribbon was a cluster of women, almost naked but for their corsets. Their eloquent thanks to Dickens and Jones were printed on each ribbon.[25] The advertisement claimed that Dickens and Jones held many hundreds of unsolicited testimonials from all over the globe that showered them with thanks (Figure 9).

Of course whether Dickins and Jones were in receipt of such testimonials is debatable. However, what is certain from reading an assortment of texts is that corsetry was an essential aspect of Victorian femininity across class lines, and in some cases, across the empire. Corset advertisements were as familiar to readers of the *Sydney Mail*[26] or even the far-flung working- and middle-class readers of the *Queensland Figaro*, as they were to cosmopolitan English readers.[27] Despite its appearance in remote corners of the empire, corsetry remained largely a 'Western' phenomenon and did not appear to have seriously threatened traditional hegemonic dress. Japanese magazines publicly lampooned and seriously criticized corsetry in the 1880s as an 'unreasonable demand of fashion'.[28] Indeed Japanese and other non-European women appear to have been among corsetry's most resistant subjects. Frances E. Russell, a staunch opponent of corsetry, noted that although there were 'no better missionaries than American women', the 'Japanese in their loose drapery and Sandwich Islanders in their motherhubbards look[ed] with amusement or contempt upon the corsets of the Christians'.[29]

While corsetry must have been a hot and cumbersome (and even publicly ridiculed) item of apparel in tropical climates, it may have been considered absolutely indispensable to many isolated European women who were far away from home and 'genteel' society. A correspondent for *The Domestic Economist* (published in 1850) reported that many British women in India were 'voluntary victims of fashion' or *living holocausts* offered at the shrines of vanity and bad taste' specifically because they clung tenaciously to garments designed for European climates. Few women in England, wrote the author, could 'conceive the discomfort, in many cases of absolute suffering that [was] undergone by many of their own sex in the East, who clothed themselves as they do in

Figure 9
Dicken's and Jones sturdy
courtil corsetry supposedly
supported those women of the
Empire who enjoyed cycling,
riding, rowing and tennis.

Europe'. Wearing corsetry in the 'East', continued the author, was 'the
height of absurdity . . . it [was] prejudicial to health and kept the body in
an absolute vapour bath'. Vanity, according the article, was the reason
why so many women refused to acknowledge the suffering caused by the
garments, and the reason why women would not discontinue their use.[30]

While simple vanity may have been a factor in the popularity of the
garment for some women in India, I would argue that the garment
was retained in tropical climes because it was a crucial physical and

psychological vector in the maintenance of female subjectivity and class identity. Corsetry may have been an important daily reminder to middle-class women in the colonies (as it was to their less fortunate imprisoned sisters) of their class origins. As such, corsetry may have helped these women preserve their sense of culture and their sense of identity as 'civilized' modern women while they remained in seemingly 'uncivilized' parts of the world. Sarah Hale, editor of *Godey's Lady's Book* and author of several etiquette manuals, suggested as much in her popular text *Manners; Or Happy Homes and Good Society All the Year Round*. In it, she encouraged the use of corsetry and made very clear that closely fitting clothes were essential in establishing, and more importantly, maintaining, a 'civilized' demeanour when conquering the empire. 'Are the mothers of men who rule the world found among the *loose-robed* women?' she asked her readers. Or were they found 'among the women who dress[ed] in closer-fitting apparel?' The nations that were 'most morally refined' observed Hale, were those in which 'the costume of men and women differ[ed] most dramatically'.[31] Tightly laced corsetry served this purpose admirably. It disciplined and contained the 'Western' body and acted as a symbol of civilization and order, as opposed to the chaos and disorder of the 'primitive' naked or semi-naked bodies of the 'unconverted'.

Female loyalty to corsetry, whether 'at home' or 'abroad', was the result of a range of very powerful class-based pressures and incentives. Clothing was, for Hale and many working- and middle-class women throughout the empire, considered a barometer of morality. It was believed, by the Victorian middle and upper classes at least, that costume could be read as easily as any text. That is, clothing was thought to reflect and indicate the morality of its occupant. Corsetry was an essential tool in the precarious pursuit and preservation of a 'respectable' figure.[32] 'Dress in general could never', insisted the influential Sarah Hale, 'be considered a silly, trifling matter . . . [when] God's word . . . clearly reveal[ed] its high import.' Dress, for Hale and many of her class contemporaries throughout the century, 'reveal[ed] more clearly than speech expresse[d], the inner life of heart and soul in a people, and also the tendencies of individual character'.[33] As a consequence of the multifaceted powers and functions of dress, few women would ever even entertain the notion of abandoning the corset, and fewer still could withstand the opprobrium that inevitably followed if it was eschewed. Pejorative cries of 'Tomboy, Hoyden and Unladylike' were, according to dress reformer Elizabeth Ward, dinned into the ears of women who disobeyed fashion directives until they succumbed to the pressure to wear corsetry.[34] Eliza Haweis's, *The Art of Beauty*, published in 1878, echoed and reinforced damning popular opinion of the uncorseted body when it declared that those women who refused 'to wear the corset . . . look[ed] very slovenly'.[35]

Advocates of the garment, and there were many, universally insisted that corsetry provided the only 'proper foundation' on which to build 'a smooth and artistic fitting dress waist'.[36] The 'smooth and artistic dress waist' or bodice, as it is currently termed, was absolutely de rigueur to women's frocks for at least seventy years and was a crucial feature of both middle- and working-class clothes. Class differences in clothing (as in corsetry) relied chiefly on the cost of the fabrics and trims rather than on the fundamental design. While the skirts, sleeves and decorative accessories of nineteenth-century gowns altered significantly in the period between 1830 and 1900, the bodice did not. Essentially, the bodice was cut so closely to the body that corsets were necessary to contain and re-shape both the chest wall and the abdomen to fit inside it. As the advice page in *The Barmaid* journal of 1891 illustrates, the smooth bodice was as much an essential fashion item for women who worked in ale houses as for their middle-class superiors. *The Barmaid*'s regular column titled 'Hints on Dress' advised readers that 'the shape and accurate fit of our underwear [is] never of greater importance than now, when our gowns fit so closely to the figure that every wrinkle in a badly made petticoat can be seen'.[37]

An examination of mid- and late-century dressmaking texts, discloses how the tight bodice or 'wasp-waisted' look was sartorially engineered by both working-class dressmakers and the better-paid *modistes*. Dress-making texts published by technical colleges for both 'trade' students and home dressmakers, frequently included illustrations that consistently showed the waist measurement being taken outside the fully clothed and already tightly corseted body.[38] Explicit instructions regarding the measurement of the waist commonly included such directions as 'tie a string around the waist . . . and measure round the waist very tight',[39] take the 'size of the waist very tightly',[40] and 'tie a tape tightly around the waist to ensure a good waist line'.[41] The creation of the minuscule circular waist was the goal of both working-class dressmakers and the *couturiers* to the middle class. However, dressmakers across the classes did not always comply happily with demands to reduce the waistline. *Queen* magazine reported that dressmakers were frequently badgered to make garments considerably smaller than their client's bodies. When these 'sensible dressmakers' (as the *Queen* dubbed them) objected, the response from clients was 'O! you make the waist of so many inches and I'll engage to get into it'. How the 'getting into it' was effected, reported the *Queen*, referring cryptically to the corset, was 'one of the secrets of the prison house'.[42] These 'secrets of the prison house' were revealed in corset advertisements that stressed that the chief objective of corsetry was to 'outline the figure, narrow the waist and give a small round effect'.[43]

Although both the design of the corset and the persuasive powers of fashionable dressmakers undoubtedly contributed to the cross-class popularity of the garment, its hegemony as a fashion item for both working- and middle-class women relied on a continuum of subtle but pervasive influences. The corset was, of course, one article of clothing within a fashion system that encompassed dress in general, manners, good breeding and wealth. As Leonore Davidoff has demonstrated, dress was of crucial importance to the construction and articulation of middle-class femininity. As Davidoff argues, even 'the correct use of a handkerchief could connote inward grace and social status'.[44] Dress operated as a vital and problematic conduit which, ideally acted, was expected to visually delineate and distinguish middle-class femininity from that of its supposedly 'coarser' incarnation in working-class women.

The role and significance of clothing in defining the parameters of feminine respectability were not simply a construction of idle middle-class women, or ambitious working-class women intent on improving their situations. Dress, and male critics – who were quick to denounce women who misunderstood, or purposely transgressed, the moral implications of appearance – sternly policed its relationship to the social order. Fashion, according to John Mather Austin, mid-century author of *Golden Steps To Respectability, Usefulness and Happiness*, was a 'particularly dangerous folly', which threatened to imperil a woman's 'good name'. A 'good name' was, according to Austin, 'everything – literally EVERYTHING!' and without it [women] were '*nothing.*' (Austin's italics). Austin warned young women and their mothers not to disregard fashion, nor to plunge into its extremes, but to study it carefully. While Austin exhorted women to cultivate 'worthier attractions than the poor gee-gaws of DRESS!', he reminded them that 'the most worthless and abandoned of the female sex' dressed the 'most gaily and fashionably'.[45] Those women considered most abandoned by Austin and his peers were actresses and prostitutes. Both groups took great liberties with fashion, including indulging in extremes of tight lacing, or conversely, and just as wickedly, abandoning corsetry altogether.[46]

Not surprisingly, in an era when moral behaviour was determined as much by dress as by actions, and when one's own reputation and that of one's family could be made or ruined by appearances, it was of tremendous importance to working- and middle-class women to be appropriately attired. Dressing well required a studious examination of fashion trends and the acquisition of correct foundation garments to underpin 'agreeable and harmonious' frocks. Ideally, middle-class female clothing reflected a husband's or a father's economic success. As mentioned earlier, restrictive clothing was instrumental in this process, for it gave women the appearance, and indeed actualized, their inability and disinclination to perform manual labour. However, finery was, to the disquiet of the middle-class women, not entirely the prerogative of the better-off.

By mid-century, middle-class Victorians expressed anxiety and resentment when working-class women aspired to, and at times achieved, the stylish appearance of middle-class women.[47] The invention and swift acceptance of the sewing machine into both working- and middle-class family homes made for the democratization of 'style'.[48] Women's magazines were also accomplices in this process. Many carried complete patterns of the latest Parisian modes, and most of these magazines published numerous illustrations and lengthy articles that carefully described how fashionable, genteel styles could be inexpensively emulated by use of the home sewing machine.[49] To complicate matters the Victorian press was peppered with accounts of what prostitutes and courtesans wore, so middle-class women had to choose their clothing, and their corsetry, very carefully to signify their status as leisured but respectable women.[50]

Consequently, in such a fashion climate, imbued with morality and tinged with competition between individual women, and again between the social orders, single middle-class women faced an extraordinarily difficult dilemma. For while their appearance had to signal their class origin and impeccable virtue, it also had to promote sexual attractiveness in order to attract an appropriate marriage partner. The tightly laced corset was vital in achieving these ends. It restricted movement, and in doing so, mechanically forbade women from any physical exertion that might be construed as coarse or 'working-class'. At the same time it threw into relief its occupant's 'sexual assets', which were then demurely enhanced by carefully chosen outer garments. The negotiation between sexual attractiveness and the cultivation of a respectable demeanour was patently a complex task, fraught with peril.

Despite both the enormous energies required and the difficulties involved in constructing and negotiating a class-specific demeanour, neither working- nor middle-class women can be considered cultural dupes of fashion in general, or of the corset in particular. Both classes were implicated in the corset industry, though this was less the case for middle-class women. The involvement of working- and middle-class women escalated in tandem with the increased popularity of the garment. In the eighteenth century men were the corsetiers. Men designed corsetry, then measured and fitted the garments to women's bodies.[51] It was thought at that time that women were unable to become corsetières because they lacked the strength required to cut the whalebone, and then to push the strips of whalebone into the canvas (or canvas-like) casings of the garment. However, by the early nineteenth century these misconceptions had been almost overturned and women increasingly became active subjects in all aspects of the corset industry. By 1805, *The Book of Trades* noted that the 'ladies dressmaker must know how to hide all defects of the body and be able to mould the shape by stays while that she corrects the body'.[52] By mid-century, a significant gender shift in that most intimate of corset procedures, being the fitting of the garments to individual women's bodies, had occurred. Many of the more sympathetic, or perhaps astute, corset retailers advised customers that only 'female attendants' worked at their 'establishments'.[53]

Women were also directly involved in the actual design of corsets. While the overwhelming majority of corsetry manufacturers in the late nineteenth century were men, many of the industry's leading firms may have begun from women's initiative.[54] Many individual women even patented garments of their own design. Martha Gibbon was the first woman to patent a corset in 1800, and hers was the only patent lodged by a woman that related to corsetry until 1843. However, a close examination of patents between 1850 and 1900 reveals that the number of female staymakers, or corsetières as they came to be known, increased markedly, especially from 1860. Certainly, by the last quarter of the century, women were strongly represented in the patents. Of the twenty-four patents lodged in 1899 that were directly related to corsetry, eleven were entered by women. Their inventions and improvements were as ingenious and as well detailed as those patents entered by men.[55] They included such devices as a 'detachable corset protector', a 'modified corset' that was an early brassière prototype, a 'gymnastic corset', being a garment submitted by an American schoolgirl who played sport, and a corset padded over the bust and hips for thin women (Figures 10

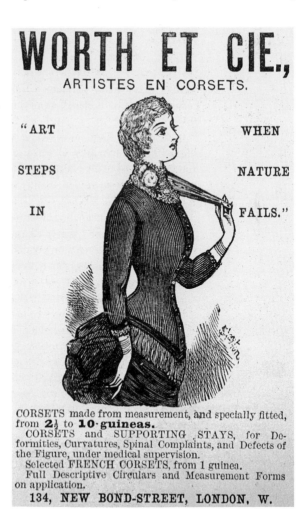

Figure 10
'Art stepping in where Nature failed' referred to padded corsets produced by Worth et cie. These corrected 'defects of the figure'. See *Illustrated London News*, 1887.

WORTH ET CIE.,
ARTISTES EN CORSETS.

"ART   WHEN

STEPS   NATURE

IN   FAILS."

CORSETS made from measurement, and specially fitted, from **2½** to **10·guineas.**
  CORSETS and SUPPORTING STAYS, for Deformities, Curvatures, Spinal Complaints, and Defects of the Figure, under medical supervision.
  Selected FRENCH CORSETS, from 1 guinea.
  Full Descriptive Circulars and Measurement Forms on application.
  134, NEW BOND-STREET, LONDON, W.

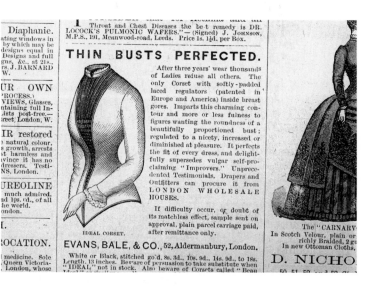

and 11). Ada Roscoe, a London actress, designed a completely reversible corset trimmed on both sides, presumably to double the life span of the corset's appeal.[56]

Clearly, while women were often cruelly contained by corsetry, many resisted that containment by attempting to alter its construction at the most basic stages of its conceptualization, via the patents. Corsetry design also offered women an opportunity to enter the male-dominated world of business.

Many of the women who submitted corset designs and modifications identified their class backgrounds and their occupations. Female corset makers were represented along with dressmakers and tailors. Some, like Ada Roscoe, disclosed unrelated occupations, while some women simply identified themselves as either 'married woman', 'spinster' or 'gentle-woman' from a particular region. The increased participation of women in the design and manufacture of corsetry may (as with the democratization of finery) have been a result of the invention and relative cheapness of the sewing machine. As mentioned earlier, the sewing machine enabled women to experiment and create garments for themselves that were possibly patterned on, or adapted from, existing commercially purchased garments, or alternately, made up from corset patterns that were provided in women's household and fashion texts.

Perhaps not surprisingly, a significant number of the corset patents lodged by women were concerned with improving the comfort rather than the strength of corsets. A design submitted by Fanny Gibson demonstrates the way in which women's intimate knowledge and experience of corsetry was translated into their corsetry designs and improvements. Gibson's 'invention' related to corsets 'designed for stout people as an abdominal support and also as an improvement of the figure'. Gibson's stays were quite unlike other garments designed for the corpulent body in that they 'provide[d] a larger space on either side of the busk so that the material [would] conveniently fit over the enlarged abdomen'. For reasons of comfort she also allowed 'a greater space between the back and the hips'. In other words Gibson's corset was bigger. More significantly still, her corset could be worn comfortably by overweight women because it did not attempt to mimic the envied and much-replicated hourglass or wasp-waisted shape. The illustration accompanying the patent revealed that it was, as Gibson explained in her specifications, designed to fit over the body, rather than compress it into the fashionable contracted contour.[57] That Gibson's garment had no pretence of a waistline made it a genuine departure from other garments designed by men to hold the bodies of heavier women. Gibson's design was obviously the result of a genuine knowledge of the requirements of women's bodies, for she was a dress-maker (Figures 12 and 13).

Unfortunately, a tendency to increase levels of comfort did not neces-sarily characterize all the patents submitted by women. Anna Maria Hatchman, a self-identified 'corset designer' of Surrey, submitted an 'improvement in stays or corsets' which was as severe and constrictive as those designed by her male counterparts. The object of this garment was to hide a large abdomen, rather than hold it, as Gibson's had done. Hatchman's article consisted of a standard heavily boned garment that differed from other designs submitted by male patentees only because of the inclusion of an extra, attached stomach section used to 'flatten the abdomen'. This section was comprised of complicated elliptical gores, reinforced with 'pieces of steel or whalebone' onto which extra bands, fastened by sturdy buckles and eyelets, were used to lever the stomach into position and contain it within a fortified wall of fabric.[58]

Most corset designs submitted by male patentees tended to favour the rigid construction preferred by Hatchman, rather than the accommod-ating properties promoted by Gibson. Often, as in the case of female patentees, the interests and the occupations of men who were interested in improving corset design were revealed in the notes included with the patent designs. Many male patentees were identified as stay- or corset-makers. (Indeed, an examination of the corset patents discloses the rising fortunes of several American, English and French corset firms.) However, many of the corset designs submitted to the patent office were from men whose occupations were, at first glance, completely unrelated to women's bodies or the construction of corsetry. Warehousemen,[59] mechanical engineers,[60] real estate agents,[61] and even dentists[62] can be found in the corset patents. This was largely because the materials used in the manufacture of corsetry were also common to many of these fields. Male patentees invariably claimed that their inventions and patterns were conceived to increase the comfort of the corseted body, but a close (and gendered) examination of patents lodged by men actually reveals that

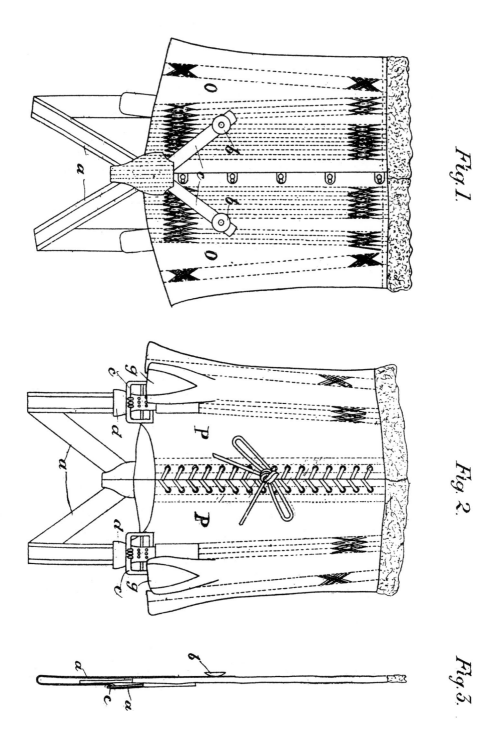

Fig.1.

Fig.2.

Fig.3.

they were most often concerned with strengthening rather than redesigning the garments to afford extra comfort.

Overwhelmingly, patents lodged by men reveal a strong interest in if not an obsession with reinforcing all aspects of the corset. Indeed the patents can be read as documents in which male fears of female sexuality or female 'escape' might be detected. Ideas, and indeed methods, of containment and control of female corporeality characterize many of men's patents. The incorporation of horsehair, felting, metal, wood, leather and wire,[63] alone or in combination, to strengthen the linings of corsetry was devised to this end. The extremely successful method of steam moulding, conceived and patented by Edwin Izod, is a good example of the popular male desire not only to resculpt but to restrain and regulate female flesh. Izod – who manufactured both corsetry and the moulds on which corsets were modelled – refined and improved the technique of stiffening the garments. His quickly pirated steam moulding process involved designing a desirable female form by packing sawdust or bran into a corset until he was satisfied its shape was perfect, and then setting the 'torso' in a solution of plaster of Paris or other suitable cement. The corset was then removed and the 'anatomically perfect' form was used to cast models of glass, china, earthenware or cast metal, into which were fitted a series of copper pipes. Corsets were designed to fit over these models. The garments were then covered in a solution of a glue/starch mixture that was baked into the fibres of the corset by steam forced through the copper pipes inside the moulds.[64] The heat-moulding process effectively set the corsets into a hard, shell-like construction. While Izod's method of steam moulding sounds primitive and conjures up notions of physical imprisonment, it was a major advancement on other methods of stiffening the garments.

Figure 12
Patent submitted by Fanny Gibson designed to accommodate the fuller figure. Although this design provided more comfort for the torso than standard garments, Gibson's corset included cumbersome perforated leather straps that 'passed around the thickest part of the buttock [to] prevent the corset from slipping up or otherwise shifting out of position.'

Figure 13
'The Duchess' corset, unlike Gibson's design, retained its hour-glass shape though intended for the fuller figure. This was made possible by the inclusion of a 'series of narrow whalebones diagonally in front…gradually curving in and contracting the corset at the bottom of the busk, where the figure was reduced and…an elegant appearance secured.' See *Illustrated London News*, 1889.

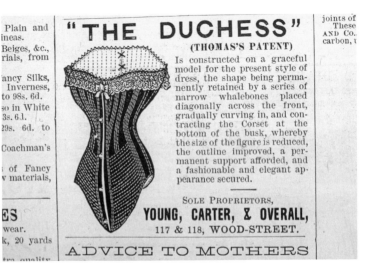

Plain and ineas.
Beiges, &c., rials, from
ancy Silks, Inverness, to 98s. 6d. so in White 3s. 6.1. 29s. 6d. to
Coachman's
of Fancy v materials,
ES
wear.
k, 20 yards

" THE DUCHESS "
(THOMAS'S PATENT)
Is constructed on a graceful model for the present style of dress, the shape being permanently retained by a series of narrow whalebones placed diagonally across the front, gradually curving in, and contracting the Corset at the bottom of the busk, whereby the size of the figure is reduced, the outline improved, a permanent support afforded, and a fashionable and elegant appearance secured.

Sole Proprietors,
YOUNG, CARTER, & OVERALL,
117 & 118, WOOD-STREET.

ADVICE TO MOTHERS

joints of These AND CO. carbon, t

A patent lodged a year earlier by George Tomlinson detailed a method
which involved 'a model of the perfect human bust' upon which was
'clamp[e]d or tack[e]d raw or partially tanned hide . . . moistened to a
plastic condition'. The hide was perforated for the sake of ventilation,
covered with shellac, then, further covered with 'felting or material to
deaden the noise consequent upon [the] crackling or indentation of the
hide'.[65] By the 1870s and 1880s, several patents lodged by men involved
the use of hydraulic pressure and newly invented 'hardening machines'
to make corsetry ever more durable.[66] Patents submitted by women were,
by comparison, characterized by attempts to lessen the impact of standard
'male-designed' corsetry on female flesh. Margaret Orr's corset, patented
in 1890, was such a garment. Orr's 'improved corset bodice' that she
considered 'especially useful for hot climates, or for wear while playing
lawn tennis or as a change after wearing ordinary stiff corsets' were
made of a 'kind of elastic (cotton) stockinet'. Orr's garment was, as she
described, suitable for wearing under tea gowns, and 'very suitable for
those [women] who object[ed] to the usual stiff corsets'.[67]

While many men corsetiers dwelled on designing a sturdy carapace for
the female body, others concentrated on 'improving' or in other words,
strengthening, the metal catches, hinges, and ribs that provided the
infrastructure and closed the garments. Normal exertion in corsetry often
resulted in the garments 'breaking'. That is, the steels, or bones (or their
substitutes) snapped when the pressure exerted by the tightly encased flesh
exceeded the strength of the corset's infrastructure. Working-class women
would, because of their increased levels of physical exertion, have broken
more steels and would therefore have been more prone to abrasions and
puncture wounds from broken corsets. Nevertheless, breaking steels and
busks were a continual problem for all classes of women who wore
corsetry. Their breakage provided a challenge for designers who recognized the pecuniary rewards that lay in wait for the manufacturer who
could supply women with a truly unbreakable garment. That corset
shields continued to be popular until very late in the century indicates
that the problem of breaking steels was never really overcome by
designers.

Corset shields were comprised of two strips of metal or bone covered
in sturdy fabric and riveted together to form an X shape. They were sewn
into the inside of the garment at crucial areas of stress. They were bought
in pairs, and as many advertisements for the devices pointed out, they
were 'simple, economical and easily put in' and 'could be had of Drapers
everywhere'.[68] The purpose of the corset shield was, according to a patent
lodged in 1893,

> to preserve [the corset's] shape and lessen liability of breakage of
> the [corset] ribs, and second to protect the body of the wearer from
> abrasion by the protruding ends of ribs in case of the breakage
> thereof.[69]

Advertisements for the shields promised that when fitted to a new corset, the garment would 'not break *over the hips* or in *front*'. Thousands of women, were said to 'wear and praise them'.[70] While many brands of corsetry claimed to be unbreakable, the popularity of corset shields indicates that they were not (Figures 14 and 15). Despite this, firms went to considerable lengths to convince women that the steels, bones and busks in their garments would not break, tear through the fabric and pierce their flesh. Visual images that conjured up ideas of enormous strength were employed in advertising strategies to convince both working- and middle-class women that their garments would not break. Chilcomb House museum holds a corset box label on which two lions unsuccessfully attempt to tear a corset apart. Some firms named their corsets with the specific intention of convincing customers of the stamina of their garments. This explains why such supposedly dainty, feminine garments were given names such as 'The Armorside',[71] 'The Hercules Patent Spring', 'The Damascus', 'The Battledore' and 'The Serpentena'. The latter claimed, like many other brands, that their 'patent[ed] coil steels [were] guaranteed not to rust or break'. Other firms abandoned the illusion completely and made a more prosaic sales point by including 'a few extra steels in each box'.[72]

Figure 14
Corset shields, such as Oktis, added a metal infrastructure to the corset ostensibly preventing the breakage of 'bones'. Women reported that when the 'bones' or 'steels' snapped they sometimes tore through the corset and pierced the body. See Woman's Life, 1899.

Figure 15
Pearl Corset Shields were said to 'double the life of a corset.' Shields were of considerable importance to working-class women who could not afford to replace worn or 'broken' garments.

Although men undeniably dominated the corset patents and the corset industry in general, there were some remarkable exceptions. Women who were corsetières made real incursions into the male-controlled field of corsetry. By mid-century, female corsetières found recognition and even fame at international trade exhibitions,[73] which allowed them access to the public world of men and commerce. Women corsetières were described in official exhibition catalogues as inventors, designers, or designers and manufacturers. Several of these corsetières or staymakers were also identified as dressmakers and tailors. The catalogue of London's *Great Exhibition of Works of Industry Of All Nations* recorded the participation of eight women corsetières in a field of nineteen competitors.[74] Some may have been of the class of '*small muddling staymakers*' disparagingly mentioned in a separate trade catalogue issued by George Roberts,[75] whose firm was also represented at the exhibition. However a combination of professional jealousy and disdain for women's involvement in public events may have motivated this comment, as several of the female firms at London's Great Exhibition appeared at other major international events held over several decades, which probably indicates their relative success. Josephine Sykes, a 'Ladies Outfitter of London', won awards for her display of 'corsets and ladies (sic) belts' at the Philadelphia

International Exhibition 1876.[76] American women were also keen to exhibit their designs at these fairs. At the exhibition, Mrs Harriet M. Chapman promoted 'buff corsets' that were padded. This made them useful (according to the general report) for women with sore breasts, 'while at the same time giv[ing] a nice appearance to those who have small-developed breasts'.[77]

While the most successful designs exhibited by women at the trade fairs appear to have differed little from those of male competitors, there were occasional successful departures in design. The 'inventor and manufacturer' Mary Sykes, of Regent Street (who may have been related to the previously mentioned Josephine), was awarded a medal for her entry of a corset weighing only 5 ounces. It had an 'elastic portion made by hand'. While the weight of other garments was not disclosed in the exhibition catalogue, that Sykes's garment was considered noteworthy for its lightness probably indicates that most garments on exhibition were substantially heavier.[78]

The great exhibitions provided women with opportunities to display and, perhaps more importantly, to publicize their corsetiering skills and their businesses at a time when few opportunities were open for them to do so. England's most beloved and well-known mid-century woman corsetière, Madame Roxy Caplin, won several awards for her corsetry designs and took the prize medal at the Great Exhibition of 1851.[79] Caplin's career can be seen as evidence of at least one woman's significant participation in and importance to the corsetry industry. Her success was, in part, due to her husband's involvement as much as to her unique designs. Monsieur Caplin was a doctor who advised his wife on the physiological impact of corsetry. Madame Caplin maintained that her garments were based on hygienic medical principles, and this found favour with exhibition judges, who were impressed by Caplin's range as much as by her supposed commitment to anatomical laws. Caplin's designs were, in comparison to those of many popular garments manufactured by large male-headed corset firms, based on a more realistic appraisal of women's bodies. The range of her garments was astonishing, and this probably added to her success. Her range encompassed garments designed for every stage of the female life cycle. These included the tiny 'child's bodice' the 'reverso tractor' for the gangly adolescent, maternity stays for '*femmes enceintes*', the 'self regulating contracting belt' for the post-partum mother, the 'medical belt or uterus supporter' for the sufferer of prolapsed uterus, and the 'double elastic corset' for the woman 'of weak constitution'.

Caplin founded a small empire on her corset designs and skilful market-ing. By 1860 she had published two texts and several pamphlets on the benefits of corsetry. Her public lectures later published as *Woman and Her Wants*, won praise from the press, whose favourable remarks were reprinted in the back of succeeding editions.[80] These texts were sold directly by the publisher and were also available at either of Caplin's salons, which were based in London and Manchester. Her Berners Street salon in London was also furnished with an 'anatomical gallery', in which an 'anatomical Venus' along with 'hundreds of magnificent models executed with utmost fidelity to nature [illustrated] every important organ of the human body'. Caplin took pains to stress to clients of a squeamish disposition that the anatomical and physiological gallery was 'quite distinct from the rest of the establishment and [that] a visit to one [did] not necessarily involve a sight of the other'. The 'whole course of embryology' was on display at the gallery, in order to teach mothers how to 'nurse, dress, and train [their] children and preserve [their] own and [their] family's health'. Corsetry played a large part in that health regime.[81] So significant was Caplin's contribution to the corset culture of mid-century London that she became immortalized in Lidstone's *Londoniad*, a text written in verse, which according to its title, gave a 'Full Description of the Principle Establishments, Together with the Most Honourable and Substantial Business Establishments in the Capital of England'.[82] Of Caplin Lidstone glowingly wrote

How shall the poet in a single lay, the glory of her age and time portray?
Suffice if for the wondering world to mark, she took from all beside the medal in Hyde Park:
The only prize that was for corsets given to any manufacturer under heaven.

Lo! the dazzling splendours of her fame advance O'er all England and the whole of France
She the beloved, who now fills Brunswick's throne
Deals with Madam Caplin – her alone.[83]

Of course few women reached the dizzy entrepreneurial heights of the ambitious and astute Roxy Caplin. Many more were directly involved in the manufacture of garments on the factory floor and in homes as outworkers.[84] Several of the major corsetry firms in Britain were in seaside towns and cities. These provided unmarried, cheap female labour on the factory floor, while sailor's wives undertook much of the outwork or sweated labour involved in corsetry production. A factory owned by Messrs Thomas of Cheapside employed almost 2,000 staff. However, it is unclear how many of the staff were women, and how many of the employees were outworkers.[85]

Charles Booth's *Life and Labour of the People in London*, first published in 1889, identified women and girls in the corsetry trade as among the most poorly paid workers in that city. In corset factories, many women were consigned to japanning busks, a 'dirty and disagreeable' operation involving the application of black lacquer to coat the strips of metal and protect them from rust. Women and girls also 'covered the steels

. . . fix[ed] clasps and put in eyelet holes with small machines'. Children were employed to 'put in eyelets, insert cords and do other light work'. At one factory visited by Booth, 'learners worked for nothing for the first month [with] the girl in charge of them getting the benefit' of any work they did. The learners were eventually put on 'piecework', which was very lowly paid and repetitive. Men cut out the cloth, and linings, of the corsets. This was better-paid work. The sewing up of separate parts of the corset, undertaken by women, was not. Fitters cut the rough edges from the garments and then sent them back to machinists for binding. The binders were usually women, and were the best-paid female members of the team. The poorly paid outwork consisted of inserting the stay bones and 'fanning' them. Fanning refers to the decorative stitching used to keep the bones in place. Booth considered this work 'light and easy' but recognized that the wages were extremely exploitative. As Booth pointed out, the higher wages made by piecework were the result of having children contribute long hours to the production of the garments.[86]

Similar conditions appear to have operated in American corset factories, but both written commentary and analysis of working conditions in corset factories has proven difficult to locate. However, *The Fourth Annual Report of the Commissioner of Labour* sub-titled *Working Women in Large Cities*, published in 1889, contains statistics that allow some conjecture. Tables within the report indicate that many city corset factories employed female children from ten years old and that the average age of beginning employment for women in the corset industry was between thirteen and fourteen years old. (This appears to have been typical of many industries that employed women and girls at this time.) The highest-paid women in these factories were corsetmakers, whose annual earnings were $304.95. Boners were the lowest-paid workers in these factories, earning $138.73 per annum. Unfortunately the report does not, of course, include the number of men employed at corset factories or their rates of pay. However, statistics provided by the report indicate that the living expenses of all women employed in the corset factories under discussion were barely met, and that very often, basic living expenses exceeded their incomes[87] (Figures 16–19).

Better incomes may have been had, at least in the 1890s, by selling corsetry on commission. In the United States, women were employed as 'lady agents' to sell corsetry, corset shields and undergarments door to door. Advertisements placed in a range of working- to middle-class magazines such as *The Designer* assured readers that 'lady agents' could not find a 'greater combination of money making articles to canvas for [nor could they] make money faster' than by selling the 'Fast Black Sateen Lustrene and Moiré Under-skirts, together with corset waists, Corsets, safety belts, [which held the menstrual linen in place] and Shoulder Braces, etc.'. The Reliance Corset Company of Michigan, which manufactured these garments, claimed that 'agents were wanted everywhere'.[88] Similar advertisements were placed by rival firms such as Madame Griswold's, a

New York-based company, whose plentiful advertisements for 'patent skirt supporting corsets' often notified readers that 'lady canvassers [were] wanted everywhere'. Like The Reliance corset firm, Griswold's promised exclusive territorial rights and claimed that a 'profitable and permanent business'[89] could be had from the sale of their garments.[90]

While corsetry operated to contain and constrain both working- and middle-class female bodies, it paradoxically provided some women with a method of escaping or resisting the confinement of both class and gender restrictions. Claims that 'lady agents' could procure a 'profitable and permanent business' were probably quite correct, particularly for those women on the American frontier whose clients were far from department stores and corsetières. Indeed, lady agents who specialized in corset sales can be seen to have successfully resisted domestic ideologies that forbade or frowned upon women's entry into the commercial realm. Whether the women involved in the corset industry were professional middle-class

Figure 18
The employees' Dining Room at the Royal Worcester Corset Company appeared crowded, but was orderly and well ventilated. The tables were set with plentiful food and drink. There is an element of what might be considered a 'contrived' respectability in evidence in this photograph. (Courtesy of Bob Trackimowicz and the Worcester Museum.)

corsetières, gentlewoman designers and inventors, or working-class saleswomen and factory operatives, all can be seen to have distinguished themselves as women with occupations at a time when the notion of an occupation was a 'core element' in the construction of *masculine* identity.[91] Interestingly, while corsetry was a significant item in the construction and articulation of a sometimes punishing, self-policing subjectivity, its careful use allowed some women to push the boundaries and limitations of class. Working-class women, such as those satirized in Mayhew's *The Greatest Plague on Earth*, understood that the cultivation of a svelte figure or *tournure* might turn the head of a 'better class' of suitor. Middle-class women, on the other hand, corseted to protect and consolidate their position rather than to escape from it, a situation that

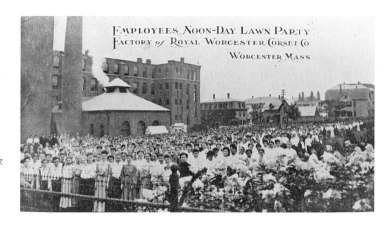

Figure 19
Employees' Noon-Day Lawn Party c.1900. This photograph of Worcester's apparently passive, contented and neatly dressed workforce, is disturbed by the inclusion of the factory's barbed-wire fence. (Courtesy of Bob Trackimowicz and the Worcester Museum.)

often meant the negotiation of complex unwritten rules around tight lacing (see chapter 4). However, for many women from all classes, corsetry was mandatory to femininity. Its use and its terrible effects began not in adulthood, but in utero.

2
Corsetry and the Invisibility of the Maternal Body

> One of the strongest reasons for the adoption of the corset, though it is not commonly avowed, is the belief that it conduces beauty and symmetry of figure. Slender forms are usually praised, and chiefly because they are associated with the litheness and undeveloped graces of youth.[1]

While middle-class Victorian culture idealized the image of the mother and her post-partum child with almost alarming sentimentality, the pregnant body was considered by polite society to be somewhat repugnant and best kept from view.[2] Pregnancy set strict parameters on both middle- and working-class women, whether they wanted the child or not. Pregnancy inevitably reduced employment prospects for working-class married women and spelled financial and moral ruin for their single sisters. Middle-class women suffered similar social and pecuniary ignominy if they had the misfortune to bear illegitimate babies, and while the lot of married middle-class women was decidedly happier than that of pregnant working-class women, their lives too were severely constrained by the maternal state. Pregnant middle-class women were ostracized by virtue of their biology. They were routinely advised that they 'must retire early to rest', avoid parties, balls, concerts and long trips on public transport.[3] Corsetry of both maternity and standard design, was commonly worn by working- and middle-class women to avoid this type of censure. Maternity corsetry was sold as early as the 1830s and, as the century closed, patterns for maternity corsets which could be made at home, and which were almost indistinguishable from standard corsets in design, were discreetly advertised in respectable magazines.[4] For pregnant Victorian women, tightly laced corsetry, whether of maternity or standard design, afforded a few extra weeks or even months of freedom in face of taboos which demanded their invisibility.

So intense were the taboos surrounding the nineteenth-century gravid uterus that they almost silenced the usually vocal medical profession. It must be pointed out that few Victorian women attended a physician or a midwife before the onset of labour because pregnancy was not considered pathological,[5] but this does not fully explain the medical failure to address the issue of corsetry during pregnancy. Physicians who ordinarily railed against corsetry in the nullipara female remained obdurately mute about the use of corsetry during gestation, though they knew of its prevalence. This contradictory textual silence was noted by Dr Bouvier, a French physician. Bouvier observed a lack of medical interest regarding foetal and maternal distress from tight lacing, but concluded that this was because their were no serious consequences from the practice to either party. Bouvier claimed to have witnessed three instances of tight lacing in pregnancy and claimed that no ill effects had been felt by mother or child. It was, he remarked

> a striking fact that the writers who have so emphatically condemned the corset as 'the evil of the age' and the active cause of pelvic congestion, of defective bile, of dyspepsia and the like, have little or nothing to say of its teratogenic influence upon the unborn infant. One is driven to the conclusion that its ill effects, in this direction at least are few; perhaps the presence of the *liquor amnii* is the great safeguard of the foetus.[6]

While Bouvier's observations regarding foetal and maternal distress from corsetry were largely unsubstantiated, his remarks on the dearth of medical literature relating to tight-lacing in pregnancy were accurate. Neither the *Transactions of the American Association of Obstetrics and Gynaecology* nor the journal of the American Gynaecological Society, *Gynaecological Transactions*, or their British counterparts, published a single article between 1876 and 1900 that discussed the dangers of wearing corsetry during pregnancy.[7] This reticence is not surprising in an era when doctors were routinely advised to avert their eyes during an examination of the pregnant woman, or drape her body so heavily that her genitals were withheld from view. One popular medical text of 1853 depicted a surgeon examining an upright, fully clothed woman whose voluminous skirts concealed not only her body and her undergarments, but the entire right arm of the kneeling physician who was 'examining' her.[8]

Taboos that silenced the medical profession similarly intimidated polite society. Even the words pregnant and pregnancy were avoided in polite Victorian company.[9] Pregnancy was, of course, the most obvious demonstration of women's carnal animality, as well as a reminder of the female body's predilection for unseemly, squeamish and occasionally painful bodily functions. Consequently, Victorian standards of decency demanded the concealment of the pregnant body and denied any public discussion of either the experience of pregnancy or its *accoutrements*. American women were as much silenced by pregnancy taboos as their British sisters. Elizabeth Edson Evans, author of *The Abuse of Maternity* published in 1875, wrote that American women often avoided 'speaking of their situation' to their nearest relatives or most intimate friends. Pregnancy was 'apt to go on under the unwholesome shadow of a great silence . . . and the candidate for maternal honours [was] so often ashamed of her altered form and countenance as to shun the sight of acquaintances'. Evans also noted that 'sarcastic remarks' were sometimes directed at women 'who ventured to walk in the streets when conspicuously advanced in pregnancy' and that these remarks were made as often by women as by men.[10]

Pregnancy taboos were implemented and obeyed for several reasons. They operated primarily to ensure that an image of womanly innocence was maintained despite evidence of sexual experience.[11] They were essential too in perpetuating the illusion (and male fantasy) of the continued 'virginality' and 'innocence' of married women[12] despite the somatic betrayal that revealed they had indulged in, and possibly enjoyed, sexual intercourse. At the most material level taboos worked to conceal from ordinary view the animalistic processes of parturition which were not in accord with demure feminine gender roles. However, several other factors worked to undermine the status of the pregnant body and the experience of pregnancy. While multiple pregnancies were once applauded, the role of the Victorian matron was, increasingly as the decades unfolded, to limit family size. Horatio Storer remarked in 1868 that

> in ancient commonwealths the most fruitful mother was considered to have deserved well of her nation . . . now on the contrary such a wife is considered as almost the greatest misfortune that can occur to a man . . . Women, [he continued] ha[d] learned to consider . . . the noblest purposes of their being as . . . a disgrace and a disaster.[13]

There appears to be an element of truth in Storer's remarks. By mid-century, women themselves began to question and sometimes reinvent the domestic and maternal role constructed for them. Limiting pregnancy was crucial to this process. While the stereotypical 'True Woman' was ideally domestic, docile and reproductive, bourgeois economic demands which escalated during the nineteenth century, required that wives limit their fertility in order to display their husbands' affluence to its best advantage.[14] Large broods of children hindered the accumulation and display of wealth. Pregnancy, while essential to the Victorian family unit, encumbered the middle-class matron's contribution to the family's social and financial status and limited her own autonomy. Pregnancy, under these circumstances, may have been viewed by some women, as their own failure to observe newly constructed roles. Taboos may have worked to hide the Victorian matron's perceived role failure as contributor to family prosperity, as much as to hide her 'unchastity'.

Pregnancy taboos may have also operated and been enforced to protect prevailing unrealistic stereotypes of masculinity that deemed 'civilized' nineteenth-century men to be both in full control of their sexual 'urges' and respectful of female virtue. This heroic and mythic stereotype was publicly attacked by feminists and moral reform groups in both Britain and America who aimed to curtail the excesses of male sexual behaviour, in and outside of wedlock. Unwanted sexual intercourse in marriage, or to use its nineteenth-century nomenclature 'legal sex slavery', was the subject of much public bitterness and criticism. American feminist Angela Heywood (perhaps that nation's most outspoken critic of male sexuality and its unbridled reign in marriage) declared in 1893 that nineteenth-century man ought to have a '*solemn meeting with, and look serious at his own penis until he is able to be lord and master of it, rather than it should longer rule, lord and master, of him and of the victims he deflowers*' (Heywood's italics).[15]

A plethora of marital advice manuals published by reformists, moralists and physicians between 1870 and 1900[16] upheld Heywood's opinions but expressed them in less confronting terms. Marital advice books were eagerly purchased by middle-class readers who were anxious to limit their families and understand the complexities of human sexuality. Most texts abhorred contraception and abortion and promoted male sexual continence 'and continence alone' as a method of family planning.[17] Numerous doctors and social commentators were alarmed by the physical deterioration of women from continued unwanted pregnancies. Dr Elizabeth Duffey, author of *The Relations of the Sexes* published in 1876, noted that she saw many patients whose 'tender delicate organs of generation were abused to such an extent by too frequent use that they became inflamed, ulcerat[ed] and render[ed] the woman an invalid'.[18] Male continence was considered the logical, civilized and Christian solution to the prevention of female debilitation and the dilemmas of contraception. 'A man of justice and honour . . . could never thus abuse the love and confidence of a wife.' To do so was to sink 'lower than the brutes'. The wife alone, wrote Henry Wright '*must decide how often and under what circumstances, the husband may enjoy . . . passional expression of his love*'.[19]

Despite the often ardent promotion of female sexual autonomy in marriage, many texts indicated that male continence was the exception rather than the rule, and that women commonly experienced 'sexual connection' and resultant pregnancies against their express wishes. 'How gross, how fatal, how general the error that woman comes to man as a wife, only as a means of his sensual indulgence!' wrote Wright. 'How few men have any other higher ideal of Marriage than that of a licensed, uncontrolled gratification of sensual passion!'[20] Under the real politik of marital sexuality, pregnancy taboos that insisted on maternal invisibility can be seen to have masked the reality of male sexual incontinence in marriage, and to have protected the fiction that Victorian men had civilized and governed their sexual appetites.

A small range of clothing, including corsets, was skilfully employed by nineteenth-century mothers to conceal their swelling bodies from common view. Interestingly, specifically designed maternity clothes were not popularly worn in the nineteenth century. Middle-class women routinely altered existing garments as the abdomen demanded and then reduced those same clothes after parturition.[21] This process, while economically advantageous, also contributed to the ideological and vestimentary conceit. The first (and very discreet) advertisements for maternity clothes did not appear in the American press until 1911[22] or in Britain until 1913.[23] To wear obviously new or apparent maternity clothing may have been viewed as a bold admission of the woman's physical and therefore mental 'unchastity'. Long shawls were worn by pregnant women to conceal their condition, while corsetry of maternal and 'regulation' design was complicit, indeed imperative, in the difficult process of disguise.

The exacting observance of nineteenth-century gestation taboos meant that corset manufacturers could appeal to customers only indirectly, using considerable discretion. Joseph Amesbury's Patent Adjustable Body Support, 'used in various conditions of the body in the single and married state', was clearly a maternity corset despite its ambiguous title and description. An illustration of the garment in the 1840 edition of *Substitutes for Stays and Corsets, Patent Body Supports*[24] shows it to be an ill-named device of stalwart and unflinching construction. It was made of buckram or similar sturdy cloth, fastened at front and back by a formidable arrangement of panels, laces, bones, straps and buckles. The front panel (shaped somewhat like an inverted 'v') ran from beneath the breasts to the pubes, and was laced either side of the abdomen. These laces were presumably loosened as the foetus demanded. The front and back sections of the 'support' could be closed 'partly with buckles and straps, and partly with the system of laces, and sometimes with buckles and straps only'. The busk also was adjustable. While the enlarged breasts may have been supported by the garment, the arrangement of buckles at the back of the corset, combined with bones and laces, must have added to the awkwardness of the increasingly cumbersome torso. Although adjustable, the existence and position of the busk would have hampered any leaning forward movement, while the already stiff fabric further reinforced with bones possibly chafed the abdomen and would certainly have clasped it firmly into an unyielding upright position.

Although Amesbury claimed the garment supported the body of the pregnant woman, in actuality it effectively upheld and supported the prevailing ideology that demanded its invisibility. Straps, buckles, laces and bones on maternity corsetry throughout the century worked to contain and imprison the unruly, fecund body, giving it the appearance of taking up less space, of appearing less 'offensively' pregnant. The design of the corset possibly reduced both the body's ability to expand and certainly the ability to move about with ease, thereby hindering its liberty in both private sphere and public arena. Amesbury's rigid garment (and other garments of similar design) can be read as a manifestation of societal embarrassment about the pregnant body, a material expression of distaste for the uncomely expanding belly. The charter of these, and similar maternity corsets, was no doubt an attempt (though possibly an unconscious and not altogether successful one) to contain and mould the pregnant form. The corseted pregnant body presented less of a visual affront to respectable Victorian society and to its double standards in regard to maternity.

Why the pregnant Victorian body was the target of ridicule and even covert hostility is puzzling, for pregnancy can be interpreted as the most significant indicator of obedience to biologically determined female gender roles. Paradoxically, while Victorian women were expected to marry and bear children, pregnancy actually transgressed the binary oppositions that attempted to neatly categorize men and women. Within the narrow confines of Victorian gender dualism, masculinity was defined as white, middle-class and in control of sexual desire. Masculine infractions of prescribed sexual behaviour did not contravene gender expectations, for male sexuality (despite protestations from moralists and feminists to the contrary) was proclaimed as naturally active, inexorable and demanding. This was not the case for women. The construction of Victorian femininity, like its masculine counterpart, was also envisioned as white and middle-class, but was further circumscribed by the decree virginal. This final stipulation, unlike the masculine sexual mandate, was inflexible. Paradoxically, while reproduction was considered the cornerstone of the Victorian family, and while post-partum motherhood was frequently exalted, the expanding 'public' female body indicated female indiscretion and an affront to public decency. The expanding physical pregnant body was the literal transgression of constructed feminine ideals that denied female carnality and demanded sexual passivity and virgin status (Figures 20 and 21).

As a result of its transgression, the pregnant body (and its post-partum lax abdomen) stood well outside the physical and moral ideals of femininity constructed and promoted by Victorian popular culture.

Figure 20
This Swanbill advertisement played on feminine insecurities regarding the loss of the 'virginal' waistline. The accompanying text stressed that 'nothing tended to age a woman more than a loss of symmetry of figure.' It also reassured women with children that with a Swanbill belt strapped about her person 'even a mother of a large family' might retain 'her natural maiden form.' See *Illustrated London News*, 1888.

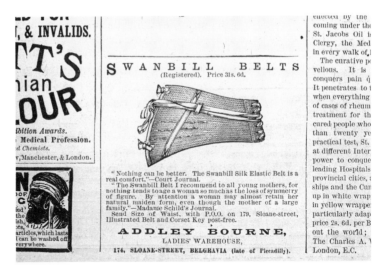

The expanding abdomen was, of course, the antithesis of that most desirable Victorian female asset, the tiny waistline. Although 'ideal' female body shape altered dramatically between 1850 and 1900, both a tiny waist and virginal demeanour were immutable aspects of its construction and expression. The delicate 'balletic' figure of womanhood so beloved by early Victorians was both slim-waisted and characterized by downcast eyes that signified sexual modesty. The icon of the ballet dancer depicted in innumerable steel engravings was actually considered the essence of femininity in England, America and France.[25] Her image was superseded in the latter decades of the nineteenth century by that of the buxom, saucy

Figure 21
Manufacturers of the Domen Belt corset assured women concerned about their matronly waistlines that the garment was unique for 'restoring, improving and supporting the post-partum figure.' See *Woman's Life*, 1899.

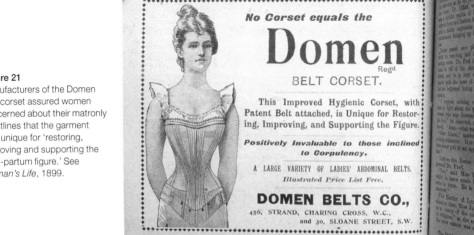

Gibson girl who at first glance appears the physical and moral opposite of her dainty predecessor. This was not the case. Though curvaceous and statuesque, the Gibson Girl's ample figure was thrown into relief by a tiny waistline, and despite her smouldering glances and suggestive posturing, she was depicted on the threshold of emergent sexuality, aware of impending sexual pleasures, but virginal nonetheless.[26] The pregnant Victorian body could offer neither the appearance of a delicate frame nor innocent if eager glances full of promise, and was marginalised in popular culture to the point of invisibility for its sins. The rarity of photographs of the pregnant Victorian woman, even in family albums, is evidence of this.

Once pregnant, the nineteenth-century female was regarded, in the few texts which acknowledged her existence at all, as little more than a uterus which literally took on a life of its own. The negation of the pregnant body is made very apparent in texts that discussed the maternal corset. These inevitably centred on the effects of constriction on the foetus rather than the impact of the corset on the mother. The foetus, which until the last trimester was cushioned from immediate pressure by amniotic fluid, was for much of the pregnancy no doubt more comfortable than its mother, whose body endured direct compression by corset at all times. This apparent and rudimentary observation was completely ignored by the garment's critics.

The refusal to acknowledge the existence of the maternal body (beyond the uterus and its contents) had serious consequences for individual women, and in an inevitable corollary, in attitudes held by pregnant women toward the foetuses they carried. In physical terms it meant that the severe constriction of the female body, at a time when it most required comfortable loose clothing, was never really addressed. The refusal to acknowledge pain endured by the corseted pregnant woman was manifested by the failure of even the most ardent dress reformists to discuss the issue of pregnancy and corsetry with any empathy toward the mother. Annie Jenness Miller, a fashion designer whose magazine *Dress* claimed to pursue 'a style of clothing for women which [did] not cause torture and disease of the body and distraction of the mind',[27] showed no sympathy for pregnant women who corseted their bodies. Miller, like most critics, assumed that vanity, ignorance and indifference led women to corset their swelling abdomens. She observed that corsets were 'grudgingly loosened a quarter of an inch at a time and [were] retained as the months passed'. Miller's despair was solely for 'the future of the child yet unborn', whose mother remained 'laced within stiff bones and steel while the very instincts of being cr[ied] out against it'. The 'instincts of being' referred to by Miller were not those of the mother, but those of the child. Mother was the invisible, negligible container for the more important subject, the foetus.

Miller's ideas were echoed in the popular American magazine *Arena*, which was written for an educated middle-class readership. Its editor, B.O.

Flower, was remarkable for his broad-minded socialist views. Vegetarian-ism, animal and human rights, child slavery, divorce, religious scepticism, trade unionism, negro [sic] and female enfranchisement were all staples of the journal and consistently reiterated in Flower's usually reflective editorial comment. Flower was an unequivocal supporter of feminism and an enthusiastic advocate of dress reform. He fully believed that 'morality, education, practical reform and enduring progress' could only occur upon women's 'complete emancipation from the bondage of fashion, prejudice, superstition and conservatism'.[28] In keeping with this desiderata the journal carried frequent articles on dress reform. Despite its radical political stand and its usually outspoken and progressive discussion of sensitive issues, *Arena* resorted to conventional arguments in its deliberations on 'maternal' corsetry that made mother both culpable and invisible.

In a lengthy essay titled 'Fashion's Slaves' published in 1891, which was primarily concerned with the evils of heavy, ostentatiously furbelowed women's frocks, Flower discussed both the popularity and the eugenic repercussions of corsetry. The corset, along with high-heeled shoes, were according to Flower 'the two most deadly foes to maternity and posterity'. Both, he added rather clumsily, were so prevalent as to be 'seen at the present time, on every hand'. Flower believed the corset constituted 'a crime against the unborn'. He lamented the individual 'loss of genius . . . of brain[s] which might have been brilliant, [now] rendered idiotic by the constant pressure of a corset'.[29] He was convinced that 'humanity' would be 'deformed and dwarfed' by women who wore fashionable dress.[30]

This kind of denunciation made moral criminals of individual women who persevered with corsetry during pregnancy, and made pregnant women, as a 'class', responsible for birth defects and 'race degeneration'. While Flower refused to break with the tradition of depicting the maternal body as both invisible and blameworthy, his discussion of the maternal body is significant. That a usually sympathetic and contemplative editor such as Flower maligned the corseted pregnant woman without any consideration of conditions that impelled her to corset, indicates that pregnancy taboos were as strong in the latter half of the century as in the beginning. His attitudes also indicate that the pregnant female body was considered no less repugnant, nor more deserving of particular care, in the late nineteenth century than it had been in earlier decades.

The demonization of the corseted pregnant woman was secured (un-wittingly) by the foetus, which was routinely depicted as enduring months of uterine torture by its narcissistic, unmerciful, maternal captor. Texts that ostensibly discussed the maternal corset were peppered with punitive metaphors of the prison that inevitably cited the foetus as prisoner and its mother, rather than the corset, as the unfeeling jailer. Influential corsetière and author Roxy Caplin propelled as much by pecuniary interests as by infant well-being, indulged in what is typical of the early 'mother-blaming' rhetoric of the garment. Caplin manufactured both maternity and regular corsets, and she hoped to persuade women to purchase specifically designed maternity models rather than loosening (or tightening) their 'fashionable' stays (Figure 22 and 23). Maternal guilt was fundamental to her sales pitch. The 'fashionable corset', she wrote in 1877 (making clear the distinction between her own maternity designs and regulation corsetry), impeded 'vital organs' and 'if it did not entirely displace the [pregnant] womb, . . . it crushe[d] and oppress[ed] the unborn babe' and made its foetal life one of serious difficulty. The baby (she continued, pre-empting Flower's rhetoric) was made 'a slave of fashion' by its mother. It was, from the moment of conception, 'fettered and starved' and subjected to 'the most painful oppressions' and, according to Caplin's calculations, 'tens of thousands of British women' made their unborn babes 'slaves of fashion' by this practice.[31]

Caplin insisted that her 'number 4 self regulating gestation corset' provided real support for the expectant mother and had none of the foetal threatening impediments of other garments. It supposedly 'answere[d] all phases of pregnancy' without un-due pressure to the foetus because of its elastic dilatable panels. Though the number 4 self regulating gestation corset seems to have been an improvement on Amesbury's Adjustable

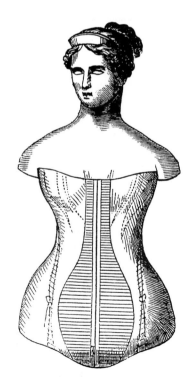

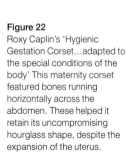

Figure 22
Roxy Caplin's 'Hygienic Gestation Corset…adapted to the special conditions of the body' This maternity corset featured bones running horizontally across the abdomen. These helped it retain its uncompromising hourglass shape, despite the expansion of the uterus.

Figure 23
Festa's Maternity Corset
Patent. This garment was more
realistically designed than the
hourglass-shaped maternity
corsets in vogue, however the
addition of bones and broad
metal busk must have been
extremely uncomfortable.

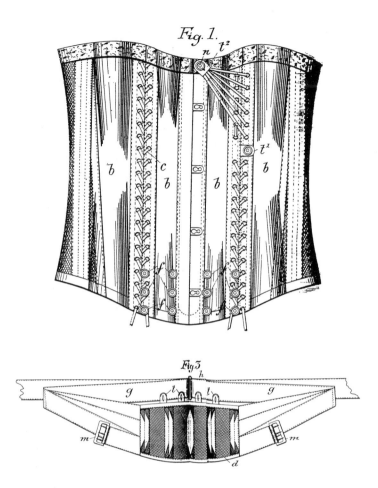

Body Support, it must be remembered that elastic's powers of expansion are matched by its powers of contraction. The corset may therefore have been as uncomfortable as or possibly even more uncomfortable than Amesbury's Body Support. Caplin understood elastic's dual abilities of expansion and contraction and capitalized on them, neatly anticipating and foiling any criticism. She inferred with the conviction of medical authority that the pressure produced by elasticized panels on the gravid body 'prevent[ed] abortion resulting from deficiencies in muscular power'.[32]

The notion that corsetry might prevent spontaneous abortion was refuted by the popular and influential physician Dr Henry Pye Chavasse. Chavasse (along with the medical profession in general) implied in a circuitous manner that tight clothing of any sort had the potential to affect the well-being of the foetus. Chavasse enjoyed considerable popularity in both America and England for his series of advice books directed primarily at the mother. His text, *Advice to a Wife On the Management of Her Own Health and On The Treatment Of Some Complaints Incidental To Pregnancy, Labour And Suckling*, was first published in 1832. *Advice to a Wife* enjoyed fourteen almost entirely unrevised reprints by 1898. The text is important for several reasons, not least of which reason is that it survived without medical editorial revision for almost thirty years. The numerous references to the dangers of corsetry during pregnancy suggest that the garment remained a feature of middle-class pregnancies until at least the end of the century.

Chavasse conceded that 'stays' were injurious to both mother and child, but his primary concerns (like those of most critics) were centred on the unborn. *Advice to a Wife* was opposed to maternal corsetry on the grounds that it caused 'cross birth' infant deformity and bearing down of the womb.[33] Chavasse acknowledged, at least, that corsets could increase soreness of nipples,[34] encourage malaise, and bring about episodical fainting, but he was unsympathetic toward women who experienced these symptoms. 'If a patient felt faint' he wrote somewhat testily, 'she ought immediately lie down flat on her back . . . stays and any tight articles of dress – if she be so foolish enough to wear either tight stays or clothes – ought to be loosened'.[35] The lady who is '*enceinte*' he wrote, observing the social niceties surrounding gestation in 1868, must remove all bones from her garments and 'wear her stays loose'. Women he continued, were not to 'screw themselves up in tight stays and dresses' because 'the child should have plenty of room'.[36]

While Chavasse recommended that the foetus was to be allowed plenty of room he made clear that mother was not. Despite his insistence that women loosen or relinquish stays during maternity, he urged them to embrace a lifestyle which acted as a 'psychic' corset that fettered their movements almost as effectively as the garments of cloth, bone and steel they had been advised to loosen. The 'psychic' corset was invoked for reasons identical to those for its material counterpart, to hide the embarrassingly distended female body from view. Pregnant readers were exhorted to limit their exercise to a morning walk about the garden or in the country, presumably out of sight.[37] Twenty five years later physicians were still advising women to remain under physical and social siege while pregnant. In 1891, Dr John Keating, author of the much-published *Maternity, Infancy and Childhood*, advised women to loosen their stays while they were pregnant and to take a daily walk, but to confine those walks to the late evening. This had the benefits, said Keating, of enabling the pregnant woman to leave the house 'without the restraints of wearing close fitting clothes'. This also ensured a 'good night's sleep',[38] and arguably avoided any public display of her uncomely pregnant body. This kind of advice, while granting perfect liberty to the baby, effectively imprisoned mother. Attempts by her to escape from the prison of her confinement (claimed a plethora of physicians) evidenced a flagrant disregard for the baby and was certain to increase the likelihood of that 'disaster', miscarriage.[39]

Although physicians (when they admitted its existence at all) unanimously concurred that the corset presented dangers to foetal well being, they were extremely reluctant to discuss its effects in detail. Interestingly, their textual silence in professional journals was undermined by their occasional declamations of maternal corsetry in publications for the general public. George Napheys, like most nineteenth-century doctors, faced an extraordinary dilemma when he attempted to discuss the corset, specifically because the most dramatic consequence of its use was miscarriage. To inform readers of this was to encourage its 'abuse' and equip women with knowledge that might allow them to control their own fertility. Napheys's best-selling text, *The Physical Life of Woman: Advice to the Maiden, Wife and Mother* (1870) reflected the usual medical obsession for the foetus, but also inadvertently divulged the potential that tightly laced corsetry had as an abortifacient. Napheys was a member of various medical and gynaecological societies and clearly understood the relationship between corsetry and miscarriage. He also recognized that pregnancy taboos (or as he put it 'false delicacy') had prohibited the discussion of corsetry's use and maternal aftermath. He claimed that he could not condemn too strongly attempts to conceal pregnancy by 'tight lacing and the application of a stronger busk', but he could not bring himself to articulate the worst case scenario of the corset's use, foetal mortality. Concealment, he wrote lamely, meant 'the child [was] placed in jeopardy'.[40]

Influential writer and physician Dr J.H. Kellog similarly castigated the use of the corset during pregnancy as 'an outrage against nature'[41] but like Napheys he was reluctant to explain why. The 'practice of some women lacing themselves in all through the period of pregnancy for purposes of "preserving their figure" [was] nothing short of an absolute cruelty, not only to themselves but to their unborn infants'. Laws, wrote Napheys, had been passed in ancient Greece to prevent tight lacing of the pregnant mother. 'What ever a woman has a right to do to her own body', he wrote (echoing the familiar almost thematic refrain of the maternal captor), the mother had 'no right to blight for all time the prospects of another being possessed of individual rights . . . although . . . a prisoner in her own body'.[42] Augustus Gardner, author of *Conjugal Sins Against the Laws of Life and Health* (1870) also believed the corset played a role in maternal debility, but his greatest sympathy was saved for the 'unborn thousands annually immolated . . . before the blood worshipped moloch of fashion'.[43]

At the time that Napheys, Kellog, Gardner and their contemporaries were self-consciously discussing or circumspectly avoiding the effects of corsetry on the pregnant body, the injurious effects of corsetry on the un-impregnated body were well known. The corset had been the subject of intense medical and scientific scrutiny since the 1860s. By 1880 both the medical profession and of course the women who wore the garments understood that the corset exerted tremendous pressure on the abdomen as well as on the chest. Using a manometer on more than fifty women Dr Latou Dickinson had shown that 'regular' stays produced between 21 lb and 80 lb of pressure per square inch on the body.[44] Dickinson's work had been replicated and further publicized by Dr D.A. Sergeant, who had shown that the corset reduced lung capacity by at least one-fifth.[45] Their work was further supported by hideous animal experiments on dogs and monkeys. The animals were corseted and the pressure on their abdomens and chests were systematically increased until they expired. These experiments, argued defenders, attempted to replicate the conditions imposed by the corset on the human frame and were discussed at some length in *Lancet*. The experiments showed that heart damage, syncope and death were related to tightly laced corsetry. Critics of vivisection by corset described these experiments as 'horrifying and wanton cruelty'. This charge was disputed by doctors who claimed that the animals did not suffer, and that similar 'compression of the abdomen and chest . . . [was] self inflicted daily by thousands of women in Great Britain without anaesthetic'.[46]

Despite the sustained professional debate and scientific research into the corset's deleterious effects on the unimpregnated body, most physicians refused to discuss the effects of the corset on foetal life or the pregnant woman in anything but the most brief and general terms. To do so would of course impinge on pregnancy taboos. Worse still, it would automatically reveal to nineteenth-century women, who were plagued by unreliable contraception, that the commonplace corset offered an almost undetectable method of disguising pregnancy and disposing of the smaller-than-average foetus if it was born prematurely, or was stillborn. Lionel Rose has briefly discussed several case histories of working- and middle-class women whose illegitimate babies were successfully concealed from families and employees in nineteenth-century Britain. Rose noted that these pregnancies were completely undetected until the accidental discovery of the infants' bodies. In almost all cases these unfortunate women insisted that the infants were born dead or died very quickly after birth.[47] Surprisingly Rose did not speculate how these women managed to conceal their pregnancies from family members and workmates. It would seem extremely likely, given that Dr Latou Dickinson's experiments showed that the standard corset exerted up to 80 lb per square inch of pressure on the torso, that corsetry was probably integral in the maternal deception and contributed significantly to the 'concealed' infant's death.

Carolyn Conley has also researched illegitimacy and infant mortality in Victorian England. Like Rose, she has shown that mortality rates of illegitimate children were extremely high. Conley remarked that many nineteenth-century women 'chose to deny the reality of pregnancy'.[48] Conley did not explain or contextualize this statement; however, Carrol Smith-Rosenberg expands on and substantiates Conley's claim. Smith-Rosenberg has shown there were historical precedents for 'denial' and that 'denial' was a particularly useful strategy in family limitation. She has shown that until at least 1860 (and as late as 1880), women, rather than the medical profession, determined whether or not they were pregnant.

Pregnancy was determined by women upon the experience of 'quickening'. Quickening was the common nineteenth-century term to describe foetal movement. Until the foetus quickened (approximately four months after insemination), the woman's cessation of menstrual periods could be construed either as an 'unnatural obstruction' or a pregnancy, depending entirely on the woman's interpretation of the biological changes experienced by her own body. The removal of an 'unnatural blockage' was not a criminal offence. Until the woman herself declared she had experienced quickening, the foetus was not accorded legal or medical human status, and both the woman and her physician felt justified in using drugs or mechanical devices to remove the 'obstruction' and bring order to her menses.[49] Recipes for the removal of obstructions were, at least until the 1880s, found in women's household advice manuals. The *Ladies' Indispensable Assistant: Being a Companion for Wife and Mother* published three recipes for this purpose.[50]

The emergence of intense and well-organized anti-abortion campaigns in the 1850s ended women's legal access to any operation or drug to remove an 'obstruction'. Enforcement of this legislation was wide-ranging and to some extent effective. A tide of texts that spelled out the dangers of abortion flooded the American and British market, but their warnings may have inadvertently promoted the use of the corset as a safer alternative. Pregnant women were reminded that laceration, puncture, irritation and inflammation of the womb were among abortion's immediate physical consequences. It was commonly claimed that neuralgia, and an assortment of frightening medical 'miseries'[51] (including insanity) followed in abortion's wake.[52] By the end of the nineteenth century, courts villainized and severely punished the pregnant woman, rather than the abortionist or supplier of abortifacients, simply because she was easier to locate and prosecute.[53] Clerics, united in their hostility to both contraception and abortion, added moral retribution to the anti-abortion campaign. Most agreed that it was 'better by far [for a woman] to bear a child every year for twenty years than to resort to such wicked and injurious step[s]' as abortion. It was 'better to die . . . in the pangs of childbirth' wrote Francis Cooke, author of *Satan in Society*, than to 'live with such a weight of sin on the conscience'.[54]

The barrage of legal, moral and medical intimidation, censure and retribution must have enhanced the corset's uncertain but latent promise of miscarriage. The corset offered a method of contraception that was possibly more effective than patent nostrums, safer than mechanical abortion and without the legal and moral repercussions of that operation. The value of corsetry was manifold. It could both hide pregnancy, sometimes until full term and, for other luckier women, conceal its successful interruption. The tightly laced corset offered an expedient method of family limitation that was instrumental in avoiding the outrage of husband, family, employers, clergy, state, and even personal 'conscience'. The extreme pressure of a tightly laced corset may have inhibited quickening and would certainly have obscured it from public notice. In reducing the effects of quickening, or forestalling the completion of pregnancy altogether, the corset allowed the pregnant nineteenth-century woman to convince herself, consciously or unconsciously, that no pregnancy had occurred and that bleeding after months of 'failed' menstruation was simply a case of cleared 'obstruction'. Moreover, if the corset failed to procure an early miscarriage, the likelihood of an infant's survival after it had been corseted throughout its term *in utero* were markedly reduced.[55] Moreover as Rose and Conley have pointed out, penalties for concealment of a dead infant were negligible in comparison to convictions of abortion.

Despite the reticence of many medical practitioners regarding the role of the corset in miscarriage, the information was nevertheless disseminated, paradoxically by those doctors and dress reformers who wanted to warn women of its dangers to the foetus. While not a medical practitioner, Angeline Merritt, author of *Dress Reform Practically and Physiologically Considered* (1852) understood the medical ramifications of corsetry worn during pregnancy. Merritt advised readers that 'under ordinary compression [of the corset] there [was] not room for anything like proper foetal development'. She believed that the practice of wearing corsetry while pregnant was the result of 'vanity prudishness [and a] mistaken and contemptible pride' and that the practice inevitably lead to malformation of the baby, haemorrhage or miscarriage. Should the baby actually survive the rigours of corsetry *in utero*, claimed Merritt, 'mother would be tormented in labour and would give birth with instrumentalities as horrid as they [were] unnatural'. The surviving child, she continued, would 'linger an inhabitant of earth only long enough to suffer needless pain'.[56]

The relationship between miscarriage, infant mortality and the corset were even more clearly explained to the reading public by Alice Stockham. Stockham was an American doctor and avid dress reformer who had none of the 'false delicacy' that had prevented Napheys and his peers from revealing the effects of tight lacing on the foetal body. Stockham blatantly announced to readers in 1883, that 'tight lacing [was] the chief cause of infantile mortality'. She noted that many girls gave birth to 'frail scrofulous children' because of 'obstructions in the respiratory system'. These obstructions, she maintained firmly, were the direct result of the corset. The corset allowed 'mother' to 'breath enough to sustain her own organism in fair condition' but it meant she did 'not inhale enough oxygen to sustain an inter-uterine being'. Stockham stated that 'many still births were explainable to this principle'.[57] She energetically reiterated (unlike her male peers) that abortion, miscarriage and foeticide were directly attributable to a 'lack of room in the pelvis' created by 'tight lacing and heavy clothing'.[58]

It is tempting to assume that Stockham's denunciation of the corset was in fact a veiled defence of the garment, a thinly disguised endeavour to publicize its properties as an abortifacient, but this was not the case. Stockham was resolutely against corsetry in general. When asked by a patient how far advanced a woman should be in pregnancy before she laid aside her corset, she replied that *'the corset should not be worn for two hundred years before pregnancy takes place'*.[59] (Stockham insisted that 'it would take that time at least to overcome the ill effects of the garment which [women] thought so essential.') Though Stockham upheld several feminist ideals (including female sexual sovereignty and male sexual continence), she was primarily concerned with the health of the foetus above the health of its mother. 'If the wearer only had to pay the penalty with pain and weakness we might hold our peace',[60] she wrote, signalling her allegiance to the foetus. 'If [the corset] were merely a female folly', she continued, 'or if its ravages were confined to its perpetrators it might be allowed to go unrebuked' but 'the murderous practice' struck 'a deadly blow at the very life of the race'.[61] Stockham, like her fellow physicians, was therefore also guilty of demonizing the pregnant woman. Like them she described the corset as an 'instrument of torture'.[62] She warned that the corset made women very ill throughout pregnancy, but maternal suffering was incidental in the text, compared to the real 'torture' imposed by the garment upon the child at the hands of its unmerciful captor, mother.

The notion that corsetry, whether of maternity or standard design, was injurious to the baby and incidentally to its mother, ran like a refrain throughout the patents for the garments. Inventors, both male and female, unanimously agreed that stays were

> constructed and formed without due regard to the state of pregnancy and as a consequence [were] the cause of great discomfort and danger arising from the undue and unnecessary pressure exerted by them [on] parts of the body which at such time . . . should have freedom for development.

Individual inventors, keen to promote their own corset designs routinely blamed both standard and maternity corsetry for producing 'displacement . . . miscarriage, premature labour, cross birth, faintings, hysteria and other evils'.[63] While an overview of Victorian corset patents reveals that both men and women were concerned about corsetry design, female designers – possibly because they had experienced the discomforts of standard and maternity corsetry themselves – revealed a more empathetic ideological position regarding maternal comfort during pregnancy. Despite this, patents lodged by female inventors frequently betrayed both a determination to hide the pregnancy, and concern that the post-partum woman achieve a slim silhouette as soon as possible after childbirth.[64] Consequently notes accompanying corset patents lodged by women were

often a curious amalgam of desires and concerns. The health of the baby
and its mother was often paramount, but there also existed a resolve to
conceal the baby's impending birth. Leonora Louise Stauder, whose patent
lodged in 1893 was intended for women who were 'enceinte and who
wished for many and obvious reasons to hide the alteration in their figure
. . . without resorting to the use of unnatural and in many cases injurious
devices', revealed the multiple and conflicting yearnings of many pregnant
women (Figure 24).

Strauder's design was characterized by an 'abdominal protector' of
flannel felt stockinet elastic that shielded the abdomen from any 'sudden

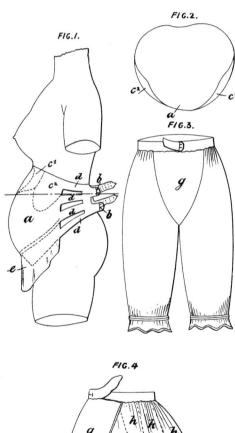

Figure 24
Leonora Stauder's 'Improved
System of Undergarments for
Women' was based on an
elaborate and unconvincing
disguise involving 'flounces,
pleating, padding, springs and
whalebone'. These were to
divert the eye 'from the
condition of the wearer.' The
patent reflects prevailing
taboos around the display of
the pregnant body.

changes of temperature' and was of a 'convenient shape and size as to completely envelope the abdomen and exact a gentle pressure thereon'. The garment appears to have offered a pliable encasement of the expanding body, but as Leonora explained it was best used in conjunction with specially cut outer clothes, for which she had also lodged a patent. The complex clothing arrangement designed by Strauder involved 'flounces, pleating, padding, springs and whalebone' to create a kind of abdominal platform which gave the illusion of flattening the stomach while diverting the eye 'from the condition of the wearer'.[65]

Many corsets designed for the pregnant and/or post-partum body abandoned the pretence of illusion and physically compressed the protruding, ideologically disruptive uterus back into the body. This was usually achieved by the inclusion of a detachable broad belt of sturdy design which sat over the stomach and which was laced or buckled into position across the abdomen. These belts were known as abdomen belts, and were a feature of many corset designs after 1860.[66] Elizabeth Mary Moore's invention, being the deceptively named Surgical Belt and Bed Stay, was designed with such a belt. Its use as a maternity corset was made clear by notes accompanying the diagram. The garment was, wrote its inventor revealingly, 'calculated to preserve a perfect figure . . . a useful surgical appliance in obstetric and other cases'. It was 'joined at the back by lacing or other suitable means' and 'provided with steel busks and strips of whalebone inserted in pockets in the ordinary manner of making stays'. The belt which 'surround[ed] the abdomen [was] provided with gussets of elastic or wire webbing'. The garment was then held into place by tapes which ran around the 'thighs and below the knees of the wearer', and these were secured by buckles'.[67]

While the complicated tapes were not a popular feature of commercially made corsetry design, the abdomen belt was clearly a success. The inclusion of a detachable or incorporated abdomen belt was often a significant sales point in many brands of corsetry. The Domen corset, whose very name was a contraction of the word abdomen, may well have been used as a maternity garment as well a post-partum corset. The Domen's widely publicized merits focused on the 'patent belt' said to be 'unique for restoring, improving and supporting the figure'[68] (Figure 25). Other maternity corsets manufactured by large corset firms such as Symingtons differed very little in construction from standard garments (Figure 26). Frequently maternity corsets, even until the turn of the century, were only distinguished from garments of standard design by the inclusion of two rows of lacing which ran either side of the abdomen, ending a little above the navel. These were supposed to be loosened as the occupant's body expanded. This was also a very popular feature of standard corset design. Belts, supports or binders were often a feature of standard corset designs. These belts were often reinforced with bones or steels. Occasionally, metal plates (as used in Madame Cave's corset) provided a completely inflexible barrier to prevent any expansion of the

"DOMEN" BELTS.
Pregnancy
Accouchement.

PERFECT FIT. GUARANTEED.

RESTORES FORMER SHAPELINESS.

Obstetric Binders for use immediately after Delivery.

"DOMEN" BELT CORSET.

A GOOD FIGURE WITHOUT TIGHT LACING !

FOR CORPULENCE

AND

GENERAL SUPPORT.

Uniting the Advantages
OF
Belt and Corset.

Illustrated Price List of large variety of Belts, Belt Corsets, &c., sent free on application to

"DOMEN" BELTS COMPANY,
456, STRAND, W.C.
30, SLOANE STREET, S.W.
Wholesale and Shipping :—61, Moor Lane, London, E.C.
Face Title-page.

stomach (Figures 27 and 28). These plates were sometimes 'set up' to perform 'galvanic action' (i.e. with magnetic inserts).

Given the extraordinary taboos around the pregnant body at this time, and given the importance of the waistline as a site of youth and beauty, it is likely that many women tightened, rather than loosened, either their maternity corsets or standard corsets as their bodies grew. Some may have purchased the heavily reinforced garments in the hope that they might eventually miscarry the foetus. Maternity corsets which did not have abdominal belts, but which favoured lacing at the front or at either side of the stomach, may have been similarly used to compress the stomach, rather than loosened to accommodate uterine expansion. Despite the inclusion of these extra potentially widening devices on maternity corsets, the advertising material which survives for these garments reveals that

Figure 26
This extant fashionable, standard, maternity corset of black silk and coloured flossing, laced at the sides for expansion (or contraction) also featured a heavy spoon-shaped busk of metal. This kind of busk, which was popular in standard corsetry from 1873–1889, curved inwards over the abdomen. Courtesy of Leicestershire Museum Services.

they were worn very tightly, with the result of simulating the unimpregnated state. Extant garments, such as those held at the Leicestershire Museum, reveal that they were almost identical in design and infrastructure to standard garments, containing as many steels or bones as ordinary corsetry. More telling still is that while maternity corsetry was ostensibly designed with the pregnant body in mind, many of these garments retained the exacting hourglass shape that characterized standard corsetry manufactured between 1850 and 1900.

Although prevailing taboos around pregnancy meant that the dangers of using corsetry during maternity were rarely articulated publicly, women clearly understood the potential for grave ill health (both to themselves and to their offspring) that the garments almost guaranteed. This begs the question of why so many women would persevere with such seemingly

Figure 27
Carlson's Patent Binder corset was frequently advertised in the opened and closed position. It was stoutly made and the attached abdominal belt potentially added even greater stress to the pelvic basin. See *Queen*, 1880.

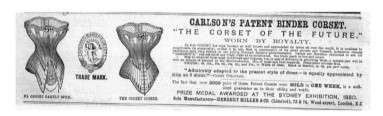

Figure 28
Madame Cave's corsetry was reinforced by rigid plates sewn into a detachable abdominal belt that buckled, rather than laced, across the lower abdomen. The advertisement claimed that the corset 'kept the figure down to its proper proportion.' Corsetry like this may well have been used to induce miscarriage. Interestingly the cave was understood by Jung to signify the uterus.

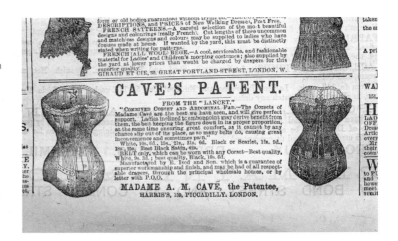

self-punishing behaviour by wearing corsetry while pregnant. The prevalence of pregnancy taboos explains only in part the popularity of the corset's use by pregnant women. Some women may have continued with corsetry despite its discomfort, fearing that to abandon the garment would jeopardize their own health. The standard corset was, after all, frequently promoted (ironically by both its defenders and its detractors) as a necessary support for the weak female frame. Some women may have believed ideas promoted by Dr Benjamin Ward Richardson, who argued that the desire to corset the body was hereditarily received and hereditarily transmitted. Richardson, writing in *Popular Science Monthly* in 1880, was convinced that while physical deformities created by the corset could not be transmitted, the 'inbred proclivity [to wear corsets] was so deep rooted [that] even if a generation of English women were made to abandon corsetry another generation, [or] perhaps two . . . would have to live before the practice was entirely abolished'.[69]

Other women may have persisted with corsetry while pregnant because they believed that their bodies had been 'weakened by civilisation' and would be made more vulnerable still by the exertions of pregnancy. Augustus K. Gardner claimed that it was a 'matter of common observation that the physical status of the women of Christendom ha[d] been gradually deteriorating'.[70] This 'fact' may have made maternal corsetry a regrettable but irreversible necessity for many women, for it was an idea that met very little opposition.[71] Indeed the theory of female physical degeneration, was vigorously promoted by a range of authoritative informants, including corset manufacturers, medical texts[72] and even popular women's magazines. Oscar Wilde (who in 1888, as editor of *Woman's World*, claimed not to advocate the corset) informed readers that the corset 'to which successive generations ha[d] become accustomed ha[d] by slow degrees deformed the figure'. Wilde further insisted that the 'compression of tight lacing and bones from wearing stays for over three quarters of a century' meant that the female body had 'lost its elasticity and [had] ceased to develop according to the laws of nature'.[73] Dr Arbuthnot Lane, author of 'Civilisation in Relation To The Abdominal Viscera, With Remarks On The Corset' published in *Lancet* in 1909, insisted that both men and women had difficulty in keeping the trunk erect, but this task was made more difficult for women *especially* because of pregnancy and the female body's naturally occurring longer abdomen and thorax.[74] These ideas were, on occasion, even reiterated by feminist doctors. The widely published physician Dr Anna Galbraith informed readers in 1911 that 'four hundred years' of corsetry had made the modern woman 'so physically degenerate that it [was] necessary to have recourse to the modiste in order to have even the appearance of a good figure and the support (of a) corset to maintain an erect position'.[75]

While the corset was cited by many doctors as a cause of degeneration of the female body, it was also blamed (unsurprisingly) as the cause of a difficult labour.[76] Dr Kellog's widely read household medical companion informed readers that 'primitive' uncorseted women (namely 'negro', [sic] Indian and other savage tribes') were spared the 'indescribable dread' of labour, because they had never known corsetry.[77] The rigours and dangers of labour experienced by American and English women were considered by many authorities as the consequence of generations of corset-wearing.[78] This could not have been reassuring information for women who had been corseted from childhood or adolescence and whose mothers' bodies, and their mothers' bodies before them, had been encased in corsets. It was, moreover, both undesirable and impossible for nineteenth-century women to 'turn back the clock' or attempt to recreate 'primitive conditions' that might or might not ensure a safe and painless labour. Caught between arguments that determined their bodies to be inherently weak and further weakened by corsetry, few women would abandon garments that purported to physically support their degenerate frames. To do so would increase, rather than decrease, the conflict and fear engendered by the garments' critics.

While the idea of constrictive maternity corsetry seemed anathema to late twentieth-century women, many middle- and working-class women in the nineteenth century employed, endured or grimly exploited 'gins of steel and cloth' from conception until parturition. While the garment was physically oppressive there can be little doubt that corsetry, whether specifically designed for the pregnant body or of standard construction, was used by many pregnant women to their own advantage. Corsets which were specifically designed for the pregnant body, while still uncomfortable, may have been important to women because their existence validated those women's experience of pregnancy which, because of prevailing pregnancy taboos, was in many ways denied. Moreover, the maternity corset discourse published in the patents and in the advertisements of reputable corsetières often stated that their garments actually offered 'the best preventative means against miscarriage'.[79] Paradoxically, such promises may have offered hope to women who were anxious to avoid miscarriage, and who believed that their bodies had been weakened by successive generations of corset-wearing.

Importantly, corsetry ostensibly designed for the pregnant body often promised to restore the 'figure to its previous form' thus circumventing, as corsetière Roxy Caplin baldly explained, 'the baneful consequences resulting from gestation'. In other words, pregnant women may have thought that retaining the corset throughout pregnancy might prevent, to a greater or lesser degree, the unflattering post-partum stretched abdomen, and enable them to cultivate the virtuous prematernal waistline after delivery. The latent promise of corsetry (either alone or in tandem with belts or binders after childbirth) to return the post-partum body to its seemingly virginal state was an alluring proposition given that the pregnant body, characterized by its protruding abdomen, thickened waistline and hips, was considered the antithesis of femininity. The tightness of the garment may have been a negligible factor in the decision to remain firmly corseted while pregnant. The compression of maternity corsetry upon the torso was probably thought by women already used to considerable constriction as no more difficult to endure than the pressures exacted by ordinary prenatal stays which, when tightly laced, exerted tremendous force.

With their regular 'stays' tightly laced both working- and middle-class pregnant women could avoid or delay the social isolation demanded of their 'condition'. The fashionable corset, at least in the early months of pregnancy, may have allowed women a few precious extra weeks of freedom in which the pregnancy was effectively hidden from sight, for the small sphere allotted to 'respectable' women in the nineteenth century contracted even further when they became pregnant. Other women, in more desperate circumstances, may have used corsetry to conceal or terminate their pregnancies, preferably before, but also after quickening. While physicians were reluctant to discuss the potential of the garment as an abortifacient, the corset's ability to limit conception was probably widely but discreetly discussed by women whose 'obstructions' had been dislodged by tight lacing and perseverance.

While the corset was utilized to the advantage of many pregnant women, it must be recognized that the garment constricted the body at a time when it most needed freedom to expand. The corset, whether worn to 'support' the pregnancy or to deny it, inevitably exerted pressure on the abdomen and chest and restricted movement. Of course, women probably used the corset as an expedient method of disguising their stomachs temporarily, by loosening their 'stays' while at home and tightening them to go out. However, corsetry must – as the third trimester progressed – have become increasingly difficult to bear, but to abandon it entirely would mean complete retirement from social life. The corset was, moreover, integral in maintaining pregnancy taboos. Its fundamental, if rarely acknowledged, charter was to reduce the size of the body, disguise 'unfeminine' bulges and prevent, whenever possible, the pregnant body from attracting public notice. In doing so the corset operated to uphold misogynist values and taboos constructed around the pregnant body to protect masculine interests. While the pregnant body indicated that the desirable trait of virgin status had been irretrievably 'lost', its regular occurrence also indicated that the prevailing notion of rugged but civilized masculine 'self-control' was a fiction.

Pregnancy made women invisible and silent but not necessarily power-less. Unlike their neurasthenic and hysteric sisters, pregnant women did not reassert or parody feminine ideals, which may in part explain why they were silenced, shunned and made invisible in popular culture. Despite their marginalization, pregnant women were not without agency. Clearly, many Victorian women hid their swelling bodies, while others understood that unwanted 'obstructions' or pregnancies might be interrupted by the application of stout and tightly laced corsetry.

3
The Child, the Corset, and the Construction of Female Sexuality

A study of the juvenile corset and the discourses that surrounded it reveals that it was an important modality in the socialisation and sexualization of nineteenth-century female children. The corset was the first item of juvenile material culture to be sexualized, and for this reason alone its existence demands investigation. Until the late eighteenth century, corsetry was worn by male and female children and adults of the middle and aristocratic classes of England and Europe. The corset was a visible outer garment of beauty and ornamentation, and its display was part of social etiquette. However, by the beginning of the nineteenth century, it seems that the corset had inexplicably become an undergarment, and by the mid-nineteenth century it was both compulsory and gender-specific.[1] The feminization of the corset, and its increasingly mandatory nature, combined with its disappearance as an outer garment, indicate that it was far more than a whimsical if long-lived fashion trend. It was, in fact, a phenomenon that swept England and America between 1860 and 1900. The popularity of the garment is indicated by the persistent advertising of the product and by the diversity, extent and longevity of debates in medical texts, women's magazines and newspapers outlining its advantages and dangers.

Because of the undeniably sexual nature of the garment, any discussion of the nineteenth-century juvenile corset must necessarily be situated within, or at least draw from, a number of larger discourses. These discourses include first-wave feminist activism, the construction of femininity, emergent theories of child sexuality, and fears of miasmic sexual contamination, since juvenile corsetry was intimately enmeshed with these and other related issues.

The decades between 1860 and 1880 appear to have been critical to the establishment of juvenile corsetry, as an essential addition to the cultivation of middle-class girlhood. However, there are occasional references that point to its use far earlier. Cecilia Ridley described the dramatic effect of 'stays' on a child of her acquaintance in 1840. Eleven-year-old Alice was 'afflicted with a pair of stays with bones which cause[d] infinite trouble and dismay to the whole household', wrote Ridley. Alice's mother had a 'gown made upon them that would astonish'. It was 'tight'-waisted, the sleeves were 'tight' and it was 'a most wax like fit and when she appear[ed] in said gown she look[ed] most awfully tall'.[2] By the 1850s, calls to modify or abolish the juvenile corset were made by both British and American dress reformers. While the 'evils' of children's corsetry were never given as much publicity as that attendant on the adult garment, reformers acknowledged the damage it did to children's bodies and discussed it intermittently. (The full impact of dress reform on juvenile corsetry was not realized until the end of the century.) Mrs Angeline Merritt, the American dress reformer wrote 'of a time when mothers . . . put deforming appliances upon daughters [of] eight, ten and fourteen years old'. Merritt believed little had changed by 1852. Mothers were 'still responsible for the vicious dressing of young girls'. They continued to 'demur greatly to the use of a corporation of stays, double gear and lacers' (sic) which according to Merritt effectively produced a 'wide deviation from the natural form which God originally conferred'.[3]

By the 1860s and 1870s, an increasing number of British and American mothers resorted to a 'corporation' of juvenile stays. The garment's primary advocates were often well known women with high public profiles. Of these, the prolific American author Marion Harland was probably the most influential. Harland wrote and published at least nineteen books. Several of these were published under the pseudonym Mary Terhune. Harland was also editor of The Homemaker magazine but it was through her best-selling texts, such as Eve's Daughters; or Common Sense for the Maid, Wife and Mother published in 1882, that she most ardently promoted corsetry for maid and mother alike. She insisted that by the time a girl had reached 'thirteen or fourteen she ought to be fitted with one of the numerous excellent bodices or corsets now in vogue'. While Harland scorned mothers who allowed their daughters to purchase a 'nineteen inch' when the child 'should wear nothing smaller than a twenty two', she defended the corset on the grounds that it 'protected the hips and abdomen, gently braced the spine and encouraged breast development'.[4]

By the 1880s magazines and women's newspapers were peppered with articles and advertisements promoting juvenile corsetry.[5] In an item titled 'Waist or No Waist' (which intimated that a waistline could not be procured without a corset), Dorothy, the fashion consultant for *Woman* magazine, wrote that 'for children and young girls up to fourteen' she could 'consciously recommend the National corset bodice'. In another column of *Woman* dealing with reader enquires, 'The Factotum' recommended to 'Inexperience' that 'the Rational Corset Bodice [was] the best for children and young girls as it [wore] very well and [was] inexpensive'.[6] The Rational Corset Bodice, according to its numerous advertisements, was ideal for those ladies who 'studied their health and that of their children'. It was, according to its manufacturers 'far superior to the ordinary, hard, stiff corsets' from which it was 'distinguished by its great pliability and the ease with which it [could] be washed'. It had the further advantage of fitting 'like a glove' and was 'especially useful for growing girls and young ladies, giving all needful support without pressure'. The Reform Corset Bodice was available in white, drab or scarlet. Scarlet was not considered an especially erotic colour but was thought to generate healthful properties.[7]

The Rational Corset Bodice was priced according to the prospective wearer's age. The model designed to fit a two-year-old child cost two shillings, while those designed for girls up to eight years old cost an extra sixpence. For young girls up to fourteen the cost rose to three shillings and nine-pence. The rational/reform child's corset at least looked more comfortable than its more curvaceous counterparts. It had the ubiquitous indented waistline but it buttoned rather than laced and this would have afforded a more comfortable fit. Illustrations reveal that it was probably corded rather than boned, but despite its supposed 'great pliability' it had the appearance of being able to stand of its own accord.[8] A number of the 'reform' or 'rational' corsets for children and adolescents were available for purchase throughout the century. While some were corded, others were quite heavily boned (see Figures 29–30). True 'reform' garments –

Figure 29
Ferris Good Sense Corset Waists generally buttoned rather than fastened with metal clasps and consequently they afforded women more comfort than standard corsetry. Few women wore them.

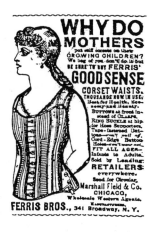

Figure 30
The Good Sense (Healthy
Children) corded waists were
designed to accommodate the
pre-adolescent body. Because
they buttoned, rather than
fastening with metal clasps,
they were looser than standard
children's garments.

that is, garments that fitted over rather than physically shaping the child's or adolescent's body – were often advertised in women's magazines which were identified as feminist and were directed at an 'enlightened' readership. Very often even these garments promised to 'support' the growing child. (see figs.37-9)

'Support' remained a principle motif of most children's corsetry advertisements until the end of the century, despite mounting evidence from clothing reform groups, independent feminists and enlightened doctors, who insisted that children's bodies did not require it. Laura Ormiston Chant, writing in a mainstream British women's magazine *Woman's World*, informed readers that girls whose muscles had been 'trained from babyhood to do their work efficiently . . . [would] not need to squeeze [themselves] into a gin of steel and whale bone for so called support'.[9] The proliferation of advertisements that relied on the concept of support, despite evidence that the body did not need it, suggests that the support promised by the garment was unconsciously understood by nineteenth-century mothers as being of an intangible 'moral' kind. It would appear that the words 'support' and 'reform' were analogous metaphors that described the perceived moral properties of the garments as much as their physical structure. (This idea will be developed more fully later in this chapter.)

It can also be argued that the spiralling popularity of the juvenile corset was in part a material response to vexing social issues created by first-wave feminist demands for education, employment and a place 'outside the hearth'. Demands for female independence challenged existing gender relations and the distribution of power. These demands were frequently perceived as alarming flights from femininity. Historian Lillian Faderman noted that the anti-feminist response to feminist claims was multiple and swift. In Britain, anti-feminist tracts began to appear as early as 1830, at least a decade before the feminist movement actually consolidated. Both American and British women were admonished, in a plethora of texts, to cultivate suitable attitudes, practise feminizing domestic arts and refrain from entering the public masculine sphere. 'There is something unfeminine in independence' wrote Mrs Sandford, author of *Woman in her Social and Domestic Character*.

> It is contrary to nature and therefore it offends. A really sensible woman feels her dependence, she is conscious of her inferiority . . . In everything that women attempt they should show their consciousness of dependence.

Anxieties generated by feminists who refused to celebrate their dependent status often coalesced in criticism of their dress. *The Mother's Magazine* warned readers that 'Amazons [were] their own executioners. They had unsexed themselves in public estimation and there [was] no fear that they [would] perpetuate their race'. An article appearing in the *Ladies Companion* that same year (1838) noted that women who sought education [would become] 'semi-women or mental hermaphrodites'.[10]

Fashion was quick to reassert the conventional feminine ideal in the realms of both the adult woman and the female child. It was also quick to reassert sex and gender difference. There were, during the nineteenth century, a range of explicit and subtle reorganizations in the material culture (or body codes) of childhood and womanhood that can be read as resistant to, and reflective of, threats to the adult social order posed by feminist demands. Body codes, explain Julia Epstein and Kristina Straub, include among other things demeanour, deportment, cosmetics and clothing. Body codes, assert Epstein and Straub, have been historically crucial to maintaining hierarchical institutions which rely on strict adherence to gender for their continuation. Body codes are used, and have historically been used, primarily to contain 'the threatening absence of boundaries between human bodies . . . that would otherwise explode the organisational and institutional structures of social ideologies'.[11]

Corsetry was a very significant body code in the nineteenth century that worked to shore up sex/gender systems which feminism threatened to destabilize. The demise of 'breeching' at a time when juvenile corsetry was becoming *de rigueur* for little girls neatly illustrates Epstein and Straub's thesis that gender fluidity is historically a source of cultural and gender anxiety. Breeching once signalled the entry of the male child to masculinity. It had been a popular rite of passage in the eighteenth century[12] but was almost abandoned by 1850. The abandonment of breeching at the time when corsetry was adopted almost solely for female children and women was not coincidental. It reveals that female rather than male gender identity was perceived as threateningly fluid and that femininity (unlike masculinity) required the implementation of boundaries to effectively define and contain it. With the disappearance of breeching, the juvenile corset became a useful tool in realizing the process of gender division. Corsetry effectively maintained bodily difference by creating or emphasizing the tiny 'feminine' waist, and it coerced gender identity by limiting the physical behaviour of girl children to that considered appropriate to their gender.

Outer garments assisted in this process. By the 1870s women's clothing was characterized by, even obsessed with, decorative detail. Assisted by the marketing of the sewing machine, gowns became sumptuous visual orgies of ribbons, bows, ruffles, lace, flowers, fur and feathers that were completely unsuited for any practical purpose.[13] Significant alterations in frock design also hindered movement. Between 1865 and 1880, boning was increased in bodices and jackets, sleeves were narrowly set into garments in a manner which precluded lifting the arms, and the bustle projected some 60 cm (2 feet) behind its wearer. This must have made even sitting down a skilful task requiring practice. Between 1870 and 1880, a closely fitted frock dethroned the bustle, but its slender skirt and 'fishtail trains' were held together from thigh to lower calf by tapes tied behind the legs to prevent a striding gait.[14] During these decades, male clothing was also undergoing a rapid and dramatic evolution. An ideology of comfort, which had its origins in England, worked to reduce confinement in masculine attire.[15] Male clothing, which had once been brightly coloured and ornamental, grew increasingly neutral and austere. The departure of men's fashion from colour, ornament and restriction and the concomitant increase in feminine *frou-frou*, reflected societal anxieties and imperatives to reinforce traditional separate spheres and preserve gender specificities.[16]

Children's clothing and other items of material culture were undergoing a similar transformation. Indeed the bodies and the clothing of female children were critical, if not paramount sites, in the decisive process of delineating and stabilizing gender. By the 1860s the clothes of girl children as young as nine, were very much miniatures of their mothers'.[17] By the 1870s, little girls' frocks, though shorter than adult costume, affected the bustles, plastrons (i.e. drapery over the chest) and *frou-frou* of their mothers' outfits and required identical underpinning[18] (see Figure 31). Fashion garments of the 1860s worn by mothers and daughters of all ages impeded movement and required corsetry to effect the ever desirable, slender waist.[19] By the middle of the nineteenth century, simply cut children's clothing (popular a century earlier) had completely vanished.[20] Little girl's clothes were, according to widely published author Harriet Beecher, 'a facsimile of the grand dame's attire, [with] flounces, fringes, bows and double skirts looped and festooned in an astounding manner'. Female children whose outer garments were suspended over hoops or crinolines (identical in shape to the crinolines of their mothers) were 'made to carry this incongruous burden totter[ing] about on high heeled boots'.[21] The trend to dress female children in impractical garments that replicated those of adult women can be read as a mechanism to ensure the reiteration and perpetuation of a particular female ideology, an ideology that reasserted traditional female role models.

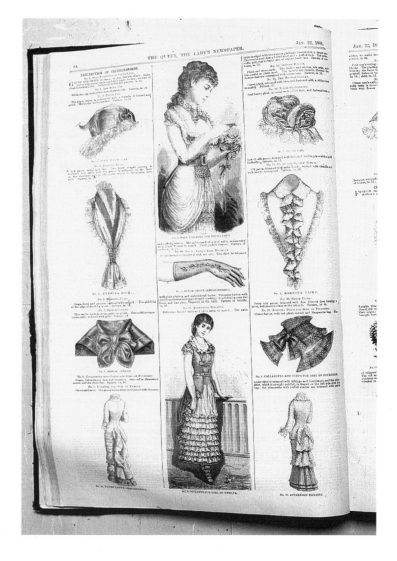

Figure 31
The frills and flounces of adult
fashions were routinely
replicated in children's and
adolescent clothes as
demonstrated in the fashion
pattern pages of *Queen*.

Juvenile corsetry was as essential to this ideology, and its reinscription, as 'precious' outer garments. Children, though largely powerless regarding the implementation of corsetry, sometimes demonstrated considerable resistance against its implementation. Occasionally, ingenious adolescent girls turned tightly laced corsetry to their own advantage. Cicely Steadman, a pupil at Cheltenham Ladies College in the 1870s, mentioned corsetry as 'a minor ailment that gave some trouble' which facilitated the 'addiction of some girls to slight fainting fits'. These fits occurred when fashion conscious young students took measures to secure an '18 inch waist'. Other canny students 'contrived a good deal of unconsciousness' and made fainting 'correspond to a surprising degree with unpopular homework'.[22]

In her delightful memoirs of a Victorian childhood titled *Period Piece*, Gwen Raverat recalled that clothing in general, and corsetry in particular, was a 'major source of rows, naughtiness, misery and all the unpleasantness' throughout her entire youth.[23] As Raverat recalled, clothing was 'imposed on us from above, without even the power of veto'. Juvenile corsetry was recalled with particular bitterness, although as Raverat kindly remarked, she did 'not believe [her] mother was more suggestive to attacks of theory [when it came to her opinion regarding juvenile corsetry] than many other parents of her time'.[24] While Raverat understood that any combat against juvenile corsetry was 'hopeless', she remembered that she '*did* rebel against stays'. Her sister Margaret, who was put into corsets at thirteen, 'ran round and round the nursery screaming with rage'. Raverat's response was markedly different. 'I ran away somewhere and took them off', she wrote, then

> endured sullenly the row that ensued when my soft-shelled condition was discovered; was forcibly re-corseted; and as soon as possible went away and took them off again. One of my governesses used to weep over my wickedness in this respect. I had a bad figure and to me they were instruments of torture; they prevented me from breathing, and dug deep holes into my softer parts on every side. I am sure no hair shirt could have been worse to me.[25]

Children's corsetry of the mid-nineteenth century fell roughly into two quite separate categories. Both remained popular throughout the nineteenth century. One kind or the other were generally worn by most middle-class girls and young women at some stage of their lives, and both styles underwent very little modification in the course of fifty years. The first of these styles was the 'reform' corset, sometimes called the corset waist or corset bodice. It was generally worn between infancy and puberty. It was usually made of buckram, calico, wool or stiff cotton cloth and was often reinforced with bones, steels or stiffened cords. It resembled a child's singlet in shape and it was designed, initially at least, to follow the contours of the torso rather than mould the child's body into a particular shape. Several versions of the reform corset included a busk. The reform corset was occasionally laced rather than buttoned, a practice that found increasing popularity as the century closed. The second category of corset will, for the purposes of this chapter, be called the standard corset. Its distinguishing feature was its hourglass silhouette, a silhouette that was very unlike that of the body of nine- or ten- year-old child. It was made of sturdy fabric, and was laced and heavily reinforced with stiffened cords; but unlike the reform corset it was designed specifically to accentuate or create (and then maintain) a tiny waistline.

Children's corsetry of both kinds was marketed from at least mid-century. Corsetière Madam Caplin advertised her juvenile corsetry range as early as 1855. She emphasized the merits of the garment in supporting the child's frame, as well as dwelling on its role in regulating the child's growth. Her 'reform' corsetry was considered very suitable for pre-pubescent girls. Caplin's use of the word 'reform' is complex. She ostensibly used the term to distinguish her 'rational' garments from the popularly worn standard, heavily boned device. Her reform corsetry was not intended, in any conspicuous way at least, to reform the moral fibre of the child. However, her descriptions of the corsets indicate that they were designed not only to support the physical body of the child, but also to be useful tools in the inculcation of appropriate gender behaviour. Her Juvenile Hygienic Corset was recommended for 'young ladies growing too rapidly' while her Juvenile Reform Corset 'laced in front [allowing the little girl] to be in a perfectly upright and natural position'.[26] This was the only acceptable comportment of polite middle-class female children. Caplin's Reverso-Tractor Hygienic Corset was also clearly intended to modify or circumvent activities deemed inappropriate. The Reverso-Tractor was designed specifically to 'prevent children standing on one leg'.[27] Caplin did not describe the Reverso-Tractor Hygienic Corset, but it is reasonable to speculate that it encased the entire torso to at least mid-thigh length. This would effectively hobble the child and preclude any un-feminine hopping, climbing or leaping games. Almost forty years later Edwin Checkley, the British proponent of physical culture, remarked that 'the iniquity of putting corsets on growing girls' was still a 'crime' and 'girls who r[a]n were still liable to be accused of rudeness(!)'.[28]

The role and effectiveness of the nineteenth-century juvenile corset as a body code is also ably demonstrated by tracing its appearance in other aspects of children's culture. Corsetry even influenced the appearance of dolls. Many dolls made between 1850 and 1900 were purchased complete with corsetry that was designed and shaped like the corsetry of adult women (see Figures 32 and 33). High-fashion children's dolls made in France, England, Germany and America, were usually corseted, and indeed dolls held in museums and in private collections which retain their nineteenth-century corsets are very highly prized. Historians Michelle Perrot[29] and Ardyce Masters have independently shown that the mid-nineteenth century was a critical period in the evolution of doll design. Dolls, says Masters, should be recognized as tools that delegate particular tasks and attitudes to children and which 'at the same time skilfully disguise the underlying motives of this delegation'. Masters asserts that dolls can be viewed as indicators of cultural anxieties and concerns, especially of anxieties connected with male fears about independent women. Occasionally, says Masters, 'events in the doll trade give away the disguise' that dolls are merely superficial playthings.[30]

Michelle Perrot has investigated 'events in the doll trade' which substantiate Masters's claims. Perrot found that during the first half of the

Figure 32
Parisian Doll in original corsetry
c.1865 (front view). Maker
thought to be Mlle Rohmer The
doll's corset of white heavy drill
is both hand- and machine-
sewn. Great attention to detail
is apparent. The corset laces
at both back and front, is
corded and shaped to tightly fit
the body of the doll. (Courtesy
of Dr Juliet Peers)

Figure 33
Parisian Doll (back view). The
detailed stitching of the corset
is picked out in red stitching
over the white drill.

nineteenth century dolls resembled the little girls who played with them, also noting that the role of the doll was that of *confidante*. However, by the mid-nineteenth century child-like dolls had vanished, to be replaced by 'fashion-plate' dolls that were replicas of curvaceous adult women with 'nipped in waists and broad hips'. The popularity of the nineteenth-century 'Barbie' was only eclipsed by baby dolls, which emerged (but did not compete with the fashion-plate dolls) a short time later. Perrot believes that the combined dominance of the entire doll *genre* by fashion and baby dolls was designed to encourage young girls to envisage maternity as a career. Masters believes that the baby-doll/fashion-plate-doll trend was actually a backlash against feminists who were subverting prevailing stereotypes of women as naturally maternal or narcissistic.[31] Fashion-plate dolls were (and still are, of course) influential in formulating childhood expectations of appearance and behaviour. The nipped-in waists and broadened hips of the 'adult' dolls would have (subconsciously at least) insinuated in female children their future role as sexual objects, and instilled in them the desire to retain or accomplish at any cost that unnatural physical feature, the tiny doll-like waist. Doll corsetry would have been instrumental in this process (see Figures 34–36).

Clearly clothes, whether on dolls or human beings, are significant objects in determining the extent and type of role socialization directed toward children. Sociologists have shown that adults actually purvey culture by providing gender-symbolic dress. Clothing is known to serve

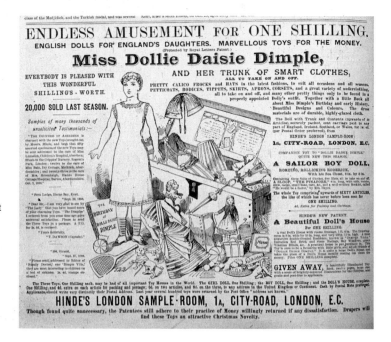

Figure 34
Miss Dolly Daisie Dimple's trunk included among other items 'skirts, aprons, corsets…[being part of] a great variety of underclothes to be found in a properly appointed dolly's outfit'. See *Illustrated London News*, 1888.

Figure 35
Doll's corset (front view) c 1895
of white and lavender courtil.
Opened to show detail of
cording. (In private collection,
Adelaide.)

Figure 36
Doll's corset (back view)
Garments like this were
frequently found on fashion
dolls. Note the metal eyelets.

both the 'macrobiological' and 'macrosocial' system. That is, gender-symbolic dress (such as frocks and trousers) assists and encourages society to attribute feminine or masculine gender attributes to particular children and then to act on those attributes when interacting with them. The importance of dress cannot be underestimated, for while it effectively delineates gender, it also serves the dual purpose of encouraging individuals to 'internalise as gendered roles a complex set of social expectations for behaviour'.[32]

Children's corsetry of the nineteenth century undoubtedly worked in tandem with 'outer clothing' to delineate gender and assist in the internalization of female gender roles. The long-lived trend of outfitting children in tight corsetry and in miniature versions of adult outer costume was not without contemporary critics, who railed against the discomfort as well as the gender limitations this kind of dressing imposed. Mrs Merrifield, British author of *Dress as a Fine Art* published in 1854, argued for reform of children's dress, which she observed, was 'fantastic in its character'. She noted that female children, were plagued by tightly laced corsets, and that these were implemented to create a small waist, a feature she considered an 'actual blemish'. Merrifield's comments were provoked by watching children of both sexes playing in a park. The costume of little girls, she observed, 'entirely destroyed their freedom of movement'. The 'stricture of their tightly laced corsets' meant that unlike the boys, who easily stooped to pick up a ball, girls were forced 'invariably to drop on one knee'.[33]

Medical arguments (rather than gender arguments), were often summoned by opponents of juvenile corsetry. Dress reformers and doctors both male and female, periodically railed against juvenile corsetry. Interestingly, dress reformers and the medical profession appear to have forged an alliance around children's corsetry as an issue, though they frequently diverged on matters associated with female suffrage and education. Dr Harriet Austin, American author of *Women's Right To Good Health* and editor of *The Laws of Life* published in 1867, noted that 'nearly every little girl five years of age ha[d] bands pinned against her chest so snugly that she [could] not take a full breath'.[34] Austin's texts were petitions for rational dress reform. The bands she referred to which prevented the complete respiration of many five-year-old American children were, of course, the bones of the juvenile corset. British dress reformers were similarly concerned by the extent of juvenile corsetry and its effect on health and respiration. *The Rational Dress Society's Gazette* of 1888 noted that large quantities of 'cheap . . . ill-made and badly cut' corsets had flooded the British market with the result that 'every little girl of ten or twelve [was] encased in stays'. Once in stays the girls had 'only about half their lungs to breathe with'. This 'semi-breathing' was apparently painless, but, reported the *Gazette*, it produced a 'lowered vitality'.[35]

The symptom of breathlessness accompanied by 'lowered vitality' was also noted by Dio Lewis, American promoter of gymnastic exercise and author of several edifying texts, including the widely read *Five Minute Chats With Girls*. Lewis observed that the corset brought about different breathing patterns between girls and boys at puberty. It was commonly held, even by medical experts, throughout the century, that girls naturally breathed using only the upper portion of the chest while boys used the entire capacity of their lungs. The corset was, of course, responsible for this misconception, for when tightly laced it constricted the lungs and made female respiration rapid and shallow.[36] Lewis warned his young readers that to wear corsetry was 'one of nine ways to commit suicide'.[37] Like many other enemies of corsetry he problematized the notion that the corset beautified the adolescent figure. 'As to a matter of beauty' he wrote 'it is a question between the creator and the dressmaker and [he took] sides with the creator.'[38]

Helen Gilbert Ecob, author of *The Well Dressed Woman: A Study in the Practical Application to Dress of the Laws of Health, Art, and Morals*, although not a doctor, similarly inveighed against the juvenile corset using medical testimony to support her arguments. Ecob made prolific but judicious use of anti-corset theories presented by respected late nineteenth-century British and American doctors such as Latou-Dickinson, Harvey Kellog, and T. Gaillard-Thomas. Ecob drew most heavily from the findings of Dr Kitchen of New York, whose views on child corsetry added a ring of scientific authority to her claims. Kitchen's medical opinion of the juvenile corset was characterized by an alarming and uncompromising condemnation of the garment.

> The appliance kills slowly [Kitchen warned] and to the unlearned imperceptibly; nevertheless the corset on the child is slow murder of the child, and if she be of a phthisical or consumptive tendency it is not so very slow a murder either.[39]

Similarly Elizabeth Duffey, author of *What Women Should Know*, was specific if not accurate in her diagnosis of the medical ailments incumbent with children's corsetry. She steadfastly maintained (as did several of her peers) that corsetry damaged the growing child's generative organs, weakened the stomach and bowels, and caused consumption. The latter was proved to be incorrect; however, at the time it seemed a logical conclusion even among trained physicians. There were after all far more female than male consumptives, and tight lacing and consumption shared some similar outward symptoms, these being discomfort, chest pain, breathlessness and a flushed appearance. Duffy wrote that mothers were culpable for much of the ill health endured by young girls. Under a heading titled 'The Evils of Stays' she wrote that '*there must be no corset worn*' by the young girl and that the enforcement of stays, rendered 'life miserable, and the sufferer incompetent to the complete and easy performance of duties assigned to her'.[40]

Feminist magazines also worked to dismantle the craze for the juvenile corset. While the influential American feminist journal *Daughters of*

America routinely carried corsetry advertisements for adults, it was never guilty of the same for children. Indeed it was in the discussion of children's clothes that the magazine's politics never faltered. Regular articles published in 1886 encouraged mothers to abandon the practice of corseting both themselves and their daughters. 'Clothing that constricts the waist interferes with breathing and digestion' wrote the editor, and 'bones and steels interfere with the pliant grace of the natural figure'. Mothers were warned that 'any girl who had been compressed by corsets from early childhood' would ultimately have both her health and her beauty seriously impaired.[41] A year later *Daughters of America* revealed that the anti-corset message had not been fully embraced and that tight lacing still occurred even within the *Daughters of America* readership. In an article titled 'What to Teach Our Daughters' mothers were advised to impart to their little girls ten important points. These included teaching them that one hundred cents made one dollar, that it was in their best interest to cultivate both a kitchen and a parlour garden, to say no and mean it, to say yes and mean it, and to understand that 'tight lacing [was] uncomely as well as injurious' to their health'.[42] Juvenile corsetry was, to the editors of this journal if not to its entire readership, a matter as important as moral or domestic guidance.

Despite the volley of reasonable arguments inveighed against it by reasonable women, juvenile corsetry remained popular, possibly because it validated various female life stages that were completely overlooked in the public sphere. Nineteenth-century descriptions of the female child in magazines, journals, health texts and advertisements were interchangeable and therefore somewhat elusive. The words 'maid', 'maiden', 'young girl', 'miss' and even 'young woman', were applicable to any female 'child' between infancy and her late teens. While fewer terms were used to describe boyhood and youth, masculinity and its maturity were much more recognizable and far less fluid. This was because the lives of male children were clearly punctuated and delineated by adolescence, increasing independence, career and marriage. Female children, by comparison, had few milestones beyond the secret biological 'storm' of menstruation to mark their increasing maturity. Unlike their brothers, middle-class female children were for most of the century denied any meaningful concept of development, autonomy and adulthood until they were married. (Even then they remained in legal infancy.) Corsetry provided concrete, if private and symbolic, recognition of the transition between pre-adolescent years, puberty and adulthood. This may, in part, explain its popularity among young women whose (publicly) constructed subjectivity was so plastic, and whose personal lives were empty of significant events that marked their emotional and physical growth.[43]

British dress reformer Lady Harberton, inventor of the divided skirt and eventual president of the Rational Dress Society in 1884,[44] left a remarkable and rare account of her own 'lived' experience of teenage years encased in corsets. Harberton's memoirs shed some light on why some female children passively or willingly accepted, or even in some cases actively campaigned for, their first tightly fitted corset. Harberton's insistence on being corseted in early adolescence appears to have been propelled by a desire to be recognized uncompromisingly as an adult. Corsetry allowed Harberton to construct her own identity, to set herself apart from the labile, merging categories of girlhood/maidenhood/adolescence. A corset cut on the lines of an adult garment would literally have physically created/imposed an adult sillouhette on her body. In maturity, she bitterly regretted her youthful decision to corset.

Harberton compared her 'bushwhacking' American childhood ('memorable for its startling gymnastic exploits') with her adolescence and adulthood that were besieged by poorly diagnosed maladies. Harberton believed many of her illnesses could be traced back to her first corset, which she candidly admitted was 'perversely followed by many of its kind'. She recalled that, upon moving to the city with her family as a young child, she had begged her mother for a corset. Her mother, who disapproved of corsetry for young girls for 'hygienic reasons' at first resisted, but then relented on the condition that the 'child' make her own. This she did, taking as her model a corset owned by a relative, that was described by Harberton as 'an elaborate work of art, one mass of fine cording and delicate stitching with one thin strip of oak in front called a busk'.

Harberton's corset was laced behind and run through with stiff cords. It was 'guiltless of steel and mostly of whalebone', but as Harberton later remarked 'you could lace yourself tighter for all that'. Her mother initially smiled at her daughter's determination, envisioning the child's defeat at such a complex sewing task, but, wrote Harberton, 'she knew little what inspiration there was in a wasp waist'. The young Lady Harberton copied the corset with 'absolute Chinese exactness', neglecting her study, play and exercise in the task 'never thinking for a moment that every stitch of that elaborate outward ornamentation would be repeated inwardly by a stitch in [her] side'. She finally finished the 'pretty barbarous thing', and though it hurt her she gave no sign. She continued to grow, 'unequally' and finally succumbed to 'side-aches' and palpitations of the heart. She recalled that she went to sleep exhausted but woke up tired, lost her country colour and shape, became pale, poetic and 'so willowy'. She 'took to writing church yard poetry, in consequence perhaps of a churchyard cough'. This was noticed in school. She 'grew round-shouldered over her desk in spite of her busk', but her slenderness was admired. No girl in the physiology class had so small a waist. She recalled that 'chunky corsetless girls measured it with envy'. The fainting fits that eventually followed her persistence with the corset rendered her interesting. For these, she noted, and the unremitting 'ugly pain in the side', physicians were called in. 'If they *thought* corsets [she wrote] they did not mention them. Doctors were delicate in those days. Not knowing what to do they bled me'.[45]

Harberton's referral to the corset as that 'pretty barbarous thing' and the recognition that her mother could not comprehend the attraction of a wasp waist, indicates that even as a child Harberton sensed that the corset held a promise of sexual or at least feminine allure. This promise was clearly explicated in corsetry texts. By the 1860s and 1870s, children's corsetry was no longer strictly perceived or promoted as a simple extension of swaddling. There began, in those decades, a subtle but marked trend in sexualizing the child's body within the corset. Children's corsetry still concerned itself with the prevention of the 'evils of early neglect'; these being such disfiguring ailments as Baker's Knee, curvature of the spine, a lounging gait and general stooping, but increasingly the emphasis of corsetry was to retain the child's tiny waist. Mothers were warned that without adequate corsetry, their daughters' abdomens might be 'weakened by a deposition of fat' in which case 'Art' [ie. corsetry] must step in to save the young girl from the social anathema of a 'chunky' waist.[46]

The objectification of the child-size waist, and the sexualization of the child that was its result, flagged a significant departure from the mandate of the eighteenth-century corset. Corsetry of that century, was, as previously mentioned, worn by adults and children of both sexes. During that era, children's corsetry was intended fundamentally to encourage good posture and strength. While the design of the eighteenth-century juvenile corset resembled that of her mothers, the adult corset differed dramatically in that the almost identical cylindrical construction also ensured that the mature breasts were shown to their fullest advantage. The 'fashionable' waist, as opposed to the real waist, was at that time a negligible sexual asset. It roamed the length of the torso until settling in 1830 at its (more or less) natural location,[47] when it became imbued with a sexual valency it had not previously experienced. The waist's ascendance as the new site of concern and adulation did not diminish the cult of the breast.[48] It heralded a new and more complete sexual objectification of the entire adult female torso, and very quickly, that of the young girl. The sexualization of pre-pubescent children was almost inevitable once the waist had been objectified, for while pre-pubescent children have little or no breast and hip development, they do naturally and generally possess that secondary sexual characteristic, a small, if undefined, waist.

The corsetry discourse from the 1860s onward made clear that the child-sized waist of adult women could only be achieved by a kind of somatic bonsai of children, barely out of infancy. The discourse crystallized in debates on the subject in *The English Women's Domestic Magazine*. There has been ongoing and recent controversy regarding the authenticity of letters that discuss juvenile corsetry published by the *EDM*. Social historian Lawrence Stone[49] believes the corset correspondence to be authentic. So too does art and fashion historian Helene Roberts.[50] On the other hand, fashion historians Valerie Steele[51] and David Kunzle[52] claim the letters represent the fetishistic interest of a limited number of corset fanciers and sadomasochistic paedophiles. Kunzle has also suggested that the *EDM* 'invented' a number of prurient letters to increase its circulation and provoke sales via the magazine's correspondence pages. The latter seems unlikely given that the target audience for the *EDM* were middle-class matrons with respectable aspirations and lifestyles. Moreover, after the *EDM*'s eventual demise, it was reincarnated for that same audience as *Myra's Journal of Dress and Fashion*, a publication both chic and above moral reproach.[53] The authenticity of the original letters is of little consequence. What remains significant is that the flood of letters that engulfed the *EDM* (whether authentic or contrived) following their initial publication is evidence that the sexual objectification of female children had been established and acknowledged by 1860, and that the child's waist was the site of intense socio-sexual interest.

So vast was the correspondence generated by the real or contrived letters in the *EDM* that the magazine published a special supplement to contain them.[54] The text was titled *Figure Training or Art the Handmaid of Nature*. While several letters in this collection were concerned with sadomasochistic aspects of juvenile corsetry, many others discussed juvenile corsetry in matter-of-fact terms entirely devoid of any titillation. *Figure Training or Art the Handmaid of Nature* was decidedly pro-corset, but it must be remembered that juvenile corsetry was almost a requisite item of middle-class girlhood by this time. Numerous letters advised mothers to corset the female child before the age of fourteen. It was believed that this would prevent a 'heavy waist' and the suffering that would necessarily accompany tight lacing at a later age. Contributors to the magazine who wrote of their own or their daughter's discomfort were shown little sympathy. Mothers who corseted their children at the age of fourteen were chided for their irresponsible behaviour for this 'allow[ed] the waist to grow large and clumsy' and made its reduction to 'more elegant proportions' in later life a painful procedure. The 'great secret' was 'to begin their use as early as possible'.[55]

One correspondent wrote that she had fitted both daughters with stays at the age of seven, the age at which she had been fitted for stays by her mother. She described these stays as consisting of 'little bone' and a 'flexible busk'. They met from top to bottom when laced so as not to 'exercise the least pressure round the chest'. Their purpose, wrote the author, was to create a 'very slight pressure at the waist . . . to show off the figure and give it a roundness', a physical attribute that seven-year-old girls do not ordinarily possess without mechanical intervention. The author recommended replacement stays as the child grew to adolescence. These were to be made a little longer and enlarged around the upper torso to accommodate the breasts, but the waist size of the corset was not to alter, 'in order that the original waist measure may be retained'.[56]

The construction of the child as potentially or actually sexual by means of corsetry brought with it profound if poorly articulated, fears. The newly sexualized and therefore potentially unruly or dangerous female adolescent body seemed suddenly to require regulation and surveillance. Ironically, the child's moral deliverance dictated that her body and its threatening sexuality be encased within ever sturdier trappings. Increasingly, corsetry became conscripted to a twofold if paradoxical mission. This mission was to achieve sexual desirability in young girls and at the same time deny, or repress sexual desire in the bodies it encompassed. The *Redresseur* Corset, described by William Barry Lord as a 'safe and efficient contrivance [for the] correction and improvement of the figure' was such a garment. It was recommended wearing for adolescent girls whose mothers had resisted the corset imperative and regretted that decision. The *Redresseur* was as punitive and regulatory as its name suggested. Unlike other 'adolescent' garments, it was devoid of lace and ribbon trims, which suggests its mandate included the repression or denial of any sexual expression. Illustrations indicate that it did, nevertheless, impose a pronounced waistline on the body (see Figure 37). While the *Redresseur* had all the compressive attributes of other corsets, it also acted as a harness that (ostensibly) improved posture. The *Redresseur* left the 'chest entirely free for expansion' with typically 'only the waist being confined at the point where restraint [was] most called for'. The garment was laced at the front and back (unlike others that at that time laced at

Figure 37
The punitive *Redresseur* corset designed to regulate the moral behaviour, as much as the body, of the adolescent girl.

either front or back) and consisted of a corset bodice with the addition of broad shoulder straps which, 'hooked together behind', brought the shoulders to their 'proper position' and kept them there.[57]

Concerns surrounding the newly sexualized pubescent child and her adolescent older sister were compounded and increased by middle-class beliefs that Victorian society was steeped in sexual transgression and licentiousness. Elizabeth Wilson has discussed the nebulous fears that permeated and frightened the middle classes of the mid- to late nineteenth century. She has located the existence of popular scientific theories that held that miasma (being invisible infectious matter floating in the air) presented a threat to community standards of health. Wilson posits that alongside threats of physical infection were fears of moral contagion that manifested and spread, miasma-like, from cities. The 'condition of women', says Wilson, became the metaphor for city life and for all that was considered dark, evil and sexually illicit in society.[58]

Middle-class fears of miasmic moral contamination were not entirely without substance. Both the American and English sex industries experienced a period of enormous growth between 1860 and 1900. Sexual depravity, in the public domain at least, was an issue as early as 1870,[59] and the female child was quickly located in the dangerous position of being both vulnerable victim and culpable agent in her own sexual misadventures. 'It is safe to say that the New York girl of ten knows far more of the world and its wicked ways than the English, German, or French girl when she becomes a wife', wrote one observer made distraught by the realization of the extent of juvenile prostitution.[60] By 1887, child prostitution was believed to have attained 'a very high degree of development in countries where inestimable advantages [were] enjoyed'.[61] By the 1890s, American pornography was swamped by paedophile imagery that predominantly exploited young female children.[62] Not surprisingly, given the internationalization of the pornography industry, there was also an abundant market in paedophile pornography in Britain. No home 'however carefully guarded, no school however select', was thought to be 'safe from [the sex industry's] corrupting influences'.[63]

Parental anxiety was increased by the apparent inability of the law to either protect children or punish offenders. A social purity booklet, published in 1886 by the Women's Temperance Publication Association for distribution at mothers' meetings, reprinted frightening extracts from the *Chicago Herald*. These reported the infliction of a *one dollar* fine (these are Temperance italics) on a man convicted 'for the enticing away of a young girl to a disreputable place'.[64] Girls 'below ten are protected in this country [wrote the Temperance Union] but what father or mother whose little daughter celebrated her tenth anniversary can bear the thought that she is now in the eyes of the law competent to consent to the most grievous and irremedial of wrongs?'[65] To stop the 'overflowing evil current' of sexual contamination seemed 'no more possible than to check the eternal progress of the glacier . . . To look for remedies from the law, from the

Church, or from the State, [appeared] hopeless ... Authority [was] practically powerless'.[66]

The perceived and actual failure of institutional reforms and commissions to reduce pornography, child prostitution and other aspects of the 'public' sexual exploitation of children was explicit. Grave fears for the sanctity of children and young women, which emanated from a perception of a menacing and predatory 'public' sexuality, were multiplied anew by the emergence of sexology in the final decades of the nineteenth century. Sexology quickly became a legitimate science and it demonized the child herself. Many theorists insisted that little girls were far more precocious than boys,[67] and that girls were capable of greater sexual perversion. Advice manuals, quasi-medical texts and 'family guides' disseminated these ideas and assisted the process of demonization. These texts contended that masturbation was an abominable and dangerous habit that was to be eradicated at all costs, particularly in little girls. Prior to 1850, discussions of juvenile masturbation focused almost exclusively on male children and the damage 'self-abuse' or 'onanism' did to the individual. However, around 1860 there began a gendered shift in focus of masturbation theory. Girls became the targets of anti-masturbation rhetoric and 'the habit' became increasingly perceived as a dangerous social, rather than individual, evil which threatened the polity as a whole.[68]

It was recognized that masturbation was 'not confined to any class but penetrate[d] all societies'. This recognition increased rather than diminished the socio/medical hysteria. Sexual threats to the child prior to this time, no matter how serious, were 'other', public, and presumed to originate from the working classes, but masturbation was known to exist in the best of homes. It 'often started at five or six years old' wrote Dr John Harvey Kellog and it inevitably lead to 'sexual disorder' and moral catastrophe. The physical ramifications of the soul-destroying vice were myriad. Declining health would quickly ensue once the habit was established and aches, nerves, loss of love for study, reduced memory, increased boldness or reserve, languor, lueccoreah, palpitations of heart, bed-wetting, St Vitus's Dance and epilepsy were its symptoms and its legacy.[69] The moral consequences were no less terrifying. 'Onanism', wrote Dr John Howe, and a *coterie* of his mid- and late nineteenth-century peers, threatened to 'dwarf the entire female organism', leaving young girls 'shy, ... squeamish and repellent'. Nymphomania was also cited as a result of the 'secret vice'. It transformed 'the most timid girl ... into a termagant, and the most delicate modesty to a furious audacity that even the effrontery of prostitution [could] not approach'.[70] Perhaps more terrifying still was the charge that it also nurtured lesbianism.[71] Renowned British and American sexologists agreed that masturbation inculcated in the young child a 'hate[red] of the opposite sex and [the] tendency to form [later] passionate attachments for other women'.[72] It was also thought to herald consumption,[73] epilepsy, hypochondria and for women especially, insanity and death. Masturbation's only cure, he wrote, was marriage or amputation of the clitoris.[74]

Clitoridectomy was by far the most appalling indicator and barometer of masculine fear of female sexuality. By the second half of the nineteenth century clitoridectomy (along with other pharmacological methods of 'prevention') was becoming increasingly popular.[75] Girls and women from middle-class backgrounds were its victims. Its cost precluded (and thus protected) working-class girls and women from this kind of 'intervention'.[76] While the use of sexual surgery seemed an efficacious method of curtailing untoward and potentially destructive female sexual behaviour, it was a method at direct odds with the middle-class ethos of stability and respectability. I would argue that stout corsetry offered a far more acceptable intervention. Juvenile corsetry acted as a chastity belt, and like its antecedent was implemented ostensibly to protect the occupant from her own carnal desire, and as a bastion against the salacious, predatory behaviour of others. Clothing was, in the mid- to late nineteenth century, considered to have protective properties. According to *fin de siècle* psychologist Carl Flugel, these protective properties were commonly extended to apply to the moral as well as the physical sphere. Flugel noted that the symbolic equation of physical stiffness and uprightness was considered integral to moral probity and firmness. 'Tightness by its firm pressure on the body' he wrote, 'symbolised a firm control over the self.' Firm, tightly fitted clothes kept 'a tight reign on passions'.[77]

Flugel's theory helps (in part) to explain the enduring popularity of nineteenth-century adolescent and juvenile corsetry. Middle-class parents, alarmed by 'miasmic' threats of moral contamination, and cognizant of the distressing and widely debated sexual theories that defined juvenile female sexuality as monstrous, might eagerly have turned to corsetry in an attempt to protect their children from their own innate carnality. They might also have hoped that corsetry would act as a barrier against moral contamination from without. After all, the durable construction of the adolescent corset, reinforced as it often was with bands of metal, bone or stiffened cord, functioned (psychically at least) as an impermeable physical container for the child's potentially explosive and destructive sexuality and as a physical barrier against 'public' sexual danger. It was, too, a far preferable alternative to surgery for various reasons. Surgery was, after all, a public admission of defeat and deviance, while substantial corsetry was a private safeguard against it. Juvenile corsetry had the advantage of economy and was instantly available in a way that surgery was not. Corsetry could be purchased as soon as the first sign of sexual interest manifested in the young child, or it could be implemented prior to that event, or at the onset of adolescence as a preventative measure. The shame unavoidably associated with sexual surgery must have added support to the ideology of 'control by corset'. Moreover sexual surgery could only protect the child from herself, a tactic that would afford little protection in an age considered by middle-class parents as saturated with dangerous and manifold sexual deviance.

This is not to say that all parents were cognizant of their own fears and underlying motives when they decided to corset their daughters. Surviving literature discussing the direct link between juvenile sexuality and its control by corset are, outside of the dubious *EDM* correspondence, rare. Presumably middle-class 'delicacy' forbade any connection between juvenile corsetry and moral protection from being discussed publicly in women's magazines or advertisements. However, fears of sexuality and its control by corsetry were occasionally articulated. George Frederick Watts, British artist and president of the short-lived anti-tight-lacing society of 1883, appears to have identified the link between the juvenile corset, sexuality and the moral control of the child. However, he did not comprehend the fears and influences that lead mothers to corset children. Watts insisted that mothers were guilty culprits who corseted their daughters for 'the gratification of a most depraved taste'. It was common, said Watts, 'for deluded mothers . . . to say, "the child is becoming a monster! She must be immediately put into stays" and then to jam her into an abomination'.[78] Watts's conclusions were of course incorrect. Conscientious Victorian matrons did not corset their daughters to appease 'depraved tastes' as he insisted, but to protect their vulnerable daughters from depravity. It is also likely that middle-class mothers (as Dr Mary Wood-Allen pointed out) corseted their female children because society had 'become so accustomed to the deformed [corseted] figure that (it) was called beautiful'.[79]

While contemporary historians have teased out the arguments and modalities used to strengthen traditional gender constructs for adult women in the nineteenth century, far less has been written about the socialization and gender construction of nineteenth-century female children and the perceived threat they presented to gender stability. An examination of texts that discuss childhood corsetry offers an insight into the way female children were socialized and the importance of their socialization in the retention of sex–gender stability. Childhood and adolescent corsetry of the nineteenth century served cultural imperatives specifically related to the construction and solidification of female gender roles. Corsetry was an integral tool in both constructing and policing juvenile female behaviour, and in the final decades of the nineteenth century it acted, in some part, to both mollify and mask cultural anxieties about child sexuality and perceptions surrounding transgressive sexual practices.

The juvenile corset was initially recruited by parents and promoted by manufacturers as necessary for the healthy development and support of the growing body. As the decades unfolded, the corset was increasingly called upon to regulate appropriate gender behaviour, then to sexualize, and eventually to protect the child's body from sexual 'contamination'. Once sexualized, the child was viewed as dangerous and powerful. These fears, though poorly articulated, were incongruously assuaged by juvenile corsetry of increasingly sturdier construction. The nascent process of juvenile female sexualization, begun by the corset, was augmented and eventually completed by the emergence of scientific theories of child sexuality. These theories increased, rather than allayed, adult anxiety by demonizing female carnality, even in its infant state. Tightly fitted juvenile corsetry was employed by concerned parents as a tangible, reassuring device that had the potential of physically divorcing adolescent children from sexual feelings that might lead to, or be precipitated by, masturbation. Juvenile corsetry presumably eased or alleviated maternal and paternal fears that female children would indulge in lustful behaviour that could ruin their lives. While compression of the torso may have effectively deadened sensation, it provided a comforting (for parents at least) symbolic barrier between their children's chastity and the flagrant loss of childhood innocence that almost characterized Victorian British and American society.

Middle-class mothers were, as Watts pointed out, complicit in the initial sexualization of their daughters, by choosing to corset them. However, in an era of little employment for women, mothers were duty-bound to produce daughters whose bodies conformed to particular standards of beauty in order to secure a good marriage. Obtaining and retaining the desired tiny waist required policing the infant body until adulthood. The pain this may or may not have precipitated cannot be quantified, although Harberton's exposé gives some indication of the long-term dull physical distress it produced. Fears of the 'chunky' waist may have affected nineteenth-century girls much as the pursuit of ideal figures do today – that is, to effectively put the girl at war with her own body. The early incarceration of the child's body in corsetry may indicate that nineteenth-century women endured an earlier and therefore longer experience of the 'battle of the bulge'. This was a battle made more difficult as the decades progressed, for by 1890 the Junoesque figure was fashionable. The Junoesque figure required that women eat more to encourage heavier arms, thighs, breasts and buttocks, but it also demanded that women retain the child-sized waist. It is quite likely that numerous conscientious middle-class mothers of the 1890s, tightened children's corsets even further, in pursuit of this wretched and impossible ideal.

4
Corsetry and the Reality of 'Female Complaints'

While several historians have attributed the plethora of Victorian 'female complaints' in part, to the prevalence of corsetry, the significance of the corset in the propitiation of those singularly nineteenth-century female ailments generically labelled by physicians as 'nerve-tire and womb ills'[1] has not received the sustained examination it deserves. Emphasis has, rather, been focused on Victorian feminine illness as a psychosomatic response to the dissatisfactions of nineteenth-century womanhood. That is, Victorian female illness has been perceived by many twentieth-century theorists as a kind of conduit in which relations between the individual and the social body were negotiated.[2] Certainly Victorian women may have somaticized personal and public cultural dissatisfaction into 'categories of self and social definition' and exploited the so-called 'fashionable diseases' to rebel against the restrictions on their lives, or to exact the attention, recognition and empowerment denied them.[3] The multiple positioning of women as both victims and agents in illness is not challenged here, nor is the notion that illness can be directly attributable to socio/cultural disadvantage. However, it would appear that the neglect of historians to deeply engage in the actual physical and mental distress consequent with 'female complaints' has led to the material reality of female illness being subsumed and negated by the theories which have been used to explain them. I would argue that the current positioning of Victorian 'female complaints' and the absence of discussion regarding the corset's role in their manufacture, perpetuates the perceived 'mythic' qualities of Victorian female illness, and thereby reinforces a fictive stereotype of the Victorian middle-class woman as a willing invalid. This chapter will foreground the role of corsetry in the creation of various 'real' and 'psychosomatic' illnesses common to middle-class Victorian women. It will juxtapose the largely female (and frequently feminist) voices that offered concise and complex political arguments countering the use of corsetry, against a range of 'mainstream' texts which either marginalized or romanticized, and therefore promoted, both the tiny corseted waist and the female illnesses which were its legacy.

Fashion historians C. Willett and Phyllis Cunnington have claimed that by 1890, many middle-class women aimed to have a waist measurement not exceeding the number of years of their age at marriage, and that most women 'intended to marry before they were twenty-one'.[4] While the fashionable ideal determined a waist size of between seventeen and twenty inches, it was an ideal rarely realized,[5] though according to abundant newspaper, journal and medical accounts many women aspired to these prescriptions. The 'innumerable evils arising from constriction of the thoracical cavity' via the corset had been the subject of feminist debate since at least 1852[6] and the 'crusade against tight lacing . . . carried on for a very long time'. In 1900, Ada Ballin wrote that the 'penalties of tight lacing' were decreasing but the practice had not been 'stamped out and [was still] very evident even to the most casual observer'. Ballin recalled a conversation at a ball with a woman who 'boasted that her waist measured only 15 inches'. As Ballin pointed out, such a tiny waist was the end result of a regime of corsetry in which 'pressure was first exerted from an early age, and gradually increased until the present condition was reached (and) the figure moulded into a hard set form'. The impression the young woman created on those who 'understood the structure of the human body' wrote Ballin, was to 'wonder that anyone so nearly resembling a wasp in figure could continue to live'.[7]

The romance of the tiny waistline also held American women in its thrall well into the final decades of the nineteenth century. Like their British counterparts, North American women suffered considerable physical damage to their bodies as a result. Harriet Hubbard Ayer (founder of the cosmetics company which still bears her name) remarked in 1899 that 'ninety nine out of one hundred American women pass[ed] through the self infliction of a waist squeezing period before they reach[ed] one and twenty'. Many women, according to Ayer, continued to 'crowd and jam' their bodies into corsets beyond the years 'allotted to ignorance and youth' to effect 'a wasp like dimension that was unpleasant to contemplate [and] excruciatingly painful to endure'.[8]

The medical profession, in a rare but fissured moment of coalition with feminists and the dress reform movement, generally insisted (in principle at least) that corsetry, particularly when tightly laced, was detrimental to women's health. However, the contemporary belief that nineteenth-century women wore corsetry despite a seamless volley of medical advice is completely unfounded. The American doctor, Charles Graham Cannaday, whose paper titled 'The Relation of Tight Lacing to Uterine Development and Abdominal and Pelvic Disease' was read before the International Medical Congress in Rome in 1894 and later published in the *American Gynaecological and Obstetrical Journal*, condemned the medical profession. As Cannadine noted, the medical profession 'lived in the presence of such an injurious custom', and yet it failed to offer 'a united protest' against corsetry. Cannaday pointed out to his distinguished audience that the identification of aetiological factors in the tide of female pelvic and abdominal ills sweeping America and Europe had been lost in 'the mad rush for scientific research and inventive methods'. His paper spelled out the appalling damage corsetry wreaked on the bodies of European and American women. He revealed to the assembled physicians what they already knew: that corsetry crushed many internal organs and was a major factor in disease. Cannaday clearly explained in point form that

1. uterine development [was] greatest from eleven to fifteen years of age.
2. tight lacing [was] usually commenced about the period of uterine development.
3. corsets as they [were] usually worn produce[d] displacement and compression and . . . [were] worn through the entire day as tight as [could] be borne.
4. displacement and compression interfere[ed] with nutrition and development of the pelvic contents.
5. badly developed generative organs diminish[ed] resistance to disease and render[ed] physiological work defective and unnecessarily painful.[9]

Cannaday's remarks were obviously dismissed or ignored by many gynaecologists and obstetricians once outside of the professional arena. While there appeared to be an acknowledgement of the dangers inherent in the use of corsetry at a professional level, the message that corsetry was anathema to good health did not successfully filter down to the general public. Cannaday's observation that there was no united medical opposition to corsetry was absolutely accurate. Many notable physicians in Britain and North America went so far as to publicly promote corsetry at meetings, in articles and advertisements placed in magazines, and in texts that were squarely directed to a female audience.

A range of conflicting and contradictory medical advice regarding the 'vexed question of stays' was even presented at a public meeting of the

British Association held in 1888. Professor Roy's paper 'Physiological Bearing of Waist Belts and Stays' did not condemn those garments, but in fact urged that 'some support was necessary' for the female body. It was only when stays were tightly laced, said Roy, that the 'evil' began. Roy's claims were supported by Dr. J. Adaine. Adaine considered moderate tight lacing as beneficial as it 'released blood from an inactive locality and left it free to be used in the brain or elsewhere'.[10] Dr. Wilberforce, who spoke at the same meeting, countered this argument and insisted that 'tight lacing and not only tight lacing, but wearing stays at all [was] an evil and a curse'.[11]

Contradictory medical beliefs regarding the healthful or dangerous attributes of corsets were also echoed in advertising material well into the nineteenth century. Dr O. Kelly LRCP of Edinburgh, along with seven other distinguished medical practitioners, recommended the Invigorator corset for 'improving the carriage and appearance of the figure *even when tightly laced*' (Kelly's italics) (see Figure 38).[12] Across the Atlantic, corset advertisements were similarly larded with medical testimonials assuring women that particular corsets were 'comfortable, elegant and perfectly healthful'. The Duplex corset advertisement, from which this quote is taken, also noted in bold type that the garment featured 'double bones, double steels and double seams'.[13] Both Dr. Warner's and Dr Scott's Electric corsets, manufactured in the United States but also sold in Britain, capitalized on and utilized the medical profession to promote their wares.

Dr. Warner's corsets, like many other brands, were given medical names such as 'Health' and 'Abdominal' to increase their medico-scientific legitimacy (see Figure 39).[14] Scott's electric corsets featured 'magnetised'

Figure 38
According to this advertisement the 'health-giving powers' of the Invigorator corset were 'assured'. Also note the convincing endorsement by Dr Gambier of the Hospital for Consumption, St Leonard's-on-Sea. See *Woman's Magazine*, 1890.

Figure 39
Advertisements for the JB side spring corset assured women that the garments were 'constructed in accordance with physiological principles' although the 'side springs' were considered by manufacturers to be 'unbreakable'.

strips of metal in their construction. According to numerous newspaper and journal advertisements in the 1880s and 1890s the garments were assembled on 'scientific principles', which by the incorporation of magnets, generated a 'health giving current to the whole system' providing an 'odic force' which 'Nature's Laws demand[ed]'. A silver-plated compass was provided with each corset allowing the wearer to test the magnetic influence of the garment. Scott's corsets were not only 'electric, unbreakable and fashioned in the true "french" shape' (ie. hourglass in design) but were available to suit any pocket, ranging in price from one to three dollars (see Figure 40). The cost of corsetry was determined by the garment's colour and the lavishness of its trim. The authenticity of Dr. Scott's credentials are difficult to ascertain. Scott may have been an entrepreneurial physician or he may simply have been a corset manufacturer who cleverly exploited the nineteenth-century enthusiasm for science and medicine. Although Scott's medical qualifications are questionable, the medical endorsement of his range of garments was not. Scott's Electric corsets were recommended by no less a personage than the American Surgeon General, Dr. William A. Hammond of New York.[15]

Advertisements placed by Warner and Scott which were lent a respectability by the endorsement of well-known men were dubbed 'mischievous'

Figure 40
Scott's used more or less
identical advertisements in
different magazines over
several years. This was
published in *Harper's Bazaar*,
13 May, 1892.

by Eliza Haweis, author of *The Art of Beauty and The Art of Dress*.
Haweis believed that medical endorsement of corsetry would be accepted
without question by the public who were 'in the main ignorant' and who
would, as a result, be 'taken in' by them. Haweis insisted that both medical
men and salesmen were directly implicated in maintaining false standards
of female beauty that jeopardized women's health. She was outraged by
corset advertisements which claimed that particular garments could be
worn 'a much smaller size . . . without injury to the figure'. Both 'trades-
men and medical men had a duty,' wrote Haweis, 'to influence women's
choice in purchasing garments and . . . [they] should recommend comfort
above appearance'.[16]

Frequently, medical texts directed toward a general readership sanctioned corsetry by maintaining an ambivalent position regarding its
hazards and its merits. *The Book of Health*, published in 1884 and drawn
from the work of eighteen respected medical contributors, wrote that
corsets composed of 'rigid bars of steel and of many whalebones' were
unnecessary to any woman who was 'neither diseased nor deformed'.
However, the authors also made clear that they 'would not go so far as
to say that stays of all kinds should be entirely given up', insisting instead
that, 'certain individuals' ought to wear 'a modified corset'. No corset
was necessary for those who were 'thin and slight of figure', stated *The*

Book of Health, but this directive was qualified by assurances that 'for the purpose of appearance and for the more ready adjustment of dress', slim women might 'wear a bodice composed of some stout material'. For women who were 'incline[d] to stoutness or prominence of the bust . . . a simple form of corset was necessary for comfort'.[17] J.M. Fothergill, author of *The Maintenance of Health, A Medical Work for the Lay Reader,* agreed. '[W]ithin certain limits the corset was not objectionable' particularly when compared to 'the older days of stays with a huge stay bone in front and eyelets at back . . . [that] required a maid' to lace up'.[18]

Similarly, Alexander Bryce M.D., author of *The Laws of Life and Health,* objected to the 'deforming corset' but still encouraged both housewives and female clerks to wear 'a sensible corset, with or without some strengthening material like whalebone or other elastic support'. The corset, claimed Bryce 'act[ed] as a brace to the spinal column [and took] the weight [of heavy clothing] from the sloping shoulder' where it had a 'tendency to contract the chest and cause a decided stoop'.[19] While Bryce insisted he supported the theories of dress reformers, he frankly confessed that he had 'not yet become a convert to the Hygienic Dress League'. Clothing promoted throughout the century by such leagues was generally loose and very unlike the tightly-fitted, torso-hugging bodices of main-stream fashions. Dress reform garments, whether called aesthetic, rational or hygienic, did not draw attention to the secondary sexual characteristics and were often reviled because they appeared shapeless by comparison to standard skin-tight fashion garments. Despite their medical training, some doctors actively promoted a dangerous fashionable appearance above health. In 1882, Dr Hunt (cited by Marion Harland in her best-selling text *Eve's Daughters: Common Sense for Maid, Wife, and Mother)* argued that while

> many volumes had been written on the subject of tight lacing [and though it had been] howled about from platforms and in all the virtuous magazines . . . the fact is the woman who affects loose garments is lazy and violates all the rules of good dressing . . . Nature 'demands' that women should have small waists, and the misery and harm . . . inflicted by the over use of corsets is only a blind, ignorant obedience to an instinct, which properly directed is graceful and natural.[20]

Occasionally, the unscrupulous behaviour of doctors who had vested financial interests in maintaining the popularity of corsetry was exposed. *The Medical Annual* of 1889 revealed that pecuniary motives led the well-known physician Dr. Landau to dismiss tight lacing as an aetiological factor in disease. *The Medical Annual* asserted that Landau's 'rather marked bias in favour of stays . . . was connected and dependent upon the main plan or method of treatment recommended by him'.[21] Despite the supposed anti-corset position held by editors of *The Medical Annual,* that text was also complicit in perpetuating the popularity of the garment. It frequently published corset advertisements from K.R. Schramm, suppliers of trusses and artificial limbs. Illustrations of Schramm's 'combined stay belt and corset' reveal that their garment could be as tightly laced, and was as heavily boned as fashionable corsetry[22] (see Figures 41 and 42).

The medical ambivalence toward corsetry was undoubtedly related, at least in part, to that profession's general opposition to feminist claims. Though many physicians enthusiastically supported dress reform on health grounds, they were suspicious and often hostile towards the larger ambitions of dress reformers who, from as early as 1850, realized that women's clothing and women's rights were almost indivisible issues.[23] Not surprisingly, female doctors who had experienced the discomfort of corsetry at some stage of their lives were, on the whole, supportive of the dress reform movement. Most were uncompromising in both their hostility toward constrictive undergarments and their defence of female emancipation and education. This does not mean to imply that all male doctors were entirely equivocal about corsetry or uniformly hostile to women's rights; however, male physicians who were sympathetic to feminist demands and who supported dress reform were clearly in the minority.

E.J. Tilt, a British gynaecologist working in the 1860s, was an enthusiastic supporter of female education and dress reform and he publicly advocated gynaecology as a suitable career choice for women.[24] However,

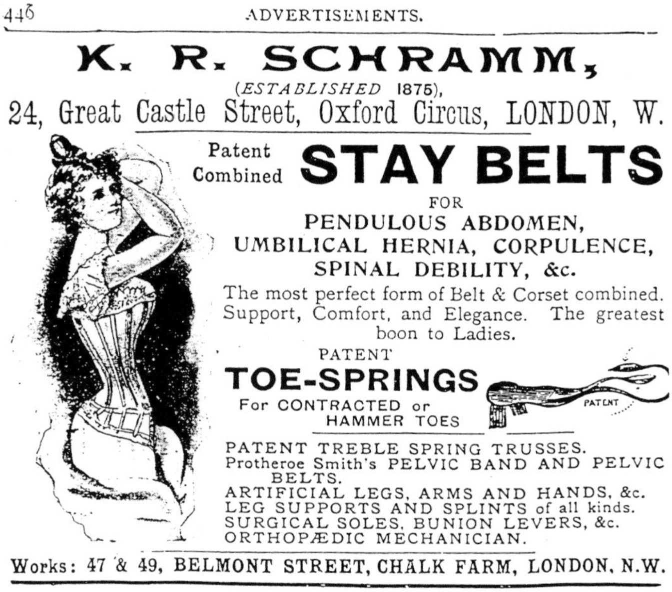

Figure 41
Schramm's stay belt advertisement simultaneously drew from, and existed as part of, the medical discourse. See the *Medical Analytical Synoptical Index*, 1887–8.

Tilt was an exception among his peers. Attitudes expressed by Dr. Benjamin Ward Richardson (some twenty years later) might be said to be more typical of those held by the medical profession, regarding female emancipation, education and female health. Richardson encouraged women to pursue higher education, but wanted it to reflect the 'truly feminine duties which [were] connected to health and happiness'. For Richardson and many of his peers, education was ideally a means of creating a more intelligent housekeeper who, once adequately informed, would not torture her body with corsetry and would actively police the habits of corsetry in other women. Equipped with a 'general study of the human body', women might become 'practitioners of the preventative (rather than curative) art of medicine', qualifying them for the title of 'sanitarian helpmate of man'. The educated woman of Richardson's utopia would 'turn pale with dread and disgust when ever she detected one of her foolish sisters strangling her body in tight corsetry and murderous belt'.[25]

While issues of corsetry, education and emancipation were often blurred and subsumed by male critics, the dress reform movement itself was from time to time undermined by ideological confusion and disputes between its own constituents. The movement reflected the opinions of members whose attitudes toward dress were motivated by a range of political and non-political positions. Several outspoken dress reformers argued that the feminist goals of financial autonomy and suffrage were absolutely dependent on the success of dress reform. Less politically motivated but no less enthusiastic members advocated dress reform purely on principles of health. Other members were motivated by a combination of desires that included health and feminist politics in varying ratios.[26]

Consequently, contradictions and altercations within the ranks of dress reform were inevitable. Occasionally, notable feminists who argued for suffrage, equal education and healthful dress actually resisted particular aspects of dress reform, some going so far as to defend frivolous fashions. Elizabeth Cady Stanton, the impelling force behind the landmark Seneca Falls feminist convention of 1848, defended female fashions, though she was careful to avoid all references to corsetry in her justification of frills and furbelows. The pragmatic Stanton insisted that 'the shortest way to a man's favour' was 'through his passions' and therefore women, whose socio-economic well-being was dependent on attracting a suitable male, should 'arrange their clothes to produce maximum stimulation of the animal nature of the opposite sex'.[27] Similar fractures and inconsistencies surfaced in the English Dress Reform movement, which, like the American chapter, was also anxious to secure larger feminist goals concerning education and suffrage. The formidable founder of the Manchester Woman's Suffrage Committee and editor of the *Woman's Suffrage Journal*, Lydia Becker, implored members at a public meeting to 'stick to [their] stays' claiming that they improved the form and gave warmth and assistance. 'Stick to your stays ladies, [asserted Becker] and triumph over

the other sex.'[28] As an important aside, Becker's loyalty to the corset may have been an attempt to dismantle personal criticism levelled at her by the news media, which seemed determined to 'unsex' her and therefore defuse her impressive feminist political authority. According to one popular newspaper, there were three sexes. These were 'Male, Female and Lydia Becker'.[29]

'How to clothe the waist' was, acknowledged American dress reformer Ira de van Warner in 1895, the 'cause of more controversy than the clothing of any other part of the body'.[30] While de van Warner was opposed to corsetry in principle, his approach to the subject was tempered by a pragmatic acceptance of the garment's popularity. De van Warner acknowledged that despite a protest against the garment that spanned sixty years, it was still impossible to convince women that the garment was responsible for almost 'all the ills and difficulties that the female flesh [was] heir to'. The fact still remained, lamented de van Warner, that 'seventy five percent of women in civilised countries [wore] corsets, and the rest usually [wore] corsets, only under other names'. De van Warner, like Becker, insisted that a properly constructed corset was a 'source of comfort, not torture' and that it was the 'essential foundation for proper dressing'. Women 'will wear corsets' wrote De Van Warner, and they always had and always would. Therefore, he reasoned, it behoved the dress reform movement to 'adapt garments to the wants of women, rather than attempt[ing] to banish them altogether'.[31] Warner's pragmatism, which was shared by several other dress reformers, points to the contested nature of dress reform[32] within the movement, specifically between individuals who opposed corsetry and those who favoured a rational adaptation of the garment. Despite occasional disagreements, most dress reformers on both continents espoused the complete abandonment of corsetry and vigorously promoted outer clothing that did not require foundation garments of metal and bone.

Because dress reform was often enmeshed within larger issues of education, emancipation and gender, it attracted and generated heated criticism from conservative factions in the wider societal *milieu*. Dress in general was a disputed and slippery arena from which both the largely male medical profession and the largely female dress reformists positioned and armed themselves to either challenge or secure a myriad of social issues. The corset, for both combatants, was a useful ally. For the majority of dress reformists and feminists, the corset represented and actualized a 'shackle of slavery'.[33] Unfortunately, women's reluctance to abandon the 'fatal object of desire'[34] demonstrated to male opponents of female emancipation an irrationality that revealed women's unfitness for the rigours of the public sphere. Declarations by radical proponents of dress reform that women's clothing, underpinned by fashionable corsetry, typified and perpetuated women's 'subject position' and 'vitiat[ed] [their] claims to equality'[35] alarmed the generally orthodox medical profession even further.

Figure 42
The Ornho corselet Belt advertisement was directed at nurses. It claimed that the belt gave a 'firm waist with entire freedom of movement' and had the advantage of being 'unbreakable'. Corselet belts had fewer bones and were smaller than standard corsets but were in many cases as rigid. See the *Hospital Nursing Supplement*, 1895.

Many physicians aligned their opinions with those of the conservative gynaecologist William Goodell, Professor of Clinical Gynaecology at the University of Pennsylvania, whose highly regarded beliefs were expounded in his often published text, *Lessons in Gynaecology*. This text, like many written for a specialized medical readership in the 1880s, was ostensibly a medical handbook, but most chapters which dealt with the treatment of discrete gynaecological ailments also offered a social critique of modern society, and found it wanting. While Goodell asserted that 'banishment of the corset . . . would be a real boon to the [health of the] sex', he preferred to attribute the plethora of debilitating female complaints experienced by mid- to late nineteenth-century women to their forays into the masculine public sphere.

Goodell maintained that a 'potent cause of [female] invalidism' was 'keeping up appearances'. Keeping up appearances entailed not only following fashion trends, but also entertaining notions of escaping the monotony and tradition of domestic obligations. Woman, he wrote, 'shines best and thrives best not in the adulation of society, not in obtrusive self exertion, but in the quiet and faithful performance of her home duties'. The 'heat and stir of life', maintained Goodell, were best suited to man's rugged nature, while the 'wholesomest passages' of woman's life were those which like the 'thesis of a symphony' were 'unpercussed and unaccented.' Goodell insisted that 'too much brain work and too little housework' spelled uterine disaster.[36] Similarly, while doctors Gaillard Thomas, Emmet, Barbour and Berry Hart, recognized that the corset had a role in female illness, they too preferred to ascribe uterine disorders to the new-fangled tendency to educate female children beyond the pleasing domestic arts. Female education that mimicked the education received by boys supposedly led to 'rapid development of brain and nervous system, precocious talent, refined and cultured taste and a fascinating vivacity'. This was, however, inevitably accompanied by 'a morbid impressibility, great feebleness of the muscular system and [a] marked tendency to disease in the generative organs'. Even when 'a course of study [was] comparatively moderate', noted the doctors, 'functional disturbances [were] of too frequent occurrence to admit a doubt to their cause'.[37]

Dress reformists and female doctors insisted otherwise. The 'dear graduates' of 1874 were stoutly defended by a coalition of feminist dress reformers and female doctors who argued that female illness was not derived from too much education but from 'the epidemic rage of fashion' and the 'unyielding steels of . . . corsets'.[38] American dress reformer Abba Gould-Woolson insisted that it was a 'ludicrous mistake to suppose a few sporadic cases of injudicious study' could be 'held accountable for the general ill health of women'. Woolson believed that if male doctors took real notice of the pernicious clothing of their patients they would quickly revise their ideas regarding the origins of ill health. Tightly laced corsetry, and skirts and petticoats that weighed heavily over hips and legs, combined with the fashion for masses of false hair, prevented women from enjoying healthy exercise. It was not that 'boys and girls are trained too much alike mentally' that made them ill, observed Woolson, 'but that they are trained too much un-alike physically, which work[e]d the harm'.[39] Mercy B. Jackson M.D. agreed. She insisted that if woman was 'to fulfil the high trusts that [would] be given her she must emancipate herself from the engrossment of fashion . . . and seek . . . the liberal education that ha[d] so long been considered necessary for her brother'.[40]

Similarly, political activist Frances E. Russell argued that clothing rather than education hampered women's health, and that fashionable clothing decreased women's prospects for social advancement. Women were, insisted Russell, 'fully able to engage in political affairs' but their demands for education, wages, and suffrage were undermined by their costume. 'Ridiculous constrictive fashions' said Russell, brought ill health and, possibly worse still, acted as 'proof of their inferiority' and pronounced a verdict against them as 'fickle, frivolous and incompetent!'[41] Russell's succinct observations were correct. Women's apparent refusal to abandon elaborate fashions in general, and the corset in particular, was frequently attributed to an inherent female narcissism that outweighed any capacity for reason. In a paper titled 'Tight Lacing Again', published in 1881 in *Lancet*, the anonymous author railed against 'the audacity of attempting to compress the trunk' in order to secure a 'wasp'-like waist. The 'monstrous . . . love of fashionable embellishment', continued the author, would prevail despite the occasional death caused by tight lacing. 'We are not greatly interested to impress (upon) beings so unreasoning and unreasonable . . . who resort to this artifice in the face of all that has been done to warn the public', he continued. He concluded that the deterrent effects of publicizing the number of deaths by tight lacing were negligible. Fashion 'would prevail' and was, to his chagrin, 'cultivated in defiance of nature and art'. [42]

These patronizing and dismissive attitudes were, on occasion, reflected in the medical perception of serious corset injury. The most commonly reported corset-related medical trauma in America was dubbed by physicians there as 'chicken breast'; a term which belittled the significance and distress of its symptoms. Chicken breast occurred when, under direct and extreme pressure exerted by the metal, bones and laces of corsetry, the ribs turned inward, overlapped the sternum and fractured. The lungs under the parts of the ribcage most severely affected atrophied and collapsed when this occurred.[43] The set of five lower ribs or 'false' ribs indirectly connected with the breast bone or sternum in front, bore the brunt of tight lacing and were at most risk of 'chicken breast'. It was an extremely painful injury that required immobilization of the ribcage for several weeks to effect a 'knitting' of the bone and cartilaginous mass. Damage to the lungs by 'chicken breast' was both potentially and actually life-threatening, for in a pre-antibiotic medical era, a punctured lung was a possible forerunner of pneumonia and death.

Medical attitudes to corset-related diseases which blamed the victim as much as the corset were also common in Britain. The majority of physicians writing in *Lancet* found it 'difficult to speak with moderation of the folly of tight lacing . . . especially as no attention [was] paid to the warnings repeated *ad nauseam* against irrational and injurious modes of dress'. Despite 'satire on one side and admonition on the other', observed one physician in 1881, there was 'little diminution in which the vagaries [were] carried, as may be proved by anyone who walk[ed] abroad during the height of the London season'.[44]

Claims by practitioners that women were obsessed with fashion and cared 'little for pathology' were, of course, quite untrue. Many women must have turned to male physicians when made ill by corsetry, but it would appear that few doctors were prepared to deeply engage with the complex issues that impelled women to corset in the first place. Claims by practitioners – that female vanity was the underlying reason for which women tightly laced their garments – reflected prevailing medical and societal assumptions about women. Positing feminine vanity as the chief impetus to corset comfortably confirmed, rather than problematizing, traditional gender behaviour, as did the recurring illnesses kindled or aggravated by use of corsets. Middle-class women were, certainly from the 1830s onward (in both Britain and North America), considered physically weaker than men and were routinely deemed to be far less intellectually capable. Within this gendered schema, female illness (whether corset-related or not) was almost naturalized, and as a result female debility was considered in many cases to be inevitable and even acceptable.

Educated women involved in medicine and dress reform fought against these gendered assumptions regarding ill health and femininity. Their work challenged claims made by male doctors that women were unconcerned about serious medical matters when it came to corsetry. Feminists within the dress reform movement were quick to capitalize on medical research in their attempts to convince women of the dangers of that garment. Indeed, it was in the published work of feminists and dress reformers that the private and largely male medical discourse around corsetry was revealed, and where important and relevant information was processed, reviewed and disseminated to women who were concerned about the destruction of female health by the corset. Many dress reform texts stand as extraordinary examples of the way complex medical knowledge written for a small, professional, largely male and decidedly *private* audience was appropriated and synthesized to make it comprehensible and accessible to a larger and very *public*, female lay reading audience. Legitimate (i.e. published) medical findings added credence to claims made by dress reformers, as did the sometimes lavish use of anatomical illustrations which were often borrowed wholesale from medical texts. Helen Gilbert Ecob (author of *The Well Dressed Woman: A Study in the Practical Applications to Dress*), was particularly adept at combing medical texts and journals and appropriating relevant material for her work. Ecob even made judicious and effective use of texts written by the most strident anti-feminist medical men of her era. While Gilbert completely ignored the anti-female education rationale posited by Drs Thomas Gaillard and Thomas Emmet, she directly and cleverly cited and expanded upon their remarks on the dangers of constrictive dress.[45]

While dress reformers like Ecob often repeated (appropriate) male medical warnings almost word for word, they approached the subject matter quite differently. 'Feminist' advice and fashion texts, sometimes written by female doctors but as often by concerned but informed women without medical qualifications, reiterated the direst male physicians' warnings but demonstrated a patience and greater understanding of corset-related 'issues' than the garment's male detractors. Catherine E. Beecher, sister of Harriet Beecher Stowe and author of *Miss Beecher's Housekeeper and Healthkeeper* (etc.), was extremely concerned about the damaging effects of corsetry on the female body. Beecher wanted to believe that the best protection against the health 'emergency' created by the tightly laced corset was to 'impress in early days, [a daughter's] obligation to the former of her body and the father of her spirit' to care for 'so precious and beautiful a casket'. However, she reluctantly conceded that spiritual persuasion was rarely successful. Beecher demonstrated considerable sympathy for mothers whose 'difficult duty it was to contend with the power of fashion . . . which in the life of a teenage girl [was] so frequently the ruling thought'. But her sympathies were also extended to the young women who corseted against their mothers' wishes. She recognized that for young women 'to be out of fashion [was] to be odd' and for a girl to be unable to 'dress as her companions [was] a mortification and grief that no argument or instructions [could] relieve'.[46] Beecher's empathic response to both mother and daughter in the face of tyrannical fashions was to adapt and modify under- and outer garments. Beecher's alternative gowns were graceful and loose and her version of the corset was a much more comfortable arrangement that supported the breasts without clamping the ribcage, stomach and hips. (see fig.49)

Empathy also characterized the writing of Anna M. Galbraith, M.D., author of numerous anti-corset popular health texts published later in the century. Galbraith's text, *Hygiene and Physical Culture for Women*, discussed the dangers of corsetry in a manner which neither sensationalized the issue nor spared readers from the grim realities of the garment's consequences. She wryly informed her reading audience that the many 'great distortions to the body from tight lacing' discovered during post mortems must have been incurred *after* death, because 'that woman has yet never been found that laced at all'.[47] While Galbraith's medical explanations of the effect of the corset on the heart, lungs, ribcage and pelvic basin were as accurate and as detailed as those of her male peers, her advice was tempered and characterized by an appeal to women's common sense. She neither patronized nor bullied nor belittled her readers. She urged them to independently assess corset-related injury to their own bodies and to act on their own observations. In doing so she attributed an intelligence to women generally denied by male practitioners, and encouraged a female agency that was antagonistic to traditional medical thought.

The [so called] 'best' corsets, explained Galbraith, were 'made of best quality steel, whalebone and French Jean' and were made so that they held their shape and 'yield[ed] to nothing'. Even when loosely worn, they 'act[ed] to a certain degree like a surgeon's splint to immobilise the thorax in case of a broken rib'. To demonstrate this analogy, and to encourage women to critically examine their own corsets in order to detect the damage they incurred, she described the construction of the contemporary garment beneath its silken and seductive carapace. Most corsets, she wrote, had an infrastructure of 'closely set whalebones and at least eight steel bands'. The heaviest pair of these steels measured from one and one-quarter to one and one-half inches wide. These were situated in the median front of the garment and were so heavy that the 'desired mold [was] given to them by machinery'. These 'strong unyielding bands passe[d] over if not presse[d] upon liver, stomach, large and small intestines'.

Galbraith explained to her readers that the damage to these organs was incurred slowly and that its effects were felt gradually and almost imperceptibly. She urged women to look at their own un-corseted naked bodies for early and obvious external signs of trauma. This advice breached standards of decency that generally discouraged or even forbade women from the immodest and brazen occupation of examining their own bodies. In urging women to examine their own unclad torsos Galbraith instigated a radical departure from traditional medical theory and practice, which located the power of determining illness solely in the hands of the (usually male) physician. Galbraith advised women to undress and minutely examine their breasts, trunk and hips for signs of trauma, which she had no doubt witnessed very often in the course of her career. 'On disrobing [wrote Galbraith] you will readily perceive a zone of compression by the purplish band on the skin from three to five inches wide, showing the creases and patterns of the undergarment.' The zone of discoloration usually extended 'from the sixth to the twelfth rib . . . which was directly over the diaphragm'. The result of this compression, she explained, meant that the ribs could not rise in forced inspiration, and that the diaphragm could not expand. The palpitations and shortness of breath that followed such constriction meant that women were 'forced to give up everything that [was] worthy of the name of exercise'. Galbraith also reminded her readers that encroachment of the chest wall on the heart caused fainting, and she made clear that tightly laced corsetry 'brought on death'.[48]

Galbraith, like many dress reformers and feminists, also refuted the ubiquitous medical fulmination that female vanity alone was responsible for the seemingly senseless injury and death caused by corsetry. Several feminist writers placed blame for the practice of tight lacing squarely with men. It was a position which, though at first seeming untenable, is in the light of nineteenth-century gender relations quite valid. Angeline Merritt, author of *Dress Reform Practically and Physiologically Considered*, insisted as early as 1852 that 'gentlemen [were] responsible' for the widespread use of corsetry. She argued that mankind had 'taught woman to believe that the chief sum of her charm and beauty consisted of possessing a genteelly contracted waist, [and] a slender tapering form'. Merritt appealed directly to men to halt 'the delusive strain of false flattery' regarding the tiny waistline, specifically because it was 'produced only by an open, designing and awful violation of physical laws [which resulted in] serious and irreparable injury to [women's] physical development'.[49] A little over twenty years later, Elizabeth Farrar, author of the frequently published text *The Young Lady's Friend*, wrote that efforts to convince young ladies that tight lacing was 'destructive of health' were completely in vain while 'the tastes of the lords of creation' went unrectified. 'Let medical men, let painters, and let sculptors teach young men that all such unnatural compression of the body is deformity', wrote Farrar. 'Let Grecian models of beauty be studied [and then] the shape of a modern belle shall no longer command admiration.'[50] Farrar's observations regarding the variety of influences that encouraged so many middle-class women to persevere with the garment were perceptive. She clearly understood that a range of powerful incentives, derived in part from both medical ambivalence and 'artistic' idealization of the corseted female body, kept women tightly bound and ill. So ill, that several fortunes were built upon the tide of female complaints[51] (see Figure 43).

The extent of tight lacing in Victorian Britain and North America continues to be topic of debate at least a century after its occurrence. Fashion historian Valerie Steele and art historian David Kunzle claim that tight-lacing was only practised by a minority of 'fetishistic' women, but there is a significant body of nineteenth-century material that challenges this. Extremes of tight lacing may have been undertaken by some women and certainly some men for explicitly sexual purposes: after all, the tightly laced corset was (and remains) a standard icon of pornography. The library of the Kinsey Institute for Research in Sex, Gender and Reproduction at Indiana University holds a large collection of nineteenth-century photographic and textual material involving sadomasochistic scenes that feature women and men in tightly laced corsets.[52] The existence of this material stands as evidence of the corset's enduring transgressive sexual valency.

However, nineteenth-century tight lacing was hardly the exclusive domain of the sexual adventurer alone. An examination of mid- and late nineteenth-century medical texts, advice texts, feminist and dress reform texts, or even a swift perusal of fashion plates that embellished nineteenth-century women's magazines, reveals that tight lacing was a practice undertaken by women across the social classes for reasons unrelated to sexual 'perversion'. In her delightful memoirs of the late nineteenth century, Gwen Raverat unintentionally averred to the popularity

Figure 43

The corseted subject of the advertisement for Lydia Pinkham's cure might have felt better had she abandoned her stays. Corsets were as fundamental to the general ill-health of Victorian women as they were to the burgeoning patent remedy industries which targeted a corseted female clientele.

FEBRUARY, 1896.]   THE "STANDARD" DELINEATOR

A PEN PICTURE

Many Women Will Recognize It

"OH, I am so nervous! No one ever suffered as I do! There isn't a well inch in my whole body! I honestly think my lungs are diseased, my chest pains me so; but I've no cough. I'm so weak at my stomach, and have indigestion horribly. Then I have palpitation, and my heart hurts me. How I am losing flesh! and this headache nearly kills me; and the backache! why, I had hysterics yesterday!

"There is that weight and bearing down feeling all the time; and there are pains in my groin and thighs. I can't sleep, walk or sit. I'm diseased all over. The doctor? Oh! he tells me to keep quiet. Such mockery!"

An unhealthy condition of the female organs can produce all the above symptoms in the same person. In fact, there is hardly a part of the body that can escape those sympathetic pains and aches.

No woman should allow herself to reach such a perfection of misery when there is positively no need of it.

Lydia E. Pinkham's Vegetable Compound acts promptly and thoroughly in such cases, strengthens the muscles, heals all inflammation, and restores the organ to its normal condition. Druggists are selling carloads of it. Mrs. Pinkham, of Lynn, Mass., will gladly and freely answer all letters asking for advice.

Mrs. E. Bishop, 78 Halsey Street, Brooklyn, N. Y., suffered all the above described miseries. Now she is well. Lydia E. Pinkham's Vegetable Compound cured her. Write her about it.

A prominent actress writes: ". . . You cannot imagine the fearful condition I was in when I first wrote to you. I was simply of no use to myself or anyone else. I had worked hard, and my nervous system was shattered from female complaint and travelling constantly. I ran the gauntlet of doctors' theories, till my health and money were rapidly vanishing. . . . . . I'm all right now, and am gaining flesh daily. I follow your advice faithfully in everything. Thank you ten thousand times for what your knowledge and *Lydia E. Pinkham's Vegetable Compound* have done for me."

If in doubt, write to Mrs. Pinkham for advice.

The LYDIA E. PINKHAM MED. CO., Lynn, Mass.

When writing to Advertisers please mention the "STANDARD" DELINEATOR.

of tight lacing in her description of the sartorial appearance of her distinguished and morally irreproachable relatives. 'Except for the most small waisted, naturally dumb-bell shaped females . . . ladies never seemed at ease', wrote Raverat. It was as if

they were not wearing their own clothes . . . their dresses were always made too tight . . . so tight that the bodices wrinkled laterally from the strain; and their stays showed in a sharp ledge across the middles of their backs.[53]

As Raverat's memoirs also candidly if inadvertently acknowledge, many women sought a tightly bound appearance without ever assuming that they were cultivating, encouraging or enacting a sexual fetish. Paradoxically, while tightly laced corsets were undoubtedly an erotic aspect of Victorian culture they also remained equally essential in the construction and maintenance of respectability, a factor which may also have led women to accept the wide range of illnesses which were almost unavoidable with their long-term use.

Medical journals published between 1850 and 1900 also point to the frequency of tight lacing among Victorian women. Although fewer women died of tight lacing in the 1890s than they had in previous decades, the *Lancet* reported that tight lacing was 'still a fruitful cause of illness' and though it no longer occupied

> a foremost place among the causes of death, the fact that it did occasionally stand in this position should be noted by those foolish persons whose false taste and vanity . . . made them the suffering devotees of a custom so injurious.[54]

The design of many brands of corsetry actually demanded that they be tightly laced. While it is often assumed that Victorian women could simply loosen the laces of the garments to reduce the pressure on their bodies, this was simply not feasible. Corsetry was carefully cut and often reinforced with at least twenty or more stiffened 'bones' or steels. Each bone or steel was tempered or curved in to a particular shape to form a gore that fitted snugly over a particular place on the torso. If the corset was loosened the garment did not maintain the desired shape, looked ungainly, and often chafed. Chafing on the abdomen and back meant that tender skin could break. Bleeding was a painful and possibly humiliating result of loosening one's corset.

Corsetry manufactured by renowned corsetière Madame Worth reveals both the size of the ideal middle-class fashionable waist in the 1880s and the popularity of tight lacing as a mainstream practice that was undertaken to achieve it. Corsets produced by Worth measured from a tiny eighteen to a not much larger twenty inches. These sizes, noted one critic, did 'not allow [the occupant] to sit down in comfort'.[55] Not surprisingly, symptoms frequently associated with wearing tightly laced corsetry included a sense of uneasiness, a sense of pelvic weight, bearing down pains toward the anus, back pain in the inguinal region, and aching of the inner thighs, all of which were 'much increased by walking'.[56]

Medical tests conducted by physician F.R. Treves in the early 1850s also point to the frequency of tight lacing among 'ordinary' women. Treves argued for dress reform specifically because he had witnessed a deluge of corset-related female complaints. He noticed in the course of his work that the 'natural' uncorseted waistline measured between twenty-six and twenty-eight inches, and he made a comparison of the uncorseted waistline with the size of dressmakers' models. The dressmakers' models, which as Treves reported 'represented the perfect female figure', had waist measurements of only twenty to twenty-one inches. This was, he accurately remarked 'a tolerably direct comment upon the extent of tight lacing, and upon the position it occupie[d] in popular taste'.[57] Treves did not ascribe any kind of sexual motive to the widespread use of tight lacing, and his work clearly positioned tight lacing as a normative rather than exceptional practice.

The popularity of wasp-waisted subjects in the fashion plates of mainstream women's magazines further indicates that tight lacing was not considered a deviate sexual practice among the majority of Victorian women who corseted. Countless illustrations in respectable women's magazines such as *The Standard Delineator of Fashion Fancywork and Millinery*, *Myra's Journal*, *Women's World*, *Queen* and similar journals, indicate that the tiny waistline was considered a very desirable and genteel physical asset. The sheer volume of mainstream representations of the tiny wasp waist in women's magazines indicates indubitably that its cultivation was not an isolated practice within the realms of private sexual fetishism.[58] Interestingly, magazine illustrations were very important in establishing and perpetuating the cult of the tightly corseted waist among 'ordinary' women. Feminists and dress reformers were aware of the power of magazines and advertising in the perpetuation of this dangerous trend. The practice was, no doubt, assisted by the traffic of fashion plates between women's magazines in Britain, France and North America[59] that featured glamorous styles using colourful lithographs of fashionable women with implausibly tiny waists.

Angeline Merritt was very critical of *Les modes Parisiennes* that graced the fashion plates of women's magazines. 'In every instance', wrote the perceptive Merritt, 'the unnatural deformity [the waist] is decked off in alluring colours, and portrayed in all the fascinating loveliness which it is possible for such burlesques on real beauty to be made to assume.'[60] Even those fashion magazines that routinely decried the tiny waist were as often guilty of its promotion. The very successful mid- to late century magazine, *Queen*, was one of many that entertained a double standard when it came to waist size and 'female complaints'. While the *Queen* had scant sympathy for 'the feelings of sinking' experienced by women in tightly laced corsets, and while it claimed to be insulted by the 'sharp tempers of the young ladies with wasp waists' to the extent that it was 'glad not to be obliged to be associated intimately with them'.[61] it consistently reinforced its dominant message that a tiny, tightly bound waist was a fashionable must by repeatedly using decorative fashion plates featuring wasp-waisted models. (see fig.51)

Despite the discomfort involved in procuring the 'unnatural deformity' of the tiny waist, many women were determined to achieve this fashionable ideal, possibly in order to resemble the fashion plates of popular magazines. They turned to dressmakers to help achieve this goal. Indeed nineteenth-century dressmakers can be seen to have been almost as implicated in perpetuating the practice of tight lacing (and its corollary serious illness) as corset manufacturers. Dress reformers, whose work will be discussed in a later chapter, urged women to ignore dressmakers for the sake of their health.[62] It was in the 'best interest of the dress-maker' to convince clients that 'they [were] breathing when they were suffocating' wrote Elizabeth Sturt Phelps. She and other reformers under-stood that 'wasp waisted fashions' which relied on 'the stiff whalebone, drawn cord, and [the] barbarous steel busk' of the corset successfully implemented the fashionable silhouette, but they reminded women that this was achieved at the terrible cost of 'imprisoning [the internal] organs'.[63]

As magazine illustrations, personal testaments, feminist textual oppos-ition to tight lacing, and the extant material culture confirm, the female waist was undeniably a crucial site of femininity. From the female waist could be read beauty or 'clumsiness', health or disease.[64] Although it was widely held that tight lacing lead to a startling range of grave female complaints, many women persevered with corsets that compressed their bodies to dangerous dimensions. Some persisted with tight lacing (as Dr Edgar Flinn explained in his 1886 text *Our Dress and Our Food in Relation to Health*) because they believed that there was 'plenty of empty space in the body', and that 'cavities existed between the organs'. These women mistakenly believed that by 'narrowing the waist [other organs] occup[ied] spare room'.[65] While this erroneous notion may have encouraged women to lace tightly, it has also been observed that even when illness was ascribed to and even accepted as a direct result of corsetry, it did not fail to dampen enthusiasm for the practice of tight lacing. Indeed it was held that tight lacing actually increased among women as its ill effects became more widely known.[66] This may have been (as historian Elaine Showalter has demonstrated) because ill health, or at least an appearance of ill health, was fundamental to the mainstream construction of nineteenth-century femininity.[67] According to Showalter, to suffer, to be ill, to be 'fading', or to be weak, were so commonplace in the lives of Victorian middle-class women as to be denoted as normative. Robust good health (in this schema) was considered a transgression of the boundaries of acceptable femininity. Female debility, on the other hand, was a sign of beauty, particularly in the 'over refined'.[68]

The corset was undoubtedly a very useful device in the creation and maintenance of a refined debilitated femininity, for it policed the waistline and to a greater or lesser extent determined the health or ill health experienced by the body within. When tightly laced the corset procured the desirable wasp-like waist, while it simultaneously forced the enclosed body to mimic, replicate and in some cases even create the idealized middle-class construct of ailing femininity. Indeed the garment was crucial in effecting and maintaining a particular and vulnerable femininity which men found so endearing in middle-class women. Until the latter decades of the nineteenth century stereotypical femininity (when not aligned perfectly with actual illness) was characterized by fragility, a construct in direct opposition to its masculine binary, identified by strength, courage and capability.

These binary oppositions in turn affected and reflected mainstream heterosexual relations, which a minority of women and an even smaller minority of men challenged. Female debility was undoubtedly admired by individual men and by the culture at large. 'Girls like[d] to look upon themselves as ethereal beings', observed one writer from the Dress Reform movement. They cared 'little about their internal arrangements as long as they did not suffer acute pain'. Young men, continued the author, enjoyed the 'sense of protecting a fragile, clinging creature who was like child and wife in one'.[69] The 'enfeebled female body' had 'always more or less been encouraged by the more robust sex, who admired in a woman a weakly dependent', wrote one masculine critic of the corset.[70] Perhaps few men were so candid in their appreciation of women's enforced (or chosen) constructed frailty than the novelist and self-aggrandizing philosopher Oliver Wendell Holmes. Holmes bare-facedly assured readers that 'a delicate woman [was] the best instrument; [because] she ha[d] such a magnificent compass of sensibilities'.[71]

Such attitudes did not go entirely unchallenged. Throughout the century there existed pockets of resistance to the dominant feminine paradigm of disability and the heterosexual ideology it supported. Although Dinah Craik, author of *A Woman's Thoughts About Woman* (published in 1859), was uncritical of women's traditional captivity in the private sphere, she resented male flattery that encouraged female invalidism. Though few men 'would be so bold as to admit this openly', wrote Craik, many 'tacitly [encourage illness in women] when they preach up lovely uselessness, false frivolity and delicious helplessness'. This kind of flattery, she added, amounted to 'poetical degradation . . . which women of common sense repudiate[d] as insulting'.[72] Harriet Hubbard Ayer was just as scornful of men who complained about, rather than celebrated, the dogged 'ill health and nervous debility' suffered by wives and female companions. Ayer bluntly maintained that men promoted the widespread situation of generalized female illness by encouraging the fair sex to secure a 'wasp waist'.[73]

Many feminists and dress reformers on both sides of the Atlantic were well aware that the corset was directly related to the wave of illness that plagued middle-class Victorian women.[74] Several dress reformers perceived the damage incurred by the corset as a matter not only of individual concern, but also of national concern. They insisted that the corset was responsible for an epidemic of female decline that had ramifications for the entire body politic. Dr. Mary Safford-Blake expressed the opinion of many dress reformers in the 1870s who feared for 'the physical degeneracy of the mothers' that originated in constrictive fashion. She believed such sartorial constriction would 'leave its impress on the sons, as well as the daughters; and in the end the national strength [would] languish under the weakness of the inheritance'.[75] Abba Gould-Woolson declared that the 'ill health of (American) country women [was] a national injury and a national disgrace' and that all 'patriotic citizens and philanthropists should do everything in their power to remove the causes which induce[d] it'.[76]

Caroline H. Dall, author of *The College, The Market and The Court; Or, Woman's Relation to Education, Labor and Law*, recognized a specific relationship between the corseted body, female ill-health and masculine desire, and sought to dismantle that relationship. Dall espoused a political stand against tight fashions and their role in the construction of an enfeebled femininity, and reiterated the theoretical position championed by Mary Woolstonecraft who condemned female fashion as a 'badge of slavery'. Dall, like Woolstonecraft before her, wished to persuade women to acquire strength of both body and mind by abandoning constrictive dress. She was convinced that 'soft phrases' such as 'susceptibility of heart', 'delicacy of sentiment' and 'refinement of taste' were 'synonymous with epithets of weakness'. Women who either succumbed to or actively constructed their feminine identity on such conceits were in reality, asserted Dall, 'objects of pity' whose refined debility would eventually make them 'objects of contempt'.[77] Clearly, few women were cognizant of Dall's political theory, dismissed it, or simply did not question a feminine role identity which, though predicated on the impairment of their health, appeared superficially at least to work in their favour.

Indeed the 'delicate bloom' and 'singular pallor' of North American girls and women in the 1890s was so ubiquitous, according to gynaecologist and Harvard professor Edward Clarke, that it had 'almost passed into proverb'.[78] Clarke reported that upon arrival in Boston, the British writer Lady Amberly remarked that she had never seen 'so many pretty girls together', adding that 'they all look so sick'.[79] Lady Harberton (founder of the American dress reform movement) believed that a national health crisis had come about because 'an appearance of incapability ha[d] come to be looked upon as a mark of good breeding'. Ill health had become, according to Harberton, 'a definite object to strive for among many classes of women'.[80] Similarly, a survey conducted by Catherine Beecher, similarly led her to believe that there was a 'terrible decay of female health all over the land and [that this] evil was . . . increasing in a most alarming ratio'.[81] Beecher had drawn up a survey of women's health, which she had distributed to her numerous friends and acquaintances across cities and towns in the United States. It was to be sent to the ten women each knew best. The respondents were asked to rate their constitutions as perfectly healthy, well, delicate, sick, invalid and so forth. Hundreds of women participated, and confirmed Beecher's suspicions. Pelvic disorders, sick headaches, and general nervousness, those staples of 'female complaints', dominated the findings.[82] Because robust good health was 'neither generally admired nor cultivated by women', British society also found itself 'encumbered by large numbers of delicate girls'. The *Rational Dress Society's Gazette* of 1887 noted that the 'feeble strength of women [was] one of the crying disgraces of the age'. Many women could not walk more than a few hundred yards without fatigue. Any exertion 'knocked them up'. They caught cold, they fainted, they had headaches. The weight of heavy clothing, artificial hair and, importantly, the fact that 'their whole bodies were pressed in tight stays' was, argued the *Gazette*, the obvious cause.[83]

Stays had been considered the obvious cause of female decline much earlier in the century. Charlotte Tonna, writing in 1845, believed that while she 'was not able to compare shapes with a wasp or an hourglass' her 'rare exemption from headaches . . . and other lady like maladies' was due to her good fortune in never having been 'submitted to the restraints of those unnatural machines', corsets. Tonna had on one occasion in her youth worn a corset under a tightly fitting ball gown. Her evening was ruined by the unpleasant choking sensations the corset temporarily imposed on her body. The experience revealed to her the unremitting torture most women endured on an hourly basis from the corset. Tonna was clearly delighted by the physical and mental confidence she experienced without the restraints of corsetry. She fully appreciated and celebrated the ease of her own body to assume 'free respiration, circulation and powers both of exertion and endurance'. She assured her readers that this was 'no trivial matter'.[84]

Angeline Merritt also made clear (in the mid-century) that tight clothing underpinned by tight corsetry effectively 'cramp[ed] and deaden[ed] the vital apparatus to a morbid incapacity', a condition which left women incapable of 'properly performing their office'. To effect a permanent cure, wrote Merritt, women 'must throw aside the now general constrictions of corsage, stays and buckram and drink unimpeded pure healthful oxygenised air'.[85] Writing in the 1870s, Abba Gould-Woolson discussed what she termed the enduring 'cult of the *invalide*', in her text *Woman in American Society*, and foreshadowing Veblen's theory of fashion, she linked female debility to trends of conspicuous leisure and conspicuous consumption. These trends demanded that gentlemen of means should demonstrate their ability to 'sustain large pecuniary damage without impairing [their] superior opulence'. Gould-Woolson wrote that she had heard a husband conclude a glowing enumeration of his wife's talents with the final remark that she was an invalid. This remark, said Gould-Woolson, allowed the man not only to demonstrate his wife's 'fine breeding' but the extent of his own 'ample means [that were] required to support such helpless elegance'. While Gould-Woolson appeared to have little sympathy for the debilitated female, she recognized that the cult of disability actually originated in genuine ill health. This was brought on, she claimed, by a rejection of energetic pursuits, the avoidance of fresh air and the adoption of constrictive fashion. Little had changed for women's health by the 1890s. Anna Galbraith was still repeating the warnings of her foremothers who had railed against the corset for reasons of health. She insisted that corsetry was directly responsible for rendering 'woman more impressionable than strong, transforming her into . . . a feeble dependant'.[86]

Feminist and dress reform claims throughout the century that the corset was largely responsible for a dazzling constellation of female complaints were, in the light of twentieth-century medical research, well founded. Actual illnesses related to the wearing of corsetry ranged from minor but never the less unpleasant ailments, such as nausea and constipation, to more dangerous eating disorders, and to morbid conditions of uterine displacement. Between these conditions existed an enormous range of diseases and injuries that to a greater or lesser extent were corset-related, or aggravated by that garment. Chlorosis and its frequent counterpart neurasthenia were both frequently subsumed under the rubric of womb ills, or female complaints,[87] and the corset was eventually traced as a presupposing factor in both ailments. (The medical terms 'chlorosis' and 'neurasthenia' were on occasion used interchangeably by some physicians.) The chlorotic girl was frequently described as feminine, smooth, white, waxy, anaemic, sluggish and sexually depressed.[88] Dr Meinert (cited in Vertue) attributed chlorosis directly to corsetry in 1893 but his conclusions were overwhelmingly rejected.[89]

Chlorosis, which has no medical analogue in the twentieth century, was also characterized by amenorrhoea, syncope and dyspnoea, being cessation of menses, fainting and breathlessness. Lesser indications of the disease included a pale bloodless face, palpitations, visible pulse in the temporal arteries, loss of breath when ascending stairs or dancing, a dislike of food (especially meat), swollen legs toward evening,[90] bilious attacks, headaches, and 'psychasthenic and functional nervous symptoms in the more mentally active and better off classes of women'. Many of its working-class victims, reported one nineteenth-century physician, sought employment as cooks or kitchen helps in basement kitchens so they could avoid the frequent stair-climbing of other occupations which increased the severity of the symptoms. Writing in 1925 about his experience as a house surgeon in London in the 1890s, Mr F. Parkes Weber realized in retrospect that chlorosis was the direct result of tight lacing. As he later pondered, chlorosis never appeared in boys, fat rather than thin girls were more affected, and prolonged bed rest, where corsets were not worn, *always* made the patient feel better, while a spell at the seaside did not. Seaside resorts, noted Weber, inevitably increased chlorotic symptoms, because women laced themselves more tightly than usual for 'strolls along the promenade'.[91]

Writing almost seventy-five years earlier, Harriet Beecher warned that not only did 'stiff corset bones' cause chlorotic symptoms but that corsetry was also largely responsible for those distresses which were 'peculiar to women'.[92] By this, Beecher specifically meant uterine displacement and uterine prolapse. The displaced or prolapsed womb is a condition in which the uterus is forced through, or collapses outside of, the cervix, protrudes into the vagina and in extreme cases, outside the body. Beecher's direct yet sensitive discussion of uterine prolapse was derived in part from having experienced this terrible condition herself. 'The pressure of the whole superincumbent mass [of the uterus] on the pelvic or lower organs induce[d] sufferings proportioned in acuteness with the extreme delicacy and sensitiveness of the parts crushed', she wrote; the 'terrible sufferings that are sometimes thus induced can never be conceived of, or at all appreciated'. Nothing that the public could be made to believe on this subject, she continued, would 'ever equal the reality'. She believed that the 'evil' (of prolapsed uterus) was 'becoming so common, not only among married women but among young girls, as to be the cause of universal alarm'.

She also recognized that the delicate (i.e., genital) nature of the illness made it particularly difficult for women to seek medical advice. Few women felt comfortable enough to admit this affliction to even their closest *confidants*. 'Many a woman', wrote Beecher, 'is moving about in uncomplaining agony who, with any other trouble involving equal suffering would be on her bed surrounded by sympathising friends.' So dreadful was the pain from uterine displacement, she reported, that many women would have exchanged it gladly for the 'horrible torments of savage Indians or cruel inquisitors' and would have considered it a 'merciful exchange'.[93]

Although prolapsed uterus was routinely treated by the medical profession by 'mechanical' means and bed rest, the relationship between the removal of the corset for extended periods of bed rest, and the subsequent return of cervical/uterine health were never directly associated. Beecher, though unqualified as a medical doctor, was adamant that emulating the wasp-like figure was the primary cause of uterine damage and insisted 'female complaints' in general were dramatically reduced or eradicated by the complete avoidance of corsetry.[94] Abandonment of the corset was a significant part of a 'water cure' favoured by Beecher that involved douches, a change of diet and mild exercise. She was largely opposed to the insertion of mechanical devices into the vagina (a solution favoured by male doctors to hold the uterus in place) unless the damage was otherwise irreparable. She was also extremely concerned for the many unmarried and married women who presented with uterine damage to male doctors, only to be to be sexually molested in the course of their treatment.

This was not a new problem, though it was rarely publicly acknowledged. Sexual assault in the privacy of a consulting room during an intimate examination was reported as a frequent occurrence as early as the 1850s.[95] Beecher's information regarding medical sexual abuse was received from her colleague and friend, a married female doctor, Mrs Gleason. During 1854 and 1855 Gleason successfully treated 130 cases of uterine prolapse,[96] which she directly attributed to corsetry: of these 130 patients, only 30 required surgical intervention to restore their health. Gleason had learned about the extent of medical sexual misconduct from her own patients and from 'the most unimpeachable sources', who well understood that the penalties for reporting sexual assault would 'inflict heavier penalties on the victims than on the wrongdoers'. Gleason and Beecher were aghast that these 'developments', as they delicately termed them, were occurring more frequently as uterine troubles escalated among women. The 'entire helplessness of [the] sex' made retribution impossible, wrote Beecher. The 'refined, delicate, sensitive woman could do nothing when thus insulted . . . The dreadful fear of publicity shut her lips and restrained every friend'.[97]

Dress reformers in Britain were also linking the corset directly to 'female complaints' such as uterine disorder and abdominal damage, but there appears to have been less recognition of the opportunities for sexual misconduct this complaint might present for unscrupulous male medical practitioners. Many women, reported the *Rational Dress Society's Gazette* of 1888, endured a range of dyspeptic disorders from wearing corsetry, but according to their medical sources it was clearly the 'delicate organs in the pelvis that suffered most'. A 'ladies doctor' reported bluntly that 'uterine derangement had increased fifty percent within the last fifteen years as a result of tight clothing, corsets and high heels'. Another apparently well-known but unnamed specialist reported to dress reform members that 'disorders of the pelvic organs' seldom occurred without entailing 'anaemia, disordered digestion, *hyperaesthesia, neuralgia* or other manifestations of nervous derangement or prostration (*Gazette's* italics).[98]

Assertions by dress reformers on both sides of the Atlantic regarding the number of women who suffered from uterine damage or displacement were not exaggerated. Even a cursory examination of mid- to late nineteenth-century British and American gynaecological and obstetrics journals reveals that the invention and improvisation of intra-uterine rings, pessaries and stems (used to lever the uterus back into position and hold it there), was the subject of unremitting professional discussion. The British gynaecologist Tilt (who advocated medical education for women) questioned both the benefit of pessaries and the enthusiasm demonstrated by doctors for inserting the devices. Although Tilt recognized that corsetry endangered the female body, he failed to make the direct connection between the symptoms of tightly laced corsetry and the symptoms of the displaced uterus. He did, however, assert that psychological conditions were mistakenly ascribed to uterine malfunction and that uterine pessaries were over-prescribed and dangerous. Tilt believed that there had been an 'undue development of this mechanical tendency' which had given rise to 'a system of uterine orthopaedics'. There was, he wrote caustically, 'no contagion . . . so catching as enthusiasm' when it came to the prescription to insert a mechanical pessary. Tilt preferred a non-interventionist approach to uterine displacement. Strength would return to weakened ligaments of the uterus, he argued, upon 'prolonged repose in a horizontal posture'.[99] Tilt concluded this because 'victims' of uterine complaints were 'free from pain at night',[100] but he did not appear to have made the connection that the corset's temporary removal might have been responsible for alleviating the symptoms of uterine distress (see Figure 45).

The feminist dress reformer and doctor Arvilla Haynes did make this connection. She insisted that the increasing numbers of women presenting with uterine and abdominal damage and disease in her practice had sustained their illnesses because of corsetry. She further claimed that the very design of uterine devices was evidence that corsets had produced the initial injury. 'Prolepses' occurred, said Haynes, when organs compressed by new sturdier corsetry designs, threw the 'weight of the contents

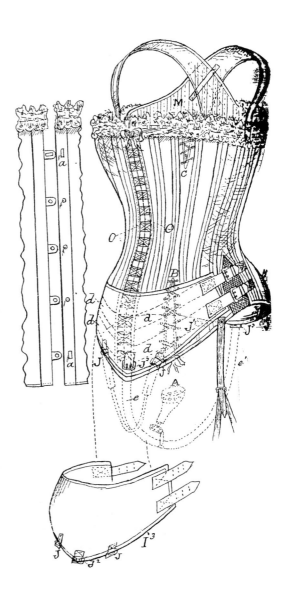

Figure 44
Patent lodged by Elizabeth Rowland in 1897 for a corset with pessary attachment that was intended to support the retroverted uterus. See following figure for details of pessary attachment.

Figure 45
Rowland's invention consisted of a 'ball and socket pessary' attached to the corset with tapes and buckles. The pessaries were 1–5 inches long 'of soft rubber, or vulcanite or other suitable material.' The abdominal belt which was part of the corset design, and which helped keep the arrangement in place, would have added pressure to the already damaged contents of the pelvic basin.

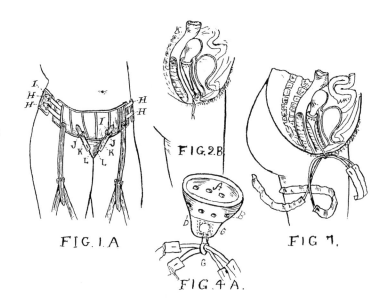

of the abdomen upon the pubic portion of the pelvis . . . and destroyed the true bearing of the body'. She pointed out that uterine devices designed to secure the displaced or prolapsed uterus back into position were designed specifically to restore that equilibrium of the pelvic basin destroyed by the corset.[101] However Haynes's theory, along with Tilt's criticism of uterine devices, was virtually ignored by the majority of doctors and gynaecologists.

Paradoxically, the corset was on occasion actually invoked to cure the very damage it incurred. Elizabeth Rowland, a 'Certified Ladies nurse and Hygienic Specialist', lodged a patent in 1897 for a corset with a pessary attached. The garment came with a range of spring stem pessaries measuring from 1 to 5 inches in length. These were to be made of hard or soft rubber, vulcanite, silver, or any other material thought suitable. The pessary could also be of cup design. The spring pessary pushed the uterus back into place, while the cup device held the prolapsed uterus *in situ* and prevented its further protrusion into the vagina. The pessary was held onto the corset by a complicated arrangement of straps and buckles. The specification reveals the corset was closed by a metal busk which would have increased the pressure on the lower abdomen as well as on the chest. The corset was of overall sturdy design, made of either elastic courtelle sateen or jean and was 'cut to fit the body perfectly'; that is, quite tightly. It laced at the back and included a detachable belt that buckled into position. It was reinforced with at least 24 steels or bones. It was clearly the kind of garment that would have made Avilla Haynes, or any enlightened doctor or gynaecologist, shudder (see Figures 44 and 45).[102]

Few, if any, male doctors or gynaecologists recognized or acknowledged the relationship between pessary design, the effects of corsetry, and uterine damage. It was, however, reluctantly acknowledged (on occasion) that uterine injury had unpleasant ramifications for men. As American physician Dr. Godman, author of 'Injurious Effects of Tight Lacing on the Organs and Functions of Respiration, Digestion and Circulation etc', admitted, tightly laced corsetry often 'rendered the conjugal condition one of unceasing disappointment and gloomy solitude'.[103] Victorian delicacy forbade a wide discussion of this side effect, but it may well have been the corset's role in reducing sexual access to wives and lovers that impelled so many male doctors to attempt a speedy 'cure', by using a device to push the uterus back into position. Discussions of uterine displacement in medical journals between 1860 and 1900 usually dwelled heavily on the treatment of the disorder and largely neglected any sustained discussion of its origin. Falls, inherent weakness of the muscles in the pelvic basin, hysteria, violent fits of laughter, straining of the bowels, abortion, difficult or protracted childbirth[104] and even 'conjugal onanism'[105] were thought to bring about uterine disorders and dislodge the womb, but gynaecology's primary and far more exciting challenge was not to detect the origins of uterine displacement, but rather to reposition that recalcitrant organ.

Rigid pessaries made of 'vulcanite, coralline or metal were the kinds most likely to be used in difficult cases',[106] while pessaries made of boxwood or of horsehair, covered in India rubber, were commonly used. These were inserted into the vagina and remained there until disintegration or removal.[107] Dr Beverly Cole, writing in the *Transactions of the Obstetrical Society of London*, promoted a spring pessary for use when 'ordinary pessaries [were] contraindicated or inadmissible'.[108] The design and manufacture of pessaries was a promising new field for many physicians.[109]

Long-running debates in British and American medical journals between 1870 and 1900 indicate that pessaries and stems of all kinds presented serious risk of injury to women's bodies. Infections, ulceration and fistulas of the vagina, cervix, uterus and bowel were commonly reported. Frequent too were the cases in which pessaries became embedded in the soft tissue of the body, destroying or damaging simultaneously the functions of the bladder, vagina and rectum. A meeting of the Obstetrical Society of London in 1876 discussed several shocking gynaecological disasters that were the result of pessary insertion. A debate ensued in which doctors alternately defended and discredited a range of devices invented and named after themselves and their colleagues. Zwanke's pessaries were the focus of much attention.[110] Dr. Godson 'feared' he was 'accountable for an immense amount of injury' because he had 'placed hundreds of Zwanke's pessaries in the last eight years'. Dr. Edis advised other 'fellows' that 'instruments [of all kinds] were too often inserted without the patient being made aware of what had been done'. The meeting discussed the methods by which embedded devices were best removed from patients. Major surgery involving anaesthesia and bone nippers were all considered. New and improved models and devices were then presented and recommended to the assembly.

In a separate discussion of the treatment of sixty-seven cases of uterine displacement published in *The Medical Press and Circular* of 1880, Dr Grailly Hewitt validated Beecher's assertions that the injury was widespread among single as well as married women. (This would of course indicate that repeated child-bearing was not a primary cause of uterine prolapse, and that corsetry was.) However, unlike Beecher, Hewitt did not make the connection between corsetry and uterine displacement. Hewitt noted that his patients were 'governesses, ladies dependent on their own exertions in various ways, and wives of curates'. Uterine dyskenesia, as Hewitt termed the condition, was so painful that it produced in many cases a 'helpless invalidism'. He reminded his peers that the physical disability incurred by distortion and displacement of the uterus, was 'not imaginary or fanciful though often [it was] erroneously so considered'.[111] Hewitt's opinions were not shared by the majority of physicians. Famous gynaecologist Braxton Hicks insisted in *Lancet* that 'generally' patients who presented with 'uterine displacement and irritability' were 'of a neurotic temperament, ill-nourished, badly feeding and much complaining'.[112] This medical misogyny was surpassed by the eminent medical practitioner, W.S. Playfair. Playfair, though reliant on uterine disorders for his income and genuinely fascinated by that organ, remained unsympathetic, even hostile toward his patients. 'Every practitioner', wrote Playfair, knew of 'cases of this kind' in which women with uterine disorders 'profess[ed] a total inability to take a healthy amount of food' and consequently manifested a wasting of the fatty tissues, anaemia, loss of appetite and dyspeptic symptoms. These women, he continued, aggravated their condition by the 'pernicious habit of deadening pain by chloral, morphia or stimulants . . . constantly crave[d] sympathy (and) victimised whole households by [their] morbid selfishness'.[113]

Playfair was an early supporter of the Weir Mitchell rest cure. He believed that uterine displacement and the hysteria supposedly arising from that displacement, was in many cases effectively cured by enforced bed rest, enforced feeding, massage, and shampooing of the body. This regime (with or without the insertion of a pessary), combined with bed rest, attention to diet and the implementation of the ill-named 'passive exercise' (whereby electric shocks were passed through the body[114]) would correct, or at least alleviate, the worst symptoms of uterine prolapse and displacement.[115] C.C. Frederick MD similarly supported the implementation of the rest cure. Unlike his peers, however, Frederick was unconvinced that bed rest and specific medical intervention (including radical surgery) actually cured neurasthenia, chlorosis and the 'nerve tire' of American women. 'Call it neurasthenia, nervous prostration, or what you will' remarked Frederick, 'pelvic disease and conditions which simulate pelvic disease' are a 'monstrous stumbling block at times to the brilliant results which our operations seem to promise.'[116] Few if any male doctors, including Frederick, directly credited the extended removal of corsetry required by enforced bed rest to the improvement or abatement of womb ills and nerve tire. Diet was considered significant, but only insofar as that under medical supervision women were forced to eat. Most women who presented with uterine displacement, neurasthenia and chlorosis were 'poor feeders' who complained of dyspepsia, nausea and constipation. These were exactly the complaints dress reformers and some enlightened general practitioners ascribed to the corset. Confined to their beds, *sans* corsetry, women were able to ingest and digest food, and eliminate bodily wastes.

Gynecologists and obstetricians embraced a peculiar 'double vision' regarding the corset. While they (like general physicians) denounced the garment from time to time, and occasionally recommended its temporary removal to alleviate acute pain, they rarely insisted on its complete banishment. At the risk of proposing a conspiracy theory, it would appear that obstetricians and gynaecologists realized that wholesale condemnation of the corset was not in their best interests. The years between 1850 and 1900 were critical for these disciplines. Both groups sought to establish themselves and their specializations as reputable during these decades. The uterine damage created by corsetry provided these men with almost unlimited opportunities to examine women, who in good health would never present for genital and rectal examinations. While (as Beecher observed) many women went about in uncomplaining agony, numerous others were driven by pain so acute that they submitted to physical examinations of the most intimate nature.

Clearly, the damaged bodies of corseted women provided the raw material of research for the new specialists. These men could not resist opportunities afforded by the corset to survey and 'own' those organs of the female body that were usually only observable during autopsy. Dr Robert Barnes could barely disguise the thrill that coursed through him when he examined the living uterus. He wanted to share those feelings of conquest and power with his colleagues. He reminded readers of *Lancet* that the uterus was

> the only internal organ so accessible. [We] can touch the uterus directly from below, we can feel its whole surface, often from behind and in front, . . . we command it by palpitation, we determine its texture, its mobility, its relation to other organs, [and] we see a part of it which gives an indication of the vascularity and other features of the whole.[117]

Whether many physicians shared the flood of crypto-sexual power experienced by Barnes is unknowable. However, what is clear is that the examination and treatment of the prolapsed or displaced uterus provided an invaluable vehicle by which individual surgeons were able to publicize their skills and immortalize their names by the invention and modification of pessaries, stems and other intra-uterine devices.[118] At a more pragmatic level, a steady succession of hard-to-cure 'uterine complaints' provided a ready source of income for practitioners. The corset was, as Dr Anna Galbraith so aptly observed 'the chief support of doctors'.[119] Insistence on its removal meant that steady incomes would dwindle, research opportunities decrease, and prestige vanish. Without the corset, obstetrics and gynaecology could not thrive, indeed those professions might, in their very infancy, have been threatened with extinction.

Corsetry received ardent support from the most unexpected quarters. While the male medical profession were in the main against the use of corsets, many significant physicians contributed both directly and indirectly to the continued popularity of the garment. While many male doctors abhorred the garment and enthusiastically and graphically described its morbid effects, their arguments were often located in medical journals directed toward a professional rather than toward a general reading audience. Moreover, despite their criticisms, their discussions of the garment were often coloured by assumptions of femininity that made the banishment of the garment seem unlikely, given that women were apparently biologically destined to privilege the cultivation of beauty above reason. As dress reformers and many mid- to late nineteenth-century doctors realized, the garment was responsible for a diverse range of short- and long-term illnesses. Constipation, chlorosis, hysteria, neurasthenia, dyspepsia, headaches, and general malaise were among its least dangerous effects. As several female physicians and dress reformers made explicit, the garment was also largely responsible for the wave of serious uterine disorders that plagued middle- and working-class women. That so many women presented for help with corset-related injury despite middle-class 'delicacy' indicates the painful and debilitating nature of 'female complaints'. In reality the large numbers of women who presented for medical help was not a true indication of the numbers of women who suffered from female uterine complaints. Other women, too poor to attend clinics, afraid of sexual assault, constrained by 'virtuous shame' or sensibly fearing the consequences of pessary insertion, probably suffered in silence. Worse still, they may have held fast to their corsets believing them to assist, rather than aggravate, internal derangement.

The failure of the medical profession to unconditionally oppose corsetry contributed not only to the perpetuation of female complaints, but to their cultural denial. This denial has been echoed in contemporary discussions of nineteenth-century female complaints which have privileged oppressive gender stereotyping as the principle causative factor in the aetiology of nerve tire and womb ills. To privilege cultural expectations above the physical causes of female complaints is a dangerous theoretical practice. This is because it trivializes or even entirely negates the material reality of pain, and thereby reduces or even obliterates the reality and history of corset-related suffering which was endured by many North American and British middle-class women.

5
Breathless with Anticipation: Romance, Morbidity and the Corset

Although tightly laced corsetry made numerous middle-class women seriously ill, the practice continued well into the twentieth century. The long reign of the corset indicates that for many women the garment had considerable benefits that outweighed its widely publicized risks. The most prosaic and apparent advantage of corsetry was its ability – whether the occupant's body had been 'trained' from early childhood, or by voluntary tight lacing in adulthood – to literally sculpt the flesh and bones, to create the much-admired 'hand-span' waist. In doing so, judicious use of corsetry enabled women to construct a femininity that reflected middle-class ideals and expectations of female gender. When tightly or even moderately laced, corsetry generated physical symptoms in the healthy middle-class female body that emulated that of the fashionable, ailing, fragile and importantly *virginal* heroines idealized by Victorian popular culture. Paradoxically, the garment's resilient appeal lay as much in its ability to contravene or transgress those ideals as in its ability to encourage the female body to emulate or obey them.

It is the contention of this chapter that middle-class women employed corsetry because of its ability to implement a range of conflicting ideological purposes. Corsetry was instrumental, indeed critical, in both reinforcing and disrupting prevailing definitions of femininity. While the physical responses of the corseted body could be perceived as acceptably and stereotypically submissive, the breathlessness, flushed or pale face, and the rapid rise and fall of the breasts could in specific circumstances be read, or experienced, by its occupant and by others as overtly sexual. In other words, the corset's longevity may have been ensured by its dual ability to create an acceptable fashionable ideal, ostensibly based on virginal reticence and refined debilitation, but with the added capability, when occasion permitted, to flagrantly sexualize the body. Seen this way it would appear that skilful manipulation of their own bodies *via* the corset enabled single middle-class women to successfully negotiate a path between prevailing and antithetical constructions of femininity, which positioned them as either virginal or dangerously sexual. However, the perception of the corseted middle-class woman as a powerful agent in the construction and manipulation of her own rather malleable sexual subjectivity is jeopardized when an examination of the socio-cultural climate in which that sexuality was constructed and articulated is undertaken.

Costume historian Helene Roberts has commenced an examination of this kind. In her landmark paper titled 'The Exquisite Slave: The Role of Clothes in the Making of the Victorian Woman', Roberts maintained that woman's role in nineteenth-century heterosexual relations was characterized by a 'submissive-masochistic pattern of behaviour'. Roberts demonstrated that corsetry, high-heeled shoes, crinolines, bustles, and even the silhouette and colour of feminine attire projected a message of a female 'willingness to conform' to this masochistic pattern. Roberts's work is incisive, but unfortunately its brevity disallowed an expansion of those ideas regarding the relationship between clothing as reflective of wider cultural values. That is, while Roberts correctly established the affiliation between feminine attire and cultural expectations of female behaviour and demeanour, she did not analyse wider cultural imperatives that assisted the construction of middle-class femininity as submissive and willing to conform.[1]

This chapter will build on Roberts's work. It will examine the way in which corsetry (in particular) reproduced existing power relations, by making women fragile and ill (or by giving them the appearance of fragility and illness). However, it will also focus on the way corsetry was integral to the processes of sexualizing feminine illness, which in turn further cemented inequitable power relationships. While I agree with Roberts that submissive-masochistic femininity was an overriding characteristic of Victorian heterosexual relationships, I contend that the construction of a submissive, feminine masochism was a reflection of a Victorian engagement with death, and, moreover, that Victorian society simultaneously reified and coped with death, by 'othering' it as feminine. Further to this I would argue that the 'othering' of death was internalized by middle-class Victorian women, and that this macabre psychic internalization contributed to the construction of a morbid female sexual subjectivity. Given these circumstances it would appear that the popularity of corsetry rested precisely on its propensity to sexualize the female body in a manner that reflected a particular and sinister historical moment, a moment in which the intersection of sexuality and morbidity coalesced. Of course, neither corsetry nor the prevailing morbid *milieu* that encouraged its use was universally accepted by middle-class women. There existed a small, sporadic, but never-the-less radical critique by feminist dress reformers who both recognized and problematized the prevailing construction of morbid romantic heterosexual relations, and who understood the role of corsetry in its construction. Despite these pockets of resistance to corsetry (which will be discussed a little later), feminist arguments were largely overridden by a *zeitgeist* that superficially condemned corsetry, but simultaneously approved of and rewarded its more immediate and apparent consequences.

The construction of a more or less morbid female sexual subjectivity, and the relationship between this sexual specificity and the corset, had its origins, analogue, indeed its *raison d'être* in the generalized and very public Victorian relationship with death. According to several nineteenth-century historians a morbid aesthetic characterized, if not entirely permeated, Victorian popular culture. This was hardly surprising in an era that predated antibiotics, and in which as a result, death was a far more frequent [and premature] companion than it is today.[2] The Victorian attention to the customs, rituals, and *accoutrements* of death point to its intense emotional and psychic valency.[3] However, the appearance of a generalized Victorian involvement with death, the psychological management of Victorian grief was clearly gendered. That is, Victorian society coped with the frequency of mortality, and its emotional and psychic toll, by routinely 'othering' death and its management to the feminine. Understanding the Victorian obsession with illness and death, and women's socially situated positioning to it, is integral in identifying both the morbidification of female sexuality and the significant role corsetry played in that construction.

Middle-class Victorian women were intimately connected to death *via* a multiplicity of cultural and physical ties. An emphasis on the funereal aspects of life and female identification with death were officially transmitted in childhood. Between 1780 and 1830 art classes for female students dwelled on the production of *memento mori*. Generations of middle-class women were possibly inculcated with notions of female morbidity in their formative years this way. Illness, dying and death, and female identification with those events, variously and inevitably afforded middle-class women an honour, respect, prestige and attention that was, in many other ways, denied them in Victorian society. As Philippe Aries, author of *The Hour of Our Death*, has pointed out, deep mourning and the dramatic Victorian productions around that event can be read as evidence of its romance.[4] Moreover, death and dying were the domain of women, for the middle classes died at home rather than in hospital, and it fell to women to tend the dying,[5] and to female friends and relatives, rather than funeral directors, to prepare bodies for burial.[6] Women were, of course, also responsible for the maintenance and policing of mourning costume,[7] for themselves as well as for immediate family members.[8]

Illness, death and mourning also lent a particular importance, even glamour, to women in the public sphere, where the processes of its othering were made absolutely explicit. Women and death became almost synonymous in cultural representations of illness and mortality that flooded Victorian society. Over and over again *female* death and dying were played out in literature, art, music and theatre. Operatic heroines inevitably died youthful deaths in dramatic or heart-wrenching finales, while romantic paintings of the era repeatedly featured tremulous, child-like dying female invalids, gazing into the great 'Beyond'. The feminine enculturation of illness and death in the public sphere (and the sexualization of that process and its expression), has been explored by several significant historians and literary critics. Art historian Bram Dijkstra has discussed the prevalence of painterly images of wan, dying or dead women in the mid- to late nineteenth century. Innumerable mid- to late nineteenth-century canvasses bore such titles as *A Shadow*, *The Sick Woman*, *The Dead Woman*, *The Dying Woman*, *The Fate of Beauty*, *Convalescence*, *The Dying Mother*, *The Death of Albine* and so forth. As these titles suggest, the contents frequently depicted women in varying stages of death or dying, but while these depictions rendered illness softly 'romantic' their subjects were also clearly positioned as objects of sexual desire.[9] The representation of the beautiful dead woman, noted Dijkstra, was a favourite device of nineteenth-century artists, one which allowed them to portray an 'animalistic female sexuality' that was at once tantalizing and tamed, safely transmogrified to the realms of the transcendental and the spiritual. These lachrymose representations of the female, which flooded the popular market in cheap print form, were remarkable as much for their themes of 'passive feminine sacrifice' as for their 'passive erotic appeal'.[10]

Themes of female death and dying were also the sustaining *leitmotifs* of innumerable Victorian novels. Sex and death provided such a significant medium of artistic possibilities in Victorian culture that, according to literary critic Regina Barreca, the 'dialectic must be recognised as one of the most influential patterns in Victorian poetry and prose'.[11] Romantic literature, directed at a middle-class female readership, frequently dwelled on the pathos of the lingering and picturesque deaths of its heroines.[12] An 'embarrassing eroticism' marked many (textual) Victorian female deathbeds, according to Nina Auerbach, author of *Private Theatricals: The Lives of the Victorians*. Auerbach points to Dickens's Little Nell, Emily Bronte's Cathy and Robert Browning's Pompilia, as examples of women whose 'lingering lushly orchestrated deaths, aroused centres of [masculine] desire' – and (I would argue) female identification. Such literate representations, existing in tandem with artistic renditions of women as eroticized corpses, or near corpses, indicated, according to Auerbach, an expression of a 'common, if uncommonly powerful cultural desire' propelled by misogyny and a kind of unconscious, peculiarly Victorian, necrophilia.[13] Female death was, as American poet Edgar Allan Poe observed, 'unquestionably the most poetical topic in the world'.[14]

Non-fiction contributed to and perpetuated the processes of morbidification of the sexual feminine. It is indicative of the saturation of macabre, misogynist values of Victorian society that popular author Oliver Wendell Holmes could publicly air his own murderous and almost necrophiliac fantasies without demur. Holmes hungered for

> a woman true as Death. A woman, upon whose first real lie, would be tenderly chloroformed into a better world, where she could have an angel for a governess, and feed on strange fruits which . . . make her all over again, even to her bones and marrow.[15]

Holmes's explicit longings can be read as representative, perhaps even typical of a cultural nexus between femininity and death, which was underpinned and shadowed by male sexual desire.

Consequently, in a society that considered female ill health as normative to femininity, and where death and dying lent women a particular if morbid prestige, and, where feminine ill health, death and sexuality were collapsed, it was an easy, if not inevitable step for middle-class women to construct or derive a femininity, indeed a particular sexual subjectivity, from those influential and celebrated cultural givens. Indeed, it was in the middle-class woman's best interest to do so. As dress reformer Abba Gould Woolson explained,

> to be ladylike was to be lifeless, inane and dawdling, and since people who [were] ill must necessarily possess these qualities of manners from a lack of vital energy and spirit, it followed that they [were] the ones studiously copied as models of female attractiveness.[16]

Corsetry was essential to this modelling process. As dress reformer Eliza Haweis noted, it gave women the fashionable appearance of 'uncertainty and unsafeness'.[17] It was a crucial item of feminine attire in this respect. This was because corsetry enabled middle-class women with reasonable diets, secure from the contagious diseases and slum conditions of their working-class sisters (the former of whome should therefore, have been pictures of health) to effect a particular demeanour, a demeanour that actually effected, or at least reflected, a physical vulnerability or debilitation that was admired and eroticised in Victorian popular culture. Moreover (as mentioned earlier), physical responses provoked by the corset had the advantage of being construed as indicative of a delicacy that revealed a retiring virginal nature, or, in appropriate circumstances such as the ball room, it enabled the female body to be read as seductive, if not completely concupiscent. In doing so, corsetry empowered women to manoeuvre within existing social constructions of femininity, and importantly, enabled them to manipulate those constructions to their own (situated) social advantage.

Corsetry was arguably the most significant weapon among an arsenal of devices employed to achieve the desired and desirable almost deathly demeanour. However, powder, rouge and lipstick (which by 1860 had lost their promiscuous *cachet*[18]) were also utilized to obtain complexions described by contemporaries as 'deathly pale'. The magazine *Nineteenth Century* doubted that the wide publicity given to the death of a well-known society beauty, Miss Gunning, who died in 'fearful sufferings entirely owing to the use and abuse of cosmetics', would deter her 'fair imitators' from so 'silly and repulsive a practice' for more than a week.[19] This was in fact a reasonable conjecture, given that by the 1860s many commercially produced cosmetic preparations were known to contain a frightening array of poisonous substances. Cosmetics, beauty washes and unguents 'infallibly contain[ed] mercury or some other destructive or injurious mineral' warned the *Ladies' and Gentlemen's Pocket Companion of Etiquette and Manners*.[20] Carbonate of lead, sugar of lead, corrosive sublimate, hyposulphite of soda, lead and mercury were known to exist in the everyday 'toilet articles with which ladies [were] daubing their faces'.[21] The dangerous propensity of mercury, lead and bismuth to be absorbed by the skin had been known for centuries, but their effects on the skin made them essential to the numerous 'preparations of white'.[22] Arsenic, which also known to be lethal, was eaten in small and presumably furtive amounts by fashion's most enthusiastic votaries[23] to achieve pellucid, ethereal, skin tones. Blue vein colouring preparations, painted over existent or non-existent veins on the temple, throat and breasts,[24] increased the effect of a diaphanous, 'soon to leave this world' complexion. 'Nothing so effectually wrote *memento mori*! on the cheek of beauty' wrote the famous actor, Lola Montez, regarding the practice of coating the face with toxic powders. 'Many a time', she continued, 'have I seen a gentleman shrink from a brilliant lady as though it was a death's head he was compelled to kiss.'[25]

The British magazine *Bow Bells* was consistently critical of fashions that made young women appear death like. Consequently it took a very strong stand against the practice of arsenic eating by reminding readers that it 'would be both foolish and wicked to take to arsenic eating to improve the complexion'.[26] Numerous women, possibly reluctant to blanche their skin with lethal cosmetics, drank a daily glass of vinegar, which was thought to both whiten the skin and reduce corpulence.[27] The laxative properties of vinegar were exploited by both the 'normal' nineteenth-century woman and her anorectic sister, for this purpose.[28] The prevalence of its use can only be guessed at. However, admonitions against drinking large quantities of vinegar were so frequent in beauty and health manuals that it can be assumed to have been widely practised.[29] *Bow Bells* implored 'young ladies' to avoid vinegar, claiming a daily glass could lead to death. The magazine urged its heavier readers to 'be boldly fat' and never to 'pine for graceful slimness and romantic pallor.' If 'nature intended you to be ruddy and rotund,' wrote the editor, 'accept it with a laughing grace which will captivate more hearts than all the paleness of a circulating library'.[30] Well-meant advice of this kind was probably to little avail when robust, cheerful rotundity and ruddy skin were antithetical to mainstream cultural constructions of feminine beauty as pale, slender and ailing. Despite protestations from magazines and beauty manuals the idealization of the indisposed female, so relentlessly perpetuated by popular culture, meant that to look ill, vulnerable and/ or near death remained, for many women throughout the nineteenth century, a goal to be achieved at almost any cost.

Corsetry was doubly useful in realizing this goal. While it is well known that the garment clasped and moulded the torso into an hourglass shape, its effect on skin tone has been left unresearched by contemporary historians. Corsetry affected the appearance of the skin in a similar manner to vinegar, arsenic eating and the application of risky cosmetics, and might as a result have been considered a safer alternative than those substances in the middle-class quest for 'romantic pallor' and slenderness. It is quite likely that the corset was used in tandem with arsenic eating, vinegar drinking and cosmetics to achieve the coveted wan appearance. Dr Andrew Combe, author of *The Principles of Physiology*, commended corsetry's ability to produce a 'fragile and airy form, a sylph like figure' and significantly, an 'interesting paleness, occasionally relieved by a touch of carnation'. He admired the 'expressive look, softly shaded by melancholy' which he attributed to corsetry, and he added almost as an afterthought, that '*most of these indications [were] precisely those of feeble health*'.[31] Other male critics of corsetry, who were genuinely aghast at the physical changes it wrought on the female body, also unwittingly perpetuated the garment's use by valorizing and romanticizing its ability to deaden the appearance. Luke Limner, author of the widely cited *Madre Natura Versus the Moloch of Fashion: A Social Essay*, published in 1874, made an impassioned plea to 'abolish that type of body bondage and cursed contrivance, the corset'. Despite good intentions, Limner, like Combe before him, undermined that message by describing his corseted subjects in a manner that at once glamorized and sexualized their subjection. '[T]he fair prisoners incarcerated in the walking white sepulchres' were, wrote Limner (reflecting the Victorian propensity to collapse sex and female death), 'externally wreathed in beauty but internally wreathed in death and bones'.[32]

Feminist critics of the garment agreed that the epidermal changes effected by corsetry signalled ill health but, unlike Combe and Limner, they did not romanticize these changes. Instead, they drew from prevailing medical knowledges to fortify their own position. Medical practitioners opposed to corsetry routinely claimed that 'red noses [were] among the injurious effects of tight lacing'.[33] The physiological explanation of this occurrence was that 'outraged blood [was] forced from its legitimate channel' by tight lacing, and 'retreated vengefully to a point where its settlement' would remain 'a source of keenest mortification'.[34] A red nose was a humiliating disfigurement in Victorian England that spoke of alcoholism and ill temper. As a consequence the 'red nose' theory of tight lacing was quickly appropriated by opponents of the garment, and reiterated in women's magazines, household advice manuals and beauty texts until the end of the century.[35] It was 'a mistake to lace [one's] stays . . . like grim death', warned the *Bow Bell*'s beauty adviser of 1864. 'Nature never intended the body to be cut into two by staylaces and she revenges it by . . . cheeks of chalk [and] noses like plums.'[36] *Beeton's* (of household management fame) agreed, calling tight lacing 'the most absurd habit ever suggested by vanity and adopted by ignorance, and the cause of [both] ill-health and a red nose'.[37]

However disfiguring the red nose might be, critics of the garment had to acknowledge that corsetry also whitened the skin. Unlike Combe, they refused to valorize this symptom of asphyxiation by referring to the pale visage in unflattering terms such as sallow, pallid, chalky, and/or flushed. To remark on these complexional changes in terms that were not unflattering might of course, encourage the practice. In her lecture to London's National Health Society in 1880, dress reformer Edith Barnett, author of *Common-Sense Clothing*, berated societal values in which the 'glow of good health' was 'viewed as coarse and unladylike'. She observed with considerable anger that the woman 'regarded with most envy' was she who wore the 'livery of disease . . . and whose waist [could] nearly be spanned by her own hands'.[38] Similarly, Combe's perception of the corseted body as an, 'airy', fragile form, was perceived quite differently by the garment's adversaries. Far from being charmingly sylph-like, tightly corseted women were described as 'wheezy, panting, die away creature[s], painful to look at . . . who faint[ed] their way through life'.[39]

In twentieth-century terms the 'die-away demeanour' of the corseted woman might be best described as an actualization, or enactment, of a morbid subjectivity. Similarly, the corset might be identified as a 'body code' that constructed (or assisted in the processes of constructing) a debilitated demeanour that contributed to a more or less morbid sexual specificity. Clearly, the sturdy composition of standard corsetry worked both to create and to impose a particular deportment of the body that both contributed to the constitution of identity and communicated normative expectations about how women should behave. Interestingly nineteenth-century critics of the garment, particularly feminist critics, read the corseted female body as a text, much as twentieth-century feminist theoreticians of the body and its fashions have done. Elizabeth Stuart Phelps, Frances Willard and Elizabeth Farrar undoubtedly read the corseted body as text. Their criticisms of fashion are remarkable for both their perspicacity and their 'freshness'. Though written almost one hundred and fifty years ago, many of their criticisms and observations can be applied to the ways in which contemporary standards of beauty oppressed the late twentieth-century female body, and to the ways in which modern women are socially positioned to make resistance to this oppression so difficult. Farrar's feminist consciousness can be identified in her description of the corseted body. 'One might read in [the] pallid cheeks, . . . hollowed eyes, . . . languid air and shrunken form', wrote Farrar, 'a lesson on the evil influences the body [has] been under.' The evils alluded to here by Farrar were twofold. First, she recognized and read the physical damage inscribed on the female body *via* the corset. Secondly, her reference to the 'evil influences' exerted on the body was a comment on prevailing social trends which made the practice of tight lacing almost mandatory for young women in middle-class society.[40]

Indeed, feminist dress reformers such as Farrar, Phelps and Willard can be seen to have pre-empted, or at least foreshadowed, twentieth-century feminist theory in their attempts to theorize the female body in both its corporeal and political sense. The work of contemporary feminist Elizabeth Grosz has startling resonances and parallels with theories posited by her nineteenth-century foremothers. Grosz has called for the implementation of a corporeal feminist analysis. Corporeal feminism is a theory that privileges the body's interiority, while also recognizing that the inscription of the body's surface is integral to the acquisition of both individual sexual subjectivities, as well as those cultural attitudes deemed appropriate by the society in which the subject is located. Corporeal feminist analysis claims that female somatic commonalities can provide an overarching 'universal' pliable enough to account for cultural, historical, class and racial specificities. That is, corporeal feminism both takes into account the biological, or universal, trans-historical elements of the biological body, and accommodates the body's capacity to be 'moulded, constructed, socially informed or culturally specified'.[41]

Both Grosz and her feminist intellectual antecedents have argued for a holistic analysis of the female body and the fashions and cultural conventions that contained and constrained it. Nineteenth-century feminist dress reformers recognized that the female body was (as Grosz has more recently expounded), a 'political object *par excellence*,' whose 'form, capacities, behaviour, gestures, movements (and) potential' have been, and remain, 'primary objects of political contestation'. Like Grosz, they believed that the body should not be perceived as a 'mere shell or black box that has no interiority'.[42] Nineteenth-century feminist dress reformers, both male and female, with a sometimes nascent and sometimes well-developed feminist consciousness, utilized what we might recognize as a corporeal analysis by maintaining that the corset simultaneously impaired the physical body and had unavoidable deleterious repercussions on its occupant's 'interiority'. Indeed these themes were fundamental to many feminist dress reform texts, and were intermittently woven through women's journals that located women's fashions as contributing to female morbidity.

'[C]old extremities, pale visages and troubled sleep' along with 'excessive nervousness of the system' were, according to many observers, 'among the frightful consequences of [the] universal practice' of tight lacing.[43] *Bow Bells* reported that corsetry 'interfere[d] not only with internal structures of the body', but also with the 'temper and feelings with which . . . beauty is associated'. Beauty was an index of 'sound health, intelligence, good feelings and peace of mind', according to the author, and tight lacing encouraged 'uneasy feelings, bitter thoughts, (and) bad temper' which exhibited 'their signature on the countenance'.[44] Similarly, Ada Ballin, writing in *Womanhood*, maintained that along with the 'usual list of ailments' incumbent with 'the pressure of tight corsets', came 'a feeling of weariness, and depression of the spirits, and [feelings of] bloodlessness'.[45] B.O. Flower, editor of *Arena*, dwelled at length on the physical constraints of corsetry, but was also concerned by the psychological dangers inherent in its use. Once the corseted woman had 'diminished her breath of life, she ha[d] just to that extent, destroyed all normal sensibility', he wrote. The corseted woman could 'neither think nor feel normally . . . pleasurable sensations and ennobling thoughts' were replaced by an 'indescribable array of aches, pains, weaknesses, irritations and nameless distresses of body, with dreamy vagaries, fitful impulses and morbid sentimentalities of mind'.[46]

Perhaps the most acute illustration of the way in which corsetry effected a morbid feminine internalization was the *Atlantic* steamer tragedy, discussed by Phelps in her stirring text, *What to Wear?* This text alternately attacked and pitied modern women who did not 'characterize' their clothes, but allowed their 'clothes [to] characterise [them]'. In a chapter titled 'Dressed to Kill' (a phrase which Phelps correctly claimed had ceased to be a metaphor) she noted that the 'strait-jacket' of the corset, and the fashionable basque waist, made women's lungs 'contract and ache'. It also made 'their breath come in uneasy gasps' and left them not only 'pallid, puny, undersized and undersouled' but psychologically undermined as well. Phelps cited the *Atlantic* steamer tragedy to make clear the connection between corsetry and tight clothing, and their combined role in conditioning women to be passive to the point of extinction. All the men on board the ill-fated *Atlantic* escaped death, but not one woman survived. 'Every effort was made to assist women up the masts and out of danger until help arrived', recalled a survivor, 'but they could not climb, and we were forced to leave them to their fate.' The tightly corseted women, whose arms were pinioned to their sides by the combination of compressed ribs and tightly set sleeves, could not lift their hands above their shoulders, and could not climb the masts to safety. While Phelps recognized that tight clothing prevented the female passengers from physically escaping their deaths, she also noted bitterly that it was

not to be supposed that women properly dressed from infancy,
acquiring the freedom and courage which a proper mode of dress
impart[ed] would have met death in such a wholesale manner.[47]

Phelps recognized that surface inscriptions on the female body, imposed
by tight clothing and the corsetry beneath it, were crucial in physical
disempowerment, as well as identity formation, and that, moreover, the
identity and/or interiority of women, was influenced, and morbidly so,
by prevailing fashions. The female body was perceived by Phelps in 1876,
just as it was perceived by Grosz decades later, as far more than a 'mere
shell or black box' which had no interiority. Nineteenth-century women's
interiority was, as Phelps's discussion of the *Atlantic* tragedy demonstrates, taken into consideration by dress reformists who understood that
female interiority was critically and morbidly influenced by the sartorial
containment and imprisonment of the body.

Feminist discussions that aimed to indicate or tease out the relationship
between cultural morbidity and femininity were remarkable for both their
breadth of analysis and, occasionally, their fearless and complex theories
regarding the (constructed) sexuality of Victorian women. The corset was
a central site of their discontent. While feminist dress reformers argued
vehemently that death was the ultimate destiny of the tightly corseted
woman, they also explored and publicized the almost enumerable array
of 'lesser' deaths corsetry inflicted. As a result, the feminist dress reform
anti-corset discourse was steeped in themes of physical morbidity but
punctuated and theoretically strengthened by sophisticated explanations
of the sensual, sexual, spiritual, intellectual and political deaths that
corsetry wreaked on a minute-by-minute basis on the female body. These
'lesser deaths' by corset were considered by feminist critics to deaden
authentic femininity, and to disempower female agency in the process.

Phelps insisted that corsetry and tight clothing undermined women's
ability to achieve political goals, or indeed any goals outside the private
sphere. She did this by pointing out the gender differences in dress and
the importance of sensible clothing in assisting women to gain political
power. 'Could your husband or your father live in your clothes . . .
conduct a business and support his family in your corsets, . . . (or)
prosecute a course of study in your chignon?', she asked uninitiated
readers.[48] Although sympathetic towards those who had been made
invalids by fashion, she wrote with an obvious and bitter resignation,
that the woman 'devoured by the backache, the headache, [and] the
heartache' who was a 'dark problem to the physiologist' presented a 'sad
problem to the political economy' and therefore imperilled any hope of
an 'ideal' society. Phelps recognized that corsetry was pivotal in physically
disempowering women, and that it inevitably undermined their desire to
act and think assertively. She also understood that the garment's role in
sexualizing the body diminished any chances of the sexes ever interacting
as equals, specifically because in sexualizing the body, corsetry unnaturally

heightened physical differences between the sexes. These differences were cited by biological essentialists antagonistic to female suffrage as evidence that women's proper sphere was domestic and reproductive, rather than political. '[S]ex over estimation' lay behind every 'innocent and ignorant compliance' with fashion, wrote Phelps. Artificial impositions such as corsetry exaggerated women's secondary sexual characteristics and positioned them as sex objects, which in turn continued inequitable and oppressive relations between the sexes. As Phelps explained reasonably, dress reformers

> do not quarrel with the desire to be agreeable, . . . nor do we quarrel with the differences in character of desire, so far as it is Nature's own. It is the unnatural differences which the distorted creed and practice of society have created which work the mischief. The subjection of one sex to the other results in making the attraction of one, the business of the other. To this, as in any system of subjection, rebellion is the only alternative.

It was widely held by dress reformers that the corset effectively destroyed, or at the very least dulled, the physical sensations of the torso. Angeline Merritt's claim that the 'general constriction of corsage, stays and buckram, . . . cramp[ed] and deaden[ed] the vital apparatus to a morbid incapacity'[49] was born out by medical practitioners who witnessed and recorded the corset's numbing effects. H.St.H. Vertue, who worked as a physician at London's Guy's Hospital in the late nineteenth century, mentioned the existence of a tiny pink ribbon kept as a memento of a forebear. The ribbon had been worn beneath the woman's corset, fastened by a decorative pin which had broken and 'unknowingly' punctured her skin. No pain was felt in the 'numb flesh', nor did the injury bleed, 'so severe was the compression'.[50]

Ada Ballin's discussion of tight lacing explains how this may have occurred. In her article 'The Penalty of Tight Lacing', she reported that if the initial pain experienced by the torso incurred by tight lacing was 'for a long while unheeded, the pain bec[ame] deadened, and finally the nerves cease[d] to give forth their warning'.[51] Abba Gould-Woolson's *Dress Reform* substantiated this claim and further established how this came about. Woolson noted that corsets were worn in the general belief that they disbursed the weight and tightness of numerous undergarments. (It was not uncommon for up to 14 bindings to be about the waist.) However, as she explained, it was 'Nature' rather than the corset that 'prevented one feeling at every motion the pull and drag of each separate binding'. Nature, rather than corsetry, relieved women 'from the sensation of pain when it bec[ame] excruciating', she wrote, while corsets only further deadened sensation 'by a compression which induce[d] partial numbness . . . [until] no one portion [was] conscious of more discomfort than the rest.'[52]

Subtle yet complex criticisms were also levelled by feminist dress reformers at the corset's ability to both construct and reinforce a particular kind of female sexuality, which they variously perceived as morbid, male-defined, perverted and in the interests of male sexual appeasement. The construction of an inauthentic or degenerate female sexuality as both product and reflection of the morbid society in which it manifested, was the theme of a startling poem published in the feminist newspaper *Daughters of America*. 'The Skeleton in Satin' offered a complex analysis of the role of corsetry in the conflation of death and the erotic. The poem was, at the same time, critical of the carnage of wild life, the masculine eroticisation of female debility, and the role of fashion in subsuming and disguising these seemingly discrete issues. The only extant copy is damaged and incomplete, however enough of the text survives to indicate the author's concerns. Stanza two describes the appearance of the current belle, and finds parallels between the death of the birds, and of women, in the quest of the fashionable ideal.

> Upon her cheeks no roses bloom,
> But in their place are rouge and paste,
> And over all there waves that plume,
> That caps the hearse and symbols death –
> A hollow sepulchre, a tomb,
> Where eyes of light and love should be,
> Beneath the quivering costly plume
> Wrung from the Bird of Paradise.

A following stanza made specific the connection between consumption (i.e. tuberculosis) and those fashions that mirrored the senseless waste of both women and bird life.

> The daintiest fabrics of the loom
> But thinly guard the consumptive's chest,
> Whilst bravely nods above the plume,
> Wrung from the songsters of our woods,
> The tottering step that tells of theume,
> That thinly guarded feet have bred,
> Are echoed by the quivering plume,
> That tells of desolated woods.

The final stanza, although fragmented, clearly links the effect of the corset on women's bodies and the way that *fashions* of debilitation resulted in *physical* reality. The author spoke of the fashionably dressed woman as 'this creature from the tomb' and of 'lowless passion'. Her face was described in the third stanza (not shown in full here) as 'o'ercaste with gaudy gloom' while her 'tightened ribs that cramp[ed] the lungs . . . feebly swell[ed] to thrill the plume'.[53] The plume so often referred to in the poem was a reference to the plumage of the birds killed for fashionable decoration, the use of those plumes on hats and fans, and the black plumage used to adorn horses that pulled the funeral hearse. Both the plumage on women's hats and on the heads of funeral horses moved identically and heralded the same meaning, and were read by the poet and the current author as the death of the [be]feathered subjects, whether women or the birds whose feathers were used to decorative effect. The hollow sepulchre and tomb was of course a reference to the fashionable woman, whose ill health was indicated by her wan complexion, tottering gait and impending death by rheum or consumption.

Orson Fowler also linked corsetry to the manufacture and expression of a particular and morbid femininity; however, he did not perceive corseted women as victims of perverse fashion trends, preferring instead to position them as dangerously seductive amoral degenerates. Fowler, frequently lampooned by twentieth-century historians for his phrenological passions, was also an ardent critic of the corset. He was one of very few 'medical' men who linked corsetry to female hysteria. Tightly laced corsets, asserted Fowler 'render[ed] women crazy', made them nervous, irritable, headachy and 'excited inordinately by trifles'. However, it was corsetry's ability to 'inflame the organs of the abdomen and thereby excite the amative desires' that threw Fowler into paroxysms of rage. 'The practice is disgraceful, immoral and murderous', he wrote, 'I wish to make women ashamed of tight lacing and this knowledge will do it. No woman who reads this will dare to be seen laced tight'. Tight lacing and the concomitant inflammation of the genitals it caused was, claimed Fowler, the reason that 'so many women got in love'.[54]

Angeline Merritt also claimed that tightly laced corsetry 'crowded the abdominal viscera into immediate contact and collision with sex organs of the pelvic cavity, creating . . . unnatural (sexual) excitement.[55] Unlike Fowler she did not position women as licentious corseted villains. Rather, her concerns were fuelled by fears that the sexual excitement potentially provoked by corsetry was at the expense of an authentic sexual response. Merritt was anxious that girls whose sexuality was beginning to awaken at adolescence might be more easily sexually exploited if their bodies were prematurely and inappropriately aroused by corsetry. She pleaded with mothers to refrain from corseting their young daughters for that very reason.

> Would you see those lovely maidens just budding into womanhood stoop from purity, inherent in their nature, become dupes of those lower propensities and passions which such vicious dressing, legitimately developed engenders?[56]

Merritt's anxieties about adolescent sexual behaviour were not driven by any desire to deny or eradicate female sexual response, but to protect it from exploitation, perversion or extinction. This is made clear by her insightful remarks that disclosed her belief in the existence and rightful expression of a 'natural', fully developed and powerful female sexuality. Merritt feared that the 'morbid excitement' (as she termed it) of the female sex organs, would lead not only to disease, but might result in 'an effeminacy of the physical system'.[57] Merritt's use of the word 'effeminacy' in the context of discussing female sexuality is telling. It indicated that Merritt believed that women had naturally occurring and potent sexual desires that paralleled male sexuality. These ideas ran counter to many medical texts of that time which asserted that 'decent' women were rarely troubled by such matters.

Anxieties surrounding the role of the corset as an agent of sexualization, morbid, perverse or otherwise, often were discursively hidden in, or formed part of, larger discussions on the 'morals' of the ballroom. Novelist Anthony Trollope was not alone in publicly and disparagingly calling the ballroom a 'marriage market'. Young middle-class women 'came out' (in the nineteenth-century meaning of that phrase) between 17 and 18, and the ball was critical both in marking this rite of passage into adulthood and in securing a successful marriage. Three years (or social seasons) were considered time enough for women to secure a suitable, if not brilliant, match.[58] Balls, dances or assemblies, as they were termed, allowed the refined and 'delicate' middle-class woman to be shown at her best advantage.[59] They also provided the perfect arena for the cultural conflation of *eros* and *thanatos* to manifest. Despite rigid formalities and the scrutiny of chaperones, the ball was often the scene of hectic romance, and intense though somewhat morbid sexual encounters. That critics deemed ballroom dancing a flagrant 'violation of the sixth commandment'[60] indicated the sexual nature of the event, and the potential it had for serious sexual transgression. The 'low corsage, the naked arm, the whirling dance . . . the unchaste public disrobing'[61] each met a barrage of condemnation. Dance was thought to hold 'insidious charms'.[62] The 'immodest pose taken in the waltz' was frequently credited with blinding its participants 'with lust'.[63] However, it was female costume that was most often blamed for feverish sexual excitement.

According to one critic, 'flimsy dresses'[64] made for 'unspeakable degradation . . . exposure and immoral exhibitions of what should [have been] reserved for the sacred and inmost privacy of the home'.[65] Low-cut ball gowns, designed to emphasize the waist and reveal a becoming *décolletage* relied on corsetry to achieve these desired and desirable but scandalous assets. The combination of heat and extended periods of dancing in tightly fitted gowns underpinned by even tighter corsetry, made weakness, breathlessness, and the automatic physiological response to thoracic asphyxiation, the involuntary and rapid rise and fall of the breasts, a commonplace sight, as well as a highly contentious issue. Comparisons between the physical response of the corseted body and the (perceived) female sexual responses of panting, flushed complexion and the rise and fall of the breasts were unavoidable. Revd Dr S. Vernon was

appalled by the overt sexual *ambience* of the ballroom and the conspicuous flirtations and unbridled female sexual responses that it appeared
to condone, encourage, and reveal. 'Music fired the heart', wrote the
alarmed Vernon,

> while heaving breasts and beating hearts were brought into close
> contact, the warm breath against the hot cheek, the electric currents
> flowing from hand to hand, [and] eye to eye, [did] the work nature
> intended for them under lawful conditions.[66]

Nineteenth-century sources demonstrate that the heaving bosom that
so alarmed Vernon and his ilk was far more than a romantic fiction, or
fantasy of religious zealots opposed to dance. Defenders of the corset,
such as the gynaecologist B.S. Talmey and sexologist Irwin Bloch,
celebrated the role of the corset in publicly rendering 'conspicuous and
prominent the specific woman's organ, the bosom'. They approved of
the effect of tight lacing which made the 'undulations' of the breasts
appear as an 'expressive and skilful rhetoric'.[67] The sexual demeanour
created by the corset on the female body was similarly praised by
Havelock Ellis. '[S]exual allurement' he noted, arose largely from the
'respiratory movement' corsetry imparted to the bosom.[68] Critics who
objected to the garment's proclivity to promote the sexual objectification
of the breasts, were, not surprisingly, reluctant to engage with the sexual
aspects of its implementation at the ball. *The Lady's Guide to Perfect
Gentility*, published in 1856, alluded to this effect as distasteful. The
author likened the 'extreme heaving of the bosom' to 'the panting of a
dying bird'.[69] Physician Frederick Treves, writing thirty years later, noted
with disapproval that anyone who had 'watched a wasp-waisted lady after
a dance' must notice 'the unsightly . . . exaggerated heaving of the upper
part of the chest'. This, he explained dryly, was 'merely an expense of
Nature's efforts to obtain a proper supply of air'.[70]

The failure of corseted lungs to inhale enough oxygen during or after
dancing, which resulted in undulating bosoms and 'heaving breasts', was
also responsible for episodic fainting at the ball.[71] *Bow Bells* advised
readers who were planning a ball that 'scents, aromatic vinegar, smelling
salts [and] water bottles . . . should be readily at hand'. These were 'to
be used in the case of a young lady fainting . . . which [was] frequently
the case in heated rooms, especially [for women] addicted to tight
lacing'.[72] Fainting in the ballroom provided a perfect domain for the
misogynist ideology of aesthetic feminine weakness and its binary
opposition, male dominance, to be enacted. Primary sources indicate that
fainting was clearly considered appropriate female behaviour. Fainting
'was feminine' observed *The Lady's Companion; or Sketches of Life,
Manners, and Morals, at the Present Day*. It was too 'a pleasure – not a
healthful one, certainly, but still a pleasure – to enjoy so much sympathy
about one, to hear expressions of concern, pity and admiration'.[73]

Fainting was, as *The Lady's Companion* revealed, an event that was laden with meaning. Though fainting at the ball received very little serious attention in the mid- to late century,[74] the *laissez-faire* attitude towards its frequent occurrence signified the existence of complex *sub rosa* attitudes regarding correct sex/gender behaviour. Fainting of 'delicate' scantily clad women, under heady candle-lit conditions, inevitably and simultaneously eroticized and reified morbid heterosexual gender relations, which were sanctioned by tradition, celebrated in popular culture and, increasingly, validated by science. Fainting reflected and confirmed prevailing sexological assertions that 'the voluntary subordination of woman under the other sex [was] a physiological phenomenon'. It justified sexologic claims that the 'passive role in procreation and traditional social conditions' made women 'necessarily associate sexual relationships with the image of subordination'. As Krafft-Ebing authoritatively declared, the image of subordination 'constituted and characterised the timbre of female emotions'.[75] In other words, fainting was the physical manifestation of cultural imperatives and values that determined passivity – to the point of unconsciousness – as the epitome of an ideal femininity.

Fainting continued to provide romantic opportunities for women to demonstrate their refined debility, and for men to perform heroic feats, well into the century. Marion Harland (the widely published mid- to late century health and beauty adviser) recalled that when 'women fainted in assemblies . . . for want of breath' they might have 'expired completely' had not 'the instant expedient in all cases been (for men) to cut the corset strings'.[76] Whether apocryphal or authentic, scenarios such as that described by Harland illustrate the Victorian propensity to 'other' death to the feminine and to eroticize that event. Fainting's valency as a cultural enactment of feminine death (or near death) revolved around the binary tensions it demonstrated. The 'life and death' appearance of fainting elicited permutations around feminine fantasies of submission and masculine fantasies of power.[77] This is evidenced by the rigidly gendered nature of the event. Men did not faint into women's arms. Women fainted into the arms of men, and in conditions that glamorized their vulnerability, vulnerability so perfect that it mimicked the complete passivity of death. Indeed, the collapse of the tightly corseted woman at the ball cannot be overestimated as a barometer of the morbidity of Victorian gender relations. In corseted female collapse can and should be read the somatic, as well as the public, intersection and conflation of Victorian misogyny, morbidity and high romance.

The gendered and inherently macabre scenarios of ballroom syncope had an even more sinister analogy (if not a direct parallel) to the romanticized and sexualized fetishization of female victims of tuberculosis.[78] The corset was as much implicated in the sexualization of the tubercular invalid as it was for her healthy sister. Tuberculosis was a disease, according to medical historian Susan Sontag, 'in the service of a romantic view of the world'.[79] In the popular imagination tuberculosis was actually thought to be an aphrodisiac, with an ability to confer extraordinary powers of seduction to its victims.[80] Well into the twentieth century, corsetry was thought to be a significant factor in its aetiology. Several theories regarding the relationship between corsetry and tuberculosis were posited and explained in popular medical texts and magazines. Dio Lewis, who favoured a gymnastic cure for consumption, directly linked the 'monstrous perversion of taste' exemplified by the 'wasp waist' created by corsetry as a major causative factor in that disease.[81] Treves claimed that 'delicate' women with a 'family tendency to lung affections could hardly adopt a more effectual plan of bringing those tendencies to fulfilment than by tightly compressing the chest'.[82] Other critics insisted that 'family tendencies' were not a prerequisite and that the corset alone could create the conditions for disease. Stays were a 'predisposing cause of convulsive coughs [and] consumption', concluded *The Lady's Guide*.[83] The 'constant irritation' of the ribs against lungs caused by corsetry was also believed to 'produce a deposit of tubercular matter'.[84] Corset-related lung injuries that resulted in any kind of 'blood spitting' were also thought to provoke the disease in women who would not ordinarily be prone to 'consumptive tendencies'.[85]

Warnings such as these, which directly or indirectly linked tightly laced corsetry to tuberculosis, did little or nothing to reduce corsetry's popularity and, according to historian Helene Roberts, may have actually served to increase the practice of tight lacing.[86] This may well have been the case. Though market forces were quick to respond to a perceived need for a safe corset alternative, the 'Sylphide or Anticonsumptive Corset' proclaimed by its manufacturer to be more 'conducive to longevity than any article yet submitted to the public' failed to capture a great share of corset sales.[87] Perhaps this was because tuberculosis, like fainting, was a decidedly gendered affliction, one that, like fainting, perpetuated and reified cultural expectations of the feminine. The tubercular body was, in the popular imagination, a female body. Its manifestation reflected the perfect expression of the Victorian *Zeitgeist* of female death and sexuality. Though both men and women died from TB, it was a singularly 'feminine' disease. When it occurred in men it was linked to masculine bohemian creativity, artistic pursuits and poetry. For both male and female victims, the disease provided a metaphoric equivalent for delicacy, sensitivity, sadness, and powerlessness[88] which were all strongly identified as feminine characteristics in the nineteenth century. Consumption's othering to the feminine was also evidenced by the general belief that the disease was (unlike diseases such as cancer) identified as a disease of liquids and of disintegration, febrilization, and de-materialization of bodily fluids, specifically mucus and blood.[89] Each of these traits and effusions can be, and was, perceived as a biological function of the female body. TB was also considered by several leading doctors to be a result both of excessive passion and of the repression of overwhelming desire,[90] characteristics which – by the late nineteenth century – were identified with female sexuality.

Tuberculosis was (as Dijkstra has shown) also romanticized and feminized in popular and 'high' art that 'fetishized the emaciation of the tubercular woman'. A 'taste for the cadaverous' along with themes of 'tormented contaminated beauty' had existed before the nineteenth century, but the nineteenth century was, according to Mario Praz, author of *The Romantic Agony*, one in which the romantic fashion for consumptive heroines had never been so popular. Edgar Allan Poe, whose own mother had died of TB, was moved to begin his 'Ode to Consumption', with the chilling line, 'There is a beauty in woman's decay'.[91] This was a motif that ran through numerous best selling novels, notably those by George du Maurier, whose tubercular heroine Trilby was admired as much for her 'waxen whiteness' as for her sexual transgressions.[92]

Interestingly, TB also signified a mark of breeding and distinction.[93] Cultural renditions and representations of the disease as romantic and exciting undoubtedly influenced its acceptance as a suitable middle-class disease and, at the same time, provided women with role models that encouraged them to emulate or even provoke its symptoms. Far from transgressing Victorian constructions of womanhood, the sexually charged consumptive woman was an indication of the chimerical nature of a constructed Victorian femininity. The sexualized consumptive might be best read as an aspect of the late nineteenth century's extreme dualistic mentality. The 'virgin and the whore', the 'saint and the vampire' were, as Dijkstra pointed out, 'two designations for a single dualistic opposition'.[94] The sexualized consumptive can be seen to have been situated somewhere near, if not completely aligned with, the vampire in this binary code. Significantly, both the virginal feminine invalid, who lived at the knife's edge of her own demise, and her supposedly salacious tubercular sister maintained romantic relationships with death: certainly, in the case of the consumptive, a complete textual/cultural imbrication with it. The oppositional nature of the dangerously sexual consumptive and her ailing (yet tubercule-free) sister made tuberculosis the perfect middle-class female disease, for it positioned its female sufferers as sexual, but not threateningly so. The sexualized consumptive exemplified all the passive, ailing feminine traits so admired by Victorian culture, traits that were enlivened by a forbidden but only potentially dangerous sexuality. The consumptive's supposed sexual desire was countered by her weakened body's inability to act on that desire; thus she did not transgress those cultural boundaries that constructed her as essentially passive and virginal.

TB or conditions that mimicked that disease provided a labile corporeal discourse of femininity, from which any number of competing and even conflicting sexual messages might be transmitted and read. Panting and heaving breasts could be assumed to denote either sexual desire or physical debility. Similarly, the flushed cheeks (whether caused by corsetry or by TB) emblazoned on a startlingly white complexion could be construed as either a modest 'celestial suffusion' or a heightened sexual awareness.[95] Tightly laced corsetry was in fact integral in the emulation of consumption's lesser and more appealing symptoms. In the latter stages of the disease, the female patient appeared to be in a state of acute sexual arousal. The tubercular woman's face was often pallid, but notable for its pronounced flush. Her body was restless and her breasts rose and fell rapidly as her lungs struggled to inhale sufficient oxygen.[96] Periods of hyper-activity in the course of the disease alternated with periods of languidness,[97] paralleling both a model of heterosexual sexual intercourse and the effect of the corset on the female body that made it appear sexually aroused. Her symptoms bore a keen resemblance to those of the tightly corseted but otherwise healthy middle-class woman, who fainted with such abandon at the ballroom.

The excitement of courting such a romantic, dangerous, transgressive, yet acceptable illness was a reality in a culture that outwardly rewarded female ill health and glamorized female death. Occasionally, the use of corsetry to mimic phthisis was too effective. According to Orson Fowler, many women died of tight lacing, believing it to be consumption. These women, wrote Fowler, undertook a 'kind of suicide by strangling themselves' while the 'real cause of death [was] overlooked [and] kept studiously out of view'.[98] Further evidence of the mainstream appropriation or imitation of TB appeared in popular texts that specifically protested against its emulation. Marian Harland advised mothers to 'show no charity to the faded frippery of sentiment that prate[d] over romantic sickness'. She urged mothers to demonstrate a 'fine scorn' for what she described as the 'popular desire' to change 'excellent health' for the 'fascination of lingering consumption'. Harland's comments and observations reveal the prevailing aura surrounding the romantic tubercular victim. The 'sensation of early decease' was, she reported caustically, 'induced by the rupture of a blood vessel over a laced handkerchief'. The handkerchief was held to the 'lily mouth' of the victim 'by an agonised parent or distracted lover'.[99]

While the blood-spitting, ailing daughter outwardly presented as a 'wan virgin', Harland's use of the words 'lily mouth' in the description of the blood-spitting woman has a sub-textual meaning that is not at first apparent. In the parlance of Victorian English flower language, lilies signified purity, sweetness and modesty,[100] but lilies were also a favourite artistic motif that denoted imminent death, or a spiritual other-worldness. The 'lily' mouth suggests both virginity and mortality. However, it is also important to recognize that while mortality was 'othered' to the feminine, Harland's description might imply that the 'tubercular' (or supposedly tubercular) woman positioned herself, whether consciously or not, as a sexual being, one whose sexual subjectivity was made more exciting by its cultural identification with an eroticized death.

Harland's 'pseudo' consumptives were, in effect, manipulating a fashionable construction of femininity and sexuality to their own advantage.

Consumption brought sustained attention of a more dramatic kind than the sympathy given to the fainting ballroom belle. Like fainting, consumption confirmed prevailing ideas around femininity and gender-appropriate behaviour. Both women who fainted at the ball and women who coughed or spat blood from corset-related lung injuries can be seen to have negotiated a set of fluid, complex and (outwardly) opposing feminine constructions. Judicious application of the corset enabled women to construct a particular kind of sexual subjectivity. Its assistance was critical in the difficult task of presenting women as sexual subjects in the world, for others as well as for themselves, at a time when overt displays of sexual behaviour were (ostensibly) frowned upon.

The consumptive woman provided a template on which women in better health might model their femininity. The tubercular woman exemplified all the passive, ailing, feminine traits so admired by Victorian culture, traits that were simultaneously enlivened by a forbidden but only potentially dangerous sexuality. The consumptive's supposed sexual desire was countered by her weakened body's inability to act on that desire; thus she did not transgress those cultural boundaries that constructed her as essentially passive and virginal. The consumptive woman 'flirted' with death, which – given the Victorian erotics of thanatos – increased her sexual valency. The corseted female body offered all this too. The tightly laced woman exhibited the romanticized symptoms of her consumptive sister, while avoiding TB's abject symptomology.[101] The corseted woman's breathless, flushed appearance mimicked the consumptive's sexualized demeanour, while her weakened body was the literal and authentic manifestation of gender roles that determined her to be passive and ailing and, when made unconscious by corsetry, appear to be near death and therefore very, very 'feminine'.

Any garment so integral to scenarios that romanticize, encourage, reify and collapse fantasies of death and sexuality must be considered fundamentally oppressive. However, women who tightly laced must also be understood to have implemented the device to achieve their own ends. Discerning application of the corset, painful and dangerous as it undoubtedly was, assisted women in making successful matches. The hand-span waist allowed the less than beautiful woman a particular sexual prestige that her healthier but heavier peers envied. The corset was, for many otherwise healthy middle-class women, an invaluable method of constructing a particular subjectivity in an era when illness was a normative, almost essential category of femininity. It was the most significant item within a range of 'devices' used to achieve a fashionably ailing demeanour. Feminist dress reformers such as Elizabeth Stuart Phelps recognized that the construction of feminine identity on illness undermined rather than strengthened female agency, in both its somatic and its political sense. Other reformers such as Merritt pointed to the 'effeminacy of the sexual system' which corsetry was thought to effect.

Paradoxically, the garment's longevity and popularity were ensured specifically by its ability to sexualize the female body in a manner that reflected a particular historical moment, a moment in which the intersection of sexuality and morbidity consolidated. Women clearly understood the importance of the garment in the creation of a morbid sexual attraction. Corsetry paradoxically animated the appeal of the ailing and otherwise insipid virgin, by provoking in her the physical symptoms that replicated those of her sexualized tubercular sister. In doing so, the corset created a space in which middle-class Victorian women could be sexual, a difficult task in an era that denied female pre-marital sexual experience, and collapsed death and romance. The tightly corseted woman, like her eroticised but dying sister, appeared innocent yet dangerous, tantalizing yet chaste, breathless with anticipation, an anticipation that mimicked or foreshadowed sexual congress, or death.

6
Not in That Corset: Gender, Gymnastics, and the Cultivation of the Late Nineteenth-Century Female Body

Although the corset, in one incarnation or another, remained an integral garment of female attire until the introduction of pantyhose in the 1960s, attempts to engineer its decline had been set in train at least a century earlier. Indeed, a series of peripatetic and at times unrelated campaigns from the 1850s worked to convince women that the corset and other oppressively tight clothing should be abandoned. Health and dress reformers, feminist education reformers with a commitment to popularizing women's sports, especially gymnastics, along with advocates of aesthetic or artistic dress, all contributed incrementally, if sometimes unwittingly, to the corset's eventual but slow decrease in popularity. Mainstream resistance to these reformers was often articulated in discourses that attacked the appearance of costume worn by the champions of sartorial change. However, rather than dwell on the adjustments in clothing design for which the reformers are more usually remembered, this chapter investigates (in part) the less frequently acknowledged aspects of the various fashion reform movements. It will focus on the progressive attitudes held by dress reformists toward the containment of the female body by the corset, and their involvement in the rise of sport as a desirable activity for middle-class women.

Debates about prevailing fashions and particularly the uncorseted body were wide-ranging and at times curiously ambivalent. Mainstream fashion texts that were critical of tightly laced corsetry, and ostensibly supportive regarding the abolition of the more tyrannical aspects of female clothing, were (somewhat paradoxically) often hostile toward women who, for whatever reasons, abandoned corsetry altogether. It would appear that anxiety generated by the uncorseted female body was possibly both a disguise and a reflection of other less well articulated fears about wider issues regarding femininity, related to increased female political activism and the changing position of women generally. Discourses involving the corset, or its abandonment, operated to facilitate public *angst* and deliberation around 'indelicate' and seemingly ominous matters involving female sexuality and its perceived threats to gender stability. Uncorseted female flesh – whether it manifested energetically beneath the tailored outfits of reform dress and (later) the gymnastic bloomers of the New Woman, or whether it reposed languidly beneath the flowing robes of the female aesthete – was considered by its critics as unruly, inadequately gendered. It was, as the century reached its close, also viewed as sexually labile and alarmingly modern.

As earlier chapters have established, corsetry was as important in the construction, performance and articulation of femininity as the elaborate gowns that covered the female body. In other words, corsetry was considered by its votaries as indispensable in the serious work of demarcating female from male, and in fetishizing femininity. Oddly, both historians of costume and historians who have documented nineteenth-century feminist activity have largely overlooked (and in some cases claimed) that matters of dress in general were of little consequence to feminist activists.[1] It has on occasion been considered that the reformation of female costume was considered a peripheral issue, or even a distraction to greater issues of female emancipation. This was certainly not the case for all nineteenth-century feminists. The long-running feminist journal, the *English Women's Review of Social and Industrial Questions*, was an ardent supporter of dress reform, and considered it central to larger issues concerning women's rights. Though the magazine admitted dress reform had almost 'died out' by 1877, it argued that sporadic interest in women's attire demonstrated the need for continued debate around women's dress. This debate, according to *The English Women's Review*, had to be the province of women alone. Men 'could not legislate for women on dress', wrote the editor, any more than they could legislate on any other important questions for women. Dress reform, wrote *The English Women's Review*, was integral to women's 'right to compete with men in every branch of industry for which their talents and education qualif[ied] them'.[2]

Individual dress reform activists often recognized the links between the body, dress reform and the wider goals of suffrage. Some believed that the impairment of women's health at the hands of fashion made dress reform an even more important issue than the vote. Dr. Mary Walker, the controversial general practitioner of the 1870s who wore bifurcated 'male' attire for her entire adult life, insisted that the 'wont of the ballot [was] but a *toy* by comparison' to the urgent need for reformed dress and for the abolition of corsetry (Walker's italics).[3] Numerous other mid- and late century feminists and their male supporters were adamant that clothing and female enfranchisement were intimately connected, and that escape from sartorial bondage was essential to achieving enfranchisement. Not surprisingly, much of the prevailing women's rights rhetoric was appropriated or shared by dress reformers and appeared in discourses around reform and rational dress. Women were exhorted to 'free' themselves and 'emancipate' their bodies from vestmental bondage. Advice dispensed by Dr Mercy Jackson in the 1870s can be seen as a good example of the use of suffragette rhetoric. Clothing in general, but especially 'corsets that encase[d] the body in a prison barred with whalebone and steel' were, noted Jackson, calculated to 'fetter women's powers'.[4] Oppressive clothing subjected the female body to 'inconvenient, unsightly and even tormenting control', a control that 'also brought into subjection . . . the noble faculties of the mind'.[5]

Mid-century arguments for dress reform and enfranchisement often centred upon popularizing the infamous Bloomer costume. The Bloomer freed the body from the enormous weight of petticoats, and the garment did not require corsetry to provide a wasp waist. Elizabeth Smith Miller, the American originator of the Bloomer or Turkish trouser costume,[6] was a women's rights activist and self-proclaimed feminist. So too was Amelia Bloomer, the garment's most significant proponent and namesake, who used her temperance magazine *The Lily* to promote the 'new' look while campaigning for enfranchisement.[7] The failure of the Bloomer to convert women to reform dress may in part be responsible for twentieth-century misconceptions that dress reform was not a significant issue for nineteenth-century feminists. The Bloomer costume of the 1850s was ridiculed and derided on both sides of the Atlantic and was, as a result, avoided by many feminists who feared it would detract from the 'cause', whether that cause was dress reform or suffrage, or both. Hostility to the Bloomer costume meant that it had largely vanished by 1860. A variant of that garment did not reappear publicly until the late 1890s with the advent of bicycling. However, issues of dress reform, trousers and their links to physical liberation and enfranchisement persisted. Dress reformers simply changed tactics to achieve the same end. Many feminist dress reformers switched their attention from popularizing bifurcated clothes to refiguring women's undergarments, and began earnest campaigns to remodel or completely banish the corset.

Influential dress reformer Abba Gould-Woolson understood the power and overwhelming pressures of mainstream attitudes and forces to undermine the progress of dress reform. She commended the 'intelligent, brave . . . and heroic' inventors of the Bloomer costume, but as she explained, the advocates of Bloomer costume had 'overrated the intelligence and courage of their followers, and they had underrated the strength of their opponents'. Woolson believed any endeavour to reintroduce Bloomer costume in the 1870s would 'invite another defeat (and) dishearten reformers in the future'. She favoured, as did many reformers, a 'complete revolution in the structure and the adjustment of the ordinary under dress as by far the most important thing to be gained'. If that could be effected 'the outward covering would in time take care of its self'.[8] Abandoning corsetry was part of that process. Reform design undergarments, sometimes actually called 'emancipation garments', which were intended to replace corsetry, almost came to symbolize women's struggle to free themselves from the constraints of fashion and to gain control over their entire persons. These goals were reflective of, if not completely identical to, those of the larger movement related to women's rights.[9]

By the 1890s, claims by dress reformers that constrictive clothing hampered political enfranchisement and women's entry into the larger masculine sphere were commonplace. Readers of *Women's Tribune*[10] counted members of the National Council of Women of the United States as part of its readership. Political activist and feminist Frances Willard was one of these readers. In an address to NCUWS, Willard linked the idea that the constraints of the corset and tightly fitting clothes destroyed female political ambition and agency, both individually and collectively. The female body, in both its political and its physical incarnation, remained central to much of the feminist discourse. Fashionable women jeopardized their constitutions, in both the physical and political sense of that word, claimed Willard, by remaining 'swathed by their skirts, splintered by [their] stays, bandaged by their tight waist[s] and pinioned by [their] sleeves'. This, she observed dryly, made 'a trussed turkey or . . . spitted goose' . . . [rather than a living soaring eagle] women's 'most appropriate [political] emblem.'[11] Yet another notable American suffragist, Frances E. Russell, also promoted the idea that dress and women's advancement were related issues. Russell insisted that women had potential to fully engage in political affairs, but the 'current mode' of constrictive dress along with women's 'fetich worship' of fashion, meant that they could not be taken seriously in the wider masculine political arena. Fashions that made women appear 'either infantile or idiotic . . . vitiate[d] (their) claim to equality', wrote Russell, for they simultaneously created and 'typified [women's] subject condition'. Russell emphasized that any desire on the part of women to progress from a state of 'mingled doll-hood and drudgery' to a 'grand new standing place of perfect equality by the side of man', required that women abandon corsets and tight clothing to establish 'the outward appearance of . . . reasonable human being[s]'.[12]

Similarly, English suffragists and dress reformers also recognized that the body, its clothing, and emancipation were inextricably linked. Elizabeth Stuart Phelps, like many English dress reform feminists, positioned the body as central to her theories of dress reform. She claimed in her *What To Wear?* that corsetry had to be abandoned because it directly sapped women's physical strength and in doing so undermined women's potential for political power. While written to encourage the adoption of rational or reformed dress, *What to Wear?* was also fully intended to be read as a critical examination of women's role in society. The introduction informed readers that the text had a 'political as well as social value' and was directed both to 'those women who ha[d] joined the women's movement, to the readers of *The English Women's Review*, and sympathisers with Miss Jex Blake . . . and Lydia Becker'.[13] Phelps's combined sartorial and political rebellion manifested in explicit advice to readers not to simply abandon their corsetry, but to torch it; she declared

> Burn the corsets! . . . No, nor do you save the whalebones, you will never need whalebones again. Make a bonfire of the cruel steels that have lorded it over your thorax and abdomen for so many years and heave a sigh of relief, for your emancipation I assure you, from this moment has begun.[14]

Public declarations by dress reformers that women should 'throw off all customs that tend[ed] to cramp them in any direction, and . . . to retain only such [garments] as liberate[d] and enlarge[d] their powers'[15] alarmed mainstream critics of reform dress. Potential for the uncorseted body to offer wider liberation than its immediate freedom from stays was unconsciously and sometimes consciously recognized, feared and resisted by authors of popular health and beauty texts. As a result, criticism of the uncorseted body as much as the new fashions promoted by dress reformers to clothe it was often linked with, and often even central to, wider criticisms of the women's rights movement. The corseted, contained, middle-class female body, was (ideally) perceived by authors of mainstream texts as tractable and obedient. It was a body that did not appear to threaten the political or sexual status quo. The uncorseted middle-class female body appeared as its potentially destabilizing, ideological opposite. *How to Get Married Although a Woman: or the Art of Pleasing Men*, published in 1892, spelled out these connections, anxieties and oppositions. Its author, a 'young widow', urged readers to remain 'womanly and womanish in every way'. She warned female readers against campaigning for women's rights, for to do so would be seen as 'usurp(ing) a man's place' and going 'out of [woman's] sphere'. If a woman had a 'leaning toward women's rights', advised the young widow, she should 'erect [her]self and lean the other way'. Those women who ignored her warnings were, she claimed, destined to 'unattractive spinsterhood . . . dress reform and the lecture platform'.[16]

Much of the reactionary writing around dress reform was, as the young widow's text demonstrates, provoked by a range of feminist issues rather than by any single cause. Many texts that were critical of dress reform were also distressed by a variety of related mid- and late century women's issues that encompassed dress reform, suffrage and, increasingly from the 1860s, the conscious development of feminine physical strength. Indeed, the actual corporeal bodies of dress reformers and feminists began to emerge at this time as a significant issue for dress reformers and mainstream opponents alike. Dress reformers insisted that their loose rational garments encouraged health and the possibility of developing real physical strength. For many dress reform critics, the adoption of rational or reformed dress, particularly those garments that did not exaggerate secondary sexual characteristics, heralded an unsexing of the female body. This sartorial unsexing of the female body, and its possible masculinization via the attainment of physical vigour such loose garments allowed, was an unthinkable breach of gender conduct, and was perceived as an encroachment upon male territory, as alarming and as dangerous as female campaigns for suffrage.

As early as 1851, a backlash against women's nascent interest in politics had begun. Even at this early stage the links between the new feminine interest in dress reform, its relationship to increased health and strength, and their combined promises of even a metaphorical escape from the private sphere had been detected. The anonymous author of *The Young Ladies' Mentor: A Guide to the Formation of Character in a Series of Letters to Her Unknown Friends*, published in 1851, was annoyed that some women claimed that 'their present sphere [was] a too contracted one and that they ought to share in the public functions of the other sex'. The author was appalled that these headstrong women proclaimed an 'equality in mental and *physical*' powers (the author's italics). This kind of equality, continued the author, made 'the sexes rivals', destroyed a maxim established by 'divine government' and therefore 'threaten[ed] family life'.[17] Horace Bushnell, author of *Women's Suffrage: The Reform Against Nature* (published in 1869), actually insisted enfranchisement would physiologically alter women, who were already demonstrating signs of their masculinization through dress. 'Suffrage', wrote Bushnell darkly, would have a series of 'probable effects'. An entire chapter was devoted to these probable effects, which included a 'sharp look', a voice that was 'wiry and shrill', a body that was 'angular and abrupt' and a character that was 'self asserting . . . bold and eager for place and power'. Female suffrage would, according to Bushnell, generate 'a race of forward, selfish politician women' whose very bodies would be markedly different from those of their previously unenfranchised sisters. The new woman would, Bushnell calculated, be 'taller and more brawny', with 'bigger hands and feet, and a greater weight of the brain'.[18]

What Bushnell feared, to a greater or lesser extent, came to pass. However, it was not suffrage that conceived a race of strong and therefore potentially emasculating women. This birth was a result of concerted campaigns by dress reformers, feminists and gymnastic teachers who, between 1850 and 1900, led a well-orchestrated and largely successful campaign to introduce schoolgirls and their mothers to the benefits and delights of disciplined exercise. Corsetry remained an impediment to this goal until very late in the century. In 1899, British suffragist and dress reformer Laura Ormiston Chant noted that one of the 'chief obstacles to ... a scientific and universal system of physical training' were mothers who opposed the gym uniform, fearing that the uncorseted gym frock would somehow make 'hoydens' of their daughters. Chant was appalled to see gymnastic exercises attempted by girls wearing 'stays ... and inappropriate underclothing' further hindered by their high heels and 'street clothes' complete with bangles (see Figure 46).[19]

As Chant's report illustrates, the cultivation of a public mentality that looked favourably on the promotion of female strength was not a seamless or unproblematic process. Indeed the very bodies of women and children, who undertook exercise that was not traditionally deemed 'feminine' became contested sites in discourses that disputed just how fit and how strong the female body ought to become. Darwinian theory, religious exhortations, eugenic arguments and theories of education[20] were frequently called upon to either justify or negate the rise of gymnastics for women. These sometimes-contradictory discourses frequently overlapped and competed for primacy in both dress reform texts that promoted rigorous exercise and mainstream texts that were alternately cautious and antagonistic toward the emergence of the physically empowered female body. The clamour of critical voices prompted by women's participation in demanding exercise routines escalated as the century drew to a close, but their origins began in the 1850s when gymnastics was introduced to Britain and North America from Germany.[21]

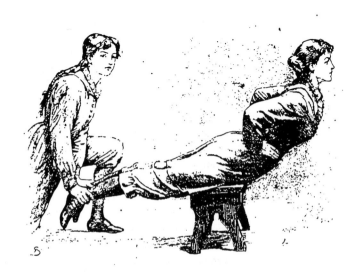

Figure 46
Gymnastic costume featuring bloomers were favored by Laura Ormiston Chant. The girls depicted in this and other accompanying illustrations are sturdy and energetic in comparison to fashion plate models of this era. See *Woman's World*, 1899.

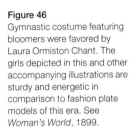

Gymnastics made a rapid if not overwhelming impact in the more enlightened educational circles in Britain and North America within little more than a decade of its introduction there. Caroline Dall, author of *The College, the Market, And the Court; or Women's Relation to Education, Labor, and Law*, noted as early as 1867 that 'as teachers of gymnastics women [were] sometimes already somewhat employed'. Dall anticipated that 'a wide field would be opened if a teacher were attached to each of [the] public schools'. She observed that this was a 'step in physical education [that was] greatly needed'.[22] By the mid-1870s, gymnastic exercise was gaining a following in many middle-class girls' schools and colleges in both North America and Britain. By 1880, the crusade for female gymnastics had, in some quarters, reached a level of 'fanatic enthusiasm'.[23] Concerns about, and resentment toward, the newly physically empowered female body accompanied this progress. Opposition to the 'gym-fit' female body was expressed even by those who had previously argued for increased physical activity for women and for the abandonment of corsetry.

Luke Limner, whose appeal against corsetry was widely cited by his contemporaries, was extremely ambivalent about gymnastic exercise which, if it was to be properly undertaken, required the participant to leave her corset off. '[W]ithout in any way wishing to render woman either Amazons or athletes we think gymnastic opportunities for growing girls – slightly indulged in – might be productive of much good', wrote Limner. However, Limner's underlying, if unacknowledged, loyalty to corsetry and its role in upholding the inequitably gendered physical status quo, was betrayed by further remarks in which he bare-facedly admitted that

> while the youthful body demand[ed] recreative work to prevent it from becoming enfeebled [by corsetry] . . . this particular state of nature ha[d] always been more or less encouraged by the robust sex who admire in women a weakly dependent.[24]

Antagonism to female gymnastics may also have arisen because of the gendered nature of that sport. Men were not significant participants in gymnastic exercise until the twentieth century. Unlike other sports engaged in by women during the nineteenth century, such as golf, tennis, riding and rowing, that were pastimes largely designed to oil the machinery of social intercourse between the sexes, gymnastics was a solitary, almost separatist activity. It was often undertaken in all-female gyms, or in classes that separated the sexes. Moreover, gymnastics was primarily concerned with cultivating the body for its own sake, rather than as an object on which to display the latest fashionable clothing. Female gymnastics was, too, a largely individual and private pursuit, except on those occasions when gymnasts doubly contravened gender behaviour by performing publicly, to demonstrate their sometimes startling feats of strength. The rise of exclusively female gymnasiums is an exceptionally interesting one.

The all-female gym offered women a space in which to explore the limits of their physicality. With a sense of pride in their newly emergent physical prowess, may have come a sense of empowerment and liberation that could inspire women to conquer other previously male- dominated fields. Despite suspicion and, at times, overt hostility to gymnastics, the sport continued to gather momentum. Clothing in general and the use of corsetry in particular was often discussed in texts that were published specifically to popularize the sport.

Dio Lewis, considered by sport historian Kathleen McCrone to be the 'leader of gymnastic reformation in America',[25] opened his Gymnasium for Ladies Gentleman and Children on the eve of the Civil War, and began his *Boston Journal of Physical Culture* that same year.[26] Lewis's widely read text, *The Musical Gymnasium for Family and Schools with Illustrations of All the Positions*, was in its ninth edition by 1867. The popularity of Lewis's system of gymnastic exercise may, in part, have been the result of his attitude to the sport and to clothing. Although his exercise routines were demanding, they could be 'performed with equal safety, propriety and success by women' as well as by men. His exercise routines were accompanied by music that was not merely 'incidental' but 'designed to stir the sources of exhilaration, mirth [and] enthusiasm'. Lewis's programme of gymnastic exercise was, in his own words, 'a sort of physical jubilee . . . and carnival of vital laws'.[27] In short, Lewis made gymnastics fun. Lewis, like most advocates of female gymnastics, promoted a loosely fitting costume. He was, also, resolutely against the use of any kind of corsetry.[28]

So too was Madame Bergman Osterberg, Lewis's British counterpart who did much to foster gymnastic training, and to promote its potential as a career for middle-class women in Britain. Osterberg began the first tertiary college of physical training in Britain in the 1880s. She absolutely forbade corsetry and demanded that her students adopt functional comfortable dress for exercise.[29] McCrone, who has examined Osterberg's role in the rise of gymnastics in secondary and tertiary schools in Britain, has argued that Osterberg's preferred gymnastic dress, sans corsetry, 'epitomised the spirit of emancipation that inspired women to break free of some of the more restrictive elements of the Victorian code of femininity'.[30] Corsetry was at that time, of course, an essential and restrictive component of conventional Victorian femininity.

Gymnastic costume was far removed from prevailing mainstream sport and ordinary street attire. Osterberg's gym costume was composed of a long-sleeved, loose, plain blue serge frock, worn to a little lower than knee length. This garment quickly 'evolved' into a box-pleated tunic, loosely sashed at the waist, and worn over stockings with sand shoes. This gymnastic outfit, which remained the universal sports costume in many schools well into the twentieth century, disguised the secondary sexual characteristics, rather than emphasizing them as conventional street attire did.[31] The importance of the sport costume, sans corsetry, was viewed by feminists as a method of resisting Victorian cultural imperatives around femininity. Dr Kate Mitchell, writing in 1890, recognized that corsetry was an important method of controlling women's behaviour. She noted approvingly that the 'pernicious habit of tight lacing' was being undermined, 'at least for the growing girlhood of England', because of the popularity of physiological classes and gymnasiums where corsetry was forbidden.[32]

The legitimacy of McCrone's assertion that sports clothing represented a resistance to the 'restrictive elements of Victorian femininity' is substantiated further when a comparison of the gym costume and mainstream underclothes and outer dress is undertaken. Gym frocks were outlandish by comparison to ordinary attire. Gym frocks exposed the stockinged legs almost from the knees down, and were sometimes worn with loose bloomers beneath. Both of these aspects of the costume affronted accepted standards of decency. Only young girls were supposed to show their legs, and bloomers, even beneath a skirt, were considered 'masculine and immodest'.[33] The lack of a cinched waistline, which was de rigueur in conventional attire, added to the costume's ability to shock. The absence of a tightly fitted bodice and the small circular waist created by corsetry made the body appear formless by comparison.

Interestingly, it is possible to trace a direct sartorial backlash against the abandonment of corsetry, the design of gym costume, and the new physical freedom advocated by leading gymnasts in the 1870s and 1880s. New corset models appeared on the market that were clearly designed to woo women who had abandoned corsetry back to a corseted existence. Manufacturers 'improved' the garments by making them far more visually appealing than they had ever been during the nineteenth century. Corsets, which had, from the beginning of the nineteenth century, operated as gender-specific apparel were, in the early 1870s, dramatically feminized even further by the incorporation of dainty embroidery and figured silks, delicate ribbons and rich trims.[34]

The colour range of corsets increased accordingly and the garments became unashamedly sexual. Brilliant colours, made possible by the invention of new chemical dyes in the 1860s, meant that corsets were no longer limited to a range of white, black, drab and pastel. Solferino, magenta and gold were choice favourites by the mid-1870s.[35] More significantly still, the corset, for the first time since the eighteenth century, became in the 1870s a high fashion item, worn *outside* the frock and forming part of the bodice. The corset bodice was very tightly fitted and ran down to a sharp point in front of the skirt that unfurled beneath it.[36] It would appear that both the re-inscription of the corset as a fashion item, beautifully adorned and worn as an outer garment, and its simultaneous glamourization and overt sexualization as an undergarment can be perceived as a direct response to trends which might have threatened its popularity. It can also be assumed that the increased and dramatic 'feminization' of corsetry indicates that gymnastics was perceived as a threat to sex and gender stability.

Despite sartorial counteractions that worked to undermine or override gymnastics, and the numerous textual responses designed to foil or at least impede its rise, Osterberg's students, assisted by an international network of dress reformers and feminists, disseminated her doctrine as gym mistresses in girls' schools, colleges and universities throughout Britain and North America.[37] Gymnastics was also popular on both sides of the Atlantic with adult women.[38] While Osterberg sensibly forbade corsetry, she also implemented a precise exercise and diet programme, designed specifically to alter the female body. This dietary regime was not intended to reduce the weight of her charges, but to increase it. This dual programme was consciously implemented for two purposes. The first of these was to attempt to overturn the lingering but still prevalent idea that femininity was epitomized by a neurasthenic physical frailty. The second and related motive was to demonstrate that tertiary education was not, as Osterberg's opponents insisted, mentally or physically debilitating.[39]

Public demonstrations by Osterberg's students to dispel these fears met a mixed reaction. The British magazine *Queen* demonstrated its support for female gymnastics by publishing positive reports of various displays held in London. These displays were not of the kind disparaged by reformers as superficial, that simply involved batons and 'musical drill', but were real exhibitions of stamina that required the flexibility and potency that could only be attained by rigorous exercise without corsetry. A 'large and influential audience witnessed a gymnastic display by lady members of the Hall Park gymnasium', noted a reporter from the *Queen* magazine in 1898. This display included high-jumping and horse vaulting,[40] feats that would have been impossible to achieve in corsetry. However, not all accounts of gymnastic displays were as enthusiastic and complimentary as those reported by *Queen*.[41] Critics of female gymnastics dubbed these events as the 'reverse of charming and detrimental to health'.[42] Despite this kind of castigation, public demonstrations of women's new found strength increased as gymnastics became, albeit sometimes grudgingly or condescendingly, accepted as a suitable activity for women. Madame Osterberg's students, undeterred by occasional public denunciations by men as 'those dreadful girls',[43] continued their public demonstrations of stamina, as did the American colleges and girls' schools that had taken up gymnastics as part of the curriculum.

An important part of Osterberg's scheme (and that of her followers) was to measure and record the increase of muscle mass of her students. This was carried out at the Anthropometrical Laboratory at South Kensington Museum by no less than the father of eugenic theory, Frances Galton.[44] Galton's records indicate that women's bodies were literally transformed under Osterberg's care. Osterberg's dietary plan, combined with exercises designed to increase muscle definition and power, increased her students' overall body mass. The physical appearance of Osterberg's students leaned, as one commentator remarked, toward 'classical' rather than contemporary standards of beauty.[45] That is, the body of the female athlete promoted by Osterberg was muscular, athletic and statuesque, and had a noticeably larger waist than her fashionably corseted smaller, sedentary sister.[46]

Significantly, it was not the expanding waistline so much as the increased muscle mass and body weight of women who undertook these programmes which aggravated late nineteenth-century critics of the uncorseted and newly empowered body. An expanded waistline did not seriously contravene femininity. It pointed rather to multiple childbirth or an indulgence in rich food, or a 'letting go of appearances', which were all considered gender-appropriate, if not desirable, feminine traits. The cultivation of muscle tissue was, however, a serious transgression of gender, for strength was considered by mainstream Victorian society as a biologically ordained prerogative of men. Between 1850 and 1900 sport was largely considered the province of working-, middle- and upper-class men. Sport was recognized as a defining and reinforcing element of masculinity,[47] as a 'legitimate avenue to virile athletic manhood'.[48] However, the Victorian cultivation of a muscled masculine sporting identity or subjectivity was a complex process, fraught with dangerous dilemmas. The 'muscled' body has, as Susan Bordo points out, historically exemplified a range of cultural meanings. Until the late twentieth century, muscularity was the province and signifier of masculine power. The muscular male physique in the Victorian era was carefully cultivated, but up to a particular point, for the overly muscular body was associated with the working or even the criminal classes. The heavily muscled male body had connotations of the chain gang and unrelenting manual labour. The muscled body was too, according to Bordo, 'suffused with racial meaning'. The muscular, sweating, male body was associated with the primitive, and the animalistic other.[49]

Given the rigidly gendered nature of muscularity and its potentially dangerous proclivity to emit the wrong cultural signifiers, it is not surprising that the cultivation of muscular bodies by middle-class women was such a controversial issue. The corseted hourglass figure of the conventional Victorian woman emphasized her breasts and hips, and was the symbolic marker of an appropriate femininity. It acted as a reassuring signifier that middle-class women courted a reproductive destiny. The corseted projection of the body and its corollary, the emphasis of its soft maternal parts, evoked a comforting promise of potential maternity.[50] The uncorseted muscular female body emitted quite different signals and transgressed gender, class and even racial norms as a result. The very processes of its cultivation involved behaviours that were considered gender-deviate. In Foucauldian terms gymnastic training involved 'the incorporation of disciplinary methods', and a 'policy of coercions' that worked to manipulate, shape and train the body into a docile obedience.[51] However, unlike the masculine subjects of Foucault's discussion whose disciplinary training inevitably augmented the 'constricting link between an increased aptitude and an increased domination', the newly strengthened bodies of women who undertook gymnastics actually stood outside of, and therefore contravened, the expectations of mainstream society. The strong athletic female body rejected the 'individual and collective coercion of bodies'. The bodies of women who had undergone rigorous exercise routines, signified and actualized a deviance from imperatives which would otherwise determine them as 'breeders'. Although the improved health that resulted from concerted exercise may actually have increased their ability to have safe pregnancies and less complicated deliveries, the altered body shape of the female gymnast and the athlete affronted traditional ideas of the ideal sexual/maternal.

This ideological transgression was as often made apparent by the attitudes as by the bodies of women who regularly trained in athletic or gymnastic pursuits. Primary sources reported that the athletic woman's body was characterized by 'an elasticity' and significantly an 'assuredness' which 'betoken[ed] muscular development and strength'. One only had to 'use one's power of observation to test the superior health and strength of modern women', wrote feminist doctor Kate Mitchell, for the modern woman 'used her muscles as easily and healthily as a man'. Mitchell attributed the new health directly to the abandonment of the 'sins of tight lacing' and the rise of 'gymnasium and physiology classes'.[52]

Interestingly, the popularity of gymnastics in particular, rather than sports in general, appears to have actually threatened the corset industry. Many sports could be played, albeit without complete freedom of movement, while wearing corsetry. However, the extreme flexibility demanded by gymnastics during exercises such as forward rolls, rope climbing and work on the parallel bars made the abandonment of corsetry essential. Market forces were quick to respond to the feminine pursuit of serious exercise. Increasingly after 1870, both large and small corset firms patented and produced garments that specifically promised to assist the body during exercise. Corsets such as the 'pliable romping bodice' and the 'school girls' athletic corset' appear to have been targeted to appease the contradictory concerns of conventional mothers who were alarmed by the rise of gymnastics in schools. They may also have been considered as a kind of sartorial concession to progressive gymnastic teachers who insisted that their charges abandon corsets for unrestricted gymnastic dress.

Many of the sport and exercise corsets designed for adult women (rather than children), such as the Mey's Helene watch spring corset advertised in the 1880s, which guaranteed to give the 'best form for exercise', differed little, if at all, from standard corset design. The Mey's Helene garment had moveable watch spring steels rather than whalebones for support. This invention was hardly new and did nothing to reduce compression of the torso.[53] The widely advertised Dermathistic corset, like the Mey's Helene, differed little from the standard design beyond the incorporation of leather facings.[54] The facings of leather prevented the bones or steels tearing through the garment when they broke under the

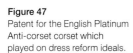

Figure 47
Patent for the English Platinum
Anti-corset corset which
played on dress reform ideals.

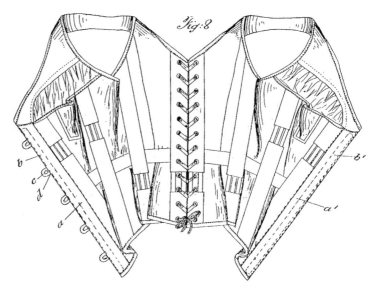

pressure of exercise. The 'Anti-Corset' corset, also promoted by its
manufacturers Herts and Son as ideal for sport, was less rigid but held
almost as many bones as standard corsetry (see Figures 47 and 48).[55]Some
brands, such as the CB Sports Corset, did nothing else but add elastic
gussets at the waist and inserted tapes inside the garments, on which were
printed 'For Cycling, Tennis and Sailing' (see Figure 49).

    The Leicester Museum's Service has a particularly good example of
the standard style of sports corset. The corset is in very good condition,
which might suggest its original owner wore it rarely and found cycling,
tennis and sailing too difficult while wearing the garment. The corset is
made of black lasting, with a white coutille lining cut over the hips, with
six elastic gores, two each at breasts, hips and waist, to provide some
flexibility of movement. Forty graded whalebones provided the garment
with a substantial infrastructure and the black lasting is beautifully
decorated with 'flossing' or 'fanning' of shell-pink silk thread.[56] Other
manufacturers of sports corsetry eliminated bones and steels entirely but
found new ways to shape and strengthen their garments.[57] William Pretty,
a corset manufacturer of Suffolk, patented a garment of standard hourglass shape that was supposedly 'improved' by the use of Aloe plant or
Mexican fibre. Pretty's Garment was 'intended especially for wear whilst
taking strong exercise'. While it had 'no bones or side steels which might
be liable to break or impede the free movement of the body' the garment
'possess[ed] great stiffness and [was] wholly unaffected by moisture.' Both
characteristics were considered by the inventor to be advantageous (see
Figure 50)[58]. Illustrations that accompanied Pretty's patent also show that
the corset was furnished with a fashionable spoon-shaped steel busk which
ran from between the breasts to the lower edge of the garment.[58]

Figure 48

The Platinum anti corset corset (or substitute corset) and the Y and N corsets depicted here were designed on similar principles. The Platinum anti-corset corset, despite its assertions of difference, still retained its 'unbreakable busk' and hour-glass shape. See *The Graphic*, 1896.

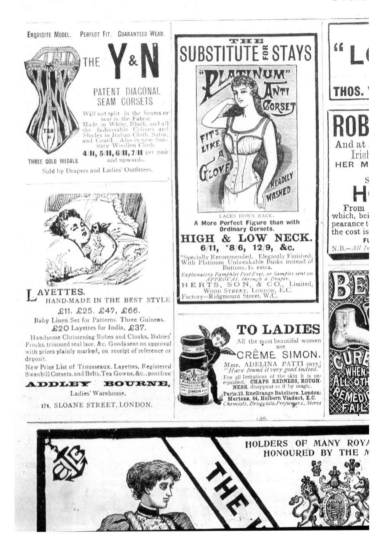

Few, if any 'exercise' corsets were designed without the ubiquitous busk, and as a consequence were criticized by reformers. Edith Barnett warned readers of her text, *Common-Sense Clothing*, that even modified garments described by manufacturers as 'hygienic' still caused 'compression enough to distort the stoutest figure. A steel plate [i.e. the busk] fixed over the abdomen and sundry lacings and straps . . . indicate[d] one course with regard to stays [warned Barnett], eschew them!'[59] Dress reformer Frances Steele cautioned readers [in 1892] against purchasing 'manufactured

Figure 49
Ferris advertisements were designed to appeal to 'young ladies' who played sport and 'attended gymnasium'. They were frequently advertised in the *Women's Tribune*, 1895.

waists' which claimed to have health-giving properties. Many of the garments, which were often sold by mail order, had 'unyielding steels at the front'.[60]

Although dress reformers were largely hostile to corsetry, they understood that some women required the breast support that corsetry provided. Several reformers designed ingenious garments and sold them, or patterns for them, through mail-order advertisements or directly through dress reform salons. These early bra prototypes were generally referred to as 'supports' and were to be worn instead of corsets (see Figure 51). The

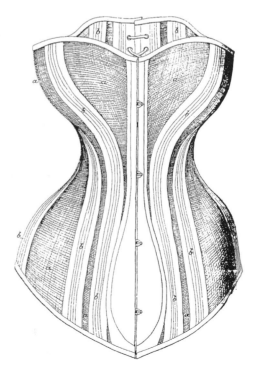

Figure 50
William Pretty's specification for a corset 'expressly designed for taking strong exercise . . . possessing great stiffness . . . and wholly unaffected by moisture.'

Perfection Supports.

Ladies will find a good substitute for the corset in Mrs. Newell's Perfection Breast Support Form which is endorsed by Mrs. Frank Stuart Parker in her lectures as the best and cheapest on the market. By its use the weight of the breasts is removed from the dress waist to the shoulders, giving ventilation and correct shape with perfect freedom of the body. The Low Form is best suited to those who only need it for support while the the High Form supplies deficiencies of figure; when ordering send bust measure. Send to the office of the WOMAN'S TRI-BUNE. Price by mail $1.00.

Figure 51
Perfection Supports were early brassières and despite their sensible no-fuss design (or because of it) they failed to capture the popular imagination. See *Women's Tribune* 1895.

FLYNT WAIST,
—OR—
True Corset.

No. 1 represents a high-necked garment. No. 2, a low-necked one which admits of being high in the back and low front. No. 3 is to illustrate our mode of adjusting the "Flynt Hose Support" each side of the hip; also, the most correct way to apply the waistbands for the drawers, under and outside petticoats and dress skirts. No. 4 shows the Flynt Extension and Nursing Waist, appreciated by mothers. No. 5, the Misses' Waist, with Hose supports attached. No. 6, how we dress very little people. No. 7 illustrates, how *the warp threads of the fabrics cross at right angles in the back*, thereby ensuring in *every waist* the most successful Shoulder Brace ever constructed.

It is universally indorsed by eminent physicians as the most Scientific Waist or Corset known.

Pat. Jan. 6, 1874.
Pat. Feb. 15, 1876.

THE FLYNT WAIST

is the only garment manufactured where the material of which it is made is shrunk before cut; the only one which in its natural construction contains a

Figure 52
The Flynt Waist had many of the features that made a corseted existence more comfortable. Emphasis was removed from the waist in this design but the wide shoulder straps that acted as a brace enforced their own restrictions. See *Woman's Journal*, 1890.

'Perfection Support' advertised in *The Women's Tribune* of 1895 was, despite its front lacing, very like brassières designed and worn in the 1950s. The Perfection Support had wide straps, and the fabric was gored rather than boned beneath the breasts to provide comfort.[61] Other reform garments that were designed to support the breasts covered the entire torso. Some were made either entirely without bones or had removable bones. The 'Flynt Waist or True Corset' was such a garment (see Figure 52). It was frequently advertised in *The Woman's Journal* in the 1890s and could be purchased by mail order. The Flynt Waist was part of a range of 'hygienic modes of underdressing' manufactured by Mrs O.P. Flynt. The 'true corset' was shaped like a singlet with sleeves, was made for both children and adults, and was completely devoid of bones. Every garment 'supported the bust from the shoulders'. The garment promised 'perfect respiration gained by freedom from compression' and was considered 'ideal' for singers, actresses, teachers of elocution or physical exercise, equestrians and invalids. 'Thousands of ladies who had been fitted by mail' were, according to the advertisements, 'constantly blessing the inventor'.[62] This may have been the case. The Flynt waist and other genuine reform corsets or brassière substitutes did not rely on compression or an infrastructure of bones or steels to provide shape to the body. They were designed, rather, to fit over the body without substantially altering its shape.

Another widely advertised garment, the Equipoise Waist, was boned, but was ingeniously designed to allow the occupant to remove the bones either 'all at once or one by one at short intervals'. The progressive removal of steels allowed the woman's body to slowly get used to the sensations of being less constricted.[63] The realistic shape of the Equipoise waist also allowed the natural expansion of the waist to occur. Despite their obvious benefits, reform or rational corsets, whether designed for sport or for everyday comfort, were generally overlooked in favour of standard corsetry (see Figures 53–55). Most women appear to have persevered with more or less standard garments when they played sports. These were, as mentioned earlier, cut on the usual waist hourglass shape, but had minor modifications, such as being cut higher over the hip to allow increased leg and hip movement (see Figure 56). This modification did little to increase the levels of comfort. The bloodied corsets held at the Wimbledon Tennis museum reveal exactly how constrictive and punishing these garments could be.

Women's escalating involvement in sport and the increasing interest in the athletic female body was evidenced in health texts that flourished in the latter half of the century. Ironically, these texts were often directed toward a male rather than a female readership. Twenty years after Osterberg's students had publicly demonstrated the transformative power of exercise, it was rare for men to state that women were incapable of enormous physical strength. However, texts that were ostensibly written to increase the stamina of both sexes promoted the cultivation of different

EQUIPOISE WAIST.

For Ladies, Misses, Children and Infants.

THIS WAIST is a perfect substitute for corsets, and may be worn either with or without the bones, which, owing to the construction of the bone pockets, may be removed at pleasure.

THE CUT represents the Waist as made for Ladies and Misses, boned and with full bust; the construction of inside of bust under fulled piece is that of a corset front, so that a corset and a perfect bust support is provided within a waist. In the Open Back Soft Waists, as made for Children and Infants, particular attention to the physical proportions and requirements of the growing little ones has been given in shaping the parts, and from the large variety of sizes, all ages can be perfectly fitted from stock.

PRICES.

Style 600,	Ladies' Whole Back, without Bones	$1.75
" 601,	" " " Bone Front only	2.00
" 603,	" Laced Back, Boned Front and Back	2.25
" 610,	Misses' Whole Back without Bones	1.50
" 611,	" " " Boned	1.75
" 621,	Children's—with out Bones	.75
" 631,	Infants' " "	.75

PATENTED. DIRECTIONS FOR MEASURING.

For Ladies and Misses, take a snug measure around waist over dress, and give it to us in inches.
For Children and Infants, take chest measure also, and state age of child.
We shall take pleasure in sending circulars to all who desire to learn more about this meritorious garment. Waists sent by mail to any part of the U. S., postage prepaid, on receipt of price, and if not satisfactory we will exchange or refund the money, if returned in good order. Mention THE WOMAN'S JOURNAL.
☞ One good Agent wanted for every City and Town in the United States. Address

GEORGE FROST & CO., 31 Bedford Street, Boston, Mass.

Figure 53
The Equipoise Waist was both corset and bust supporter, and was manufactured both with and without bones. The design of the garment allowed the bones to be removed as women desired. See *Woman's Journal*, 1890.

kinds of physical strength. These differences were determined by traditional gender expectations. By the 1890s mainstream texts were clearly instrumental in ascribing gender to the muscular body. William Anderson's *Physical Education: Health and Strength, Grace and Symmetry*, published in 1897, encouraged both men and women to participate in gymnastics, but for gender-specific reasons. Anderson was associate director of the

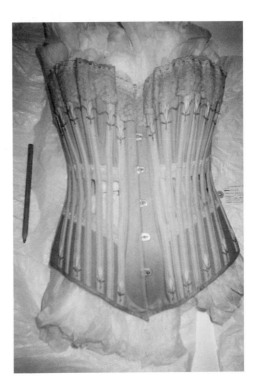

Figure 54
Extant Symington's Ventilated Corset c. 1885 allowed some ventilation but only at the waist. (Courtesy of Leicestershire Museum Services)

Yale University gymnasium and president of the Anderson Normal School
of Gymnastics. He claimed that 'the idea which regarded physical training
as un-feminine [was] a thing of the past' and insisted that 'the pale angular
flat chested' women so often seen in drawing rooms would blossom
into 'plump neck[ed] creature[s] [with] well developed bust[s]' if they
exercised for an hour a day. This would, according to Anderson, result
in male admiration and possibly love. His female readers were, however,
cautioned to avoid 'heavy weight lifting' not because they could not

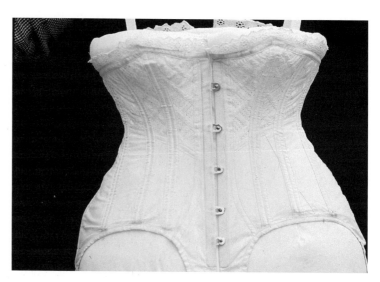

achieve this, or because it might damage their health, but because weight lifting was 'incompatible with grace'. The musculature of female gymnasts, according to Anderson, would, unlike the muscles of their male counterparts, become 'sluggish and [curiously] rigid, even when in repose'. Anderson recommended that female participants use the 'light elastic apparatus'. This would not increase muscle density but instead make their muscles 'pliable and quickly responsive'. Exercise for women was, in Anderson's opinion, less about muscle definition and the development of strength, and far more about the cultivation of gender-appropriate attributes. Exercises appropriately modified for the female sex made feminine 'eyes brighter, the colouring of the face more beautiful . . . the step more elastic and springy, and the carriage of the body more queenly'.[64]

William Blaikie's *How To Get Strong and Stay So*, published in 1880, which also promised to increase the stamina of both sexes, was as corporeally sexist as Anderson's. Blaikie's text, while directed to men, contained a chapter on women's health in which he simultaneously celebrated and undermined the extremes of physical stamina the female body could achieve. *How To Get Strong and Stay So* gave a detailed description of the French gymnastic troupe, the Young sisters, who toured Britain and astonished audiences with their feats of strength. Nathalie Young was not a 'woman of extreme build', yet she could lift extraordinarily heavy weights above her head. Her sister climbed 'slack rope' and, during one performance, challenged a group of twenty sailors to do the same. Nathalie 'wore out the whole twenty on aggregation of feet higher than St. Peters Cathedral in Rome', wrote an awed Blaikie. This was due to her 'great strength and either handedness and the athletic power of pinching a rope with sinews of [her] lower limbs'. While Blaikie was clearly astonished by the Young sisters, he questioned the desirability of their strength and seemed particularly afraid of the stamina that exhibited itself in the women's arms.[65]

That Blaikie's anxieties centred on women's arms rather than their legs, can be explained, in part, by prevailing fashions. The arms, shoulders and upper chests of fashionable belles were often completely uncovered in formal evening dress. Arms, rather than legs, were legitimately displayed. Arms were less overtly sexualized than legs and were therefore an acceptable focus of attention by women and their male admirers. Harriet Hubbard Ayer gave detailed descriptions of the ideal feminine arm. Like Blaikie, she disliked the 'lumpy arm of athleticism' and urged women to cultivate 'beautiful' arms. These were 'round, soft, smooth, white and plump, not fat . . . taper[ing] gently to the hand with an adorable little curve at the small delicate wrist'.[66] As both Blaikie's and Ayer's texts make clear, bare arms and shoulders could be 'read'. In their lineaments could be deciphered a measure of an individual woman's commitment to either a traditional feminine ideology or a potential or actual infraction of femininity that was betrayed by upper-body muscularity.

While gentle exercise for the female body was always commended in mainstream texts, most authors concurred with Blaikie and Ayer that 'the distinct protuberances of the athlete were to be avoided' by female readers at all costs.[67] Ayer's text was one of many that set out gentle exercises that were designed to make women's bodies conform to a stereotypical feminine shape. Health and beauty texts, whether written by reformers or by more conventional authors, both worked to either reinforce or alter prevailing standards of feminine beauty as determined by the body. The prevalence of these texts, and the diversity and polarization of opinion demonstrated within them, indicate the enormous stresses under which femininity was labouring from mid- to late century. Body shape and physical strength were often central issues in mainstream and reform advice manuals.

While texts such as Blaikie's urged women to remain physically 'soft' and mentally deferential to prescribed gender roles, reform texts were simultaneously urging readers to abandon corsets and other items of gender-fetish clothing, specifically in order to construct or rebuild their musculature, in some cases until their body shape was actually altered. This is not to say that reform texts consciously encouraged women to exercise in order to look like men; indeed, the reverse was true. Reform texts dwelled on the importance of physical strength for women, but were often scrupulous to point out that women would not lose their feminine charm in doing so. Abba Gould-Woolson reported that 'it [was] often asserted that they who preach dress reform for women, desire[d] merely that they . . . dress like men. Heaven forbid!' was her response. While Gould-Woolson defended the 'utility' of men's clothes, she took considerable care to defend sartorial femininity, and enthusiastically discussed the colours and textures of fabric that could be used in reform dress.[68] 'Beauty', wrote Woolson emphatically, had to be incorporated into 'remodeled garments'.[69]

Despite such attempts to convince detractors that increased musculature, combined with the abandonment of corsetry and the adoption of reform dress, offered no threat to prevailing masculinities, the nervous reaction particularly from male critics continued unabated. Anxieties around the presumed 'masculinization' of the female form were made explicit in mainstream magazines, texts and newspapers that urged women to abandon serious exercise and competitive sports. The attacks were as formidable as they were multi-faceted. They included veiled medical threats, insistences that the muscular female body spelled the beginning of race suicide, ridicule of the newly athletic body shape, insinuations and eventually outright accusations that the empowered female body harboured the seeds of sexual perversion and lesbianism.

Late century English novelist Oliver Wendell Holmes, who abhorred the 'excessive development of the muscular system' in women, attempted to dismantle women's interest in physical education by the use of medical threats. Holmes informed his female readers (without a shred of medical evidence to substantiate his claims) that exercise was of questionable value for women and that muscle development was to be avoided at all costs. According to Holmes the muscles were 'great sponges that suck[ed] up and ma[d]e use of great quantities of blood, [which meant that] other organs suffer[ed] from the want of their share'.[70] The organs thought to be jeopardized by muscle development, were, of course, the uterus and the ovaries. Fear surrounding damage to these organs was often expressed in racial rather than individual terms. Theories of reproductive impairment and the problems this presented to 'race' were used by both proponents and opponents of female gymnastics, well into the twentieth century. Arguments from dress reformers who promoted rigorous exercise, and mainstream authors who believed it was masculinizing, grew increasingly more complex as knowledge of the body, eugenic theory and social Darwinism unfolded.

Disputes centring on the development of female strength and its potential to increase or decrease the advancement of the species continued well into the century. Dr W.L. Howard, author of *Confidential Chats With Girls,* was adamant that 'no girl between the ages of 14 [and] 20 years should ever train for physical contests, or any form of athletic competition'. As late as 1911 adolescent girls were cautioned that the womb hung on 'silken threads, [and] any rough play, strain or carelessness at the time of menstruation' could 'ruin [them] for life'.[71] These claims were in direct contrast to arguments forwarded by dress reformers who, from at least mid-century, insisted that gymnastic exercise and vigorous sports increased women's overall and life-long health. Angeline Merritt, writing in 1854, before the theories of eugenic inheritance were widely articulated, had already formulated an opinion regarding physical deterioration over the decades. Merritt understood the connection between oppressive female dress and what she perceived to be a decline in the health of the 'civilized' races. Tight lacing in particular, according to Merritt, had 'alarmingly deteriorated [the] race in both physical and mental stature; and unless checked in its onward career, [would] soon destroy it!'[72] Reformers of later decades, armed with unfolding 'scientific' discourses emerging about race, appropriated the jargon and the knowledge used in these discourses to substantiate their own arguments about the condition of the race and its relationship to corsetry.

By 1899 reformers insisted that concerted exercise, the abandonment of corsetry and the popular use of modified costume would 'cut the chain of hereditary ... evil' caused by fashions that 'cribbed, cabined and confined' and which, over generations, had created a 'degenerate type of [female] body'. Gymnastic exercise and the avoidance of corsetry would, according to reformers, prevent another generation of 'sickly, stunted forms, ugly faces, [and] ugly natures' that threatened to 'punish' future generations.'[73] Exercise performed in comfortable uncorseted dress was, they intoned, essential for the well-being of the 'race of the future'.[74] Reformers also proffered sophisticated criticisms of corsetry and its relationship to eugenic health that were tailored to undermine arguments forwarded by individual women who chose to corset. Women who argued they had a 'prescriptive right to suffer for an ignoble cause' if they 'chose' to wear corsetry, were reprimanded by reformers such as Edith Barnett, who responded that corseted women could 'scarcely argue . . . for their right to entail suffering upon future generations'.[75]

While feminist dress reformers argued succinctly within a framework of progressive 'evolutionary theory' for the abolition of corsetry, their opponents were similarly appropriating aspects of social Darwinism to support the notion that corsetry was vital to women's physical well-being and continued evolution. Paradoxically, while theories of evolution generally presupposed change, they were used most often to argue against women's changing status within Victorian society. Indeed, as historian Lorna Duffin has pointed out, science and the prevailing social values of the Victorians became 'hopelessly entangled'.[76] Middle-class women could be considered (within theories of social Darwinism) as less evolved than men. Not only were their mental faculties supposedly less pronounced than in males, but their physical bodies were (supposedly) naturally frail or at least weaker by comparison. The terminology employed by corsetières reflected this. The metal strips or bones in corsets were often referred to as supports, while corset advertisements repeatedly promised to 'support' and at times even to strengthen the internal organs of the body. Both uses of the word 'support' in the patois of corsetry reflected the gendered Darwinian corporeal dualism. Corsetry designed to 'support' the body, whether during exercise or in repose, reflected the notion that the female body was less evolved than its masculine counterpart. Corsetry perpetuated the idea that the female body actually required an artificial infrastructure to keep it upright, to prevent it from collapsing into uncertain shape and uncomeliness.

Feminist dress reformers recognized the Darwinian inferences of corset manufacturers and promoters and worked to discount their claims. Abba Gould-Woolson repudiated such ideas as specious, claiming that if corsetry was essential to womankind, then God's intelligence had to be questioned. Gould-Woolson reasoned that if the female body really required corsetry to remain upright then 'one half of God's humanity [was] a hopeless failure'. God was able to 'construct man so that he should be equal to all the requirements of the life conferred upon him', wrote Gould-Woolson with her tongue firmly in cheek, 'but woman came forth from his hand wholly incompetent to maintain herself erect, . . . thus one skeleton sufficed for men, but . . . women . . . had to be propped up externally by another skeleton strapped about it'.[77] Lady Harberton concurred. She simply claimed that 'no creature ha[d] yet appeared on this earth which as a species require[d] a mechanical support for its own body'.[78]

The popularity of biological determinist arguments that legitimized and promoted the Victorian notion of female fragility and masculine strength can be explained, says historian Ruth Bleier, by the bias that permeated, and still permeates, scientific discourse. It is important, says Bleier, to recognize that a 'consistent and profound bias shapes scientific theories in general and theories about women in particular'. Bleier claims that when social movements are (or were) perceived to threaten the social order, corresponding scientific theories emerge (or emerged) that defend (or defended) the gendered status quo. Science, at these particular times, says Bleier, argues for presumed biological origins, permeated by an andro-centric bias consisting of 'premises and interpretations . . . universalistic assumptions, an acceptance of innate natures and a separability of biology from culture'. These biological determinist arguments emerge, says Bleier, as 'dominant explanations' during periods of unrest and during struggles for autonomy, particularly when women's issues are involved.[79]

The emergence of theories premised on biological determinist arguments and buttressed by universalistic assumptions can, not surprisingly, be detected in arguments for, rather than against, corsetry. One article that demonstrates Bleier's conclusions admirably, was written by Frances Billington, and published in *Woman* magazine in 1890. The author relied on the citation of traditional medical science to bolster her view that women required corsets. (She was an opponent of dress reform beyond its most superficial amendments.) Billington found a worthy advocate for her cause in Dr Thomas Nunn, FRSC, who was a well-known consult-ing surgeon at the Middlesex hospital. Nunn drew upon theories of race and class to justify and promote the use of corsetry. He argued that the 'possession of a slender waist was a question of race' and that the 'long slim figure of a typically well proportioned woman of the day [was] an evolution'. Nunn explained that the tiny waist of the middle-class English woman was a result of heredity, rather than corsetry alone, and he 'inferentially associate[d] high mental ability with a small waist'. He further claimed that,

> as intellectual faculties had largely relieved the strain of hard phys-ical exertions, . . . women's muscles had become smaller and more and more flexible. Thus a woman of graceful proportions . . . probably spr[a]ng from a well endowed ancestry, whose natural talents . . . had save[d] them from running only to muscular devel-opment and therefore towards intellectuality.

This view was, according to Billington, 'not likely to commend itself to the "strong minded" who hitherto regarded a small waist as a con-temptible form of female weakness and vanity' and who 'looked upon their own numerous inches as a conclusive proof of their superiority, because they more closely approximated . . . the sex they deride[d] but mimic[ked]'. It was, she continued, 'somewhat cruel to shake this firm faith by such a scientific deduction but [dress reformers would] no doubt regard a mere male doctor's theory as of small weight'.[80]

Much of the criticism of the uncorseted female body, was, as the century progressed, articulated within wider criticisms directed at those women who, toward the end of the 1880s, self-consciously considered themselves 'New Women'.[81] These women were, as Carroll Smith-Rosenberg has shown, educated, ambitious and most frequently single. In an era when the most pressing feminine middle-class goal was to marry brilliantly, the conscious pursuit of single-hood was enough to make the middle-class woman who purposely avoided marriage an object of suspicion. As Smith-Rosenberg noted, the New Woman and her behaviour became central to arguments about the naturalness of gender and even the legitimacy of the bourgeois order. By insisting on her own social and sexual identity (framed in the rhetoric of the women's-rights movement), the New Woman effectively and blatantly repudiated the status quo. Consequently, she was perceived as the very symbol and manifestation of feminine disorder and rebellion.[82] The New Woman's resistance to the 'old order' was perhaps most easily observed in her renunciation of fashionable 'feminine' dress. As Kaja Silverman has succinctly argued, 'clothing not only draws the body so it can be seen, but also maps the shape of the ego'. Moreover, continues Silverman, 'every transformation within a society's vestimentary code implies some kind of shift within its ways of articulating subjectivity'. The body and the clothing of the New Woman remain a very good example of this semiotic.

New Women frequently eschewed the frilly extremes of fashionable frocks, favouring and appropriating the less cluttered lines and less oppressive suits promoted by dress reformers. The New Woman's dress contested dominant values and gender demarcations. It operated as a 'sub-cultural flag'[83] that indicated her allegiance to a new paradigm of female beauty. The New Woman's psyche was blatantly 'written on the surface of her body' both by her musculature and by her choice of clothing.[84] This made her an obvious and easy target of attack. Elizabeth Walker, reformer and author of *The Dress Reform Problem: A Chapter for Women*, understood the power of costume to be read, and therefore to be held up to ridicule. She warned followers of dress reform in the 1880s that 'when not carefully applied' dress reform costume would 'bring upon the wearer the contemptuous epithet "ridiculous old guy".'[85] This kind of gendered insult was meant as a slight not only against dress reform clothing but also against the New Woman's apparent intellectual and material rejection of traditional gender roles.

Woman, the conservative middle-class magazine whose logo 'Forward: But not Too Fast', summed up its editorial stance on the New Woman, frequently lambasted her style of dress. Dorothy, the magazine's fashion consultant, reassured readers that she would not subject them to 'tirades against corsets . . . or spring upon them [a partiality] for unmitigated trouser costumes'.[86] Dorothy's venom toward what she considered inappropriate dress revealed that it was the New Woman's appearance, as much as her gender transgressive behaviour, that was the cause of concern. The magazine was alarmed at this perceived threat to the social order by the New Woman's abandonment of feminine fashions and ladylike pursuits. As a result, the body of the New Woman, beneath its reform clothing, was also frequently the locus of critical attention by the magazine's writers. The un-named author of an article titled 'The Virile Girl' published in that magazine in 1890 berated those women who attempted to 'break down the sex distinctions' in order to 'escape the limitations of . . . gender'. These remarks were intended to belittle the New Woman's body as much as her choice of dress which, worn without standard corsetry, devoid of excessive frou-frou, and made up in dark and 'sensible' colours, stood well outside prevailing fashionable trends.[87] The 'whole brood of restless females', continued the author, was 'trying to be mannish'.[88]

Seven years later, *The Lady's Realm*, another conservative British magazine directed at a middle-class readership, admitted that it too would 'never understand the "New Woman" [and her] total disregard for those female fripperies and fascinating gee-gaws which [were] so typical of womanliness'. Men did not like to see a 'weak imitation of themselves', warned the author. *The Lady's Realm* consoled itself, and possibly its readers, with the assertion that the longer the New Woman 'remained a devotee of the anti-corset league . . . the more surely she would come around'.[89]

The mainstream press was on the whole, similarly critical of reform dress. It fuelled anxieties that dress reform and exercise spelled the 'unsexing of women' and the disassembly of male superiority. 'Manly Women', as the athletic devotees of dress reform were often termed, were pilloried in articles that nervously reported (and some times stated outright) that women who adopted 'manly occupations . . . sports and . . . imitations of male garments' were intent on gaining a 'share in the political life of men, . . . [and] in the government of their country'.[90] New women were of course at that time campaigning vigorously for suffrage. As sport historian Susan Cahn has observed, 'the female athlete took her place alongside politically minded suffragists and feminists, . . . and together they formed a threatening cadre'.[91]

While the New Woman's education and ambition clearly made her an intimidating peer of man,[92] her strengthened body represented another dark, if ill-defined, multifaceted menace. This is not to say that all New Women were muscular or pursued sporting activities that altered their anatomy; however, those who did and whose bodies were altered by rigorous exercise met specific attacks engineered to bring their sexuality into disrepute. This was because the empowered body of the New Woman actually disrupted the conventional construction of Victorian gendered sexual subjectivities, based, to a greater or lesser extent in the mid- and late nineteenth century, on physical difference. In other words the athletic New Woman's body disturbed the delicate mechanisms of conventional heterosexual norms. The strong female body challenged, even undermined, masculinities that had been, until that time, studiously constructed around a 'natural' physical superiority to a frail, feminine and significantly heterosexual 'other'. By the end of the century, critics of female athletics blatantly claimed its adherents would acquire masculine bodies and masculine sexual interests as well. *Lippincott's Monthly Magazine*'s report of a successful female athlete in 1911 was couched in sexual imagery that was clearly linked to female 'perversion'. It described the athlete 'with her muscles tense and blood aflame . . . play[ing] the 'manly role'.[93] The numerous accusations of mannishness directed at the New Woman indicate that she was perceived to have distanced herself not only from 'normal' women but also from heterosexual men. It suggests too that those men, who feared the supposedly masculine New Woman also suspected that their exclusive role in initiating and controlling sexual relations was in jeopardy.[94]

The female athlete, particularly in the early twentieth century was, as Cahn points out, emblematic of a modern type of womanhood. Her body, freed from corsetry, strengthened by exercise and dressed in clothing which was not primarily designed to emphasize her secondary sexual characteristics, was as a consequence perceived as dangerously ambiguous, sexually labile and new. Accusations that female muscularity was manly or unsexing were, in part, designed to scare the New (modern) Woman back into a constrained, conventional and presumably corseted existence. The uncorseted body of the 1850s was similarly viewed as a threat to established femininities, though the hysteria around female sexuality was less pronounced. Throughout the century the corset operated to control women on a number of levels. It limited their movement to a range of acceptable gestures, dissipated their physical resources, and enforced a particular construction of sexuality upon them that assisted societal demands that they remain obedient, reproductive subjects. The emergence of female gymnastics was a significant area of resistance to these cultural imperatives. The gymnastic movement re-visioned women's exercise programmes, and enthusiastically and successfully repositioned women from decorative dilettantes on the sports field to powerful athletes.

Gymnastics successfully created a new and modern femininity, one that was not predicated on a tiny waistline and cumbersome frocks. It was of course only one aspect of Victorian femininity in an era when many competing aspects of femininity coexisted. Nevertheless, it was a startling affront to prevailing models of femininity, because of its apparent disdain for conventional sartorial as well as corporeal codes of conduct. In an era when the well-fitted corset was a barometer of heterosexual morality, the uncorseted body of the female gymnast was unruly and transgressive. Paradoxically, much of the success of gymnastics can be attributed to that sport's directive that corsetry be abandoned. For many women, gymnastic exercise would have been the only time that the corset could be 'legitimately' forsaken. This may, in part, have accounted for the popularity of the sport. The female gymnast, assisted (in some cases unwittingly) by the various dress reform movements, can be seen to have actually embodied feminist dress reform theory, and in doing so seriously threatened the corset's hegemony in the construction of Victorian womanhood.

7
Corsetry, Advertising, and Multiple Readings of the Nineteenth-Century Female Body

Advertising played an integral role in the popularity and longevity of corsetry. It often revealed more about prevailing socio-cultural attitudes than about the items that were for sale. Nineteenth-century advertising selectively 'reflected, mediated and reinforced preferred meanings taken from the overall cultural knowledge at hand'.[1] The shared similarities between nineteenth- and twentieth-century advertising makes the deployment of contemporary analyses of representation a particularly useful exercise. Indeed, a critical examination of Victorian corsetry advertisements, informed by twentieth-century critics writing in the fields of popular culture, including film, advertising, pornography, and art provides a surprising optic on the rationale and popularity of a garment that was so universally worn and yet understood by so many critics as inherently oppressive. Moreover, a contemporary analysis of nineteenth-century corset advertisements quickly dismantles prevailing perceptions of them as quaint quasi-erotic trivia, and recasts them as significant documents of social history from which attitudes toward sexuality in general, and female sexuality in particular, can be gleaned. Once seen this way, corset advertisements can be recognized as major forerunners to the sexual objectification of women in the public realm in the twentieth century.

By the 1880s few publications were without corset advertisements of some kind, and by the 1890s corset advertising saturated public reading space. Corsetry advertisements appeared in women's magazines as well as newspapers and journals designed for general consumption. They appeared too in smaller publications such as theatre programmes, dance programmes, trade union journals, and religious magazines. Interestingly corsets were, according to Frank Presbrey author of *The History and Development of Advertising*, the first item of apparel to be advertised in a systematic, businesslike fashion in the United States.[2] Corsetry advertisements of the mid- to late nineteenth century were marvels of technical skill. Their sometimes striking detail was, until the late 1870s, produced by fine line wood engravings.[3] Corsetry advertising was as financially rewarding in Britain as it was in North America. *Godey's Lady's Book and Magazine*, a nineteenth-century middle-class women's journal that regularly published corset advertisements, reported that twelve million corsets were sold in Britain in the early 1860s.[4]

Corset advertisements on both sides of the Atlantic drew from and were informed by a diverse range of nineteenth-century cultural vectors. The breadth of their creative licence was as breathtaking as their ubiquity. An astonishing range of cultural informants were often appropriated, fused, even bastardized in single advertisements for the garment. Amalgamations of Greek and Roman myths, along with references to biblical stories, sometimes simultaneously furnished the stuff of many corset advertisements. Many of these eclectic intertextual cultural fusions were also notable for their mimicry of the traditions of high art. Others reflected more prosaic earthly matters as they tapped into and exploited social advances that were effected by or affected women. The rising nineteenth-century feminine interest in sport, discussed in Chapter 6, was echoed in corset advertisements that depicted women on horseback,[5] rowing and playing tennis. Even trends in sexology were shadowed in corsetry advertisements. Advertisements published in the mid-century hinted, spoke of and at times even illustrated supposed female coquetry, but by the late century corset advertisements, particularly those directed toward the young carnally experienced matron, commonly evinced strong sexual narratives in which female protagonists demonstrated autonomous, powerful sexual subjectivities.

The increasing involvement of women in tertiary education was, to a far lesser extent than issues of sexuality, also reflected in corset advertisements. Y&N corset advertisements published in the *Illustrated London News* (and elsewhere) in the 1890s were clearly designed to appeal to the New Woman who was (at least when perceived by corset manufacturers) deemed to be more interested in her education than in her figure. The academic signifier in these advertisements was a pair of glasses, a cheap and effective device still used by advertisers today to indicate the presence of a functioning intellect. Y&N advertisements usually featured a line drawing of a corseted young woman whose bespectacled face turned in contemplative profile not to a nearby mirror, as many corseted advertising subjects were wont to do, but rather into the distance toward her presumably academic career.[6] (see fig.73) Curiously, the Y&N corset company was the only one that chose to show its corseted subjects wearing glasses. Perhaps this was because by the 1890s educated women were increasingly abandoning constrictive undergarments (see Figure 57). Nevertheless by the late 1890s, corset advertisements were devised to appeal to every coexistent, even competing, femininity produced by the Victorians. The New Woman, the balletic or clumsy adolescent, the dainty housewife, and the haughty Gibson Girl could each see herself in advertisements designed to both effect and reflect these stereotypes.

Dr Warner's corset firm revolutionized corset advertising in both Britain and North America. Until Warner's 'revolution', corsetry advertisements typically consisted of small discreet advertisements that were occasionally illustrated by simple line drawings of the garment. As technological skills in the printing industry were developed, corset advertisements grew more sophisticated.[7] Warner's firm appears to have been the first corset company to understand that the public glamorization of the garment and its occupant would increase sales. They first advertised their garments in the 1870s in both religious and secular magazines. Early advertisements consisted of a diagram of two women, one in a rusted corset and another in Warner's rustless garment. (The metal infrastructure of corsets made them difficult to wash and dry without being spoiled by rust marks.) Warner also appears to have pioneered the 'panoramic' type of advertisement. By 1888 full-page advertisements depicting stylish fully clothed women in smart drawing rooms discussing the merits of Warner's corsetry were widely published in magazines across North America. Smaller

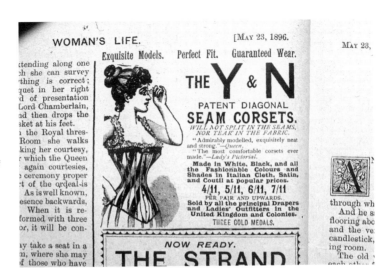

Figure 57
Y&N's corseted 'New Woman' pondering a more intellectual if not more comfortable future with her corset firmly in situ. See *Woman's Life*, 1899.

advertisements on the covers of various North American magazines
soon followed. A four-page advertisement for Warner's corsetry in a
standard magazine was the earliest use of so much space by one advertiser
in any one periodical. Several American corsetry firms quickly followed
Warner's advertising initiative. R&G corsets began buying quarter pages
in women's magazines such as the widely read *Ladies Home Journal*,
eventually taking the coveted back page of that magazine at the cost of
$4000 per insertion.[8]

Corsetry advertisements were tailored to appeal to distinct groups
of women. Tasteful constraints evident in advertisements published in
feminist and suffrage journals meant that their advertisements often
differed markedly from mainstream publications. American feminist
journals such as *The New Century for Women* (published by the women's
committee of the Women's Building at the Philadelphia Centennial Exhibition), along with other pro-feminist magazines such as *The Woman's
Journal*, *The Woman's Standard*, *The Woman's Tribune*, and *Daughters
of America*, all regularly published corset advertisements, but these were
usually of 'rational' or 'reform garments'. These were less constrictive
than standard corsets.[9] However, this was not always the case. Advertisements placed by Warner's for their Coraline corsets were an exception.
The Coraline was boned, busked, and closed by back lacing and a seam
of metal fasteners in front. Warner's advertised in several suffrage journals
but used the least constrictive garments from its range in these advertisements. Accompanying text in these advertisements emphasized the
supposed health benefits of the garment. Similarly, *Daughters of America*
published advertisements for Duplex corsetry that was far from rational
in design. However, the strength of the garments was the predominant
sales theme, rather than their beauty or their power to enhance the figure.

Whether the advertised corsets were of rational or standard design,
most corsetry advertisements published by feminist magazines were
characterized by their 'matter of fact' descriptions and wholesome, even
progressive illustrations. Advertisements for the Delsarte corset waist and
Ferris Good Sense corsets are examples of this type of advertising. Both
used advertisements that showed women in active pursuit of exercise or
outdoor adventure. The simple sketches favoured by the Delsarte corset
company showed subjects enjoying a range of callisthenic exercises which
were possible while wearing the Delsarte corset waist. Arguably the most
convincing of these advertisements consisted of an illustration of a young
woman gracefully bending to touch her unshod toes, a feat that would
have been physically impossible in standard corsetry.[10]

Advertisements placed by the Ferris Good Sense corset company
similarly portrayed women as active, energetic subjects. Ferris's corsetry
advertisements of the 1890s were specifically designed to appeal to 'young
ladies who r[o]de bicycles, play[ed] tennis, or attend[ed] gymnasium'.
Line drawings that accompanied the text showed competent women
exuberantly participating in these and other outdoor pursuits, such as

horse riding and boating.[11] These activities could, of course, only be enjoyed in the outdoor and masculine public sphere. This is a significant aspect of these advertisements, for corset advertisements published in the mainstream press usually featured women in idealized indoor settings, rather than in active outdoor activities (see Figure 58). In other words, advertisements published in mainstream newspapers and journals persistently reflected traditional gender-related assumptions and values[12] and in doing so reinforced rather than altered or questioned these assumptions about women's rightful sphere.[13]

Mid- to late nineteenth-century corsetry advertising was given considerable impetus in both Britain and North America by a succession of industrial and manufacturing exhibitions. While these events primarily specialized in demonstrating major technological advances and the agricultural wealth of the nations involved, they also provided a venue for showcasing less spectacular products of those nations, including corsetry manufactured by both small and large firms. Unfortunately, advertising material published by corset companies for these exhibitions has proved almost impossible to locate. However, a surviving flier distributed by Madame Griswolde's corset company at the Philadelphia exhibition in 1876 indicates that her firm, at least, used simple advertising techniques that relied on little more than an illustration of a streamlined but very

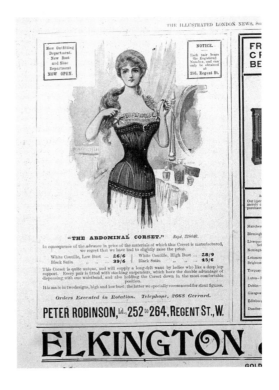

Figure 58
The Domen clad woman in the privacy of her bedroom in *Woman's Life*, 1899.

curvaceous corseted torso.[14] This method was also favoured by English corsetiere George Roberts, in advertising material for his garments, published for London's Great Exhibition.

Both Madame Griswolde's flier and George Roberts's illustration were actually typical of the most enduring nineteenth-century method of depicting the corseted body. As mentioned earlier, initial (illustrated) corsetry advertisements featured simple line drawings of an isolated and supposedly uninhabited corset. While this method of advertising corsetry seems innocuous and unremarkable by standards of the late twentieth century, the early illustrated corset advertisements probably transgressed the boundaries of Victorian standards of (public) decency. While no written record of the public response to the early advertising of this most intimate garment survives, it is apparent that corset advertisements differed significantly, even radically, from other advertisements of intimate female apparel. A comparison of advertisements featuring drawers (or bloomers as they were sometimes called) with corset advertisements reveals these dramatic differences. Drawers were generally advertised far more discreetly than corsetry. Drawers were never depicted as if on an actual body. They were inevitably shown as flat two-dimensional garments. Furthermore, they were usually shown folded in order to conceal the crotch from view, which fashion historians assert was a measure employed to avoid any direct visual reference to the genitals.[15]

Corsetry advertisements in comparison to underpants advertisements were positively titillating, for they revealed – even accentuated – every curve of the female torso, and in doing so inevitably hinted at sexual availability. Corsets, unlike underpants, were never illustrated as folded up, nor were they ever represented as empty, two-dimensional garments. An imaginary but fulsome torso was always apparent within, fleshing them out (see Figures 59 and 60). From the late 1870s corsetry advertisements often had an entire, or at least 'upper half', female figure sketched into the garment. Despite the popular inclusion of a figure in many of the later advertisements, the invisibly embodied depiction of the garment was never really displaced; and the curiously embodied yet unembodied torso remained a staple image within the genre until early in the twentieth century. Numerous corset manufacturers used both the physically inhabited and supposedly physically uninhabited garment simultaneously in their advertisements (see Figure 61).

By the 1880s, corset advertisements in Britain and North America were frequently characterized by far more elaborate diagrams. Entire pictorial narratives became popular, in which women and their corsets were portrayed enacting a range of intimate female experiences. For the feminist historian, these advertisements initially appear as tantalizing visual evidence of what Carroll Smith-Rosenberg has described as and termed a 'female world of love and ritual'. Numerous corset advertisements appeared as sympathetic, and sometimes even bold expressions of femininity and even of specifically female desire. The protagonists were

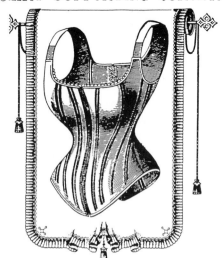

Figure 59
George Roberts' rigid and
somewhat scientifically
calculated corset which
paradoxically enclosed an
invisible but bulging torso.

Figure 60
The empty yet fully embodied
diagram of Madame Griswold's
Skirt Supporting Corset.

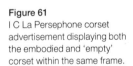

Figure 61
I C La Persephone corset
advertisement displaying both
the embodied and 'empty'
corset within the same frame.

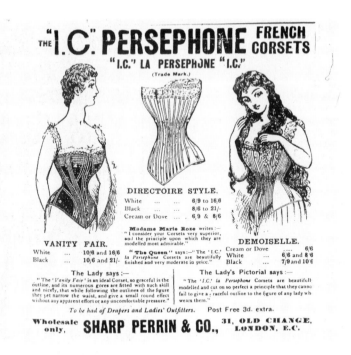

often shown engaged in conversations and actions that outwardly had little or nothing to do with men. (see fig.79) At first glance, corset advertisements could easily be read as expressions of an (almost) 'separatist' trope within nineteenth-century advertising. They featured only women and girls; rarely were men ever actually present in them.

The images of femininity portrayed in these advertisements were diverse and sometimes curiously touching. Women and girls of all ages were represented. Illustrations of sisterly scenarios in which young women appeared to be earnestly discussing matters of the corset and similarly confidential matters were used to increase sales of garments designed for teenagers and young women, while depictions of mother/daughter 'bonding' were frequently commissioned in advertisements for juvenile corsetry. Advertisements directed towards young adult women and early middle-aged matrons were similarly characterized by their privileged glimpse into the private realm of women. Several advertisements featured cosy scenes of women enjoying afternoon visits. This spectatorial aspect was further escalated by the dramatic sexualization of the subjects depicted in advertisements of the late 1890s (see Figure 62).

Whether the corseted advertised subjects were situated in the bedroom, the parlour, or on those rare occasions out of doors, all appeared to be successful in their mission to achieve popularity, prestige and sexual desirability. Indeed, the corseted subjects were often depicted as pleasing

Figure 62
Whitely corsets were costly, luxurious and richly coloured. Corsets of sky blue, maize, pink and mauve-coloured brocades featuring silk floral designs were worn under evening wear. These garments were favoured by women who were presumably aware of the garment's ability to charm and not simply to support.

themselves as much as others in this quest. Moreover, while these advertisements appeared in a wide range of publications that were written for male as well as female readers, each advertisement presumed, at least on first consideration, a female rather than a male gaze. However, as film critic Barbara Creed has warned, the 'field of visions is full of traps' and the 'erotics of spectatorship' and its analysis are perilous.[16] For while the corset advertisements appeared to speak of the feminine, to speak from – and confidently about – a particular femininity and even of a female sexual specificity, it must be remembered that men devised these advertisements to promote corset sales to women. This means that any yearning to read corset advertisements as visual affirmations of female sexuality, or as an optic into Smith-Rosenberg's nineteenth-century female world of love and ritual, must be tempered with the notion that they might also be read more sceptically as evidence of male wish fulfilment. Indeed, as Annette Kuhn asserts, the construction and subsequent commodification of female sexuality in both advertising and pornography has been facilitated by the masculine hegemony of female representation. As a consequence, says Kuhn, representations of women 'inevitably bear the traces of capitalist and patriarchal social relations in which they are produced, exchanged and consumed'.[17]

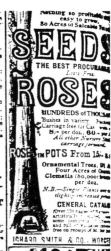

Laura Mulvey's work (which focuses on representations of the twentieth-century female body) is also extremely useful when examining nineteenth-century representations of the corseted woman.[18] As Mulvey has pointed out, men are usually the authors of female representation and women are more often merely the scribes. This was as true of the nineteenth-century world of advertising as it has been of the twentieth. In practice, the nineteenth-century male hegemony of popular representation of women meant that it was men who usually constructed and therefore controlled depictions of female sexuality. Further to this, as Mulvey points out, male constructions of the sexual female serve masculine desires and fantasies, and it is not surprising under these conditions that sexualized representations of women were, and still are, often publicly positioned to elicit, allow, and encourage male voyeurism.

Many nineteenth-century corset advertisements were frankly sexual. Most were informed by male rather than female expectations and understandings (or misunderstandings) of the female body and its desires. Corset advertisements were, too, very public property. A surviving pamphlet produced by George Roberts's Stay Warehouse in London in 1851 is a particularly good example of both the prevailing male hegemony of female representation in the nineteenth century, and the tendency of advertisers to make the semi-naked female form visually accessible to men as much as to women.[19] Roberts's catalogue included a large illustration of his three-storey 'stay warehouse' in which the massive plate glass windows on the ground floor were filled from ceiling to floor with countless corsets. These were pinned to the far wall of the display in rows, on body forms placed on shelves attached to the front of the wall, while still more corsets were laid flat on the shelves below. The effect was dazzling, even by current advertising standards. Every inch of the display was crowded with corsets shown at various angles.

Corset advertisements published in magazines and journals were at times even more blatantly positioned to catch the male public eye. Advertisements for garments produced by the Y&N corset company were regularly published between advertisements for tobacco, shirt studs, cigars and other 'masculine' as well as feminine commodities.[20] Advertisers may have thought men might persuade wives and lovers to purchase Y&N corsets because of this. For whatever reason, the placement of corset advertisements in between other advertisements directed at men allowed, even invited, male readers to examine corseted models with ease and without detection (see Figure 63). On occasion, the corset itself was used to sell other goods manufactured for male usage. Old Gold cigarettes used an image of the corset in place of the words 'of course it is' in its slogan 'Of (corset) is a treat to smoke Old Gold cigarettes'.[21] The diagram of the corset in this advertisement was marginally bigger than the picture of the cigarettes. Its comparatively larger size indicates the importance of the garment in popular culture. The advertisement's use of the corset also indicates the popular commodification of women's bodies in

Figure 63
Corsetry sometimes appeared somewhat incongruously between items designed for male consumption, enjoyment and purchase. See *Today Magazine*, 1896.

Figure 64
This Old Gold corsetry
advertisement, published in the
Illustrated London News 1899,
took up half a quarto size
page.

Victorian society, and flags an underlying if unacknowledged attitude, being that women's bodies were considered as accessible and as interchangeable as other purchased pleasures, such as cigarettes (see Figure 64).

Curiously, the very advertisements ostensibly designed to appeal to and encourage heterosexual subjectivities may also have appealed to some lesbians[22] in quite a different way. A number of corset advertisements featured two corseted women at a time and these women were often depicted touching each other, with either an arm about the waist, or with one woman's hand placed on her companion's hip. Women, whether lesbian or heterosexual do, of course (as the preponderance of women's fashion magazines in both the nineteenth and twentieth centuries indicate), enjoy consuming representations of other women. Diana Fuss, in 'Fashion and the Homospectatorial Look', has gone so far as to claim that the fashion industry and the images it produces provide a 'socially sanctioned structure in which women are encouraged to consume, in voyeuristic [and in some cases vampiristic] fashion', images of other women.[23] Images of women, particularly in fashion rather than make-up advertisements, says Fuss 'harness . . . taboo (homosexual) desire', albeit in constant pursuit of pre-oedipal nostalgia.[24] Psychoanalytic explanations aside, it is quite feasible that nineteenth-century female viewers, both lesbian and heterosexual, may have identified with the women depicted in corsetry advertisements in a straightforward quest to emulate them. Others may have emotionally aligned themselves with these images, seeing in them a reflection of the close and affectionate same-sex ties, or same-sex longings.

Other women, lesbian or not, may have sexually objectified the subjects within these advertisements. These women may have reversed and appropriated the gaze (as defined by Mulvey) 'for their own pleasure' (see Figures 65 and 66).[25]

While John Fiske is notable for his discussion of the polysemic potential of television commercials, his work is also very useful when discussing the potential for lesbian readings of nineteenth-century corset advertisements. Fiske convincingly argues that television speaks meaningfully to a 'cross cultural audience and at the same time take[s] into account divisions within particular societies'.[26] Nineteenth-century corsetry advertisements may also have had this kind of power and appeal. Of course, most Victorian women probably accepted the dominant values portrayed in corset advertisements. That is, they did not challenge the 'preferred [heterosexual] meaning' or the promises of [heterosexual] romance proffered by the manufacturers and advertisers. However, other women who identified (either consciously or unconsciously) as lesbian may have 'read' these advertisements quite differently. Few culturally sanctioned representations of women circulated in 'decent' middle-class Victorian society that validated lesbian relationships. As a result, lesbians may have employed what Fiske has called an 'oppositional' readings of

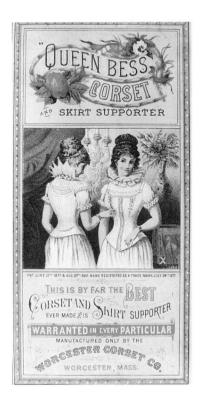

Figure 65

The subjects of this Queen Bess advertisement may have been perceived quite differently by lesbians and heterosexual women.

Figure 66
According to the
accompanying text a lady
could 'lie down with ease'
wearing Dr Warner's corsets.
Women in these and similar
advertisements often displayed
a physical intimacy between
women and in doing so offered
potential for lesbian readings.

corsetry advertisements, ascribing to the illustrations of embracing, semi-clad, corseted women a pleasing, even reassuring re-inscription of same-sex affection and love.

The flood of corset imagery, though potentially provocative to the Victorian middle-class sensibility, found acceptability because it was part of a larger artistic tradition of representing women. Little academic analysis exists which looks at the depiction of women in nineteenth-century advertising, but fortunately several academics and art historians have examined the depiction of women in nineteenth-century art. Feminist incursions into art history that dwell on the representation of the female nude in the nineteenth century have established that Woman was routinely objectified for the pleasure of the male spectator as a 'consumable object of desire'.[27] Despite the 'lowbrow' status of corset advertisements in comparison with high-art depictions of the unclad female form, it is clear that both types of representation were informed and infused by identical values and referents. Indeed, because of their fundamental shared similarities, corset advertisements should be viewed as a trope within the larger artistic canon that encompassed the female nude in art, architecture and sculpture. By the nineteenth century, the female 'nude' had become a genre within high art, and her depiction was commonly used to represent ideals of art, beauty and justice. Art schools, salons, and art critics encouraged artistic conventions that assisted in the creation of nudes specifically contrived not to offend Victorian standards of decency. The nude of Victorian high art was usually part of a 'classical' study, already held in esteem in the public imagination; and to increase her acceptance and justify her exposure, any realistic features such as pubic hair were scrupulously avoided.[28]

The female nude's popularity and public acceptability, whether it appeared in high art or advertising, derived much of its legitimacy from the craze for Greek statuary[29] which swept Britain and North America in the early part of the century. The importation of the Elgin marbles to Britain in 1807 by Thomas Bruce (the seventh Earl of Elgin) created enormous interest in Greek culture. This manifested in a short-lived trend in fashion styles and a far more enduring admiration of Greek architecture. The wide interest in antiquity was increased and further expanded by the discovery of the Venus de Milo, which was universally regarded as a great masterpiece. The consequent acceptance of Greco-Roman statuary made it impossible for concerted campaigns against nudity (whether in art or advertising) to succeed. Artists and advertisers alike quickly understood that the nude or semi-nude female body was invested with integrity when it was presented in either a religious, classical or mythological setting.[30] The conventions that dictated appropriate representation of the nude female body in high art (no matter how spurious or flimsy the connections) were just as quickly co-opted in advertising to legitimize depictions of the semi-naked corseted female body.

Sewell's Rival Corset company capitalized on Greco-Roman antiquities to sell its garments. Sewell's advertisements, published in the 1870s,[31] featured an image of a stony, corseted Venus de Milo, whose shapely hips were thinly veiled by classical drapery (see Figures 67 and 68). Madam Caplin, Britain's foremost corsetière at mid-century, also used classical images to advertise her wares. Both mature and juvenile subjects were depicted as armless corseted statues in her text *Health and Beauty* (see Figure 69). This kind of representation must have infuriated dress reformers, who argued throughout the century for a return of Greco-Roman fashion styles that did *not* cinch the waist or require corsets for effect.

The plundering of classical icons, myths and legends in corset advertisements succeeded because Greco/Roman myths and legends were understood, admired and widely circulated in the popular culture of middle-class Victorians. The widespread inclusion of serious studies of Greek and Latin in public and private schools after 1800 made for a familiarity with the pantheon of gods and goddesses which proliferated in Victorian art and advertising.[32] The Corset Sylphide, manufactured by the Robinson corset company,[33] and Sharp and Perrin's best-selling corset, the I.C. Persephone (I see Persephone)[34] were both named after goddess figures, and their naming was no doubt intended to evoke the

Figure 67
Sewell's Rival corset advertisement featuring the whalebone-clad Venus de Milo was published in Sylvia's Home journal, 1884.

Figure 68
Drew's inimitable A La Grecque corsets capitalized on the Victorian fascination with Greco-Roman culture. Advertising like this must have infuriated dress reformers who were arguing for the abandonment of corsets and the adoption of loose, comfortable dress based on authentic Greek and Roman costume.

awe and glamour a classical forebear might bring. On occasion, the corseted women of these illustrations were actually depicted as glamorous mythological creatures. Y&N's diagonal seam corset advertisements often featured an intricate depiction of a corseted siren whose curvaceous body, astonishing hair and scaly mermaid hips emerged from the sea triumphantly before a halo of radiant light (see Figure 70). The Weingarten Brothers similarly used cultural metaphors to sell their garments. Their Erect Form corsetry advertisements,[35] published at the turn of the twentieth century, featured three marmoreal beauties reminiscent of a gathering of muses who were draped and partially veiled by a transparent, gauzy swathe (see Figure 71).

Figure 69
This marmoreal corseted bust advertised Roxy Caplin's corsetry in *Health and Beauty*, published in 1866.

While Weingarten's advertisements appear innocuous enough, indeed possibly more modest than other depictions of the corseted body, they can also be read as highly exploitative representations of femininity. As Ludmilla Jordanova has convincingly argued, any public 'unveiling' of women can be read as an expression of 'masculine desire allied to fantasies of ownership and display'. Unveiling women publicly is not just a prelude to sexual possession, says Jordanova, but an 'encounter with [the] risks and dangers . . . excitements and pleasures' associated with women's

Figure 70
Y and N's late century appropriation and domestication of myths and legends resulted in high kitsch advertisements of this kind.

WEINGARTEN BROS
MERICA'S Leading Rich Form & La Vida CORSET!

Figure 71
Weingarten's swathed beauties demonstrated a range of glances, and corsetry, in *Ladies Field*, 1902.

bodies. Jordanova's arguments, though concerned with images of women as representatives of scientific, legal or humanistic thought, can be applied equally well to corsetry advertisements. Indeed, even more than the 'classical' representations of women critiqued by Jordanova, the corseted representations of women were, because of the widely acknowledged sexual *puissance* of the garment, explicit reminders of the intimate 'excitements and pleasures' associated with women's bodies.[36]

By the latter decades of the century both art and advertising were richly sown with classical allegories and metaphors woven about women's bodies. Marina Warner's *Monuments and Maidens* has explained this abundance of female allegorical figures as the method by which women's bodies have historically facilitated the exchange of goods, ideas, and shared aspirations. The 'symbolic form of the female figure', says Warner, whether it manifests in quasi-realistic sculptures, or whether it appears as artistic renderings of abstract ideas, can be viewed as a 'tap root' which even today 'runs down deep in classical Christian culture'.[37] Warner's belief that the use of 'symbolic woman' can be seen as a 'tap root' directly connected to classical Christian culture (and deeply enmeshed with consumerism) is borne out in particular advertisements placed by Warner Brothers' corset firm in both British and North American magazines in the 1880s. Warner's advertisements were often characterized by curious amalgamations of both Christian and pagan referents. The Coraline Corset advertisements, placed by that firm from the 1880s to the end of the 1890s, were almost invariably accompanied by one or two cupid- or angel-like figures. Early advertisements featured two of these beings. One was usually winged and peeped from inside the garment above the breasts while another, devoid of wings, carried a star-tipped wand, and gazed admiringly at the waistline of the garment (see Figure 72).[38]

Figure 72
Warner's corset advertisement featuring the double cupids in *Harper's Bazaar*, 1881.

Figure 73
Warner's corset advertisement
with the single cupid elevated
to putti status, in the *Woman's
Journal*, 1889.

The figures within these widely circulated illustrations may have been recognized, metaphorically (or at very least subliminally) by the educated Victorian woman or man, as part of a mythic narrative in which the corset (fully but invisibly embodied) represented Venus, with her son (Eros) by her side as the cupid. The inclusion of cupid imagery within Warner's corsetry advertisements also operated to suggest that glances of love and admiration from more earthly suitors might follow once the corset was purchased and worn. By the late 1880s, Warner's had largely dispensed with the standing cupid figure in its advertisements, but retained the peeping winged cupid within the garment.[39] This lent a peculiarly religious aspect to the advertisement. The peeping cupid appeared to be disembodied, with only a pair of feathery wings to support its head. This figurative disembodiment of the cupid elevated the image from that of Greco/Roman myth and re-inscribed it as the Christian religious putti, being the winged, angel-headed spectre that hovers above members of the holy family in Renaissance religious art (see Figure 73).

By far the most elaborate amalgamation of the sacred and profane in corset advertising was an advertisement published by Warner's later in the century. In this advertisement several religious and mythological signifiers were juxtaposed to create an Edenic scene reminiscent of the Fall. (see fig.93) The advertisement was staged in a walled garden that could easily be read as the Garden of Eden. A small tousle-haired naked child or cupid, standing in a pair of adult boots, hosed the Warner's corset that was suspended in a tree. The corset in this advertisement can be seen to represent an apple, which in turn represents the body of the first woman and temptress, Eve. The child can be read as either a cupid or as Adam, the first man, while the hose is the obvious phallic device of Eve's impregnation. Interestingly, the inability of the hose to dampen, spoil or penetrate the corset might have been a whimsical device on the part of the advertisers to suggest that had Eve been adequately corseted by the brothers Warner, the human race might have been saved from the ignominious consequences of the Fall (see Figure 74). Less irony characterized advertisements for Madame Dean's Spinal Supporting corsets, which flagrantly appropriated religious iconography. In this advertisement, angels (reminiscent of renaissance depictions of seraphim) bore a corset above a cluster of adoring women, who raised their arms in *homage* to Madame Dean. A testimonial within the advertisement continued the religious fervour. Mrs M. Papes of Iowa revealed to readers that she had been an invalid for six years and, despite travelling extensively and fruitlessly in the pursuit of health, had never received 'as much benefit as [she] had in a few weeks wear of . . . Madame Dean's corset'. It was, she intoned, 'a *godsend*' (advertisement's italics) (see Figure 75).

Less whimsical and less religious by far, were advertisements for children's corsetry. (see figs.95-98) These were designed to appeal to mothers whose daughters ranged from three years old to mid-teens. These advertisements at first appear as glimpses into private moments of

Figure 74
The corset advertisement at its polysemic best, as apple, as Eve and as armour against the Fall.

mother-daughter bonding; however, mother-daughter bondage is probably a more accurate description of the rituals illustrated within these advertisements. In the Perfect Health corset advertisement, a small child who appears to be as young as three or four, admires her newly corseted, appropriately child-like figure in a small mirror held by her mother. Although the corset is of a rational, rather than standard design, and although the child's waist is not seriously constricted by the garment, the inference is that the child is learning an important lesson about her body, the lesson being that the child's body both requires and is enhanced by its new garment. The advertisement visually implies that the child has begun her life's commitment to corsetry, and that through judicious corseting she too will become as successful, as maternal, and as shapely as her mother. More sinister readings can also be divined in this maternal scene, for the advertisement is an instruction to both mothers and daughters regarding the application of the appropriate technology of female gender. Within the advertisement, mother is depicted as having fitted the garment to her daughter's body and as having transmitted the knowledge of its application to the child (see Figure 76 and 77).

The advertisement for Harness' Electric Corsets shown in Figure 77,[40] like all of this type which use mother/daughter vignettes or alternately

MADAME DEAN'S SPINAL SUPPORTING CORSETS.

They support the Spine, relieve the muscles of the back, **brace the shoulders** in a natural and easy manner, imparting **graceful carriage** to the wearer without discomfort, **expanding the chest,** thereby giving **full action to the lungs,** and **health** and **comfort** to the body. Take the place of the ORDINARY CORSET in every respect, and are made of fine Coutil, in the best manner, in various styles and sold by agents everywhere at **popular prices. Mrs. Wm. Papes,** Keota, Iowa, says:—I have been an invalid for six years, have travelled extensively for health, yet never received as much benefit as I have in a few weeks wear, of your MADAME, DEAN'S CORSET. I am gaining strength all the time, and could not do without it. It has proven to me a *godsend.*

FREE Our new book entitled: "Dress Reform for Ladies" with elegant wood engraving and Biography of **Worth,** the **King of Fashion,** Paris; also our **New Illustrated Catalogue** sent **free** to any address on receipt of two 2-cent stamps to pay postage and packing.

AGENTS WANTED for these celebrated Corsets. No experience required. Four orders per day give the agent **$150 monthly.** Our agents report from four to twenty sales daily. $6 to older sister/younger sister scenarios, literally and figuratively illustrate a punishing female ritual, not unlike the more frequently researched and critiqued rituals of femininity such as foot binding or clitoridectomy. Mary Daley refers to these kinds of culturally sanctioned ritual as 'Sado-Ritual Syndromes'.[41] The practice of corseting female children can be seen as another culturally specific kind of sado-ritual. Corsetry was, after all, instituted, like clitoridectomy and foot binding, to regulate and sculpt the female body into a shape that was widely admired by men. Rituals of female mutilation, whether involving the foot, the waist or the clitoris were (and are) instituted and perpetuated to appease male fantasies of power, ownership and sexual desire.

Typically, as in those other culturally specific sado-rituals such as foot binding and clitoridectomy, women were co-opted as active agents in enacting the practice of corseting female children. The female complicity in the sado-ritual of juvenile corseting is evident in corset advertising. Women are represented as the ritual's chief protagonists and as instrumental to its application to small female children. Of course, women in all countries that have practised, or continue to practise, sado-rituals on their own children do so because they understand only too well that these cruelties were (and are) necessary if female children were (and are) to become acceptable brides. In patriarchal cultures (be they Victorian Britain or nineteenth-century China) where marriage was the only realistic future for women, mothers had little choice but to mutilate their daughters in order that they survive. And, as in foot binding, clitoridectomy and juvenile corseting, men were able to deny any part of the blame or moral responsibility, because 'women did it to themselves'. This male abnegation is apparent in advertisements involving mother/daughter corsetry. All male responsibility for the act is erased, and mother is scape-goated. It is Mother in these advertisements, rather than a patriarchal society, who transmits the culture of the corset and implements the cruel but supposedly necessary technology of gender upon the child. Of course, this is not immediately apparent in juvenile corset advertisements. The enactment of this peculiarly Victorian and Western sado-ritual is veiled by safe domestic signifiers,

Figure 75
This late century Madame Dean corset advertisement demonstrates the wonderful skill of the engraver and (possibly) a gentle self-parodying and peculiarly Victorian humour.

Figure 76
Both advertisements illustrate mother's role in the sado-ritual of Victorian children's corsetry. Note the use of household images in these advertisements (such as the potted aspidistra) which help normalize juvenile corsetry as appropriately domestic, middle-class and healthy.

Figure 77
Both advertisements illustrate
mother's role in the sado-ritual
of Victorian children's corsetry.
Note the use of household
images in these
advertisements (such as the
potted aspidistra) which help
normalize juvenile corsetry as
appropriately domestic,
middle-class and healthy.

such as the potted aspidistra, or the familiar array of feminine accoutrements upon the dressing table.[42]

Other advertisements for children's corsetry were more obviously
sexually loaded. The origins of Figure 78 are unclear. This advertisement
has not been cited at any other source than its secondary point of publication, being Cecil St Laurent's text, *The History of Ladies' Underwear*.
This may suggest that the image was not an advertisement but a pornographic representation. The ambivalence of the origin of this image does
not undermine its value, but rather, adds weight to the notion that corsetry
was understood to sexualize female children. The image contains elements
common to both pornography and advertising and operates quite
convincingly within both genres. It features seven female children and
two adult maids who adjust the children's corsetry. The youngest corseted
child is a toddler of about one or two, the oldest a teenager. Every child
from the youngest to the oldest wears a corset. This image, whether it is
a 'legitimate' advertisement or whether it is drawn from the lexicon of
the pornographer, is an indisputable graphic illustration of what Abigail
Solomon-Godeau has described as 'the power of patriarchy to register
its desire within the designated space of the constructed feminine'.[43]
That is, the women and children depicted within this image are socially

Figure 78
The inclusion of the *armoire* in the background of this illustration suggests it is of French origin. The multiple views of the juvenile corseted body and the provocative pose taken by the figure right of centre suggest that this image is cheap child pornography. I have been unable to locate any details regarding its original publication.

constructed obedient subjects, whose psychic, and even physical construction, serves and reflects patriarchal desire. The image has not been devised for the appreciation of female consumers, although it is an advertisement (or image) that features garments of interest to, and worn exclusively by, women and girls. Instead, the image serves masculine desires and fantasies, specifically those of the voyeur and the paedophile. The inclusion of the mirror, along with the positioning of the subjects within the illustration, allowed for multiple aspects of the children's bodies to be displayed for the delectation of the voyeur. The paedophile was similarly served by this image. Whether the paedophile's/voyeur's predilection was for the infant, the toddler, the pre-pubescent child or the young teen, his optic desires at least, could be satisfied.

Most nineteenth-century corset advertisements were not as blatantly sexual or perverse as that described above. Nevertheless, nineteenth-century corset advertisements can still be read as a critical moment in advertising sexism. Prior to their publication, women were rarely depicted in the press (at least outside of the pornographic canon) as naked or semi-naked subjects. The public sexualization of the female body in corsetry advertising was, as explained earlier, a response to and reflection of a range of cultural imperatives that brought female nudity from the private into the public realm. While the importation of the Elgin marbles can be seen to have initially heralded a legitimization of female nudity, sexologic theories that emerged later in the century can be seen to have been similarly influential. Arguably the most significant intellectual imperative regarding the public sexualization of women in art and advertising was the renaissance in the belief of female sexuality.[44]

By the 1890s, the female body and its carnal desires were the focus of theoretical attention that was reflected in Victorian art and in advertising. The influence of sexological thought rapidly coloured a range of 'popular' depictions of women, according to art historian Bram Dijkstra. Dijkstra has demonstrated that autoerotic themes that featured women flourished in late Victorian art, and he maintains that the emergence of female eroticism in art had its origin in the rediscovery of female sexuality. This artistic and theoretical rediscovery was, as Dijkstra points out, actuated by sensational claims by sexologists of the 1870s and 1880s regarding women's supposed autoerotic tendencies.[45] Certainly, by the 1880s William Acton's mid-century assumption that female sexuality was negligible or non-existent was largely repudiated and by the 1890s sexologists more or less agreed that women and even female children were sexual beings. Sexologic theory had, thanks to the popular press and increased literacy of the working classes[46] extended beyond the elite sexologic intelligentsia to reach and influence a large, literate and enthusiastic audience. Corsetry advertisements, though devoid of any informative text regarding the actuality of female sexual expression, can nevertheless be read as a reflection in this shift of consciousness regarding female sexuality.

A survey of advertisements placed by a range of corset companies in both Britain and North America between 1850 and 1900 quickly reveals the increasing sexualization of corseted subjects, particularly toward the end of the century. Depictions of corseted women earlier in the century were 'comely' rather than sexually alluring. These early representations showed their subjects in 'negative' space (by this I mean a depiction without any contextualizing background) or within 'neutral' domestic space such as a parlour or beside a curtain in a room other than a bedroom. Women in late-century advertising were far more sexualized. This sexualization manifested in two distinct and yet related ways. While the corseted subjects of the late century were not actually wearing less than they had in earlier advertisements, their bodies were drawn in far more provocative positions (see Figure 79). As the century closed, advertisements for standard corsetry (which initially positioned women either in the domestic sphere or in 'negative space') removed their subjects from the drawing room or parlour, and situated them in that heartland of the private sphere, the bedroom.

The actual physical positioning of the diagrammatic corseted women in these advertisements (in comparison to representations of corseted women earlier in the century) increased and accentuated their new sexually charged representation. *Fin-de-siècle* corseted subjects frequently appeared immobilized in front of a bedroom mirror, frozen in a kind intimate narcissistic reverie (see Figure 80). The tendency of advertisers to position the subject's limbs in a provocative manner (which will be discussed in

Figure 79
This PD corset illustration of the haughty, sexually provocative Gibson Girl lookalike was published in *Woman's Sphere*, 1904.

Figure 80
Numerous late-century advertisements featured women gazing endlessly into mirrors, or positioned their subjects beside bedroom mirrors waiting for approval. See *Illustrated London News*, 1899.

detail a little later) combined with the location of the subject in the bedroom made them undeniably sexual. Paradoxically, the intrinsically intimate, private, image of the corseted woman inhabited a visual and intellectual space that was very public. Indeed, corset advertisements, possibly more than any other kind of advertisements, took the most intimate signs of feminine domesticity and sexuality and 'delivered them into the public realm' for general consumption.[47]

So pronounced was the sexualization of some corseted subjects that there was little difference between corset advertisements and popular pornography of the era. Pornographic imagery, whether contemporary or Victorian, has its own distinct set of characteristics that have been located and discussed by several late twentieth-century historians and cultural studies theorists. These characteristics are also evident in many Victorian and Edwardian corset advertisements (see Figures 81 and 82).

Figure 81
Late Victorian erotic postcard. Note the position of the arms in both this figure and Figure 82. Raising the arms above and behind the head levers the breasts into an upright position favoured by pornographers and advertisers alike.

Figure 82
Late Victorian erotic postcard.

A comparison of corsetry advertisements and one or two 'typical' erotic postcards of the 1890s might suffice for argument's sake, as an example of the similarity between corsetry advertisements and Victorian pornography. In both 'saucy' postcards the corseted women's hair is 'down'. This indicates to the viewer that we see the women secretly, in a private moment, for middle-class adult women wore their hair 'up' outside of the bedroom. It is important to note the placement of the women's heads and limbs in these illustrations. The arms of the postcard models are held above and behind the subjects' heads. Kuhn asserts that this position (which is a staple of the pornographic repertoire of poses) speaks frankly of a contrived sexual availability. The positioning of women's arms this way produces the apparently irresistible effect of situating them as physically vulnerable and sexually provocative. Positioning the arms behind the head is also a device used repeatedly in corsetry advertisements.

The gaze of the subject, whether she is a porn star or the subject of a 'legitimate' advertisement is (according to theorists Kuhn and Mulvey) just as important as the positioning of the model's limbs, and is enmeshed with the gaze of the viewer or spectator. The models in the postcards gaze at the camera specifically to encourage, rather than challenge, the viewer or spectator. The previously cited Weingarten corsetry advertisement (Figure 71) featuring three women (with its allusions to classical drapery that help validate it as art rather than pornography) demonstrates a range of glances that are common to the pornographic canon. Using the techniques of analysis posited by Mulvey and Kuhn, the 'gazes' can be interpreted in particular ways. As Mulvey explains,

> in their traditional exhibitionist way women are simultaneously looked at and displayed, with their appearance coded for a strong visual and erotic impact so that they can be said to connote *to-be-looked-at-ness*.[48]

The corseted subjects within the Weingarten advertisement illustrate both exhibitionism and an appearance coded for erotic impact. Their semi-nude state alone indicates this. Each of the subjects within this advertisement can be seen to conform to Mulvey's useful concept that describes the depiction of women this way as being in a state of *to-be-looked-at-ness*. The woman on the right of the illustration invites the spectator with the direct look of the exhibitionist. The central figure has her eyes downcast, an attitude which can be read as a surveillance of her own body for others, while her corseted companion averts her eyes. The gesture of the averted gaze, according to Kuhn, licenses the spectator to look at the woman's body without guilt; allowing him or her to enjoy the subject unobserved, which adds to the vicarious thrill of voyeurism.[49] The combination of the gaze, the placement of the limbs and the inclusion of 'classical drapery'[50] all blur the distinction between advertisement and pornography within this image. This blurring of signifiers and boundaries recurred over and over again in corset advertisements.

The fetching *déshabillé* evident in the advertisement for Prima Donna Corsetry similarly encapsulated several of the devices of the Victorian pornographer that also manifest in the saucy postcards (see Figure 83). In the advertisement the subject's hair is 'down', indicating a private glimpse into her boudoir. Her body is exposed and her arms are held invitingly behind her head. Her eyes and smiling countenance give frank permission for the viewer to gaze unchallenged, and her body is positioned very much like the body of the *demimondaine*. The role of corset advertising in the democratization of the semi-pornographic representation of

Figure 83
This SL Prima Donna Corset advertisement, with its corseted subject in a stereotypical erotic pose, was published in the *Church of England Messenger*, 1897.

women was practically complete by the 1890s. By this time there was very little difference between images of women in corset advertisements and the corseted women of 'naughty' postcards. The Prima Donna corset illustration that entertained so many of the hallmarks of pornography, was widely published. This one was found in the *Church of England Messenger.*[51]

While nineteenth-century corset advertisements of this kind can be seen to be the forerunners of mainstream twentieth-century sexism (culminating perhaps in the 'page three' girls in trashy newspapers), other Victorian corsetry advertisements can be seen to have foreshadowed much more violent and distressing images of women that surface in such contemporary films as *Boxing Helena*, a film in which the plot turns upon the objectification, sexual fetishization and eventual dismemberment of a captive woman. This film is cited as an extreme example of objectification taken to its most appalling conclusion. It is not my intention to discuss any details of this film here. It is cited because it calls forward the parallels between women 'objectified in pieces' in films of the twentieth century, and the way the objectification of dismembered women's bodies was figuratively articulated in mid- to late nineteenth-century corset advertisements.

Corsetry advertisements that were without a visible body can and should be read as being as sinister as movies such as *Boxing Helena*. That is, advertisements that used illustrations of empty corsets, but which clearly contained a woman's torso to 'fill them out', operated – at a sub rosa level at least – as violent representations of female dismemberment. It is very apparent, particularly in Warner's allegorically charged advertisement set in the Garden of Eden, or in the advertisement for Madame Griswold's curvaceous carapace, that even isolated, seemingly uninhabited corsets stood for, indeed became, an ideal body to be admired or envied. Complex synechdochal processes were at work here in which corsetry advertisements that featured an illustration of an 'uninhabited' corset simultaneously came to stand for the part it represented, as an emblem for an entire woman, and finally even as an emblem of the entire female sex. In other words, corsetry advertisements that used the uninhabited yet embodied corset constructed their own system of knowledge in which the corset, even when devoid of any visible torso, was synchronously an illustration of itself and a representation of the female torso it contained, as well as a symbol of the entire woman, and in the case of Warner's Edenically situated corset, of womankind.

The polysemy inherent in these images does not make them essentially morbid or distressing. The problematic aspect of these advertisements is their proclivity to bisect the female body. Representations of the partial or bisected body have been the fruitful subject of discussion by Helen Posner and Thomas Laqueur. Both agree that the body is an instrument par excellence in the exploration and assertion of broad-ranging and individual cultural values. In his work on medical representations of the body, Laqueur has maintained that representations of the body can be read as texts that reflect the specific cultural values held by the society in which its representations are produced. The importance of the body as a site of cultural values was similarly recognized by Posner. Their interrogation of images of the body, particularly of contemporary images of the bisected body, form the basis of a remarkable catalogue documenting a major exhibition of modern art and sculpture held in Cambridge in 1993, titled *Corporal Politics*. While the catalogue and the contents of the exhibition did not mention corsetry and its role in literally and figuratively fracturing the nineteenth-century female body, both Posner's and Laqueur's observations can be usefully appropriated to unpack a range of unexplored and somewhat dark issues regarding the representation of women in Victorian corsetry advertisements.

Laqueur[52] and Posner prefaced the catalogue of this exhibition with essays that independently discussed both the concept and the result of the representational fragmenting of the human body.[53] The art work under discussion in the catalogue included representations of the human body invaded by HIV Aids virus, the mental and physical result of amputation, and the body deformed by illness and accident. Laqueur noted reasonably that the body has provided one of the greatest political arenas of all time, and although civilization had historically hidden the body from view, it had at the same time managed to obsessively explore the hidden body. One method of exploration, explained both authors, was to examine the body in individual pieces. I would argue that Victorian corsetry advertisements, particularly those which were devoid of any visible physical body, were used this way. That is, corsetry advertisements functioned as a disguised (or at least oblique) but culturally sanctioned avenue of examining areas of the female body that were generally withheld from view. Corset advertisements allowed the female body to be obsessively and secretly examined, paradoxically in a very public way. Illustrations of the corset, particularly when the garment appeared as an isolated uninhabited image, were often meticulously drawn. While sometimes drawn to reveal only a direct frontal view, many other advertisements revealed a range of perspectives, so that those areas not immediately visible to the eye were revealed to the viewer. Commonplace were the advertisements in which several different perspectives or views of the corset/ body were featured.[54] Various planes of flesh beneath the arms, the small of the back, lower back, stomach, hips, and upper buttocks were, via corsetry advertisements, exposed to a very public gaze this way.

Posner's essay on human fragmentation also developed the idea that the decontextualised, fragmented body 'speaks'. She maintained that the dismembered body is essentially a body that denotes vulnerability and anxiety. Like Laqueur, she situated the body as a 'highly charged metaphor for the psychological, social, political and physical assaults on the individual'. Representations of the dismembered body, said Posner, can and should be read as the site of investigation of 'urgent concerns' including sexism, sexual identity, sexual oppression and loss. When the body is represented as dismembered/fractured/in pieces, argued Posner, there necessarily occurs an assault on the integrity of the whole body, and from this assault inevitably arises a sense of disconnection. Laqueur concurred with this observation, asserting that the fragmented body 'adrift and decontextualised, separated from its whole [was] not silenced by its dismemberment' but made a powerful claim that 'there [was] something to be said' about its condition.[55]

Linda Nochlin, writing about the work of French artist Manet in an article unconnected to the *Corporal Politics* catalogue, has also discussed the meanings that inhere to artistic renderings of the partial body, more specifically the partial or dismembered female body. Like Laqueur and Posner, Nochlin associated the depiction of fragmentary images of the body as a kind of 'wilfulness and deliberate provocation' on the part of the artist, rather than an inability or simple disinclination to 'complete' the picture. As Nochlin asserts, the partialism or fragmentation of women in Manet's work was a method of portraying 'sexually suggestive undertones'. As Nochlin also explained, Manet's use of synecdoche was a 'brilliant realist device', which made the viewer aware of the 'nature of the actual power structure underlying the worldly goings on' in his paintings.[56] From the ideas posited by Nochlin, Posner and Laqueur, it can be concluded that the portrayal of the body in pieces can be understood (whether it manifests in Victorian or modern art) as an assault, albeit a merely visual one, on the body.[57]

The almost ubiquitous fragmentation of the female body in corsetry advertisements can be similarly construed as an assault, but of a gender-specific kind. Fragmenting the flesh of either men or women, whether representationally or literally, can be seen as a violent act or representation of that act. However, when the female rather than the male body is fragmented, the assault becomes (as Nochlin suggests) a specifically sexual assault. The sexual issues involved in bisecting women's bodies are issues that have been discussed quite rigorously by Laura Mulvey. In her landmark article titled 'Visual Pleasure and Narrative Cinema', published over twenty-five years ago, Mulvey recognized and teased out the sexual connotations and imperatives behind the fragmentation of women's bodies.[58] Her initial work in this area, though it discusses the fragmentation of women's bodies in the cinema, has particular relevance to the examination of corsetry advertisements. It is entirely feasible that the fragmented female body that characterized so many nineteenth-century corset advertisements was actually a forerunner to the cinematic fragmentation of the female body in the late twentieth century. Mulvey's psychoanalytically based article maintained that the almost epidemic 'cinematic fragmentation' of women's bodies, in which the camera 'worshipped in close-up' the hair, eyes, shoulders, thighs and almost any other part of the female body deemed attractive, amounted to a scopophilic fetishism.[59] It is this corporeal dismemberment and its corollary, sexual fetishism, which are the most outstanding and troubling aspects of corset advertising (see Figure 84). The female body has of course a long history of objectification. On it, according to Marina Warner, have been projected the 'fantasies and longings and terrors of generations of men, and through them of women, in order to conjure them into reality or to exorcise them into oblivion'.[60] Corsetry advertisements stand as evidence of these fears, but more frighteningly still, the images of female dismemberment so common within these advertisements can be read as a diagrammatic annihilation both of male fears and of the bodies of the women that evoked them.

When understandings of 'authorship' and the gendered power of public representations of the disrobed female body are considered, initial readings of corsetry advertisements are indubitably and radically transformed. The twentieth-century concept of these advertisements as bygone curios that allude to feminine specificity (or even of empowered nineteenth-century female sexuality) is quickly dissolved when they are examined in the light of feminist scholarship. Corsetry advertisements neatly encapsulated the longings and terrors of male fears of female sexuality, and though this was unacknowledged by the society which produced them, corset advertisements allowed at least a diagrammatic resolution of those

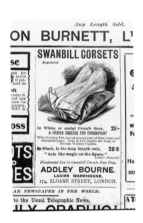

Figure 84
The Swanbill corset advertisement in which the body/corset reclines on a pillow, appearing at once vulnerable, dismembered and penetrable. *See The Graphic*, 1900.

fears. The scrupulously illustrated images of women's bodies encased in corsetry that contained and safely tamed women's bodies placated anxieties, but conveniently sexualized the corseted subjects within. Images that used only fragments of the female body, or invisible but nonetheless 'apparent' sections of women's bodies were more brutal by far. These diagrams reduced women to fractured fetish objects by a process of illustrative and psychic dismemberment. These advertisements stand as indisputable visual evidence of Victorian misogyny repeated, enacted and celebrated in the everyday realm of commerce and culture.

Conclusion

Whether she lived in London or Philadelphia, in the life of the middle-class Victorian woman the corset was a 'universal'. The abundance of texts published on both sides of the Atlantic which either advocated or decried the garment indicate its popularity, particularly between 1850 and the turn of the century. While *Bound to Please* has examined the role of the corset in constructing and constraining the lives of middle-class women, the corset operated in a similar way for working-class women. The plethora of instruction manuals published in the early part of the century directed toward working-class women, that included patterns and detailed instructions on how to make corsetry, are evidence of the garment's cross-class popularity. The eventual mass production of cheap corsets in the 1870s and 1880s further democratized the garments. Though men were involved in the manufacture of corsetry, women made up the bulk of the largely invisible labour force in the garment's production. Paradoxically, the lives of the often ill-paid corset factory operatives were probably made even more taxing by wearing the very garments produced by their own labour. For these women, however, the corset may also have been a very useful ally in the cultivation, indeed in the sculpting, of a svelte body – a body that might potentially attract a suitor from a better class. The avoidance of a 'chunky' working-class waist and the cultivation of an elegant middle-class tournure that might attract a well-heeled husband relied on firm corsetry as much as on tasteful gowns and good grooming in the mid- to late nineteenth century.

A range of powerful forces kept both working- and middle-class women 'bound', even after marriage. When moral values were measured (initially at least) on appearances, and when popular culture at large insisted that a well-corseted body was evidence of a well-trained mind, it is not surprising that firmly, if not tightly, laced corsetry was de rigueur. Women of both classes were in large part responsible for contracting the waist to elegant but dangerous proportions, but as early- and mid-century reformers Angeline Merritt and Abba Gould-Woolson pointed out, men were deeply implicated in this practice because they publicly admired and praised the tightly bound body. The 'hand-span waist' was just that. The term derived from the ability and inclination of men to completely encircle the corseted female waist with two hands. The survival of the term 'hand-span waist' into the twentieth century indicates the enormous cultural valency this practice had in the Victorian era. The term's survival in everyday parlance points to the continuance of Victorian standards of beauty which still determine that a child-size, well defined waistline is worthy of 'aesthetic' merit. The appearance of the tiny waist in current fashion magazines is evidence that the waist remains a site of sexual objectification; while the endurance of the corset as a pornographic icon indicates that current sexual practices, in some circles at least, locate the waist as a site of fetishism.

The garment's popularity in the Victorian era rested on a number of complex contradictions, which increased rather than diminished its allure. The most basic of these was the garment's ability to alter the shape of the body. Women who believed their bodies and prospects were blighted by embonpoint could reduce the appearance of their girth by way of the corset. Other women 'cursed' by slender 'underdeveloped' busts and hips could disguise their lack of curves by choosing corsetry that was specially designed and padded in those areas of greatest 'lack'. Whether she was of slight, medium or heavy build, the decent Victorian woman was obliged to corset. This was because the garment operated to keep the flesh still. Any movement of female flesh (beyond that permitted by the limbs in ordinary perambulation) was considered slovenly. Corsetry prevented any uncomely wobbling of the stomach, buttocks and breasts. In exceptional circumstances when the breasts were 'legitimately' exposed, the corset enhanced and facilitated their rise and fall, a sight widely admired in the ballroom but occasionally considered scandalous. The Victorian aversion, even revulsion, toward any visible movement of the stomach and buttocks of the female sex may explain why the brassière, which was promoted from quite early in the century by dress reformers, failed to find a market. The entire female torso, in broad daylight at least, required anchoring and stabilizing if it was to appear decent and suitably asexual. Although the corset was invoked to restrict any movement that might suggest overt sexuality, it was simultaneously instrumental in creating a body shape that was deemed sexually attractive and distinctly feminine. Female children, generally powerless (though sometimes resisting) agents in the construction and articulation of gender, were (and remain) essential to its perpetuation. Female children were the crucial spoils of the Victorian gender battle, and the juvenile corset was an integral cannon in the armoury of both gender-differentiation and stability. Efforts to consolidate gender in female children were patently apparent in many aspects of their material culture, including outer clothing and dolls, but corsetry was of paramount importance in this regard. Corsetry restricted the movement of female children to that considered appropriate, and when worn over a period of years physically prevented the expansion of the ribs, abdomen and waist. That no equivalent garment existed for male children reveals that femininity rather than masculinity was considered dangerously labile and in need of marshalling. Indeed Victorian femininity appeared to require urgent reinstatement, consolidation and containment. Female children whose bodies were encased in corsetry in their formative years ideally survived as adults whose ribcages and waistlines were small, and whose demeanours were far from threatening. After the 1860s there appeared a specific range of children's corsetry that was designed and implemented less to 'support' the body of the growing child than to prevent its expansion at the waist. That juvenile corsetry literally imposed a shapely waistline upon the usually androgynous shape of little girls suggests too that a sexualization of the juvenile female body was being enacted, albeit for future 'use'. The contentious semi-pornographic letters published in the *English Domestic Women's Magazine* in that decade illustrate the new sexual status of the child's body as much as the role of the corset in its creation.

The implementation of sturdy corsetry at an early age, for whatever reasons, made for ill health in adulthood. Encased in tightly fitted corsetry, in some cases even overnight during periods of growth in adolescence, meant that the bodies of many women failed to develop in a healthy manner. Both medical and feminist/dress reform texts published between 1850 and 1900 reveal that many North American and British women 'cabined in corsetry' from childhood to adulthood suffered a dreadful range of short- and long-term illnesses and injuries, both psychic and physical. It is not surprising that 'morbid impressibility' was a constant companion of many women, whose bodies (from early youth) were subjected to up to eighty pounds of pressure per square inch via the corset. Neurasthenia, chlorosis, depression and feelings of anxiety and unease were the mental legacy of the long- term use of corsetry. Its physical inheritance included nausea, dyspepsia, vomiting, eating disorders, head-aches, malaise, chest and back pain, fractured ribs and grave uterine disorders. The 'tide of female invalidism' that manifested on both sides of the Atlantic was, according to feminist doctors, undeniably related to corsetry. Occasionally male physicians also railed against corsetry; however, their voices were muted by the cultural acceptance of female complaints as being normative to femininity. That female debility was thought by the culture at large to be an acceptable expression of woman-liness explains in part why so many women endured corset-related illness, and why the medical profession could or would not galvanize a coherent and unified attack on the garment.

The escalation of female complaints among young and otherwise 'well' women allowed unheard-of access to that most mysterious organ, the uterus. Continued access to the uterus enabled the careers of numerous men to flourish. It may have been in the best interests of many doctors *not* to have forbidden its use, for without corsetry thriving opportunities to examine the uterus and to 'own' knowledge of that organ would vanish, and the steady escalation of consultation fees would dwindle. The corset was, after all, as dress reformer Dr Anna Galbraith astutely remarked, 'the chief support of doctors'.

Despite the ability for corsetry to diminish health so dramatically, it did not entirely victimize the women who wore it. Pregnant Victorian women, who were arguably in the most unenviable and dangerous position when it came to the compulsion to corset, even managed to turn the garment to their own advantage. Corsetry worked to disguise the ideologically transgressive fecund body. Garments actually designed to support the enlarged abdomen in reality actually worked to contain and disguise it. In an era notable for stringent pregnancy taboos a tightly laced corset allowed some middle- and working-class women to continue to engage in activities outside the home until quite late in their pregnancies. Standard corsetry, which seems to have been more often worn throughout pregnancy rather than specially designed maternity stays, inevitably inflicted physical punishment on the body of the pregnant woman. Explicit accounts written by female doctors and dress reformers arguing against the use of corsetry in pregnancy, spelled out its aftermath, being 'cross birth' miscarriage, abortion and stillbirth. However, even these appalling effects of the garment were capitalized on by women who were unfortunate enough to find themselves fettered by an unwanted pregnancy. When more tightly laced than usual, corsetry was for some women a desperate, not entirely reliable, but often undetectable method of birth control. Tightly laced corsetry may well have been responsible for the decline in middle-class birth rates of the 1880s, which corresp-onded to the increasingly harsh penalties for abortion and reduction of access to birth-control technology.

Corsetry was too, as dress reformers and feminist doctors pointed out, responsible for a kind of self-imposed morbid subjectivity. In an era when women's ill health and even death were romanticized in art, literature and music, corsetry became an invaluable tool in 'safely' mimicking, even creating, a demeanour that at least gave the appearance of 'refined debility'. Corsetry whitened the skin as dramatically as cosmetics. When tightly laced it enforced rapid and shallow respiration that made the breasts rise and fall in a manner considered pleasing by admiring swains. Fainting, that most feminine of physiological responses, was the inevitable consequence of tight lacing and exercise. Adult women fully understood the consequences of tight corsetry and laced in order to provoke these somatic responses. I would argue that women often understood the subtleties, contradictions and ambiguities that could result from the judicious use of corsetry. That is, middle-class Victorian women realized that corsetry enabled them to enact a range of feminine behaviours deemed appropriate in Victorian society. Corsetry assisted women to cultivate an appearance of being morally refined, but at the same time it enabled them to transgress prevailing moral restrictions that denied them any kind of sexual expression outside of marriage. The tightly bound, scantily clad, unconscious body of the unmarried and supposedly guileless and innocent Victorian belle was an undeniably sexual body. It successfully manifested all the hallmarks of submissive heterosexuality described in approving and patient detail by Victorian sexologists. The manifold uses and meanings of corsetry made it an essential item of clothing for the majority of Victorian women, for whom it was often a lifetime companion. In an era when the lives of middle-class women were closely circumscribed, and when female sexuality was generally positioned as either non- existent or voracious, the corset operated to construct, maintain and police a femininity that was both sexually alluring and controlled. The corset was then, the garment par excellence in the construction and articulation of Victorian femininity.

Notes

Introduction

1. H.H. Richardson, 'The Bathe: A Grotesque', in Dale Spender (ed.), *The Penguin Anthology of Australian Women's Writing*, Penguin, Victoria, 1988, pp. 470–3.
2. S. Brownmiller, *Femininity*, Simon & Schuster, London, 1986, p. 19.
3. H.H. Ellis, *Studies in The Psychology of Sex: Sexual Selection in Man*, F.A. Davis and Co., Philadelphia, 1918, p. 172.
4. E.M. Webb, *The Heritage of Dress: Being Notes on the History and Evolution of Clothes*, Times Book Club, London, 1912, p. 241. Webb notes that wooden busks splintered and penetrated the flesh, took skin off the waist and broke the ribs.
5. W.B. Lord, *The Corset and the Crinoline: A Book of Modes and Costumes*, Ward, Lock and Tyler, London, 1865, p. 209.
6. C. Willett and P. Cunnington, *The History of Underclothes*, Faber & Faber, London, 1951, p. 114.
7. Webb, *The Heritage of Dress*, p. 240.
8. S. Mendus and J. Rendall (eds), *Sexuality and Subordination: Interdisciplinary Studies of Gender in the Nineteenth Century*, Routledge, London, 1989, p. 2.
9. M. Vicinus (ed.), *A Widening Sphere: Changing Roles of Victorian Women*, Indiana University Press, Bloomington, 1977. Vicinus convincingly argues that Victorian women were not always passive victims, but neither were they entirely free from this stereotype.
10. C. Smart (ed.), *Regulating Womanhood: Historical Essays On Marriage, Motherhood and Sexuality*, Routledge, London, 1992, pp. 7–8. See L. Bland, 'Feminist Vigilantes of Late Victorian England', in Smart (ed.), *Regulating Womanhood*, pp. 33–52.

11. The notion that decent middle-class women were asexual beings was spelled out in popular texts such as that written by William Acton. Possibly the most famous is titled *The Functions and Disorders of the Reproductive Organs in Childhood, Youth, Adult Age, and Advanced Life, Considered in their Physiological, Social and Moral Relations*, John Churchill, London, 1862. See especially p. 112.

12. The polarization of attitudes regarding female sexuality and its expression can be found in R.G. Walters (ed.), *Primers for Prudery: Sexual Advice to Victorian America*, Prentice Hall, New Jersey, 1974. Walters noted that similar competing discourses around female sexuality existed in both Victorian Britain and North America. See pp. 8–11.

13. Edward Shorter, *A History of Women's Bodies*, Penguin, Middlesex, 1982, pp. 28–31.

14. Madam Roxy Caplin, *Health and Beauty: or Corsets and Clothing Constructed in Accordance with the Physiological Laws of the Human Body*, Kent and Company, Holbourn Hill, 1855, pp. 46–7.

15. Ibid., p. 16.

16. B. Eirenreich and D. English (eds), *For Her Own Good: 150 Years of the Experts' Advice to Women*, Anchor Books, New York, 1978, p. 109.

Chapter 1

1. J. Perkin, *Victorian Women*, John Murray Publishing, London, 1993, p. 95.

2. W. Mayhew (ed.), *The Greatest Plague of Life or the Adventures of A Lady in Search of a Good Servant by one who has been 'almost worried to death'*, David Bogue, London, 1847, p. 86.

3. *The Family Economist: A Penny Magazine Devoted To The Moral, Physical, and Domestic Improvement of the Industrious Classes*, vol. 2, 1849, p. 20.

4. P. and A. Mactaggart, "Ease, Convenience and Stays, 1750–1850", *Costume*, no. 13, 1979.

5. Anon., *The Workwoman's Guide, Containing Instructions to the Inexpensive in Cutting out and Completing those Articles of Wearing Apparel & etc. Which are Usually made at Home; Also Explanations on Upholstery, Straw platting* (sic) *Bonnet Making, Knitting*, London, 1838, pp. 81–2.

6. Mrs T. Willmot, *The Young Woman's Guide Containing Correct Rules for the Pursuit of Millinery, Dress and Corset Making: Illustrated by Lithographic Plans With Many Useful Remarks to Young Women and Servants of Every Denomination*, London, 1841. See also Mrs J.M. Howell, *The Handbook of Millinery Comprised in a Series of Lessons for the Formation of Bonnetts, Capotes,*

Turbans, Caps, Bows and Etc; To Which is Appended a Treatise on Taste and the Blending of Colours. Also an Essay on Corset Making, J.L. Cox and Sons, London, 1847. This text spelled out the exact steps in making corsetry at home for those that could not afford, or chose not to purchase, corsets from a professional staymaker.

7. See an example of these patterns in *The Young Englishwoman*, August 1875, p. 583.

8. *Harper's Bazaar*, 24 August 1872, p. 565.

9. *Harper's Bazaar*, a magazine intended for a middle-class clientele, similarly published corset patterns for children, young women and matrons early in the century, but these decreased and eventually disappeared almost entirely after 1880. See examples of these patterns in *Harper's Bazaar*, 24 August 1872, p. 565.

10. See advertisements placed in *Woman's Life*, 21 January 1899, p. 291.

11. Both the leaflets for the Pretty Maid corset and the box that held it can be seen in the Leicestershire Museums Service, Leicestershire.

12. Symington also produced a garment called the 'home-made corset'. This was likely to have been another low-cost model. While no 'Home Made' corset exists in the Symington Collection, the surviving box in which it was packaged suggests that the garment was pre-cut and that it originally included the catches, laces and bones to be made up by the purchaser at her home.

13. The Symington Collection held by Leicestershire Museum Services has a splendid collection of these handbills.

14. A. Buck, *Victorian Costume and Costume Accessories*, Ruth Bean, Bedford, 1984, p. 86.

15. See Dermathistic advertisement in *Woman*, 1 March 1890, p. 15.

16. See for example advertisements for the Duplex Corset in *Daughters of America*, vol. 1, no. 8, July 1887, p. 12.

17. E.M. Webb, *The Heritage of Dress Being Notes on the History and Evolution of Clothes*, Times Book Club, new and rev. edn, London, 1912, p. 4.

18. *Woman*, 26 June 1890, p. 5.

19. F.B. Smith, *The People's Health 1830–1910*, Croom Helm, London, 1979, p. 393.

20. See George Roberts's substantial self-published corset catalogue, *An Address to the Ladies*, London, 1851, p. 11.

21. See the *Catalogue of the Chilean Exhibition at the Centennial of Philadelphia*, Valparaiso, Mercurio Printing Office, 1876, p. 4.

22. I am indebted to Ms Jane May, Keeper of Decorative Arts at Leicestershire Museum Services, who informed me of the existence of this corset and who unearthed this garment from the impressive Symington's collection which she oversees.

23. Ventilating and ribbon corsets were ideal for this purpose. Ventilating corsets were constructed with panels of mesh between the infra-structure of bones, while ribbon corsets that had the appearance of

being made entirely of ribbon were in reality dainty cages of metal disguised by the attractive ribbon finish.

24. See *Great Exhibition of Works of Industry Of All Nations, 1851: Official Description and Illustrations Catalogue*, exhibition no. 49, William Clowes and Sons, London, 1852, p. 580.

25. L. De Vries, *The Wonderful World of Victorian Advertisements*, John Murray and Sons, London, 1968, p. 66.

26. See Dr Scott's corset advertisement in the *Sydney Mail*, 29 May 1886, p. 1109.

27. Many firms boasted that their garments were available at 'Drapers, Ladies' Outfitters, and Stores throughout the United Kingdom and Colonies'. See for example the advertisement for Brown's Patent Dermathistic corset in the *Queensland Figaro*, 15 October 1887, p. 629.

28. J. Meech-Pekarik, *The World of the Meiji Print: Impressions of a New Civilisation*, Weatherill, New York, 1986, p. 191. I would like to thank Dr Vera Mackie for bringing this information to my attention.

29. *Arena*, vol. 3 February 1891, no. 3, p. 352.

30. Anon., *The Domestic Economist and Advisor in Every Branch of the Family Establishment*, January 1850, p. 17.

31. S. Hale, *Manners; Or Happy Homes and Good Society All the Year Round*, J.E. Tilton and Company, Boston, 1868, pp. 39–44. Hale's italics.

32. However, as one nineteenth-century commentator noted, 'the defence of virtue by the corset could not be depended on, concluding from the number of discarded stays found on park benches and on seats of fiacres'. See Cornelia Skinner cited in G. Schwarz, 'Society, Physician and the Corset', *Bulletin of the New York Academy of Medicine*, vol. 55, no. 6, June 1979, p. 564.

33. Hale, *Manners; Or Happy Homes*, pp. 39–44.

34. E. Ward, *The Dress Reform Problem: A Chapter For Women*, possibly self-published, Bradford, *c.*1870, pp. 46–7.

35. Mrs E. Haweis, *The Art of Beauty and the Art of Dress*, Garland, New York, 1878, pp. 48–9.

36. I. De Ver Warner MD, 'Clothing', in M. Harland (ed.), *Talks Upon Practical Subjects*, The Warner Brothers, New York, 1895, pp. 117–19.

37. See 'Hints on Dress' in *The Barmaid*, 31 December 1891, p. 21.

38. M. Thomas and A.S. Goodchild, *Dress Cutting and Making for County Council and other Technical Classes: Tailor System*, John Williamson and Company, London, *c.*1890. See p. 8.

39. T. Hawkins, *Self Teaching Directions for the London ABC Tailor System of Dress Cutting*, rev. edn, W. Staker, Ludgate Hill, *c.*1880, p. 2.

40. A.M. Banks, *Instructions for Drafting Bodice Patterns (from the Sussex System)*, London, *c.*1900, np. See 'How to take Measurements' on second page.

41. Mrs H. Grenfell and Miss Baker, *Dress Cutting Out With Diagrams on Sectional Paper: A Simple System for Class and Self Teaching*, Longmans, Green and Company, London and New York, 1888, p. 18.

42. "Fashionable Clothing" in *Queen*, 19 June 1880, p. 553.

43. See Persephone advertisement in *Myra's Journal*, 1 January 1890, np.

44. L. Davidoff and C. Hall, *Family Fortunes: Men and Women of the English Middle Class, 1780–1850*, University of Chicago Press, Chicago, 1987, p. 397.

45. J.M. Austin, *Golden Steps To Respectability, Usefulness, and Happiness: Being a Series of Lectures to Youth of Both Sexes, On Character, Principles, Associates, Amusements, Religion, And Marriage*, Derby, Miller and Company, Auburn, 1850, pp. 22–4.

46. T.C. Davis, 'The Actress in Victorian Pornography' in K. Garrigan (ed.), *Victorian Sexuality: Representations of Gender and Class*, Ohio University Press, Athens, OH, 1992, pp. 99–133.

47. Ibid., pp. 17–18.

48. The domestic sewing machine was preceded by an expensive, complicated and cumbersome industrial machine, but by the early 1860s, small portable machines were available and, while expensive, their democratization was made inevitable by the introduction of time payment plans. By the mid-1860s women's magazines carried numerous advertisements for sewing machines. While the sewing machine was frequently advertised as 'for family use', women and girls were most often its operatives.

49. See for example almost any copy of *The Standard Delineator of Fashion, Fancywork and Millinery*, between 1860 and 1900.

50. E. Wilson and L. Taylor, *Through the Looking Glass: A History of Dress From 1860 to the Present Day*, BBC Books, London, 1989, p. 14.

51. Hogarth's lithographs of 'The Staymaker' reveals this process. An illustration of 'The Staymaker' along with a discussion of men's role in eighteenth-century staymaking can be found in E. Ewing, *Dress and Undress: A History of Women's Underwear*, B.T. Batsford, London, 1978. A more recent discussion of the eighteenth-century corset can be found in L. Sorge, '18th Century Stays: Their Origin and Creators' *Costume*, no. 32, 1998, pp. 18–32.

52. *The Book of Trades* cited in Mactaggart, 'Ease, Convenience and Stays', *Costume*, no. 13, 1979, pp. 46–7.

53. Roberts, *An Address To The Ladies*, p. 5.

54. The extraordinary success of Symington Brothers corset firm originated with the skills of corsetière Sarah Gold, whose cottage industry

was 'mechanized' by her husband William Symington in the 1850s. See introduction to Christopher Page's text, *Foundations of Fashion: The Symington Collection 1856 to the Present Day*, Leicestershire Museums Publication, London, 1981.

55. Corset patents by men included complete designs, but were as often related to individual components of the garment.

56. See patent numbers 5105, 5964, 6314, 6417, 10,739, 13,891, 20,415, 21,272, 22,682, 22,801, in *Patents for Inventions: Abridgments for Specifications, Class 41, Wearing Apparel*, Patent Office, London, 1899.

57. See Patent no. 22,676, *Patents for Inventions*, 1892, pp. 1–3.

58. See 'Improvements in Stays or Corsets' patent no. 12,071, *Patents for Inventions: Abridgements for Specifications, Class 41, Wearing Apparel*, 1891.

59. See for example patent no. 15,733, 1891.

60. See for example patent no. 24,963, 1898.

61. See patent no. 11861, 1893.

62. See for example, patent no. 5741, 1892.

63. These items were incorporated either alone, but more often in combination, between the inner and outer layers of fabric which made up the garments. See for example George Davies's design, patented in 1864 (being patent no. 2378) which 'combine[d] strips of wood with leather and other substances' to 'replace whalebone.'

64. See patent no. 20, 1868.

65. See patent no. 2056, 1867.

66. See for example patent no. 3283, 1871.

67. See patent no.14,256, 1890.

68. The corset shield advertisement cited here was seen at the Gallery of English Costume, Platt Hall, Manchester. The advertisement was taken from *Woman's Life Magazine* of 1897. No page number or specific date was included with this cutting. The museum accession number for this advertisement is E/24/11.

69. See patent no. 11861, 1893.

70. See the *Standard Delineator of Fashions, Fancywork and Millinery*, May 1895, p. 93.

71. The Armorside was frequently advertised in *The Standard Delineator of Fashions, Fancy Work and Millinery*. See May 1895, p. 93.

72. Apart from the box held at Chilcomb House, the corset labels and boxes discussed in this paragraph are part of the Symington Collection held at the Leicestershire Museum's repository.

73. Many of the male-headed firms also exhibited shoes, stockings, leather goods and rubber goods along with their corsets. This may have been because many of the materials used in their production were common to all articles.

74. *Great Exhibition of Works of Industry Of All Nations, 1851: Official Description and Illustrations Catalogue*, William Clowes and Stons, London, 1852. See pp. 676–80.

75. Roberts, *Address to Ladies*, p. 4. These are Roberts's italics.

76. *Philadelphia International Exhibition 1876, Official Catalogue of the British Section, Part 1*, London, 1876. See pp. 170–8.

77. *United States Centennial Commission, International Exhibition, 1876, Reports and Awards, Group viii*, Philadelphia, 1877. Interestingly, a brassière was exhibited at this event but received little applause. It was exhibited by George Frost and Company, a Boston firm. It was called the 'Emancipation Corset' and was described in the report as reaching 'only the breasts'. It was recommended for young women.

78. Ibid., p. 579. Sykes's corset was exhibition no. 43. Another competitor, Charlotte Smith (exhibition no. 119), displayed a 'symmetrical corset' that enabled the wearer to regulate the pressure of the stays.

79. E. Ewing, *History of Children's Costume*, Charles Scribner's Sons, New York, 1977, p. 79. Caplin was also credited by Dr Elizabeth Blackwell as the first person to have made the corset 'tolerable in the eyes of a physician'. See p. 79 of Ewing for this citation.

80. R. Caplin, *Woman and Her Wants: Four Lectures To Ladies*, Kent and Company, London, 1860. See end pages.

81. See final pages of Caplin's revised edition of *Health and Beauty*, published in 1864, regarding the anatomical gallery.

82. Lidstone, J.T.S., *The Londoniad: Giving a Full Description of the Principle Establishments, Together with the Most Honourable and Substantial Business Establishments in the Capital of England & &*, published under universal patronage, London, 1856, pp. 246–7.

83. Sarah Levitt brought the extant copy of *The Londoniad* to my attention. I am indebted to Ms Levitt's advice and generosity regarding information pertaining to the elusive Roxy Caplin. Ms Levitt is currently completing a biography of Roxy Caplin for the *New National Dictionary of Biography*. At the time of my research, Ms Levitt was senior curator of the Gunnersbury Park Museum.

84. This was because the goods required for corsetry were often imported. Access to whalebone was also a significant factor in the placement of factories, particularly before its replacement by metal, featherbone, stiffened cord, cane and other substitutes in the third quarter of the century. Many of the skills used in corsetmaking were similar to those required in sailmaking, which was often a major enterprise in Victorian coastal cities. Bristol's industrialization is an example of this hybridization of skills. Bristol was a large centre for corsetry, canvas supplies, sails and ropes required by shipping. My thanks to Ms Alison Carter, curator of the Chilcomb House Museum, who alerted me to the connections between the location of corset industries and sailmaking.

85. Mactaggart, 'Ease, Convenience and Stays', *Costume*, p. 50.

86. Charles Booth, *Life and Labour of the People in London*, first published 1889. This citation is from the 1969 reissue, ed. A.M. Kelly, Macmillan, New York, pp. 270–3.

87. *Fourth Annual Report Of The Commission Of Labour, 1888. Women Working In Large Cities*, Washington, 1889. See especially pages, 142, 134, 140, 141, 561 and 582 for relevant tables.

88. The *Designer*, May 1899, p. 114.

89. *The Standard Delineator of Fashions, Fancywork and Millinery*, May 1895, p. 93.

90. Female canvassers were, in some cases, given training to fit the garments. This would of course have greatly increased the customer's chances of finding corsetry that suited her and increased the likelihood of repeat sales for the lady agent. Moreover, the purchase of corsetry from a friendly neighbourhood saleswoman, while convenient, might also have circumvented the embarrassment of sending orders to male clerks in distant cities. While saleswomen sold a range of personal garments, including petticoats and safety belts, it would appear that corsets and corset waists made up the majority of such door-to-door sales.

91. Davidoff and Hall, *Family Fortunes*, p. 272.

Chapter 2

1. Gould-Woolson, Abba, *Dress Reform: A Series of Lectures Delivered in Boston, On Dress As It Affects The Health of Women*, Robert Brothers, Boston, 1874, p. 208.

2. See for example E.E. Evans, *The Abuse of Maternity*, Lippincott, Philadelphia, 1875, which discussed the disdain provoked by the sight of pregnant women in 'ordinary society'. See especially pp. 28–32. Evans's book was an attempt to increase fertility rates in the middle classes. She stressed in the footnotes that there were also 'numerous instances' of women who did not hide their pregnancies until very late in their term.

3. H.P. Chavasse, *Advice To A Wife On The Management Of Her Own Health And On The Treatment Of Some Of The Complaints Incidental To Pregnancy, Labour, And Suckling* (rev. edn by F. Barnes MD, consulting physician to the British Lying-in Hospital), J. and A. Churchill, London, 1898, p. 141.

4. *Queen*'s pattern service published diagrams and details of corsetry in the 1880s. The patterns for satin stays may have been maternity corsets. One of the two pairs illustrated in the February 1880 issue was laced at both sides and had an additional row of lacing from just above the median line of the waist, which ran to the lower edge of the garment as a zip might. This pattern and the accompanying design also laced at the sides rather than the back, and cost one shilling and sixpence. The *Queen: The Lady's Newspaper And Court Chronicle*, 13 March 1880, p. 236.

5. A. Oakley, *The Captured Womb: A History of the Medical Care of Pregnant Women*, Basil Blackwell, New York, 1984, pp. 11–28.

6. Dr. Bouvier, *Bulletin de l'Académie Médicale*, vol. 18 (Paris, *1852–53*), pp. 355–89.

7. Three articles were published regarding tight lacing in similar journals during 1875 and 1876. None discussed the effects of tight lacing on pregnancy but were instead concerned with 'atrophy of the ovaries' and general disease.

8. J.H. Miller, '"Temple and Sewer": Childbirth, Prudery and Victoria Regina*', in A.S. Wohl (ed.), *The Victorian Family: Structure and Stresses*, Croom Helm, London, 1978, pp. 23–43, p. 34.

9. See Miller, '"Temple and Sewer"', pp. 32–3 regarding the reluctance of working-, middle- and upper-class society to discuss pregnancy and childbirth without recourse to euphemisms.

10. Evans, *The Abuse of Maternity*, pp. 28–32.

11. L. Davis, *Virginal Sexuality and Textuality in Victorian Literature*, University of New York Press, Albany, 1993. Davis has shown that 'virginality' was a masculinist construct used to survey and control female sexuality.

12. B. Welter, 'The Cult of True Womanhood', in M. Gordon (ed.), *The American Family in Socio-Historical Perspective*, St Martin's Press, New York, 1978, pp. 313–34. Welter has discussed the importance of chastity in the single state and the difficulties preserving that 'innocence of spirit' once married. See pp. 317–8.

13. H. Storer, *Why Not? A Book for Every Woman [and] A Book for Every Man*, Lea and Shepard, Boston, 1868, pp. 111–12.

14. C. Smith-Rosenberg, *Disorderly Conduct: Visions of Gender in Victorian America*, Oxford University Press, Oxford, 1985, p. 224.

15. A. Heywood cited in L. Gordon, 'Voluntary Motherhood; The Beginnings of Feminist Birth Control Ideas in the United States', in M. Hartman and L.W. Banner (eds), *Clio's Consciousness Raised: New Perspectives on the History of Women*, Harper and Row, New York, 1974, pp. 60–1.

16. Smith-Rosenberg, *Disorderly Conduct*, p. 243.

17. Storer, *Why Not?* p. 114.

18. E. Duffey, *The Relations of the Sexes*, Arno press reprint, New York, 1876, p. 215.

19. H.C. Wright, *Marriage and Parentage: Or The Reproductive Element in Man As A Means to His Elevation and Happiness*, np, Boston, 1855, p. 243.

20. Ibid., pp. 111–12.

21. N. Tarrant, 'A Maternity Dress of about 1845–50', *Costume*, no. 14, 1980, pp. 117–20.

22. R. Bailey, 'Clothes Encounters of the Gynaecological Kind: Medical Mandates and Maternity Modes in the U.S.A. 1850–1990', in R. Barnes and J. Eicher (eds), *Dress and Gender: Making and Meaning in Cultural Contexts*, Berg Publishers, Providence, 1992, p. 255.

23. Tarrant 'Maternity Dress', p. 118.

24. Cited in J. Haller and R. Haller, *The Physician and Sexuality in Victorian America*, University of Illinois Press, Urbana, 1974, p. 157. Haller did not mention (or perhaps he failed to recognize) that this garment was a maternity corset.

25. L. Banner, *American Beauty*, Knopf, New York, 1983, p. 63.

26. Ibid., p. 157.

27. Miller's fashion reform and her magazine (first published in 1887) were 'heartily endorsed' by *Popular Science Monthly*. See *Popular Science Monthly*, Literary Review, vol. xxxii, 1887–8, p. 850.

28. B.O. Flower, editorial, *Arena*, vol. 4, no. 3, August, 1891, p. 384.

29. B.O. Flower, 'Fashion's Slaves', *Arena*, vol. 4, no. 4, September, 1891, pp. 401–30. See p. 418 for this quote.

30. Ibid., p. 416.

31. Madam Roxy Caplin, *Women in the Reign of Queen Victoria*, William Freeman, London, 1877, p. 311.

32. Madam Roxy Caplin, *Health and Beauty: or Corsets and Clothing Constructed in Accordance with the Physiological Laws of the Human Body*, Darton and Co., London, 1855 pp. 46–7.

33. Chavasse, *Advice to a Wife*, pp. 125–6.

34. Ibid., p. 162.

35. Ibid., p. 164.

36. Ibid., p. 126.

37. Ibid., Even this small pleasure, was to be 'cautiously pursued', p. 9.

38. Keating cited in Bailey, 'Clothes Encounters' in Barnes and Eicher, *Dress and Gender*, p. 254.

39. Chavasse, *Advice to a Wife*, p. 172.

40. G. Napheys, *The Physical Life of Woman: Advice to the Maiden, Wife and Mother*, Bailliere, Tindall and Cox, Philadelphia, 1870, p. 175.

41. J.H. Kellog, *Ladies' Guide in Health and Disease: Girlhood, Maidenhood, Wifehood, Motherhood*, Echo Publishing Company, Melbourne, 1900, p. 413.

42. Ibid., p. 46.

43. A.K. Gardner, *Conjugal Sins Against the Laws of Life and Health*, J.S. Redfield, New York, 1870, p. 29.

44. Dickinson cited in Haller, *The Physician and Sexuality*, pp. 168–70.

45. Cited in A. Galbraith, MD, *Hygiene and Physical Culture For Women*, Dodd, Mead and Company, New York, 1895, p. 233. Both Dickinson and Sergeant were frequently cited in women's physical culture texts as well as more scientific journals, including Lancet and *Popular Science Monthly*.

46. See 'Experiments of the Hyderabad Commission on Tight Lacing as a Cause of Death in Chloroform Anaesthesia' in *Lancet*, 21 June 1890, pp. 1366–93 for details of vivisection by corsetry.

47. L. Rose, *The Massacre of the Innocents: Infanticide in Britain 1800–1939*, Routledge & Kegan Paul, London, 1986, pp. 39–40.

48. C. Conley, *The Unwritten Law: Criminal Justice in Victorian Kent*, Oxford University Press, Oxford, 1991, pp. 113–15.

49. Smith-Rosenberg, *Disorderly Conduct*, pp. 218–19.

50. Anon., *Ladies' Indispensable Assistant: Being a Companion for the Sister, Mother, and Wife*, New York, 1851, p. 14. These involved easily procured drugs and herbals involving guaiacumin and strong decoctions of seneca.

51. Gardner, *Conjugal Sins*, pp. 226–7.

52. Storer, *Why Not?* pp. 96–7.

53. C. Smart, 'Disruptive Bodies and Unruly Sex: The Regulation of Reproduction and Sexuality in the Nineteenth Century', in Smart (ed.), *Regulating Womanhood: Historical Essays on Marriage, Motherhood and Sexuality*, Routledge, New York, 1992, p. 18.

54. N.F. Cooke, *Satan in Society*, C.F. Vent, Baltimore, 1876, p. 26. A. Gardner's *Conjugal Sins Against the Laws of Life and Health*, E. Edson Evans's *The Abuse of Maternity* and D. Lewis's *Chastity: or Our Legal Sins* W. Tweedie and Sons, Philadelphia, 1874, are just a few of many texts which replicated these ideas.

55. M. Davies has discussed the effect of corsetry on the fluctuation of Victorian birthrates in his well researched paper, 'Corsets and Conception: Fashion and Demographic Trends in the Nineteenth Century', *Journal of Comparative Studies in Sociology and History*, vol. 24, 1982, pp. 611–41. I would, however, dispute Davies' conclusions that Victorian women were unaware that corsetry was to blame for declining birthrates.

56. A. Merritt, *Dress Reform Practically and Physiologically Considered*, Jewitt Thomas Publishers, Buffalo, 1852, pp. 49–51.

57. A. Stockham, *Tokology: A Book For Every Woman*, L.N. Fowler and Company, Ludgate Circus, 1883; 1900 edn cited, p. 31.

58. Ibid., p. 240.

59. Ibid., p. 104. Stockham's italics.

60. Ibid., p. 102.

61. Ibid., p. 107.

62. Ibid., p. 102.

63. See patent lodged by C. Joyce of Middlesex, Patent no. 3543, 1874, p. 2. The object of Joyce's invention was to 'give increased safety and comfort both to mother and offspring during the state of pregnancy' and more specifically to reduce lumbago and weakening of the back. To this end his garment included 'elastic panels' either side of the busk from below the breasts to edge of corset approximately three inches wide. Elastic panels over the hips were added with side lacing. Back lacing remained in place, and although this system of lacing allowed for potential expansion, the garment still retained the straight metal clasp and busk at the front.

64. Several other women chose to design corsetry that allowed ease of breast-feeding. See for example M.A. Devenish, who lodged a patent in 1884 that differed from other designs in that it was 'formed with two openings at the breast part of the corset' that were not laced over the bosom area. Riveted steels shaped the cups of this garment but their placement and riveting allowed them to be opened as required to feed the baby, without having to remove or unlace the side panels or cups of garment. See Devenish's Improvements in Corsets, patent no.10,702, in Patents for Inventions: Abridgments for Specifications, Class 41, Wearing Apparel, Patent Office London, 1884, p. 2.

65. Patent no. 15,229, of 1893, lodged by L.L. Stauder of London.

66. See for example Patent no. 22833, of 1895, submitted by E.S. Browett, whose design featured an abdominal belt 'light in weight – attachable to any corset and thoroughly efficient in all cases in which an abdominal belt is necessary or desired'. The belt was made of 'courtil jean, with or without elastic inserted, and with or without a protective plate in front'. Other maternity corset patents include patent no. 538, of 1880, by W. Thomas, patent no. 3543, of 1874, by C.F. Joyce, patent no. 4341, of 1877, patent no. 9727, of 1896, by G. Festa.

67. Patent no. 4327, of 1883, by E.M. Moore, invention of 'Surgical Belt and Bed Stay'.

68. *Woman's Life*, 29 July 1899, p. 324.

69. B.W. Richardson, 'Dress in Relation To Health', *Popular Science Monthly*, 1880, vol. xvii, pp. 182–99.

70. Gardner, *Conjugal Sins*, p. 19.

71. Dr K. Mitchell, author of 'Are Women Physically Deteriorating', published in *Woman*, 1, March, 1890, disagreed. Mitchell believed 'modern women' were 'yearly improving in structure beauty and general health'. She attributed this to improved diet and the popularity of exercise in gymnasiums.

72. T.A. Emmet, Surgeon to the Women's Hospital and author of several texts including *The Principles and Practices of Gynaecology*, J. & A. Church, London, 1885, p. 22, insisted that degeneration was in evidence across all classes and was due to education for girls which taxed the female economy.

73. O. Wilde (ed.), 'February Fashions', *Woman's World*, February 1888, p. 190.

74. W. Arbuthnot Lane, 'Civilisation in Relation To The Abdominal Viscera, With Remarks On The Corset', in *Lancet*, vol. 2, 13 November 1909, pp. 1416–18. Lane claimed that falling viscera commonly lead to toxic stasis, a condition which could be rectified by adequate corsetry. See p. 1418.

75. A.M. Galbraith, MD, *Personal Hygiene and Physical Training for Women*, W.B. Saunders Company, Philadelphia, 1911, p. 248.

76. There was, wrote Stockham, 'no country, no class, [or] no tribe, where childbirth was attended by so much pain and trouble as in America'. Most American women, she continued, endured through the '280 days of pregnancy, disease and suffering'. Stockham, *Tokology*, p. 15.

77. Kellog informed readers that it was 'chiefly among the middle and higher classes of society that the pangs of childbirth [were] felt and the dangers of maternity [were] experienced'. He attributed this to middle-class women's refusal to acknowledge the 'immutable laws of nature'. Kellog, *Ladies Guide*, p. 411.

78. Stockam, *Tokology*, p. 37.

79. See 'Monsieur and Madame Caplin's Descriptive List of Hygienic Corsets, Belts, & directed to mothers of families and Ladies in General', in *Great Exhibition Catalogue* 1861.

Chapter 3

1. G. Schwarz, MD, 'Society the Physician and the Corset', *Bulletin of the New York Academy of Medicine*, Second Series, vol. 55, no. 6, June, 1979, pp. 551–90. Texts of the 1850s still made fleeting references to the existence of the male corset but from the middle of the century onward, men's corsets were virtually non-existent, sporadically advertised and overwhelmingly ridiculed as effeminate and pretentious. Corsets for male children suffered a similar decline.

2. Ridley cited in H. Roberts, 'The Exquisite Slave', *Signs*, vol. 2, no. 3, Spring 1977, p. 560.

3. A. Merritt, *Dress Reform Practically and Physiologically Considered*, Jewitt Thomas, Buffalo, 1852, pp. 147–9.

4. M. Harland, *Eve's Daughters; or Common Sense for Maid, Wife and Mother*, John R Anderson and Henry S. Allen, New York, 1882, pp. 350–1.

5. These generally appeared within advertisements for adult corsetry.

6. *Woman*, 8 March 1890, p. 15.

7. E. Ewing, *History of Children's Costume*, Charles Scribner's Sons, New York, 1977, p. 98. Red flannel, notes Ewing, was believed to prevent chills and rheumatism.

8. See *Myra's Journal*, 1 January 1890, p. 1.

9. Mrs Laura Ormiston Chant, 'The Gymnasium for Girls', *Woman's World*, 1899, pp. 329–32.

10. Both texts cited in L. Faderman, *Surpassing the Love of Men: Romantic Friendship and Love between Women from the Renaissance to the Present*, The Women's Press, London, 1981, pp. 234–5.

11. J. Epstein and K. Straub (eds), *Body Guards: The Cultural Politics of Gender Ambiguity*, Routledge, New York, 1991. See introduction.

12. The breeching ceremony involved dressing the child in a 'beautiful party frock' presenting him to relatives then removing him from the room, cutting off his ringlets, dressing him in male-identified clothing (usually a sailor suit) and then returning the 'breeched' child to the assembly. See G.E. Evans, 'Dress and the Rural Historian', *Costume*, no. 8, 1974, pp. 38–40.

13. Roberts, 'Exquisite Slave' p. 566.

14. E. Wilson and L. Taylor, *Through the Looking Glass: A History of Dress from 1860 to the Present Day*, BBC Books, London, 1989, pp. 21–2.

15. P. Perrot, *Fashioning the Bourgeoisie: A History of Clothing in the Nineteenth Century*, Princeton University Press, Princeton, 1994, p. 110.

16. G. Fischer, 'Who Wears the Pants? Women, Dress Reform and Power in Mid-Nineteenth Century United States', unpublished doctoral thesis, Indiana University, 1995, pp. 72–3.

17. P. Cunnington and A. Buck, *Children's Costume in England: From the Fourteenth to the end of the Nineteenth Century*, Adam and Charles Black, London, 1965, p. 207.

18. Ibid., p. 210.

19. J. Laver, *Children's Fashions in the Nineteenth Century*, B.T. Batsford, London, 1951, p. 4. Laver also pointed out that while mothers and daughters were both subjected to the crinoline in earlier decades, that contraption at least had the advantage of freeing the legs, disbursing the weight of the underclothes and by virtue of its design, giving the appearance of a slender waist.

20. Ewing, *History of Children's Costume*, p. 70.

21. Miss Beecher, *Miss Beecher's Housekeeper and Health Keeper: Containing Five Hundred Recipes For Economical and Healthful Cooking: Also Many Directions For Securing Health and Happiness*, Harper and Brothers, New York, 1876, pp. 292–3.

22. Cited in J. Perkin, *Victorian Women*, John Murray, London, 1993, p. 94.

23. G. Raverat, *Period Piece*, Faber & Faber, London, 1960, see especially pp. 253–7.

24. Ibid., p. 47.

25. Ibid., p. 259.

26. Madam Roxy, Caplin, *Health and Beauty: or Woman in Her Clothing Considered in Relation to the Physiological Laws of the Human Body*, rev. edn, Kent and Co., London, 1864, p. 34.

27. The Reverso-Tractor Hygienic Corset and the Juvenile Hygienic Corset also cited in J. Haller and R. Haller, *The Physician and Sexuality in Victorian America*, University of Illinois Press, Urbana, 1974, p. 152.

28. E. Checkley, *A Natural Method of Physical Training: Making Muscle and Reducing Flesh without Dieting or Apparatus*, G.P. Putnam's Sons, London, 1892, pp. 118–19.

29. M. Perrot, 'The Secret of the Individual' in G. Duby and G. Duby (eds), *A History of Private Life*, Belknap, Harvard University Press, 1990. See pp. 524–5.

30. A. Masters 'The Doll as Delegate and Disguise', *Journal of Psycho-history*, vol. 13, no. 3, Winter, 1986, pp. 293–308. See p. 293 for this quote.

31. Ibid., pp. 304–5.

32. J. Barnes and M.E. Roach-Higgins, 'Definition and Classification of Dress: Implications for Analysis of Gender Roles', in R. Barnes and J.B. Eicher, *Dress and Gender Making and Meaning in Cultural Contexts*, Berg, Providence, 1992, pp. 8–29. See pp. 15–19.

33. Mrs Merrifield, *Dress As A Fine Art: With Suggestions On Children's Dress*, John P. Jewett and Company, Boston, 1854. Mrs Merrifield also cited in E. Ewing, *History of Twentieth-Century Fashion*, Batsford, London, 1974, pp. 75–6.

34. H. Austin, MD, *American Costume or Woman's Right To Good Health*, F.W. Hurd and Company, New York, 1867, p. 9.

35. *The Rational Dress Society's Gazette*, July 1888, p. 2.

36. D. Lewis, *Five Minute Chats With Young Women and Certain Other Parties*, Harper and Brothers, New York, 1874, p. 15.

37. Ibid., p. 144.

38. Ibid., p. 30.

39. Dr Kitchen cited in H.G. Ecob, *The Well Dressed Woman: A Study in the Practical Application to Dress of the Laws of Health, Art, and Morals*, Fowler and Wells, New York, 1892, p. 28.

40. E. Duffy, *What Women Should Know: A Woman's Book About Women*, Philadelphia, 1898, Arno repr. 1974, pp. 40–2.

41. *Daughters of America*, vol. 1, December 1886, p. 1.

42. Ibid., February 1887, p. 7.

43. A.S. Macleod discusses the fluidity of nineteenth-century women's lives on the American frontier, from girlhood to maturity. Female childhood, though adventurous, was nevertheless predictably domestic, and girls were socialized to anticipate marriage and maternity. Macleod discusses these issues in the context of juvenile fiction of the era, which for girls, was 'intensely domestic and interior'. Fiction written for boys, by comparison, revolved around encounters with the outside world, in which rites of passage such as careers in the military and other active adult adventures were celebrated and played out. It was not until the end of the century that juvenile fiction for girls included other options for women. See A.S. Macleod, 'The Caddy Woodlawn Syndrome', in *A Century of Childhood: 1820–1920*, New York, 1984, pp. 65–96.

44. S.M. Newton, *Health, Art and Reason: Dress Reformers of the Nineteenth Century*, John Murray, London, 1974, p. 103. Newton notes Harberton's presidency, but the attribution to Harberton as inventor of the divided skirt is in *Arena*, vol. 6, no. 5, October 1892, p. 621.

45. See *Arena*, vol. 6, no. 5 October 1892, pp. 621–44. For Harberton's observations see pp. 630–2.

46. W.B. Lord, *Figure Training or Art the Handmaiden of Nature*, Ward, Lock and Tyler, London, 1871, p. 23. Baker's Knee was described as an affliction which manifested as an 'inclining inwards of the right knee joint until it closely resembled the right side of the letter K'. Bakers' assistants were supposedly deformed this way by carrying heavily laden baskets on one side of their bodies. See pp. 39–40.

47. Perrot, *Fashioning the Bourgeoisie*, p. 27.

48. R. Perry and L. Jordinova have both examined the cult of the breast in the eighteenth century. Perry's article 'Colonising the Breast: Sexuality and Maternity in Eighteenth Century England' in J.C. Fout (ed.), *Forbidden History, the State, Society and the Regulation of Sexuality in Modern Europe*, University of Chicago Press, Chicago, 1990, pp. 112–16, discusses the economic appropriation of the maternal breast. Jordinova discusses the sexualisation of the maternal breast and the gendered assumptions common to medical and other literature of that century. See Jordinova, *Sexual Visions: Images of Gender and Science*, Harvester Wheatsheaf, New York, 1989, pp. 29–30.

49. L. Stone, *The Family, Sex And Marriage In England 1500–1800*, Harper and Row, New York, 1977, p. 671.

50. Roberts draws from the *EDM* correspondence in her previously cited article.

51. Valerie Steele, *Fetish: Fashion, Sexuality and Power*, Oxford University Press, Oxford, 1996, pp. 59–60.

52. See D. Kunzle's response to H. Roberts's assertions in 'Dress Reform as Antifeminism: A Response to Helene E. Roberts "The Exquisite Slave: The Role of Clothes in the Making of the Victorian Woman"', *Signs*, vol. 2, no. 3, pp. 570–9.

53. C. Breward, 'Feminism and the Problem of the Late Nineteenth-Century Fashion Journal', *Journal of Design History*, vol. 7, no. 2, 1994, pp. 71–89. See p. 71.

54. Lord, *Figure Training or Art*, pp. 210–11. The exact date of publication is unknown. The copy cited here was an original copy, and had 1871 pencilled into the front cover. Lord cited several of the *EDM* letters so this text was probably published soon after the infamous correspondence.

55. C. Walkley, *The Way to Wear 'em: 150 Years of Punch on Fashion*, Peter Owen, London, 1985, pp. 49–50.

56. Lord, *Figure Training or Art*, p. 40.

57. Ibid., p. 211.

58. E. Wilson, *The Sphinx in the City: Urban Life, The Control of Disorder, and Women*, Virago Press, London, 1991, p. 39.

59. C.-A. Hooper 'Child Sexual Abuse and the Regulation of Women: Variations on a Theme' in Carol Smart (ed.), *Regulating Womanhood:*

Historical Essays on Marriage, Motherhood and Sexuality, Routledge, New York, 1992, pp. 53–77. See p. 56.

60. Mrs L. Frank, *Rents in our Robes*, Clark and Co., Bedford, N.Y., 1888, p. 10.

61. L. Beale, *Our Morality and the Moral Question*, J. and A. Churchill, London, 1887, p. 66.

62. G.G. Stocktay, *America's Erotic Past*, 1868–1940 Greenleaf Classics, California, 1973, introduction.

63. N.F. Cooke, *Satan in Society*, C.F. Vent, Baltimore, 1876 (repr. Arno, New York, 1974), pp. 187–93.

64. The disreputable place was probably a saloon, a dance hall or a brothel. See *Some Legal Aspects of the Question*, pamphlet by Women's Temperance Publication Association, London, 1886, p. 5.

65. Ibid., p. 12.

66. Beale, *Our Morality*, p. 85.

67. Janet Oppenheimer, *'Shattered Nerves': Doctors, Patients, and Depression in Victorian England*, Oxford University Press, Oxford, 1991, p. 186.

68. S. Fishman, 'The History of Childhood Sexuality', *Journal of Contemporary History*, vol. 17, 1982, pp. 269–83. See p. 270.

69. J.H. Kellog, *Ladies' Guide in Health and Disease: Girlhood, Maidenhood, Wifehood, Motherhood*, Echo Publishing, Melbourne, c.1900, pp. 145–65.

70. Cooke, *Satan in Society*, p. 112.

71. Dr A. Moll claimed to have treated a 'tribade' whose lesbianism had been called forth by masturbation at the age of five. A. Moll, *Perversion of the Sex Instinct, A Study of Sexual Inversion*, Julian Press, Newark, 1899 (reprinted 1931), p. 144.

72. B.S. Talmey, *Woman: A Treatise on the Normal and Pathological Emotions of Feminine Love*, The Stanley Press Corporation Publishers, New York, 1906, p. 95.

73. J. Howe, MD, *Excessive Venery, Masturbation, and Continence*, Birmingham & Co., New York, 1883, pp. 95–102.

74. Ibid., p. 110.

75. E.H. Hare, 'Masturbatory Insanity: The History of An Idea', *Journal of Mental Science*, vol. 108, no. 452, January 1962, pp. 2–25. Clitoridectomy, first performed in England in 1858 by the surgeon Isaac Baker Brown, was employed to cure sexual disorders including masturbation, hysteria and other neurasthenic disorders thought to be related to sexual dysfunction.

76. B. Barker-Benfield, 'Sexual Surgery in Late Nineteenth-Century America', *International Journal of Health Services*, vol. 5, no. 2, 1975, pp. 279–99. Benfield points out that working-class women and the insane provided the raw material of experimentation but once the operation was refined, castration procedures were commodified and sold to the middle classes. p. 288.

77. J.C. Flugel, *Psychology of Clothes*, Hogarth Press, London, 1930 (repr. 1950) pp. 76–7.

78. G.F. Watts, *George Frederick Watts: His Writings*, vol. 3, Macmillan, London, 1912, pp. 218–23. These remarks originally appeared in an article titled 'On Taste in Dress' in *The Nineteenth Century* magazine in January 1883, pp. 45–57.

79. M. Wood-Allen, MD, *Almost a Woman*, Signs Publishing Co., Melbourne, *c.*1890, pp. 23–4.

Chapter 4

1. C.C. Frederick, MD, 'Neurasthenia Accompanying and Stimulating Pelvic Disease', *Transactions of the American Association of Obstetricians and Gynaecologists*, vol. viii, 1895, pp. 351–5. See p. 355 for this term, used first by Dr. Goodell, to describe the many variants of neurasthenia, hysteria, chlorosis, etc.

2. A. Vrettos, *Somatic Fictions: Imagining Illness in Victorian Culture*, Stanford University Press, Stanford, 1995, p. 13.

3. D.P. Herndl, *Invalid Women: Figuring Feminine Illness in American Fiction and Culture, 1840–1940*, University of North Carolina Press, Chapel Hill, 1993. Herndl summarizes these positions admirably. See p. 25.

4. C. Willett and P. Cunnington, *The History of Underclothes*, Faber & Faber, London, 1951, p. 126.

5. Ibid., p. 113.

6. A. Merritt, *Dress Reform Practically and Physiologically Considered*, Jewitt Thomas, Buffalo, 1852, pp. 49–50.

7. A. Ballin, 'The Penalty of Tight Lacing', *Womanhood*, vol. 3, no. 16 March 1900, p. 265–6.

8. H.H. Ayer, *Harriet Hubbard Ayer's Book: A Complete and Authentic Treatise on the Laws of Health and Beauty*, Springfield 1899, repr. Arno, New York, 1976, pp. 269–70.

9. C. Cannaday, MD, 'The Relation of Tight Lacing to Uterine Development and Abdominal and Pelvic Disease', *American Gynaecological and Obstetrical Journal*, vol. 5, 1895, pp. 632–40. See p. 635 for the point summary.

10. 'Stays', *The Rational Dress Society's Gazette*, October 1888, p. 4.

11. Editorial note, *Gazette*, October 1888, p. 1.

12. *Woman*, 13 November 1890, p. 40.

13. Duplex were frequent advertisers in the feminist newspaper *Daughters of America*, see vol. 1, no. 8, July 1887, p. 12.

14. Dr. Warner's corsets were favoured by Marion Harland, who though despising the tightly laced corset, recommended that women adopt corsetry of some kind. Warner specialized in traditionally shaped hourglass garments. The Warner corset advertisements cited here were

found in the end pages of Marion Harland's *Talks Upon Practical Subjects*, Warner Brothers Publishers, New York, 1895.

15. This advertisement was one of many published extolling the virtues of Scott's electric corsets in *Harper's Bazaar*. It was also cited in Schwarz, 'Society, Physicians and the Corset', *Bulletin of the New York Academy of Medicine*, vol. 55, no. 6, June 1979, p. 579.

16. E. Haweis, *The Art of Beauty and the Art of Dress*, Garland, New York, 1978, pp. 121–2.

17. M. Morris, *The Book of Health*, Cassell, London, 1884, pp. 508–11.

18. J.M. Fothergill, *The Maintenance of Health: A Medical Work for the Lay Reader*, G.P. Putnam and Sons, New York, 1875, p. 81.

19. A. Bryce, *The Laws of Life and Health*, Andrew Melrose, London, 1912, pp. 325–6.

20. Dr Hunt, cited in M. Harland, *Eve's Daughters; Or Common Sense for Maid, Wife, and Mother*, 1982, pp. 353–6.

21. *The Medical Annual*, London, 1889, p. 514.

22. *The Medical Annual Synoptical Index*, 1887–1898. See unpaginated advertising section in end pages. The advertisements were illustrated and prominent, and appeared in end pages of the texts as well as the indexes. Corselets, being smaller versions of the corset, were also advertised sporadically in nursing journals such as *The Hospital Nursing Supplement*. The Ornho corselet belt was recommended by Madame Sarrante, a 'Paris Woman Doctor of some reputation'. The advertisements stated that the Ornho was porous and resilient, and gave a 'firm' waist with entire freedom of movement, but was 'unbreakable'. See *The Hospital Nursing Supplement*, 31 August 1895.

23. R.E. Riegel has discussed this further in his article 'Women's Clothes and Women's Rights', *American Quarterly*, vol. 15, 1963, pp. 390–401.

24. E.J. Tilt, *A Handbook on Uterine Therapeutics and of the Diseases of Women*, John Churchill and Sons, London, 1868, p. 2.

25. B.W. Richardson, MD LLD FRS. 'Woman as Sanitary Reformer', *Fraser's Magazine*, vol. xxii, 1880, pp. 667–83. See pp. 671–82 for these quotes. Once 'woman' had sufficiently mastered the rudiments of anatomy she ought to be 'tempted', wrote Richardson, to 'study that deadly, lively domain . . . the kitchen'. pp. 676–7.

26. S.M. Newton discusses these disruptions in *Health, Art and Reason: Dress Reformers of the Nineteenth Century*. John Murray, London, 1974. See chapter titled 'New Attitudes to Reform', pp. 115–134.

27. Ibid., p. 391.

28. Becker cited in *Rational Dress Society's Gazette*, October 1888, p. 1. The *Gazette* politely described Becker's remark as an 'interesting contribution' which was sure to bring before the public an opportunity to discuss the 'vexed question of wearing stays'.

29. Amaury de Reincourt, *Woman And Power in History*, Honeyglen Publishing, Bath, 1974, p. 315.

30. I. de van Warner, MD, 'Clothing', in Harland (ed.), *Talks Upon Practical Subjects*, New York, pp. 110–31.

31. Ibid., pp. 117–19.

32. The American journal *Arena*, published the proceedings of the International Council of Women, along with the proceedings of other international feminist organizations specifically concerned with dress reform.

33. J.H. Kellog, *The Evils of Fashionable Dress and How To Dress Healthfully*, Office of the Health Reformer, Michigan, 1876, p. 5.

34. This term was used by an unnamed physician in a two-page woman-blaming article in *Lancet*. See 'Tight Lacing', *Lancet*, vol. 1, 28 May 1881, p. 877.

35. F.E. Russell, 'Woman's Dress', in *Arena*, vol. 3, February 1891, pp. 352–60. See p. 352 for this quote.

36. W. Goodell MD, *Lessons in Gynaecology*, 3rd edn, F.A. Davis, Philadelphia, 1887, pp. 548–9.

37. D.B. Hart, MD, and A.H.F. Barbour, MD, *Manual of Gynaecology*, 5th edn, W. and A.K. Johnson, Edinburgh, 1897, p. 100.

38. An example of the coalition between feminists reformers and female doctors can be found in A. Gould-Woolson's text, *Dress Reform: A Series of Lectures Delivered in Boston, On Dress As It Affects The Health Of Women*, Roberts Brothers, Boston, 1874. Doctors Mary Stafford, Caroline E. Hastings, Mercy B. Jackson and Arvilla B. Haynes presented (and later published) their papers along with Woolson, after a series of large public lectures, in which both dress reform and women's rights were discussed. See p. 23.

39. Gould-Woolson, *Dress Reform*, p. 177.

40. Dr M.B. Jackson, in Gould-Woolson, *Dress Reform*, See p. 88.

41. F.E. Russell, 'Woman's Dress', *Arena*, vol. 3, February 1891, pp. 352–60. See p. 352.

42. 'Tight Lacing Again', *Lancet*, vol. 1, 10 January 1880, p. 75.

43. Cited in J. Haller and R. Haller, *The Physician and Sexuality in Victorian America*, University of Illinois Press, Urbana, 1974, p. 170.

44. Anon, 'Tight Lacing', *Lancet*, 28 May 1881, p. 877.

45. H.G. Ecob, *The Well Dressed Woman: A Study in the Practical Application to Dress of the Laws of Health, Art, and Morals*, Fowler and Wells, New York, 1892, pp. 28–9.

46. Miss Beecher, *Miss Beecher's Housekeeper and Healthkeeper*, Harper and Bros, New York, 1876, p. 243.

47. A. Galbraith, MD, *Hygiene and Physical Culture for Women*, W.B. Saunders, Philadelphia, 1911, p. 224.

48. Ibid., pp. 229–33. Interestingly, H.St. Vertue, MD noted that as late as the 1950s consultants still saw 'many an abdomen . . . bearing the vertical imprints of steels, [and] epigastrium[s] reddened and

ridged with horizontal grooves'. See H.St. Vertue, 'Chlorosis and Stenosis', *Guy's Hospital Report*, no. 104, 1955, pp. 329–48; see p. 347 for this quote.

49. Merritt, *Dress Reform*, p. 160.
50. E.W. Farrar, *The Young Lady's Friend*, John B. Russel, Boston, 1837; repr. 1873, p. 168.
51. See S. Stage, *Female Complaints: Lydia Pinkham and the Business of Women's Medicine*, W.W. Norton and Company, New York, 1979.
52. See for example the large collection of photographs at Shelf 4, Row 4, Berger 6 'Fetish Corset and Shoe' – 1942. The Kinsey also holds several mid- to late nineteenth-century texts that dwell on tight lacing as a sexual fetish. See for example the compilation from the *English Women's Domestic Magazine* titled *Figure Training or Art the Handmaid of Nature c.*1865, or for twentieth-century corsetry fetishism (Anon) *Figure Training Fundamentals, etc.* published in 1952 which contains illustrations taken from *Figure Training or Art the Handmaid of Nature*. Other fictitious (often biographical) texts held at the Kinsey regarding corsetry as fetish include (Anon) *Stays and Gloves: Figure Training and Deportment by means of the Discipline of Tight Corsets, Narrow Heeled Boots, Clinging Kid Gloves, Combinations and Etc.* (1909).
53. G. Raverat, *Period Piece*, Faber & Faber, London, 1960, pp. 258–9.
54. 'Death By Tight Lacing', *Lancet*, vol. 1, 14 June 1890, p. 1316.
55. Waist measurement cited in Edgar Flinn, FRCS, *Our Dress and Our Food in Relation to Health*, M.H. Gill and Son, Dublin, 1886, pp. 22–4.
56. Tilt, *Handbook*, pp. 262–3.
57. F.R. Treves, FRCS, 'The Dress of the Period', a lecture delivered on behalf of the National Health Society, *Medical Tracts*, Dublin, 1851, p. 15.
58. Kunzle admitted that enormous numbers of mass-produced corsets in the nineteenth century specifically advertised their ability to be tightly laced. See Kunzle, *Fashion and Fetishism: A Social History of Corsets, Tight Lacing and Other Forms of Body Sculpture in the West*, Rowman and Littlefield, New Jersey, 1982, p. 45.
59. E.J. Coleman, 'Boston's Athenaeum for Fashions', *Dress: Journal of the Costume Society of America*, no. 5, 1979, pp. 25–32. Coleman's paper outlines the internationalization of fashion in women's magazines in the early to mid-nineteenth century.
60. Merritt, *Dress Reform*, p. 64.
61. *Queen*, 19 June 1880, p. 553.
62. E.S. Phelps, *What to Wear?*, Samson, Low, Marston, Low, and Searle, London, 1874, pp. 14–15.
63. Ibid., p. 53.
64. K. Montague, 'The Aesthetics of Hygiene: Aesthetic Dress, Modernity, and the Body as Sign', *Journal of Design History*, vol. 7, no. 2, 1994, pp. 91–112.

65. Flinn, MD, *Our Dress and Our Food*, p. 3.

66. C. Willett and P. Cunnington, *English Women's Clothing in the Nineteenth Century*, William Heinemann Limited, London, 1937, p. 308. Also cited in Roberts, 'The Exquisite Slave', *Signs*, p. 562.

67. E. Showalter, *The Female Malady, Women, Madness and English Culture, 1830–1980*, New York, 1985, p. 122. As Showalter demonstrates, much of this attitude was derived from and underpinned by Darwinian thought that denoted women as 'lesser' beings than 'man' (sic) (see pp. 122–3).

68. H. Michie, *The Flesh Made Word: Female Figures and Women's Bodies*, Oxford University Press, Oxford, 1987, p. 20.

69. 'Editorial Note', *Rational Dress Society's Gazette*, October 1883, p. 3.

70. L. Limner, *Madre Natura Versus The Moloch of Fashion: A Social Essay*, Chatto & Windus, London, 1874, p. 109. Limner understood and was repelled by the role played by corsetry in creating female infirmity. Limner was a pseudonym for John Leighton.

71. O.W. Holmes, *The Autocrat of the Breakfast Table: Every Man His Own Boswell*, Ward Lock and Company, London, 1865, p. 115.

72. D. Craik, *A Woman's Thoughts About Woman*, Hurst and Blackett, London, 1859, pp. 4–5.

73. Ayer, *Harriet Hubbard Ayer's Book*, p. 271.

74. Frances Russell commented that American women were a 'nation of invalids' for want of dress reform. See Russell in 'Notes and Announcements' in *Arena*, February, 1891, vol. 3, no. 3, p. 385.

75. M.J. Safford-Blake, MD, 'Dress Reform', in Gould-Woolson, *Dress Reform*, see p. 15.

76. Ibid., p. 175.

77. C.H. Dall, *The College, The Market, and The Court: or Woman's Relation to Education, Labor and Law*, Lee and Shepard, Boston, 1867, p. 86.

78. Clarke cited in O. Moscucci, *The Science of Woman: Gynaecology and Gender in England, 1880–1929*, Cambridge University Press, Cambridge, 1990, p. 104.

79. E.H. Clarke, MD, *Sex in Education: Or a Fair Chance for The Ladies*, James R. Osgood, Boston, 1873, p. 21.

80. Lady Harberton, 'Symposium On Women's Dress', *Arena*, vol. 6, no. 5, October 1892, p. 621.

81. Beecher cited in Herndl, *Invalid Women*, p. 20.

82. Beecher's findings and methodology are cited, discussed, but then refuted, by Ann Douglas Wood in 'The Fashionable Diseases: Women's Complaints And Their Treatment In Nineteenth Century America', in M.S. Hartman and L. Banner (eds), *Cleo's Consciousness Raised New Perspectives on the History of Women*, Harper and Row, New York, pp. 1–22. See pp. 2–3.

83. 'On Fashion', *Gazette*, no. 3, October 1888, pp. 2–4.

84. Charlotte Tonna, *The Works of Charlotte Elizabeth*, M.W. Dodd, New York, 1845, pp. 10–11.
85. Merritt, *Dress Reform*, pp. 154–5.
86. Galbraith, *Hygiene and Physical Culture*, p. 245.
87. R. Porter, *A Social History of Madness: The World Through the Eyes of the Insane*, Tavistock Publications, New York, 1989, p. 118. The neurasthenic woman was a cultural norm of the nineteenth century, noted Porter. He described the hysteric or neurasthenic as a 'tight laced' woman and 'privileged inferior' but did not make any connection between the tightly laced female body and the physical and mental effects manifesting in that body because of its tightly laced condition.
88. Vertue, 'Chlorosis and Stenosis', p. 340.
89. Ibid., p. 337.
90. C.G. Mercer and S.D. Wangensteen, '"Consumption, heart disease, or whatever": Chlorosis, a Heroine's Illness in *The Wings of the Dove*', *Journal of the History of Medicine and Allied Sciences*, vol. 40, 1985, pp. 259–85. See pp. 262–3.
91. F.P. Weber, MA, MD, FRCP, 'Two Diseases Due To Fashion In Clothing: Chlorosis and Chronic Erythema Of The Legs', *British Medical Journal*, 23 May 1925, pp. 960–1.
92. Beecher, *Miss Beecher's Housekeeper and Healthkeeper*, p. 249.
93. Ibid., p. 249.
94. Mrs Beecher hinted at this in her text *A Treatise on Domestic Economy for the Uses of Young Ladies at Home, At School*, J.B. Ford and Company, 1870. Direct assertions regarding the role of the corset and 'female complaints' were also made in Beecher's text, *Letters to the People On Health and Happiness*. This was published in 1856. These claims are made more clearly still in *Miss Beecher's Housekeeper and Healthkeeper*, published in 1876.
95. See W. Hosmer, *The Young Lady's Book; or Principles of Female Education*, Auburn, Derby and Miller, New York, published in 1851, which advocated that obstetrics and gynaecology be the province of female doctors alone. Hosmer devoted a full chapter to the abuse of young women by gynaecologists. See pp. 187–206.
96. C. Beecher and H. Beecher Stowe, *Principles of Domestic Science; As Applied To The Duties and Pleasures of Home; A Text-book For the Use of Young Ladies in Schools, Seminaries, and Colleges*, New York, 1870, pp. 137–40.
97. Beecher, *A Treatise on Domestic Economy For the Use of Young Ladies*, p. 138. Beecher discusses the prevalence and effects of medical sexual assault in her chapter titled 'Letter Nineteenth: Abuses of Medical Treatment', pp. 134–40.
98. 'Why Women Age Rapidly', *Gazette*, no. 1, April 1888, p. 4–6.
99. Evidence of medical enthusiasm for pessaries was demonstrated at the American National Exhibition of 1867, where a display of several

hundred pessaries, (deemed by Tilt as useless or dangerous) was well received. Despite Tilt's prestige as a gynaecologist his protestations against the uterine pessary were almost entirely overlooked. See Tilt, *A Handbook on Uterine Therapeutics*, pp. 251–5.

100. Ibid., p. 271.

101. A.B. Haynes, MD, in Gould-Woolson (ed.), *Dress Reform*, pp. 110–11.

102. See 'Improvements in and connected with Pessaries, and Supports for the Treatment of Malpositions of the Uterus', patent no. 9955, 1897.

103. Godman cited in Haller and Haller, *The Physician and Sexuality*, p. 165.

104. Tilt, *A Handbook*, p. 257.

105. Goodell ascribed several womb ills including chronic ovaritis to this origin. See Goodell, *Lessons in Gynaecology*, pp. 561–3.

106. When pessaries were employed, wrote Britain's eminent gynaecologist Braxton Hicks, they were 'almost certain to be brought into contact with the ovaries and consequently [caused] much distress'. See J. Braxton Hicks, MD, FRS, FRCP, 'On A Cause of Uterine Displacement, Not Hitherto Mentioned, Contra-indicating the Use of Pessaries' in *Lancet*, vol. 1, 20 March 1886, pp. 537–8.

107. Report from the Obstetrical Society of London, in *Lancet*, vol. 2, 23 October 1875, p. 594.

108. This device consisted of a common or Hodge pessary, but was less curved to better adapt to the floor of the vagina. To either lateral arm of the pessary a segment of a watch spring was attached measuring about one and a half inches in length. These springs supported, at their distal extremity, 'a bar of vulcanite or celluloid – this latter to occupy the fornix of the vagina and uterus posteriorly'. See 'Spring Pessaries' in *Transactions of The Obstetrics Society of London*, vol. 23, 1881, pp. 238–9.

109. Dr E. Van De Warker of New York favoured the insertion of a self retaining intra-uterine stem of his own design. This device 'consist[ing] of a hard rubber stem, two and a half and three quarter inches long . . . slightly bulbed at the extremity' simultaneously forced the uterus into position and pulled the upper portion of the vagina into place. Van De Warker claimed that his modified stem was superior to that promoted by other doctors, because it was cheaper to manufacture and required less complicated machinery for its insertion. See Ely Van Der Warker, M.D., 'A New Self Retaining Intra-uterine Stem', *New York Medical Journal*, vol. xviii, no.4, October 1873, pp. 361–2.

110. Dr Galabin of Guy's Hospital reported a case in which a woman presented at the hospital for removal of a pessary inserted six years earlier. She had suffered from a fetid discharge and haemorrhage for a year prior to admission. Three unsuccessful attempts were

made to remove the pessary. A fourth required anaesthesia. The pessary was almost 'unrecognisable'. It was found 'very deep in the vagina . . . embedded in phosphatic calculite'. The 'base of the bladder was destroyed, and bladder, vagina and rectum, thrown into one common cloaca'. The Zwanke's pessary was finally extracted by 'pressing together one wing out of the rectum and the other out of the bladder'. Dr Galabin maintained it was 'very dangerous to recommend a Zwanke's pessary without making sure that the patient (understood) how to remove it herself, and (that she) must do so every night'. Dr Galabin, 'Fistule Caused By Zwanke's Pessary', *Transactions of the Obstetrical Society of London*, vol. 19, 1877, p. 202.

111. Dr G. Hewitt, 'Sixty Seven Cases Of Uterine Displacement Treated During Seven Years', *Medical Press and Circular: A Weekly Journal of Medicine and Medical Affairs*, January–June, 1880, pp. 519–20.

112. Braxton Hicks, 'On A Cause of Uterine Displacement', pp. 537–8.

113. W.S. Playfair, 'Systematic Treatment of Nervous Prostration And Hysteria Connected with Uterine Disease', *Lancet*, 28 May 1881, pp. 857–9. See p. 858 for this quote.

114. *ibid.*, Playfair described this treatment as a valuable subsidiary method of exercising the muscles of the debilitated woman. The process involved wetted sponges and electric poles placed on all the muscles, four inches apart. The electrical shocks began with the feet, and were given over the entire body except the head. 'There is no doubt that this is painful and disagreeable', wrote Playfair, but it is 'a question of utility'. See p. 858.

115. A report published in *Lancet* by the Clinical Society of London reveals the frequency of this injury, betrays the medical perception of the condition as 'hysterical' and outlines its treatment. The report discussed 'a typical and extreme instance of the affection not uncommon in gynaecological practice' in which a woman lost 4 stone, ceased menstruation and got bedsores, because her 'uterus was displaced by accident'. After its reposition via mechanical means, and obligatory bed rest, her appetite improved and she recovered. There was no mention of the corset in this article. See 'Acute Hysterical Vomiting Due to Displacement of the Uterus', *Lancet*, 19 June 1880, pp. 952–3.

116. C.C. Frederick, MD, 'Neurasthenia Accompanying And Stimulating Pelvic Disease', *Transactions of the American Association of Obstetrician and Gynaecologists*, vol. viii, 1895, pp. 351–5.

117. R. Barnes, 'Observations: Introduction to Clinical Detection on the Diseases of Women', *Lancet*, vol. 1, 3 January 1880, p. 6. Barnes, like several of his peers, claimed that the uterus was responsible for neuralgia, hysteria, epilepsy and paralysis. Though supposedly 'fearing the wrath' of his contemporaries Barnes also insisted that the uterus was responsible for 'not a few cases of insanity'.

118. P. Branca, *Silent Sisterhood: Middle Class Women in the Victorian Home,* Croom Helm, London 1975. In her discussion of the nineteenth-century proliferation of medical interest in the female body, Branca noted that between 1800 and 1900 four hundred different vaginal speculums were developed. There was too, observed Branca, an excessive use of medicated tampons and a 'fantastic variety of pessaries'. See pp. 63–4.

119. Galbraith, *Hygiene and Physical Culture*, p. 237.

Chapter 5

1. H. Roberts, 'The Exquisite Slave: The Role of Clothes in the Making of the Victorian Woman' *Signs*, vol. 2, no. 3, Spring 1977, p. 557.

2. P. Jalland has pointed out that there were two major 'turning points' regarding attitudes to death and mourning, the first of was the secularization of religion that occurred in the decades after 1870. The second turning point, which saw a dramatic decline in the rituals of mourning, was the First World War. See the final chapter of Jalland's text, *Death in the Victorian Family*, Oxford University Press, Oxford, 1996. See especially p. 371.

3. S. Kern, author of *The Cult of Love: Victoria to the Moderns*, Harvard University Press, Cambridge, Mass., 1992, disagrees. While Kern acknowledged that a 'ritualised memorialising of death' was typical of the Victorians, he claimed this ritualization indicted an inauthentic grief. See pp. 391–3. I do not entirely agree. While the pomp and circumstance of public funerals may have been little more than ceremony, Victorian women's poetry is often characterized by genuine, heartfelt grief, sustained by repeated loss.

4. P. Aries, *The Hour of Our Death*, Penguin, London, 1981, pp. 411–12.

5. *Doctor Death: Medicine at the End of Life*, An Exhibition Catalogue produced by curators at the Wellcome Institute for the History of Medicine, London, January 1997, p. 9.

6. Jalland, *Death and the Victorian Family*, p. 221. Interestingly, middle-class women were discouraged from attending the actual burial. I would argue further, that this shielded men from any perceived threats to their masculine identity, should they lose control and cry at the event.

7. The feminine internalization of death, and death's 'othering' to the feminine can also be detected when discussing the Victorian predilection for *memento mori*, which was chiefly worn and treasured by Victorian women. See Martha Pike, 'Mourning in Nineteenth Century America', in Ray Browne (ed.) *Rituals and Ceremonies in Popular Culture*, Bowling Green University Press, Ohio, 1980, pp. 296–315.

8. Mourning corsetry was also part of that attire. George Roberts, stay manufacturer, opened a special 'mourning stay' department in his three-storey corset warehouse and shop in 1851. Roberts's self-published catalogue was produced for distribution at London's Great Industrial Exhibition of 1851. See p. 9 of the catalogue.

9. B. Dijkstra, *Idols of Perversity; Fantasies of Feminine Evil in Fin de Siècle Culture*, Oxford University Press, Oxford, 1986, pp. 45–64.

10. Ibid., p. 56.

11. R. Barreca (ed.), *Sex and Death in Victorian Literature*, Macmillan, London, 1990, pp. 1–7. Contributors to this text have examined a number of popular poets and writers including, Rossetti, Tennyson, Bram Stoker, and Thomas Hardy.

12. D. English and B. Ehrenreich, *For Her Own Good: 150 Years of the Expert's Advise to Women*, Anchor Books, New York, 1978, pp. 108–9.

13. N. Auerbach, *Private Theatricals: The Lives of the Victorians*, Harvard University Press, Cambridge, Mass., 1990, pp. 90–4.

14. Poe cited in M. Praz, *The Romantic Agony*, Oxford University Press, Oxford, 1933. The edition cited here was published in 1970. See p. 27.

15. O.W. Holmes, *The Autocrat of The Breakfast Table: Every Man His Own Boswell*, Ward Lock, London, 1865, p. 243.

16. A. Gould-Woolson, *Women in American Society*, Robert Brothers, Boston, 1873, p. 192.

17. E. Haweis, *The Art of Beauty and the Art of Dress*, Garland, New York, 1978, p. 120.

18. L. Banner, *American Beauty*, Knopf, New York, 1983, p. 44.

19. W. Paget, 'Common Sense in Dress and Fashion', *Nineteenth Century*, March 1883, pp. 458–64. See pp. 459–60.

20. *By an American, Ladies and Gentlemen's Pocket Companion of Etiquette and Manners with the Rules of Polite Society, To Which is Added Hints of Dress, Courtship, Etc.*, no publisher, New York, *c.* 1850, p. 75.

21. C. Rogers, *Secret Sins of Society*, Union Publishing Co., Minneapolis, 1881, pp. 261–3.

22. R. Corson, *Fashions in Make-up: From the Ancient to Modern Times*, Owen, London, 1972, pp. 316–18.

23. Banner, *American Beauty*, p. 41.

24. Corson, *Fashions in Make-up*, p. 354.

25. Montez cited in Corson, *Fashions in Make-up*, p. 326.

26. *Bow Bells*, 29 January 1968, p. 11.

27. Banner, *American Beauty*, p. 41.

28. T. Habernas, 'The Psychiatric History of Anorexia Nervosa and Bulimia Nervosa: Weight Concerns and Bulimic Symptoms in Early Case Reports', *International Journal of Eating Disorders*, vol. 8, no. 3, 1989, pp. 259–73. See p. 266.

29. Early nineteenth-century texts also linked the drinking of vinegar to consumption. See for example Anon, *The Art of Beauty, or the Best Methods of Improving and Preserving the Shape, Carriage and Complexion Together with the Theory of Beauty*, Knight and Lacey, London, 1825, pp. 80–2.
30. *Bow Bells*, 12 April 1865, p. 286.
31. Combe cited in Roberts, 'Exquisite Slave', *Signs*, p. 561.
32. L. Limner, *Madre Natura Versus the Moloch of Fashion: A Social Essay,* Chatto & Windus, London, 1874, p. 117.
33. See *English Women's Domestic Magazine*, vol. 1, New Series, May 1860–April 1861, p. 192.
34. M. Harland, *Eve's Daughters; Or Common Sense For Maid, Wife, and Mother*, Anderson and Allen, New York, 1882, p. 348.
35. A. Ballin, 'Penalty of Tight Lacing', *Womanhood*, vol. 3, no. 16 March 1900, pp. 265–6.
36. 'Miss Surly on Tight Lacing' in *Bow Bells*, 14 September 1864, p. 163.
37. S. Beeton, *Beeton's Cookery Book for the People, and Housekeeping Guide to Comfort, Economy and Health*, Ward Lock, London, 1871, p. 73.
38. Edith Barnett, *Common-Sense Clothing*, Ward Lock, London, *c.* 1880, p. 72.
39. 'Miss Surly', *Bow Bells*, 14 September 1864, p. 163.
40. Mrs J. Farrar, *The Young Lady's Friend*, John B. Russel, Boston, 1837 (repr. 1873), p. 129.
41. E. Grosz, 'Notes Towards a Corporeal Feminism', *Australian Feminist Studies*, no. 5, Summer, 1987, pp. 1–17. See particularly pp. 1–7.
42. Ibid., pp. 1–7.
43. E. Thornwell, *The Lady's Guide to Perfect Gentility*, Derby and Jackson, Cincinnati, 1856, p. 137.
44. *Bow Bells*, 22 April 1868, p. 307.
45. Ballin, 'Penalty of Tight Lacing', p. 265.
46. Flower, *Arena*, vol. 4, no. 4 September 1891, p. 413.
47. E. Phelps, *What to Wear?* Sampson, Low [et al.], London, 1874, pp. 14–18.
48. Ibid., p. 14.
49. A. Merritt, *Dress Reform Practically and Physiologically Considered*, Jewitt Thomas, Buffalo, 1852, pp. 154–5.
50. H.St.H. Vertue, 'Chlorosis and Stenosis', *Guy's Hospital Report*, no. 104, 1955, pp. 329–48, see p. 333.
51. Ballin, 'Penalty of Tight Lacing', p. 265.
52. A. Gould-Woolson, *Dress Reform: A Series of Lectures Delivered in Boston, On Dress As It Affects the Health of Women*, Roberts Bros, Boston, 1874, p. 202.
53. Anon 'The Skeleton in Satin', *Daughters of America*, vol. 1 December 1886 p. 1. The final destroyed stanza reads thus:

—this creature of the tomb
—ain reasoning, lowless passion.
—of breast, the songster's plume,
—of man thy name is Fashion.

54. O. Fowler, 'Tight Lacing or the Evils of Compressing the Organs of Animal Life', *Medical Tracts: 1896–1898*, London, 1898, pp. 33–6.

55. Merritt, *Dress Reform*, p. 61.

56. Ibid., pp. 147–9.

57. Ibid., p. 61.

58. Trollope cited in Daniel Pool's, *What Jane Austin Ate and What Charles Dickens Knew: From Fox Hunting to Whist – the Facts of Daily Life in Nineteenth-Century England*, Simon and Schuster, New York, 1993, p. 52.

59. H. Evans and M. Evans, *The Party that Lasted 100 Days, The Late Victorian Season, a Social Study*, Macdonalds and Janes, London, 1976, pp. 82–96. This text discusses the frequency of social events and explains the differences between a dance, a ball, a kettledrum, etc.

60. Anon, *Immorality of Modern Dances*, Everitt and Francis Co. and S.F. Maclean, New York, 1904, pp. 31–2.

61. F. Willard, 'Dress and Vice', *Philanthropist*, May 1887, p. 8.

62. Revd Dr S. Vernon, *Amusements in the Light of Reason History and Revelation, Being a Collection of Sermons*, Walden and Stowe, New York, 1882, pp. 99–100.

63. This quote is from T.A. Faulkener's, *From Ballroom to Hell*, published in 1894, and was cited in Anon, *Immorality of Modern Dances*, see pp. 31–2.

64. M.B. Williams, *Where Satan Sows His Seed: The Card Table, The Wineglass, The Theatre, The Dance: Plain Talks on the Amusements of Modern Society*, Fleming H. Revell Co., New York, 1896, p. 57.

65. Willard, 'Dress and Vice', p. 8.

66. Vernon, *Amusements, etc.*, pp. 98–100.

67. Bloch cited in B.S. Talmey, *Woman: A Treatise on the Normal and Pathological Emotions of Feminine Love*, Stanley Press, New York, 1906, p. 10.

68. H. Ellis, *Studies in the Psychology of Sex*, F.A. Davis Co., Philadelphia, 1918, p. 172.

69. Thornwell, *The Lady's Guide*, p. 133.

70. F. Treves 'The Influence of Dress on Health', in Malcolm Morris (ed.) *The Book of Health*, Cassell, London, 1884, p. 512.

71. So frequent was the occurrence of fainting during the early part of the century that it was satirized in verse, interestingly by the poet Byron, who was often held responsible for encouraging and romanticizing female debility. Wrote Byron candidly: 'But where an English woman sometimes faints, Italian females don't do so outright; and then come to themselves almost or quite; which saves much hartshorn

salts, and sprinkling faces. And cutting stays, as usual in such cases.' Cited in Paul Muldoon, *The Essential Byron*, Ecco Press, New York, 1988, p. 51.

72. 'The Ball', *Bow Bells*, 8 May 1867, p. 354.

73. From 'Angelinas Fainted' a short story published anonymously in *The Lady's Companion; or Sketches of Life, Manners, and Morals, at the Present Day* (edited by a lady), H.C. Peck and T. Bliss, Philadelphia, 1852. This gentle and amusing satire cautioned women not to faint too often. Angelina had 'wonderful powers of syncope' but was warned by a maiden aunt not to faint too often. 'I can confess it now', remarked the aunt, 'I used to enjoy the excitement and therefore went off at every reasonable opportunity.' See pp. 56–7.

74. 'Cut her laces' was the typical response when 'some unfortunate succumbed' according to P. Cunnington and C. Willet, authors of *Feminine Attitudes in the Nineteenth Century*, William Heinemann Limited, London, 1935, pp. 340–1.

75. K. Ebing cited in R. Hauser, 'Krafft Ebing's Psychological Understanding of Sexual Behaviour', in R. Porter and M. Teich (eds), *Sexual Knowledge, Sexual Science: The History of Attitudes to Sexuality*, Cambridge University Press, Cambridge, 1994, pp. 210–27. See p. 212.

76. Harland, *Eve's Daughters*, p. 351, also cited in Haller, *The Physician and Sexuality*, p. 151.

77. E. Bronfen and S.W. Goodwin (eds), *Death and Representation*, Johns Hopkins University Press, Baltimore, 1993, p. 20.

78. TB, consumption or phthisis as it was variously known affected men and women, but women rather than men were more often killed by its contraction. One in ten female adolescents contracted TB in Victorian Britain, and it was the leading cause of death for adult women, accounting for a massive 40 per cent of deaths in women over twenty-five. See E. Shorter, *A History of Women's Bodies*, Penguin, Middlesex, 1982, p. 231.

79. S. Sontag, *Illness as Metaphor*, Farrar, Straus and Giroux, New York, 1977, p. 69.

80. While this was a widely spread belief, there were occasional disputes regarding its ability to create a consuming sexuality. J. Howe, author of *Excessive Venery, Masturbation, and Continence*, Birmingham and Co., New York, 1883, believed 'onanism' was the cause of phthisis, asthma and epilepsy. He also noted that 'the erotic tendencies [of the consumptive] antedate[d] the phthisis'.

81. Lewis's wife had suffered from the disease. See D. Lewis, *Weak Lungs and How to Make Them Strong or Diseases of the Organs of the Chest, Their Home Treatment by the Movement Cure*, W. Tweedie and Sons, Boston and London, 1863, p. 13 and p. 146.

82. Treves, 'Influence of Dress', p. 19.

83. Thornwell, *The Lady's Guide*, p. 136.

84. J.H. Kellog, *The Evils of Fashionable Dress and How to Dress Healthfully*, Office of the Health Reformer, Michigan, 1876, p. 9.

85. Ballin, 'Penalty of Tight Lacing', p. 265.

86. Roberts, 'Exquisite Slave', p. 562.

87. Advertised in *Queen*, 4 July 1863. Also advertised sporadically in *EDM* during that year.

88. Ibid., pp. 61–4.

89. Ibid., p. 13.

90. Sontag, *Illness as Metaphor*, pp. 24–7.

91. Poe cited in Praz, *Romantic Agony*, p. 27.

92. Dijkstra, *Idols of Perversity*, pp. 34–6.

93. Ibid., pp. 24–9.

94. Ibid., p. 334.

95. R.B. Yeazell, *Fictions of Modesty: Women and Courtship in the English Novel*, University of Chicago Press, Chicago, 1991, pp. 65–6. Yeazell demonstrates that blushing was seen as a physical bodily discourse that could replace language. As a consequence the blush, or flush, was widely discussed in female conduct literature. Blushing was thought to be both the 'woman's heart – and her other organs – made visible'.

96. Ibid., pp. 18–19.

97. Ibid., p. 11.

98. O.S. Fowler, 'Intemperance and Tight Lacing Founded on the Laws of Life As Developed by Phrenology and Physiology', paper 2, in *Medical Tracts 1896–98*, London, 1898, p. 33.

99. Harland recognized that the idealization and mimicry of TB resulted in part from its perception as a malady of the 'better' classes. Pretentious displays of blood-spitting were, she wrote, 'bathos and vulgarity' practised by 'the low minded parvenu who, because foibles [were] more easily imitated than virtues, copie[d] the mistakes of her superiors in breeding and sense'. Harland, *Eve's Daughters*, cited in Joan Jacobs Brumberg, *Fasting Girls: The Emergence of Anorexia Nervosa as a Modern Disease*, Harvard University Press, Cambridge, Mass., p. 172.

100. J. Marsh, *The Illuminated Language of Flowers*, Balance House, New York, 1978, p. 40.

101. Dying consumptive patients were known to have repulsive breath caused by the physical decay and the putrification of the lungs.

Chapter 6

1. K. McCrone, author of *Playing the Game: Sport and the Physical Emancipation of English Women, 1870–1914*, The University Press of Kentucky, Lexington, 1988, maintains that feminists sympathized with dress reform but did not see it as a 'significant theme'. While I

would contest this view, McCrone is correct in pointing out that some feminists eschewed rational dress, fearing it would 'damn their causes even further'. See p. 22.

2. *English Women's Review of Social and Industrial Questions*, no. xlv, 15 January 1877, p. 7.

3. M. Walker, MD, *A Woman's Thoughts About Love, Marriage, Divorce, etc.*, Miller, New York, 1871, p. 66.

4. Ibid., See especially pp. 77–8 for discussions of corsetry.

5. M.B. Jackson, 'Lecture 111', in A. Gould-Woolson, *Dress Reform*, Roberts Bros, Boston, 1874, pp. 68–97. See p. 70 for this quote.

6. The Turkish or Bloomer costume comprised a loose tunic, gently sashed at the waist, that fell below the knees and covered comfortable wide trousers that were gathered at the ankle. See Robert Riegel 'Women's Clothes and Women's Rights', *American Quarterly*, vol. 15, pp. 390–401.

7. Ibid., p. 392. Riegel's paper is an example of the way several costume historians have elided the importance of feminist dress reform activity into larger feminist concerns, while simultaneously charting sartorial 'victories' made by feminist dress reformers. See p. 401.

8. Gould-Woolson, *Dress Reform*, pp. vii–xi of the introduction.

9. D.J. Warner, "Fashion, Emancipation, Reform, and the Rational Undergarment", *Dress: The Journal of the Costume Society of America*, no. 4, 1978, pp. 24–9, see p. 24.

10. *Women's Tribune*, a substantial American feminist journal of the 1890s, which was devoted to suffrage reform, carried a regular column titled 'Health, Beauty and Dress' in which rational garments designed for the 'business woman', as well as her domestic sisters, were illustrated and discussed. See for example *Women's Tribune*, 30 May 1891, p. 174.

11. Willard cited in 'A Costume Wanted', *Woman's Standard*, vol. vi, no. 8, April 1892, p. 6.

12. F.E. Russell, 'Woman's Dress', *Arena*, vol. 3, February 1891, pp. 352–60.

13. Phelps, *What To Wear?*, Sampson, Low, et al., London, 1874, see p. iv of introduction.

14. Ibid., p. 66.

15. Jackson, 'Lecture 111', p. 70.

16. By a Young Widow, *How To Get Married Although a Woman: Or The Art of Pleasing Men*, J.S. Ogilvie, New York, 1892, p. 126.

17. By a Lady, *The Young Ladies' Mentor: A Guide to the Formation of Character in a Series of Letters to Her Unknown Friends*, H.C. Beck and Theo Bliss, Philadelphia, 1851, pp. 224–5.

18. H. Bushnell, *Women's Suffrage: The Reform Against Nature*, Charles Scribner and Company, New York, 1869, pp. 135–6.

19. L.O. Chant, "Gymnasium for Girls", *Woman's World*, 1899, pp. 329–32.

20. Many of the New Woman's opponents were not hostile to women's education with a component of exercise, as long as women's general education contributed to their construction as 'bright well informed housekeeper[s]'. See for example W.M. Thayer, *Womanhood: Hints and Helps for Young Women*, New York, *c.* 1895, p. 46.

21. G. Fraisse and M. Perrot (eds), *A History of Women in the West*, iv. *Emerging Feminism from Revolution to World War*, Harvard University Press, Cambridge, Mass., pp. 337–8.

22. C.H. Dall, *The College, the Market, And the Court: or Woman's Relation to Education, Labor, and Law*, Lee and Shepard, Boston, 1867, p. 232.

23. Y. Knibiehler, 'Bodies and Hearts', in Fraisse and Perrot (eds), *A History of Women in the West*, p. 338.

24. L. Limner, *Madre Natura Versus the Moloch of Fashion: A Social Essay*, Chatto & Windus, London, 1874, p. 109.

25. McCrone, *Playing the Game*, p. 6 of introduction.

26. R. Park, 'Sport, Gender and Society in a Transatlantic Victorian Perspective', in J.A. Mangan and R. Park (eds), *From Fair Sex To Feminism: Sport and the Socialisation of Women in the Industrial and Post Industrial Eras*, Frank Cass, London, 1987. See p. 5 and p. 65.

27. D. Lewis, *The Musical Gymnasium for Family and Schools with Illustrations of All The Positions*, 9th edn, W. Tweedie and Sons, London, 1867, introduction and pp. 5–6.

28. Lewis blamed many lung diseases, including TB, on corsetry and called it a 'cruel invention [that] ought at once and forever be abandoned'. See Lewis, *Weak Lungs and How to Make Them Strong, etc.*, W. Tweedie and Sons, London, 1863, p. 146.

29. McCrone, *Playing the Game*, p. 223.

30. Ibid., pp. 224–8.

31. Costume historian A. Mansfield has attributed the evolution of the sports uniform almost directly to the Rational Dress Society. See A. Mansfield, 'Dress of the English Schoolchild', *Costume*, no. 8, 1974, pp. 46–50.

32. Dr K. Mitchell, 'Are Women Physically Deteriorating?', *Woman*, 1 March 1890, pp. 2–3.

33. Thayer, *Womanhood*, p. 159.

34. A. Buck, *Victorian Costume and Costume Accessories*, Ruth Bean, Bedford, 1984, p. 86.

35. P. Cunnington and C. Willet, *The History of Underclothes*, Faber & Faber, London, 1952, p. 153. By the late nineteenth century combinations of apricot and peacock blue silk, and silk brocade were considered very elegant evening corset wear. See p. 125.

36. J. Laver, *Taste and Fashion From the French Revolution to the Present Day*, George Harrap and Company, London, 1945, p. 63.

37. By 1915 Osterberg's students had taken positions at Bryn Mawr, Girton, Newnham, University College Cardiff, Glasgow University,

St Andrew's University and the Women's college at Baltimore. See p. 96 of Paul Atkinson, 'Fitness Feminism and Schooling', in Sarah Delamont and Lorna Duffin, *The Nineteenth Century Woman: Her Cultural and Physical World*, Croom Helm, London, 1978, pp. 92–134. Atkinson has discussed the rise of gymnastics in British and North American schools from the mid- to late nineteenth century, and has examined the roles of other important female sports educators such as the Misses Buss and Beale and Dr Elizabeth Garrett Anderson.

38. *Saturday Review,* an American newspaper published in 1890, reported the growing trend in North America for 'athletic training for women', particularly in the exclusively female gymnasiums and directly attributed this to the British trend in female gymnastics. The *Review* also noted that, as under Osterberg's regime, each woman was carefully measured before commencing a fitness course in order to 'ascertain the muscular development of the various parts of the body'. Exercises were added until the woman 'blossomed into a lithe, elastic, muscular, little woman'. See *Saturday Review* cited in an article titled 'American Women's Athletics' in *Woman*, 20 November 1890, p. 14.

39. E. Clarke, a leading and influential education theorist and author of *Sex in Education: Or A Fair Chance For the Ladies*, New York, 1889, insisted education 'sapped the delicate bloom' of female students. He urged women to think less of cultivating their minds and assured them that the cultivation of their looks was a 'legitimate aspiration'. See p. 29. Education, claimed Clarke in a kind of biological determinist, social constructionist 'doublespeak', had to be 'tailored for the sexes', for while the 'cerebral processes by which the acquisition of knowledge [was] the same for each sex . . . the mode of life which [gave] nurture to the finest brain, and so enable[d] those processes to yield their best results [was] not the same for each sex'. See p. 21.

40. *Queen*, 6 April 1895, p. 612.

41. Advertisements for gymnasiums were also scattered throughout the *Queen*. McPherson's Gymnasium was, according to advertisements placed by that establishment, under 'royal patronage' and 'special consideration was shown to ladies and children'.

42. E. Sandow, 'Physical Culture for Women', in *Womanhood*, July 1899, pp. 857–9.

43. MacCrone, *Playing the Game*, pp. 222–3.

44. Park and Mangan, *From Fair Sex to Feminism*, p. 40.

45. Ibid., p. 44.

46. 'Stays', *Rational Dress Society Gazette*, October 1888, pp. 4–5. Statistics gathered by the Rational Dress Society from staymakers and sellers found that the average size of women's waists had actually decreased, over a period of twenty-five years. They attributed

this to tight lacing, lowered vitality brought about by tightly laced parents, as well as the prevention of full respiration and the lack of eating adequate food that tight lacing encouraged.

47. P. Atkinson, 'The Feminist Physique: Physical Education and the Medicalisation of Women's Education', in Mangan and Park, *From Fair Sex to Feminism*, p. 59.

48. S.K. Cahn, *Coming on Strong: Gender and Sexuality in Twentieth-Century Women's Sport*, The Free Press, New York, 1994, p. 10.

49. S. Bordo, 'Reading the Slender Body', in E.F. Keller, M. Jacobus and S. Shuttleworth (eds), *Body/Politics: Women and the Discourses of Science*, Routledge, New York, 1990, pp. 83–113. See p. 94 for this discussion.

50. Ibid., p. 208.

51. M. Foucault, *Discipline and Punish: The Birth of the Prison*, Pantheon Books, London, 1977, pp. 136–7.

52. *Woman*, 1 March 1890, p. 2.

53. This information taken from a Mey's Helene corset box label at Leicestershire Museum which has a large collection of these labels, including the 'School Girls' Athletic Corset' and the 'Pliable Romping Bodice'.

54. Cunnigton and Willet, *History of Underclothes*, p. 125.

55. The Gallery of English Costume in Manchester has an excellent example of the 'Anti-Corset' Corset. See artefact registration number 66.42/13 or photograph 27a.39.f.

56. Leicestershire Museum's Service. See Symington Collection, accession number B61.

57. Two major themes ran through the corset patents between 1850 and 1910. These were 'improvements' to strengthen the bones and steels to prevent them from breaking, and concerted attempts to make the garments less sweaty.

58. See 'Pretty's In the Manufacture of Corsets' being patent no. 1854 in *Patents for Inventions: Abridgements in Specifications, Class 141, Wearing Apparel*, Patents Office, London, pp. 2–3, 1884.

59. E. Barnett, *Common-Sense Clothing*, Ward Lock, London, *c.*1880, p. 74.

60. F.M. Steele and E. Livingstone, *Beauty of Form and Grace of Vesture*, B.F. Stevens, London, 1892, pp. 95–6. This text offered several alternative garments to women wishing to eschew corsetry. These were issued under the Newell patent and available at the dress reform rooms in Chicago by mail order. See appendix A and B at the back of the book for advice regarding the removal of corset bones.

61. *Women's Tribune*, 16 March 1895 p. 44.

62. See The Flynt Waist advertisement cited here in *Woman's Journal*, 15 November 1890, p. 368.

63. See the Equipoise Waist advertisement cited here in *Woman's Journal*, 15 November 1890, p. 368.

64. G. Anderson, MD, *Anderson's Physical Education: Health and Strength, Grace and Symmetry*, A.D. Dana, New York, 1897, pp. 26–9.

65. W. Blaikie, *How To Get Strong and Stay So*, Sampson, Low et al., London, 1880, pp. 62–3. While this strength of body and muscle definition was an acceptable goal for his male readers, Blaikie maintained that it would be an 'undesirable goal for most women'.

66. H.H. Ayer, *Harriet Hubbard Ayer's Book*, 1902, repr. Arno, New York, 1976, p. 244.

67. Steele and Livingstone, *Beauty of Form*. The moderate Delsarte and Checkley exercises provided gentle toning without muscle development, according to Steele, pp. 79–80.

68. Gould-Woolson, *Dress Reform*, pp. 148–9.

69. Ibid., pp. 155–6.

70. O.W. Holmes, *Over the Teacups*, Sampson, Low, Marston and Co., London, 1894, p. 181.

71. W.L. Howard, MD, *Confidential Chats with Girls*, Edward J. Clode, New York, 1911, p. 84.

72. A. Merritt, *Dress Reform Practically and Physiologically Considered*, Jewitt Thomas, Buffalo, 1852, pp. 160–1.

73. Chant, 'Gymnasium for Girls', *Woman's World*, 1899, pp. 329–32.

74. A.J. Miller, cited in 'Symposium on Women's Dress', *Arena*, vol. 6, October 1892, p. 644.

75. Barnett, *Common-Sense Clothing*, p. 71.

76. Duffin, 'Prisoners of Progress: Women and Evolution', in Delamont and Duffin (eds), *The Nineteenth-Century Woman*, pp. 57–90. See p. 57.

77. Gould-Woolson, *Dress Reform*, p. 201. Gould-Woolson recommended that women wear a brassière-like contraption that they could make themselves, if they felt their breasts needed support.

78. Lady Harberton, *Reasons for Reform in Dress*, Hutchings and Crowley Ltd, London, *c.* 1885, p. 12.

79. R. Bleier, *Science and Gender: A Critique of Biology and Its Theories on Women*, Pergamon Press, New York, 1984, pp. vii–viii.

80. M.F. Billington 'Waists and Stays', *Woman*, 26 June 1890, pp. 4–5.

81. C. Rover, *Love, Morals and the Feminists*, Routledge & Kegan Paul, London, 1970, similarly suggests that the New Woman's radical intellectualism encompassed matters from suffrage to sexual politics.

82. C. Smith-Rosenberg 'Discourses of Sexuality and Subjectivity; The New Woman 1870–1936', in Martin Duberman, Martha Vicinus and George Chauncey Jr. (eds), *Hidden From History: Reclaiming the Gay and Lesbian Past*, Penguin, New York, 1989, pp. 264–80. See especially pp. 265–6.

83. K. Silverman, 'Fragments of a Fashionable Discourse', in Tania Modleski (ed.) *Studies in Entertainment: Critical Approaches to Mass Culture*, Indiana University Press, Bloomington, 1986, pp. 139–52. See especially p. 193.

84. J. Finkelstein has discussed what she perceives as the inescapable power of dress in the late twentieth century to reveal the interiority of its occupants. My use of the phrases 'contour of the psyche' and 'written on the surface of the body' are taken from her text, *After a Fashion*, Polity Press, Cambridge, 1996, p. 6.

85. E. Walker, *The Dress Reform Problem: A Chapter for Women*, Hamilton Adams and Co., London, 1880, p. 7.

86. Dorothy (pseud.), 'Dress Reform', *Woman*, 29 March 1890, p. 6.

87. Dress reformers could be as scathing of the modern belle as the authors of mainstream texts were of rational dress. Phelps described fashionably dressed middle-class women as 'one panorama of awful surprises ... upholstered and ornamented ... bundled and not draped ... a meaningless dazzle of broken effects'. See *What to Wear?*, p. 14.

88. 'The Virile Girl', *Woman*, 5 April 1890, p. 11.

89. 'London and Paris Fashions', *Lady's Realm*, December 1897, pp. 689–90.

90. 'Manly Women', *Saturday Review* 22 June 1889, pp. 756–7.

91. Cahn, *Coming on Strong*, p. 20.

92. Smith-Rosenberg, 'Discourses', p. 266.

93. *Lippincott* article cited in Cahn, *Coming on Strong*, p. 8.

Chapter 7

1. T. Millum, *Images of Woman: Advertising in Women's Magazines*, Chatto and Windus, London, 1975, p. 11.

2. F. Presbrey, *The History and Development of Advertising*, Greenwood Press, New York, 1968, pp. 403–4.

3. L. de Vries, *The Wonderful World of Victorian Advertisements*, John Murray and Sons, London, 1968, p. 6.

4. 'An Article on Corsets' *Godey's Lady's Book and Magazine*, no. 68, 1863–4, p. 527

5. This advertisement was one of a series showing women actively enjoying sport. This advertisement for Ferris corsetry appeared in *Women's Tribune*, 7 November 1891, p. 29.

6. See Y&N corset advertisement in *Illustrated London News*, 7 January 1899, p. 36. The same advertisement also appeared repeatedly in *Woman's Life*. See for example *Woman's Life*, 23 May 1896, p. 447.

7. The invention of the half-tone plate in the late 1880s made the reproduction of photographs possible in newspapers and periodicals, and by the late century this process was often used to illustrate the garments with a dramatic realism.

8. F. Presbrey, *History and Development of Advertising*, p. 403–4.

9. See *Daughters of America*, 1 July 1887, p. 12.

10. Delsarte were frequent advertisers in *Woman's Tribune*: see *Woman's Tribune*, 22 August 1891, p. 272.

11. The Ferris advertisement cited here was published in *Woman's Tribune*, 29 August 1891, p. 278.

12. J. Winship, *Inside Women's Magazines*, Pandora Press, London, 1987. By the late nineteenth century women were highly identified with consumption; indeed several major magazines began as trade journals. See pp. 24–5.

13. H. Damon-Moore, *Magazines for the Millions: Gender and Commerce in the Ladies' Home Journal and the Saturday Evening Post, 1880–1910*, State University of New York Press, Albany, 1994. Damon-Moore describes the processes in which female gender norms and commerce became entwined in the late nineteenth century, by examining the evolution and rise of women's magazines. See pp. 2–21.

14. 'Madame Griswold's Skirt Supporting Corset' flier cited in Deborah Jean Warner, 'Fashion, Emancipation, Reform, and the Rational Undergarment', *Dress: Journal of the Costume Society of America*, no. 4, 1978, pp. 24–9. See p. 28 for this advertisement.

15. A. Carter, *Underwear: A Fashion History*, B.T. Batsford, London, 1992 p. 54.

16. B. Creed, *The Monstrous Feminine: Film, Feminism and Psychoanalysis*, Routledge, London, 1993. Creed's landmark work untangles conventional sexual myths perpetuated in films and television that position women as essentially devouring and evil.

17. F. Borzello, A. Kuhn, J. Pack and C. Wedd, 'Living Dolls and "real women"', in A. Kuhn, *The Power of the Image: Essays on Representation and Sexuality*, Routledge & Kegan Paul, London, 1985, pp. 9–18. See p. 10.

18. While Mulvey herself has reconsidered and refined theories of the 'male' gaze (particularly the notion that the male gaze is active and the female gaze is passive), her initial work on the hegemony of male spectatorship and fetishization of the female is still legitimate when examining corsetry advertisements. For criticisms of Mulvey's sexual division of the gaze, see Mary Ann Doane, *Femmes Fatales: Feminism, Film Theory, and Psychoanalysis*, Routledge, New York, 1991, pp. 20–2.

19. Roberts, *An Address To The Ladies*, corset catalogue, London, 1851, p. 11.

20. *Today* magazine, 21 March 1896, p. ii.

21. 'Old Gold' advertisement, *Illustrated London News*, 27 May 1899, p. 741.

22. I use the word lesbian cautiously here, given that until the early twentieth century the word was more or less confined to medico/sexologic literature, and was interchangeable with the terms 'sapphist' or 'female invert'. Romantic friendships were recognized by the Victorians, but were thought in the main to be asexual, because as Lillian Faderman points out, 'good women had no sex drive, therefore

there could be no sexual union between them'. See Faderman, *Surpassing the Love of Men: Romantic Friendship and Love Between Women from the Renaissance to the Present*, The Women's Press, London, 1985, p. 156.

23. D. Fuss, 'Fashion and the Homospectatorial Look', *Critical Inquiry*, no. 18, Summer 1992, pp. 713–37. See p. 713.

24. Ibid., p. 734.

25. M.A. Doane briefly discusses then disavows this process, in *Femmes Fatales: Feminism, Film Theory, Psychoanalysis,* Routledge, New York, 1991, pp. 20–1.

26. J. Fiske and J. Hartley, *Reading Television*, Routledge, London, 1989, p. 101.

27. J. Clarke, 'The Female Nude: The Objectification of Women in Art', *Ormond Papers: A Journal of Arts and Sciences*, vol. 11, 1994, pp. 97–111. See p. 98.

28. Ibid., p. 99.

29. R. Jenkyns, *The Victorians and Ancient Greece*, Basil Blackwell, Oxford, 1980, p. 135. See Jenkyns's chapter, 'The Consequences of Sculpture', pp. 135–54.

30. R. Pearsal, *Tell Me, Pretty Maiden: The Victorian and Edwardian Nude*, Grange Books, London, 1992, pp. 20–2.

31. Sewell's advertisements cited here belong to the Mactaggart manuscript collection held at the Gallery of English Costume in Manchester. While this collection is of considerable merit it has very little documentation, which has meant that few items within the collection (specifically corsetry advertisements) have been sufficiently documented at the time of their collection. Many corset-related items collected by the Mactaggarts were cut out of nineteenth-century magazines without complete details being recorded. Illustration cited here is listed as Mactaggart 19.E.43.

32. M. Warner, *Monuments and Maidens: The Allegory of the Female Form*, Picador, , London, 1985, p. 236.

33. The 'Corset Sylphide' advertisement cited here found in *Illustrated London News*, 22 April 1899, p. 597.

34. The I.C. Persephone advertisement cited here was regularly advertised in *Myra's Journal*. See 1 January 1890, p. 23.

35. Weingarten advertisement discussed here was cited in Norah Waugh, *Corsets and Crinolines*, B.T. Batsford, London, 1954, p. 108.

36. L. Jordanova, *Sexual Visions: Images of Gender in Science and Medicine between the Eighteenth and Twentieth Centuries*, Harvester Wheatsheaf, New York, 1989, pp. 96–7.

37. Warner, *Monuments and Maidens*, p. xix

38. See for example the advertisement for Warner's Coraline corset in *Woman's Journal*, 15 June 1889, p. 191.

39. Ibid.

40. The Harness Electric Corset was one of many appliances that capitalized on the Victorian fascination with electric currents and magnetic

fields. This advertisement was cited in Alison Carter's, *Underwear: A Fashion History*.

41. M. Daley, *Gyn/Ecology: The Meta Ethics of Radical Feminism*, The Women's Press, London, 1991, pp. 135–77.

42. Those very items may, however, also be read as a table of instruments laid out for the sadist.

43. Abigail Solomon-Godeau, 'The Legs of the Countess', in E. Apter and W. Pietz, (eds), *Fetishism as Cultural Discourse*, Cornell University Press, Ithaca, 1993, pp. 266–306. See p. 269. Soloman-Godeau's fascinating article examines the pornographic photographs of the Countess de Castiglione, and concludes that despite the countess', authorship of these images the photographs present a 'fundamental contradiction' for she endlessly 'reproduced herself [on film] as a work of elaborately coded femininity'. See p. 278.

44. B. Caine, *Victorian Feminists*, Oxford University Press, Oxford, 1992. See pp. 248–59 for an excellent summary of the late nineteenth-century feminist contribution to the controversial and very public discourse on female sexuality.

45. B. Dijkstra, *Idols of Perversity: Fantasies of Feminine Evil in Fin-de-Siècle Culture*, Oxford University Press, Oxford, 1936, pp. 145–7.

46. J. Carey, *The Intellectuals and the Masses: Pride and Prejudice among the Literary Intelligentsia, 1880–1939*, Faber & Faber, London, 1992, pp. 5–6.

47. A. McClintock, *Imperial Leather: Race, Gender and Sexuality in the Colonial Contest*, University of Indiana Press, Bloomington, 1995, pp. 208–9. I am indebted to McClintock for this idea. Her text, which does not discuss corsetry, examines the ways in which Victorian soap advertisements 'traffick[ed] promiscuously across the threshold of public and private'.

48. L. Mulvey, *Visual and Other Pleasures*, Indiana University Press, Bloomington, 1989, p. 19.

49. A. Kuhn, *The Power of the Image: Essays on Representation and Sexuality*, Routledge & Kegan Paul, London and Boston, 1985, pp. 28–33.

50. As Marina Warner points out, to disrobe the male body publicly is to leave it vulnerable. The exposed female body on the other hand is made both vulnerable and sexual by its disrobing.

51. *Church of England Messenger*, 1 January 1897, p. 13.

52. T. Laqueur, 'Clio Looks at Corporal Politics', in *Corporal Politics*, Beacon Press, Boston, 1993, pp. 14–22.

53. H. Posner 'Separation Anxiety', in *Corporal Politics*, See pp. 22–30. The exhibition includes work by L. Bourgeois, R. Gober, A. Messager and others. Posner described their work as fragmented forms that ranged from the archetypal to intensely personal and autobiographical. See p. 22 for fuller details.

54. See *Harper's Bazaar*, 6 April 1895, p. 274, for such an advertisement, which was reproduced frequently that year.

55. Laqueur, *Corporal Politics*, pp. 14–15. Laqueur offers a convincing discussion of the 'medical gaze'.

56. L. Nochlin, *The Politics of Vision: Essays on Nineteenth-Century Art and Society*, Harper and Row, New York, 1989, p. 91.

57. Interestingly H. Clayson's *Painted Love: Prostitutes in French Art of the Impressionist Era*, Yale University Press, New Haven, 1991, also looks at the representation of women in French art and dwells at length on Manet's *Nana*. However, Clayson does not recognise that the numerous renditions of Nana in her ubiquitous blue corset may be read as a fragmentation (let alone a violent objectification) of the subject's torso. See pp. 74–8.

58. L. Mulvey's 'Visual Pleasure and Narrative Cinema' was first published in *Screen* 1975 and republished in *Visual and Other Pleasures*, London, 1989. See pp. 14–26.

59. J. Fiske, *Television Culture*, Routledge, London, 1989, p. 225.

60. Warner, *Monuments and Maidens*, p. 37.

Bibliography

Primary Sources

Abel, L, Mrs, *Woman in Her Various Relations Containing Practical Rules for American Females, the Best Methods for Dinners, Social Parties etc with a chapter for Young Ladies and Invalids. Hints on Body, Mind and Character with a Glance at Women's Rights, Women's Wrongs, Professions, Costumes and Parties*, W. Holdredge, New York, 1851.

Adams, D.W.H., *Celebrated English Women of the Victorian Era*, F.V. White & Company, London, 1884.

Acton, W., *The Functions and Disorders of the Reproductive Organs in Childhood, Youth, Adult Age, and Advanced Life, Considered in their Physiological, Social and Moral Relations*, John Churchill, London, 1862.

Alger, W.R., *Friendships of Women*, Roberts Brothers, Boston, 1894.

Alibert, Dr, *Tribadism and Sapphism*, Rue Etienne Marcel, Paris, *c.* 1900.

Allbut, T.C., MD, & W.S. Playfair, MD, *A System of Gynaecology*, Macmillan and Co., London, 1896.

Allen, C., *The Sexual Perversions and Abnormalities*, Oxford University Press, Oxford, 1940.

Allen, F.L., *Only Yesterday: An Informal History of the 1920s*, Bantam Books, New York, 1931.

Ames, M.C., *Ten Years in Washington. Life and Scenes in the National Capital, As a Woman Sees Them*, Queen City Publishing Company, Cincinnati, 1874.

Anderson, W.G., *Anderson's Physical Education: Health and Strength, Grace and Symmetry*, A.D. Dana, New York, 1897.

Anon., *Argentine Figure Training*, no publishing details, *c*.1940.

——, *Beauty is Power*, G.W. Carleton and Company, New York 1871.

——, *Behaving or Papers on Children's Etiquette*, D. Lothrop and Company, Boston, 1877.

——, *Bindery Girls Protection Union Souvenir*, no publisher indicated, Chicago, 1891.

——, *Curiosa of Flagellants: Facetious Anecdotes of Ladies*, privately printed, 1930.

——, *Decorum: A Practical Treatise on Etiquette and Dress of the Best American Society*, J.A. Ruth and Company, Philadelphia, 1879.

——, *Etiquette for Gentlemen: A Guide to the Observances of Good Society*, Ward, Lock & Co. London, *c*.1925.

——, *Etiquette for Ladies: A Guide to the Observances of Good Society*, Ward, Lock & Co. London, *c*.1925.

——, *Figure Training Fundamentals for Women of Distinction and Discernment*, Naboman and Company, Los Angeles, 1952.

——, *Figure Training Reminiscences or the Use of Tight Corsets, Gloves, and High Heels in the Achievement of Fashionable Excellence*. No publishing details, thought by staff at the Kinsey Library to have been a privately published reproduction of an English book originally published between 1890 and 1900.

——, *How to Dress or Etiquette of the Toilette*, Ward Lock and Tyler, London, *c*.1860.

——, *How To Dress On Fifteen Pounds a Year: As A Lady By A Lady*, Frederick Warne and Company, London and New York, 1873.

——, *How to Dress Neatly and Prettily on Ten Pounds a Year By One Who Has Done it for Ten Years*, G.W. Allen, London, *c*.1870.

——, *How To Train the Figure and Attain Perfection of Form*, The Central Publishing Company, London, 1896.

——, *Immorality of Modern Dances*, Everitt and Francis Co. and S.F. Maclean, New York, 1904.

——, *Ladies' Indispensable Assistant: Being a Companion for the Sister, Mother, and Wife*, publication details incomplete, New York, 1851.

——, *Manners of Modern Society: Being a book of Etiquette*, Cassell, Petter and Galpin, London, New York and Paris, 1880.

——, *Six Years Labour and Sorrow: In Reference to the Traffic in the Souls and Bodies of British Girls*, Dyer Brothers Morgan and Scott, London, 1885.

——, *Stays and Gloves: Figure Training and Deportment, by means of the Discipline of Tight Corsets, Narrow Heeled Boots, Clinging Kid Gloves, Combinations and Etc.*, publisher not revealed, London, 1909.

——, *The Art of Beauty or the Best Methods of Improving and Preserving the Shape Carriage and Complexion Together with the Theory of Beauty*, Knight and Lacey, London, 1825.

——, *The Ugly Girl Papers; or, Hints for the Toilet*, reprinted from *Harper's Bazaar*, New York, 1874, p. 225.

——, *The Workwoman's Guide, Containing Instructions to the Inexpensive in Cutting Out and Completing those Articles of Wearing Apparel 4 etc. Which are Usually made at Home; Also Explanations on Upholstery, Straw Platting, Bonnet Making, Knitting*, London, 1838, pp. 81–2.

——, *The Young Ladies' Book: A Manual of Elegant Recreations, Arts, Sciences and Accomplishments*, Henry G. Bohn, London, 1859.

——, *Ultra High Heel Boots and Shoes*, typed notes, hand-tinted illustrations, *c.*1900.

Aretz, G., *The Elegant Woman, from the Rococo Period to Modern Times*, translated by James Laver, Harcourt Brace and Co., New York, 1932.

Austin, H., MD, *American Costume Or Woman's Right To Good Health*, F.W. Hurd and Company, New York, 1867.

Austin, J.M., *Golden Steps To Respectability, Usefulness, and Happiness: Being a Series of Lectures To Youth of Both Sexes, On Character, Principles, Associates, Amusements, Religion, and Marriage*, Auburn, Derby, Miller and Co., Auburn, 1850.

Ayer, H.H., *Harriet Hubbard Ayer's Book: A Complete And Authentic Treatise On The Laws Of Health And Beauty*, Springfield, 1899, reprint Arno, New York, 1976.

Azel, A., MD, *Sex in Industry: A Plea for the Working Girl*, New York, James R. Osgood & Co., 1875.

Bachelor, A., *Wanted, A Wife*, Daniel V. Wein & Co., New York, 1904.

Bain, A., *Mental and Moral Science: A Compendium of Psychology and Ethics*, Longmans Green and Company, 1884.

Ballantyne, J.W., MD, *Manual of Antenatal Pathology and Hygiene, The Embryo*, William Green and Sons, 1904.

Ballin, A., *The Science of Dress in Theory and Practice*, Sampson Low, Marston, Searle and Rivington, London, 1885.

——, *Personal Hygiene*, F.J. Rebman, London, 1894.

Banks, A.M., *Instructions for Drafting Bodice Patterns* (from the Sussex System) London, no publishing details, *c.*1900.

Barnett, E.A., *Common-Sense Clothing*, Ward Lock, London, *c.*1880.

Bayard, M. (ed.), *Weldon's Practical Fancy Dress for Ladies*, vol. 111, Weldon and Co., London, undated appears to be *c.*1900.

Beale, L., *Our Morality and The Moral Question*, Reprint, Arno Press, New York, 1974. First published by J. and A. Churchill, London, 1887.

Beam, L. & R.L. Dickinson, *The Single Woman: A Medical Study in Sex Education*, Williams Norgate Ltd., London, 1934.

Beecher, C. and H. Beecher Stowe, *Principles of Domestic Science; As Applied To The Duties and Pleasures of Home; A Text-book For the Use of Young Ladies in Schools, Seminaries, and Colleges*, J.B. Ford and Company, New York, 1870.

Beecher, H.W., Mrs, *Motherly Talks With Young Housekeepers: Brief Articles on Topics of Home Interest and About Five-hundred Choice Receipts For Cooking*, J.B. Ford and Company, New York, 1873.

Beecher, Miss, *Miss Beecher's Housekeeper and Health Keeper: Containing Five Hundred Recipes For Economical and Healthful Cooking: Also Many Directions For Securing Health and Happiness*, Harper and Brothers, New York, 1876.

Beecher, Mrs, *A Treatise on Domestic Economy for the Uses of Young Ladies at Home, at School*, J.B. Ford and Co., 1870.

Beeton, S., *Beeton's Cookery Book for the People, and Housekeeping Guide to Comfort, Economy and Health*, Ward Lock, London, 1871.

——, *Samuel Beeton's Book of the Laundry: Or the Art of Washing, Bleaching, Cleansing, etc.*, Ward Lock, London, 1871.

Bell, E.A, *Fighting the Traffic in Girls*, no publishing details, 1910.

Bell, R.H, *Woman From Bondage to Freedom*, The Critic and Guide Co., New York, 1921.

Berry Hart, D., MD and A.H. Freeland Barbour, MD, *Manual of Gynaecology*, 5th edn, W. and A.K. Johnson, Edinburgh, 1897.

Bigelow, M., *Sex Education: a Series of Lectures Concerning Knowledge of Human Life*, The Macmillan Company, New York, 1920.

Bingham, T., *The Girl That Disappears: The Real Facts About the White Slave Traffic*, The Gotham Press, 1911.

Blackwell, E., MD, *The Religion Of Health*, John Menzies, Edinburgh, 1878.

Blaikie, W., *How To Get Strong and Stay So*, Sampson, Low, Marston, Searle and Rivington, London, 1880.

Bloch, I., *Ethnological and Cultural Studies of the Sex Life in England, Illustrated* (by Subscription to Cultured Adults Only), Falstaff Press, Inc., New York, 1934.

—— *Sexual Life in England: Past and Present, A History of British Sexual Mores*, Wehman Brothers, London, 1938.

Boehn, M. von and O. Fischel (trans. G. Thompson), *Modes and Manners of the Nineteenth Century As Represented From the Pictures of the Time*, J.M. Dent and Sons Limited, London, 1927.

Booth, C., *Life and Labour of the People in London*, Second Series: Industry, *Dress, Food, Drink Dealers, Clerks, Locomotion and Labour*, Macmillan and Company Limited, 1903. First published 1896 as volume vii of *Life and Labour of the People*.

Brinton, D. and G. Napheys, *Personal Beauty: How To Cultivate It And Preserve It In Accordance With The Laws Of Health*, W.J. Holland, Massachusetts, 1870.

Brockett, L., MD, *Woman: Her Rights, Wrongs, Privileges, and Responsibilities,* Publication details incomplete. Text first published 1879. This edn republished by Books For Libraries Press, New York, 1976.

Brown, H., MD, *The Wife: Her Book,* Sisley's Limited, London, 1907.

Bryce, A., *The Laws of Life and Health,* Andrew Melrose, London, 1912.

Burgess, C., *The Sex Philosophy of the Bachelor Girl,* Advanced Thought Publishing, Chicago, 1920.

Bushnell, H., *Women's Suffrage: The Reform Against Nature,* Charles Scribner and Company, New York, 1869.

Butler, J., *Women's Work and Women's Culture: A Series of Essays,* Macmillan and Company, London, 1869.

By a Fellow of the Royal College of Surgeons, *Kallos, A Treatise on the Scientific Culture of Personal Beauty and the Cure of Ugliness,* Simpkin Marshall and Company, London, 1883.

By a Lady, *The Workwoman's Guide, Containing Instructions to the Inexpensive in Cutting out and Completing those Articles of Wearing Apparel & etc. Which are Usually made at Home; Also Explanations on Upholstery, Straw platting* (sic) *Bonnet Making, Knitting,* Simpkin, Marshall and Company, London, 1838.

By a Lady, *The Young Ladies Mentor: A Guide to the Formation of Character in a Series of Letters to Her Unknown Friends,* H. C. Beck and Theo Bliss, Philadelphia, 1851.

By a Lady, *Woman, Her Dignity and Her Sphere,* American Tract Society, New York, 1870. The name 'Lizzy Bates' is pencilled in as author on an original copy.

By a London Physician, *The Ladies Physician: A Guide for Ladies in the Treatment of their Ailments,* Cassell and Company, Ltd, London, Paris and Melbourne, 1895.

By a Number of Experts, *A Practical Guide to Corset Cutting and Making,* John Williamson and Company, Limited, London, 1930.

By a Reading Architect, *Knickerbockers for Both, A Lively Letter or Two on Dress Reform,* F. Starkey, Reading, *c.*1890.

By a Woman, *Woman's Rights and Duties,* John W. Parker, London, 1860.

By a Young Widow, *How To Get Married Although a Woman: Or The Art Of Pleasing Men,* J.S. Ogilvie, New York, 1892.

By an American, *Ladies' And Gentlemen's Pocket Companion Of Etiquette and Manners With The Rules Of Polite Society To Which Is Added Hints Of Dress, Courtship, Etc.,* No publisher shown, New York, *c.*1850.

Calthrop, D.C., *English Dress from Victoria to George V,* Chapman & Hall, Ltd., London, 1934.

Caplin, Madam Roxy, *Health and Beauty: or Corsets and Clothing Constructed in Accordance with the Physiological Laws of the Human Body,* Kent and Co., Holbourn Hill, 1855.

——, *Woman and Her Wants, Four Lectures to Ladies,* Kent and Co., London, 1860.

——, *Health and Beauty: or Woman in Her Clothing Considered in Relation To the Physiological Laws of the Human Body*, rev. edn, Kent and Company, London, 1864.

——, *Woman and Her Work, The Needle: A Lecture Given by R.A. Caplin*, William Freeman, London, c.1870.

——, *Women in the Reign of Queen Victoria*, Dean and Son, London, 1877.

Carpenter, E., *The Intermediate Sex: A Study of Some Transitional Types of Men and Women*, George Allen & Unwin, London, 1908.

Carrington C., *A Paradox on Woman Wherein It Is Sought To Prove That They Do Not Belong To The Human Species*, no publisher, Paris, 1798.

Catalogue of Exhibits and *Gazette*, from The Rational Dress Association, Reprinted by Garland Publishing, Inc., New York, 1978.

Catalogue of the Chilean Exhibition at the Centennial of Philadelphia, Valparaso, Mercurio Printing Office, 1876.

Chance, J., *The Cost of English Morals*, Noel Douglas, London, 1931.

Chavasse, H.P. , *Advice To A Wife on the Management of Her Own Health and on the Treatment of Some of the Complaints Incidental to Pregnancy, Labour, and Suckling* (rev.edn by F. Barnes, MD, consulting physician to the British Lying-in Hospital), J. & A. Churchill, London, 1898.

Checkley, E., *A Natural Method of Physical Training: Making Muscle and Reducing Flesh Without Diet or Apparatus*, G.P. Putnam's Sons, London, 1892.

Chesterton, C., Mrs, *Women of the Underworld*, Stanley Paul & Co., London, 1928.

Chisholm, C., *The Medical Inspection of Girls in Secondary Schools*, Longmans Green, and Co., London, 1914.

Clarke, E.H., MD, *Sex in Education: Or A Fair Chance For The Ladies*, James R. Osgood, Boston, 1873.

Collins, C., *Love of A Glove*, Fairchild Publishing Co., New York, 1945.

Colonial and Indian Exhibition Official Catalogue, William Clowes and Sons, London, 1886.

Combe, A., MD, *Treatise on the Physiological and Moral Management of Infancy for the Use of Parents*, Maclachlan and Stewart and Company and Simpkin, Marshall and Company, London, 1840.

Conger-Kaneko, J., *Woman's Voice An Anthology*, the Stratford Company, Boston, 1918.

Cooke, N.F., *Satan in Society*, C.F. Vent, Baltimore, 1876, reprint edn, Arno Press, New York, 1974.

Craik, D., *A Woman's Thoughts About Woman*, Hurst and Blackett, London, 1859.

Crawley, E., *Dress, Drinks and Drums: Further Studies in Savages and Sex*, Methuen & Co., London, 1931.

Creighton, L., *Memoir of a Victorian Woman: Reflections of Louise Crieghton, 1850–1936*, Indiana University Press, Bloomington (ed. by J.T. Covert) 1994.

Criminal Law Amendment Act, 496740, Vigilance Committee and Their Work: containing THE NEW LAW FOR THE PROTECTION OF GIRLS with Suggestions as to its Enforcement, London, 1885.

Daies, J.E., MD, *Prize Essay on the Laws For the Protection of Women*, Longmans, Brown, Green and Longmans, London, 1854.

Dall, C.H., *The College, The Market, and The Court: or Woman's Relation to Education, Labor, and Law*, Lee and Shepard, Boston, 1867.

Deems, C.F., *What Now? For Young Ladies*, American Tract Society, New York, 1869.

De La Santé, Madame, *The Corset Defended*, T.E. Carter, London, 1865.

Denham, H.W., MRCS, *The Use and Action of Stays on Disease and Development of the Female Figure*, John Churchill, London, *c.*1860.

DeWitt Talmage, Revd T., *The Marriage Ring, A Series Of Sermons On The Duties Of The Husband And Wife And On The Domestic Circle*, J.S. Ogilvie, New York, 1886.

——, *Woman: Her Power And Privileges, A Series Of Sermons On The Duties Of The Maiden, Wife And Mother, And Of Their Influence In The Home And Society*, J.S. Ogilvie, New York, 1888.

Dillon, J., *From Dance Halls To White Slavery*, Padell Book and Magazine Company, New York, 1941.

Dingwall, E.J., *The Girdle of Chastity: A Medico-Historical Study*, George Routledge and Sons, London, 1931.

Duffy, E.B., *The Relations of the Sexes*, 1876, reprint, Arno Press, New York, 1974.

——, *What Women Should Know; A Woman's Book About Women*, 1873, reprint, Arno Press, New York, 1974.

Eaton, T.T., *Talks on Getting Married*, Baptist Book Concerns, Louisville, 1891.

Ecob, H.G., *The Well Dressed Woman: A Study in the Practical Application to Dress of the Laws of Health, Art, and Morals*, Fowler and Wells, New York, 1892.

Edited by a Lady, *The Lady's Companion; or, Sketches of Life, Manners, and Morals, at the Present Day*, H.C. Peck & Theo. Bliss, Philadelphia, 1852.

E.D.M. (pseud.), *Figure Training, or Art the Handmaid of Nature*, Ward, Lock and Tyler, London, 1871.

Elliot, G., *Understanding the Adolescent Girl*, Henry Holt Co., New York, 1930.

Ellis, H.H., *Studies in the Psychology of Sex: Sexual Selection in Man*, F.A. Davis Co., Philadelphia, 1918.

——, *Psychology of Sex: A Manual for Students*, William Heinemann Medical Books, London, 1933.

Emmet, T., MD, *The Principles and Practices of Gynaecology*, J. & A. Church, London, 1885.

Evans, E.E., *The Abuse of Maternity*, Lippincott, Philadelphia, 1875, reprint, Arno Press, New York, 1974.

Farrar, D., *Temperance Reform As Required By National Righteousness and Patriotism*, James Nisbett and Company, London, 1899.

Farrar, John, Mrs, (née Elizabeth Ware Rotch), *The Young Lady's Friend*, John B. Russel, Boston, 1837 (repr. 1873).

Finck, H.T., *Romantic Love and Personal Beauty: Their Development, Causal Relations, Historical and National Peculiarities*, Macmillan and company, London and New York, 1887.

Finot, J., *Problems of the Sexes*, David Nutt, London, 1913.

Fletcher, E.A., *The Woman Beautiful: A Practical Treatise in the Development and Preservation of Women's Health and Beauty and the Principles of Taste in Dress*, W. M. Young, New York, 1899.

Flinn, E., *Our Dress and Our Food in Relation to Health*, M.H. Gill and Son, Dublin, 1886.

Flugel, J., *The Psychology of Clothes*, Hogarth Press, London, 1950, reprint of 1930 edn.

Forel, August, *The Sexual Question*, Rebman Company, New York, *c*.1930.

Fothergill, J.M., *The Maintenance of Health: A Medical Work for Lay Readers*, Putnam, New York, 1875.

Fourth Annual Report of the Commissioner of Labor, 1888, Working Women In Large Cities, Government Printing Office, Washington, 1880.

Frank, L. Mrs, *Rents in Our Robes*, Clark and Co., Bedford, N.Y., 1888.

Frank, M.H., *Eugenics and Sex Relations*, Books, Inc. New York, 1937.

Gaillard T., MD, *A Practical Treatise on the Diseases of Women*, Henry C. Lea's Sons, Philadelphia, 1880.

Galbraith, A., MD, *Hygiene and Physical Culture for Women*, Dodd, Mead and Company, New York, 1895.

——, *Personal Hygiene and Physical Training For Women*, W.B. Saunders Company, Philadelphia, 1911.

Gallichan, W.P. , *A Text Book of Sex Education for Parents and Teachers*, T. Werner Laurie Ltd, London, 1918.

——, *Sexual Apathy and Coldness in Women*, The Stratford Co., Boston, 1928.

——, *The Poison of Prudery: An Historical Survey*, T. Werner Laurie Ltd., London, 1929.

——, *The Great Unmarried*, Frederick Stokes Co., New York, *c*.1910.

Gardener, G.E., *Plain Talk: A Pamphlet on The Population Question and The Moral Responsibility Of Woman In Maternity*, G.E. Wilson, Chicago, *c*.1890.

Gardner, A.K., *Conjugal Sins Against the Laws of Life and Health*, J.S. Redfield, New York, 1870; reprint, Arno Press, New York, 1974.

Gasquoine, H.C., *The Truth About Woman*, Dodd, Mead and Company, New York, 1913.

Gibbon, Lloyd, Mrs, *A Treatise on the Use and Effect of Anatomical Stays*, Brentford Printer, no publisher, London, 1809.

Gilbert, O.P. , *Women in Disguise*, John Lane the Bodley Head, Ltd, London, 1932.

Gill, E., *Clothes: An Essay Upon the Nature and Significance of the Natural and Artificial Integuments Worn by Men and Women*, Jonathan Cape, London, 1931.

——, *Trousers the Most Precious Ornaments*, Faber & Faber, 1937.

G.M.G., *The Stage Censor: An Historical Sketch 1544–1907*, Samson Low, Marston and Company, London, 1908.

Goodell, W., MD, *Lessons in Gynaecology*, 3rd end, F.A. Davis, Philadelphia, 1887.

Gould, A., *The Science of Regenerative or Sex Enlightenment: A Study of the Sacred Laws that Govern the Sex Forces*, Advanced Thought Publishing Co., London, 1913.

Gould-Woolson, A., *Dress Reform: A Series of Lectures Delivered in Boston, On Dress As It effects The Health of Women*, Roberts Brothers, Boston, 1874, reprint Arno Press, 1974.

——, *Women in American Society*, Robert Brothers, Boston, 1873.

Graves, A.J., Mrs, *Women in America, Being an Examination into the Moral and Intellectual Condition of American Female Society*, Harper and Brothers, New York, 1843.

Great Exhibition of Works of Industry Of All Nations, 1851: Official Description and Illustrations Catalogue, William Clowes and Sons, London, 1852.

Grenfell, Mrs H. and Miss Baker, *Dress Cutting Out with Diagrams on Sectional Paper: A Simple System for Class and Self Teaching*, Longmans, Green and Company, London and New York, 1888.

Griffith, E., *Modern Marriage and Birth Control*, Methuen and Co., London, 1937.

——, *Sex in Everyday Life*, George Allen & Unwin, 1938.

Gueber, H., *Yourself and Your House Wonderful*, The Uplift Publishing Co., Philadelphia, 1913.

Hale, S.J., *Manners; Or Happy Homes and Good Society All The Year Round*, J.E. Tilton and Company, Boston, 1868; reprint, Arno Press, New York, 1972.

Hall, G., *The Pitfalls of the Ballroom*, Laird and Lee Publishers, Chicago, 1901.

Hall, S., *Adolescence: Its Psychology and Its Relations to Physiology, Anthropology, Sociology, Sex, Crime, Religion and Education*, vols 1 and 2, D. Appleton and Company, New York, 1904.

Harberton, Viscountess, *Reasons for Reform in Dress*, Hutchings and Crowley Ltd, London, *c.*1885.

Harcourt, C., Mrs, *Good Form For Women: A Guide to Conduct and Dress on All Occasions*, The John C. Winston Company, Philadelphia, 1907.

Harland, M., *Commonsense in the Household: A Manual of Practical Housewifery*, Charles Scribner's Sons, New York, 1882.

——, *Eve's Daughters; Or Common Sense For Maid, Wife, And Mother*, John R. Anderson and Henry S. Allen, New York, 1882.

——, *Our Daughters: What Shall We Do With Them? A Talk To Mothers*, G.W. Carleton, and Company, New York, 1879.

——, *Secrets of A Happy Home*, The Christian Herald, New York, 1896.

——, Harland, M. (ed.) also published as M. Terhune and M. Harland, *Talks Upon Practical Subjects*, Warner Brothers, New York, 1895.

Haweis, E., *The Art of Beauty and The Art of Dress*, Garland, New York, 1978.

Hawkins, T., *Self Teaching Directions for the London ABC Tailor System of Dress Cutting*, rev. edn, W. Staker, Ludgate Hill, c.1880.

Hayes, J.W., *The Draper and the Haberdasher: A Guide to the General Drapery Trade*, Houlston and Sons, London, 1878.

Himes, N.E., *A Medical History of Contraception*, Gamut Press, New York, 1936; reprinted 1963.

Hirschfeld, M., *Sexual Pathology*, Emerson Books Inc., New York, 1940.

Holliday, R., *Unmentionables From Fig Leaves to Scanties*, Ray Long and Richard R. Smith, New York, 1933.

Holmes, O.W., *Over The Tea Cups*, Sampson, Low, Marston and Company, London, 1894.

——, *The Autocrat of the Breakfast Table: Everyman His Own Boswell*, Ward Lock and Company, London, 1865.

Hosmer, W., *The Young Lady's Book or, the Principles of Female Education*, Auburn: Derby and Miller, New York, 1851.

Howard, W., MD, *Breathe and Be Well*, Edward J. Clode, New York, 1916.

——, *Confidential Chats With Girls*, Edward J. Clode, New York, 1911.

Howe, E., *Invisible Anatomy: A Study of Nerves, Hysteria and Sex*, Faber & Faber, London, 1940.

Howe, J.M., *Excessive Venery, Masturbation, and Continence*, Birmingham & Company, New York, 1883.

Howell, M., Mrs, *The Handbook of Millinery Comprised in a Series of Lessons for the Formation of Bonnetts, Capotes Turbans, Caps, Bows and etc; To which is Appended a Treatise on Taste and the Blending of Colours. Also an Essay on Corset Making*, Cox and Sons, London, 1847.

Humphrey, Mrs, *How To Be Pretty Though Plain*, James Bowden, London, 1899.

Hunt, A., Mrs, *Our Grandmother's Gowns*, Field and Tuer, Leadenhall Press and Company, London, c.1870.

Isobel, *The Art of Beauty : A Book for Women and Girls* by a Toilet Specialist, C. Arthur Pearson Limited, London, *c.*1890.

Jacobus, X., *Crossways of Sex: A Study of Eroto-pathology*, British Bibliophiles Society, Paris, 1904.

Jaeger, G., *Clothing and Bedding Reform for Men, Women and Children*, Waterloo and Sons Limited, London, 1884.

Jerome, H., *The Secret of Woman*, Chapman and Hall, Ltd, New York, 1923.

Jessop, C.M., *Dress and Health and Appeal to Antiquity and Common Sense*, Eliot Stock, London, 1869.

Judd, Mrs, *Mrs Judd's Illustrated Hand-book for Self Instruction in the Art of Dress Making, Fitting & with Model Busts and Patterns*, self published, London, 1855.

Jullien, L., *Libertinism and Marriage*, F. A. Davis Co., Philadelphia, 1901.

Kellerman, A., *Physical Beauty How to Keep It*, George H. Doran Company, New York, 1918.

Kellog, E.E., Mrs, *Social Purity: The Purity Pledge, A Talk To Girls*, International Tract Society, Melbourne, *c.*1900.

Kellog, J.H., *Ladies' Guide in Health and Disease: Girlhood, Maidenhood, Wifehood Motherhood*, Echo Publishing Company, Melbourne, *c.*1900.

——, *The Evils of Fashionable Dress and How To Dress Healthfully*, Office of the Health Reformer, Michigan, 1876.

Key, E., *The Morality of Woman*, The Ralph Fletcher Seymour Co., Chicago, 1911.

Kisch, H., MD, *The Sexual Life of Woman in its Physiological, Pathological, and Hygienic Aspects*, Heinemann, London, 1926.

Knopf, O., *The Art of Being a Woman*, Little, Brown Co., Boston, 1932.

Lawrence, J. (pseud. for L.J. McCauley) *The Single Woman*, Duell, Sloan, Pearce, New York, 1915.

Leland, C., *The Alternate Sex or the Female Intellect in Man and the Masculine in Woman*, Funk and Wagnalls Company, New York, 1904.

Leslie, E., *Miss Leslie's Behaviour Book: A Guide and Manual For Ladies* Originally published by T.B. Peterson and Brothers, Philadelphia, 1859; reprint, Arno Press, New York, 1972.

Leslie, F., Mrs, *Rents In Our Robes*, Bedford, Clarke & Company, New York, 1888.

Lesser Columbus (pseud.), *Greater Bristol*, Simpkin, Marshall, Hamilton, Kent and Company Ltd, London, 1893.

Lewers, A., *A Practical Handbook of the Diseases of Women*, 5th edn, H.K. Lewis, London, 1897.

Lewis, D., *Chastity: or Our Legal Sins*, Tweedie and Sons, Philadelphia, 1874; reprint, Arno Press, New York, 1974.

——, *Five Minute Chats With Young Women and Certain Other Parties*, Harper and Brothers Publishers, New York, 1874.

——, *The Musical Gymnasium for Family and Schools with Illustrations of all the Positions*, 9th edn, W. Tweedie and Sons, London, 1867.

——, *Weak Lungs and How to Make them Strong, or Diseases of the Organs of the Chest, Their Home Treatment by the Movement Cure*, W. Tweedie and Sons, Boston and London, 1863.

Lidstone, J.T.S., *The Londoniad: Giving a Full Description of the Principle Establishments, Together with the Most Honourable and Substantial Business Establishments in the Capital of England & &*, Published under universal patronage, London, 1856.

Limner, L. (pseud. for John Leighton), *Madre Natura Versus The Moloch of Fashion: A Social Essay*, Chatto & Windus, London, 1874.

Lombroso, C., *Criminal Man: According to the Classification of Cesare Lombroso*, G. Putnam's Sons, London, 1911.

——, *The Female Offender*, Appleton & Co., New York, 1898.

Lord, W.B., *The Corset and the Crinoline: A Book of Modes and Costumes*, Ward, Lock and Tyler, London, 1865.

——, *Figure Training or Art the Handmaiden of Nature*, Ward, Lock and Tyler, London, 1871.

Lowney, E.B., *Herself: Talks with Women Concerning Themselves*, Forbes & Co., Chicago, 1920.

Mackirdy, Archibald, Mrs and N.W. Willis, *The White Slave Market*, Stanley Paul & Co., London, *c.*1900.

Madame Schilde's Winter Fashions Biannual Illustrated Catalogue of Parisian Patterns for Ladies and Children. Useful Garments by Madame Schilde, self-published, 1878–9.

Mantegazza, P. , *Physiognomy and Expression*, Contemporary Science Series, London, 1911.

Mayhew, H. (ed.), *The Greatest Plague of Life: Or The Adventures of a Young Lady in Search of a Good Servant by One Who has Been 'almost Worried to death'*, David Bogue, London, 1847.

McFadden, B., *The Power and Beauty of Superb Womanhood*, Physical Culture Publishing Company, New York, 1903.

Mencken, H.L., *In Defence of Woman*, The Freelance Books, New York, 1918.

Merrifield, Mrs, *Dress As A Fine Art: With Suggestions On Children's Dress*, John P. Jewett and Company, Boston, 1854.

Merritt, A., *Dress Reform Practically and Physiologically Considered*, Jewitt Thomas Publishers, Buffalo, 1852.

Mirkland, W., *The Joys of Being a Woman and Other Papers*, Houghton and Miflin, Boston, 1918.

Moll, A., *Perversions of the Sex Instinct, A Study of Sexual Inversion*, Julian Press, Newark, 1899 (repr. 1931).

Morris, M., *The Book of Health*, Cassell, London, 1884.

Napheys, G., MD, *The Physical Life of Woman: Advice to the Maidens Wife and Mother*, Balliere, Tindall and Cox, Philadelphia, 1870, p. 175.

——, *Modern Surgical Therapeutics: A Compendium of Current Formulae, Approved Dressings and Specific Methods For Treatment*, 7th edn, Bailliere, Tindall and Cox, London, 1881.

Nichols, T.L., MD, *The Herald of Health Almanac*, published by the Sanitary Depot, London, 1877.

Niemoeller, A.F., *Essays of an Erotologist, Some Observations on Little Known Aspects of Sex: Sex and Clothing*, Haldeman-Julius Publications, Girard, Kansas, 1946.

O'Sullivan, M.U., *The Proclivity of Civilised Woman to Uterine Displacements: The Antidote*, Stillwell and Company, Melbourne, 1894.

Parke, R., *Human Sexuality, A Medico Literary Treatise on the Laws, Anomalies and Relations of Sex with Special Reference to Contrary Sexual Desire*, Professional Publications Co., Philadelphia, 1908.

Pearce, M.K., *Leaflets for Mothers' Meetings: Some Legal Aspects of the Question*, Social Purity Series, Women's Temperance Publication Association, Chicago, c1890.

Pearse, F., MD, *Modern Dress and Clothing in its Relation to Health and Disease*, Wyman and Sons, London, 1882.

Phelps, E., *What To Wear?*, Sampson, Low, Marston, Low, and Searle, London, 1874.

Ploss, H.M. and P. Bartels, *Woman: An Historical Gynaecological and Anthropological Compendium*, vols, 1–4, C.V. Mosley Co., New York, 1936.

Prospectuses of the Greater London Exhibition, William Clowes and Sons, London, 1851.

Raverat, G., *Period Piece*, Faber & Faber, London, 1960.

Rayne, M.L., *Gems of Deportment and Hints of Etiquette: The Ceremonials of Good Society, Including Valuable Moral, Mental, And Physical Knowledge, Original and Compiled From the Best Authorities, With Suggestions On All Matters Pertaining To The Social Code. A Manual of Instruction for the Home*, Tyler and Company, Indianapolis, 1882.

Reynolds, J., MD, *The Limiting of Childbearing Among The Married*, reprinted from the Transactions of the American Gynaecological Society, 1890.

Robbins Pennell, E., *The Feasts of Autolycus: The Diary of A Greedy Woman*, John Lane, London and New York, 1896.

Roberts, G., *An Address To The Ladies*, self-published corset catalogue, London, 1851.

Rogers, C., *Secret Sins of Society*, Union Publishing Co., Minneapolis, 1881.

Roth, B., MD, *Dress: Its Sanitary Aspects*, John Beale and Company, Brighton, 1880.

Sangster, M.E., *Winsome Womanhood*, Fleming H. Revell Co., New York, 1900.

Scharlieb, M., MD, *A Woman's Words to Women on the Care of Their Health in England and India*, Swan Sonnenschein and Company, London, 1895.

Schilde, Marie, Madame, *Old English Costumes*, S. Miller, London, 1883.

Shaftesbury, E., *Sex Magnetism: Lessons in the Cultivation of Magnetism of the Sexes*, Ralston University Press, Meriden, Connecticut, 1925.

Sladdin, W.H., *Shoulderology! Bustology!*, Simpkin Marshall, Hamilton, Kent and Company Limited, London, 1896.

Smith, P. J., *The Soul of a Woman: An Interpretation of the Philosophy of Feminism*, Paul Elder and Co, San Francisco, 1916.

Spring, G., DD, *The First Woman*, M.W. Dodd, London, 1852.

Steele, F.M. & E.A. Livingstone, *Beauty of Form and Grace of Vesture*, B.F. Stevens, London, 1892.

Stekel (or Steckel), W., *Bisexual Love: The Homosexual Neurosis*, The Gorham Press, Boston, 1922.

——,*Sadism and Masochism: Disorders of the Instincts of the Emotions*, Vision Press Limited, London, 1943.

Stillwell, R., Revd, *Dress Pride and Beauty: A Plea for Plainness and Naturalness*, William Briggs, Toronto, 1896.

Stockham, A.B., *Tokology: A Book For Every Woman*, L.N. Fowler and Company, London, *c*.1900, first published 1883.

Stone, A., MD, *The Women of the Streets*, Burton Publishing Company, Missouri, 1919.

Stopes, C., *British Freewomen: Their Historical Privilege*, Swan and Sonnenschein and Company, Paternoster Square, 1894.

——, *Contraception: Its Theory History and Practice*, London, Putnam and Co. Ltd, London, 1946.

——, *Wise Parenthood*, G.P. Putnam's Sons, Ltd., London, 1926.

Storer, H.R., MD, *Why Not? A Book For Every Woman [and] A Book for Every Man*, Lea and Shepard, Boston, 1868; reprint, Arno Press, New York, 1974.

Strahan, S., MD, *Marriage and Disease: A Study of Heredity and the More Important Family Degeneration*, Kegan, Paul, Trench and Trubner Co. Ltd, 1892.

Stuart, J.B., *On Beauty: Three Discourses Delivered in the University of Edinburgh with an Exposition of the Doctrine of the Beautiful According To Plato*, Sutherland and Knox, Edinburgh, 1858.

Sylvia (sic), *How To Dress Well on a Shilling a Day: A Ladies' Guide to Home Dressmaking and Millinery*, Ward, Lock and Tyler, London, 1863.

Talmey, B.S., *Woman: A Treatise on the Normal and Pathological Emotions of Feminine Love*, The Stanley Press Corporation Publishers, New York, 1906.

Thayer, W., *Womanhood: Hints and Helps for Young Women*, New York, *c*.1895.

The British Section at the Vienna Universal Exhibition, 1873, J.M. Johnson and Sons, London, 1873.

The Crystal Palace and Its Contents, Being an Illustrated Cyclopaedia of the Great Exhibition of the Industry of All Nations, W.M. Clark, London, 1852.

The Great London Exhibition, Reports by The Juries on the Subjects in the 36 Classes into which the Exhibition was Divided, William Clowes and Sons, London, 1863.

Thomas, M. and A. Goodchild, *Dress Cutting and Making for County Council and Other Technical Classes: Tailor System*, John Williamson and Company, London, 1890.

Thornwell, Emily, *The Lady's Guide to Perfect Gentility*, Derby and Jackson, Cincinnati, 1856.

Tilt, E.J., *A Handbook on Uterine Therapeutics and of the Diseases of Women*, John Churchill and Sons, London, 1868.

Tonna, C.E., *The Works of Charlotte Elizabeth*, M.W. Dodd, New York, 1845.

Treves, F. FRCS, *The Dress of the Period: A Lecture Delivered on Behalf of the National Health Society*, Hodges and Smith, Dublin, 1851.

Trollope, A., *The Way We Live Now*, Oxford University Press, Oxford, 1982 [1875].

Tuke, D.H., *A Dictionary of Psychological Medicine*, J.A. Churchill, London, 1892.

Uzanne, Octave, *The Fan*, J.C. Bain, London, 1884.

——, *The French Woman of the Century: Fashions, Manners, Usages*, George Routledge and Sons, New York, 1887.

Veblen, T., *The Theory of the Leisure Classes: An Economic Study of Institutions*, Unwin Books, London, 1970; first published New York, 1899.

Vernon, S., *Amusements in the Light of Reason History and Revelation Being a Collection of Sermons*, Walden and Stowe, New York, 1882.

Von Hartman, E. and A. Kenner, *The Sexes Compared, Etc.*, Swan Sonnensschein & Co., London, 1895.

Walker, Alexander, *Beauty in Women Analysed and Classified With A Critical View of the Hypotheses of the Most Eminent Writers, Painters and Sculptors*, Thomas D. Morrison, London, 1892.

Walker, A., Mrs, *Female Beauty as Preserved and Improved by Regimen, Cleanliness and Dress*, Thomas Hurst, London, 1837.

Walker, E., *The Dress Reform Problem: A Chapter For Women*, Hamilton Adams and Company, London, *c.*1880.

Walker, E.C., *What the Young Need to Know: A Primer of Sexual Rationalism*, M. Harman, Chicago, *c.*1910.

Walker, F. (ed.), *United States Centennial Commission International Exhibition 1876: Reports and Awards, Groups viii*, J.B. Lippincott and Co., Philadelphia, 1877.

Walker, I., *Dress as it Has Been Is and Will Be: Discussing with Particularity Recent Innovations and Forecasting the Tendency of Male Drapery from What We Know, Together With All That is Practical Today*, Isaac Walker, New York, 1885.

Walker, M., *A Woman's Thoughts About Love, Marriage, Divorce, etc.* Miller, New York, 1871.

Ward, E.M., *The Dress Reform Problem: A Chapter For Women*, no publisher, Bradford, *c*.1870.

Ward, H., *Memories of Ninety Years*, Hutchinson and Company, London, 1924.

Watts, G.F., *George Frederick Watts: His Writings*, vol. 3, Macmillan, London, 1912.

Webb, E.M., *The Heritage of Dress: Being Notes on the History and Evolution of Clothes*, Times Book Club, new and rev. edn, London, 1912.

Webster, A., *A Housewife's Opinions*, Macmillan and Company, London, 1879.

Weininger, O., *Sex and Character*, William Heinemann, New York, undated possibly *c*.1920.

Wells, R., *Manners Culture and Dress of the Best American Society, Including Social, Commercial and Legal Forms*, King Richardson and Co., Cincinnati, 1894.

Weldon, Mrs, *Weldon's Practical Crochet*, Weldon and Co., London, *c*.1895; Dover reprint, 1974.

Westermark, E., *The Future of Marriage in Western Civilisation*, The Macmillan Company, London, 1937.

Willard, F.E., *Occupations For Women*, The Success Company, New York, 1897.

Willett, C. and Cunnington, B., *Feminine Attitudes in the Nineteenth Century*, William Heinemann Ltd., London, 1935.

Williams, M., *Where Satan Sows His Seed: The Card Table, The Wineglass, The Theatre, The Dance; Plain Talks on the Amusements of Modern Society*, Fleming H. Revell Co., New York, 1896.

Willmot, T., Mrs, *The Young Woman's Guide, Containing Correct Rules for the Pursuit of Millinery, Dress and Corset Making: Illustrated by Lithographic Plans with Many Useful Remarks to Young Women and Servants of Every Denomination*, J.L. Cox and Sons, London, 1841.

Wise, D., Revd, *The Young Ladies Counsellor: Or Outlines and Illustrations of the Sphere, the Duties and the Dangers of Young Women*, J.S. Publishers and Stationers Co. Ltd, Otley, 1888, pencilled into first page.

Wood-Allen, M., MD, *Almost A Woman*, Signs Publishing Company, Melbourne, *c*.1900.

——, *Ideal Married Life: A book for All Husbands and Wives*, Fleming and Revel and Company, Chicago, *c*.1900.

Worth et Cie corsetières, *Corset, Trousseau and Layette List*, Regent St, London, *c*.1885.

Wright, H.C., *Marriage and Parentage: Or the Reproductive Element in Man as a Means to his Elevation and Happiness*, no publisher, Boston, 1855.

Journal articles

Anon., 'Death from Tight Lacing', *Lancet*, 14 June 1890, p. 1316.

——, 'Experiments of The Hyderabad Commission on Tight Lacing as a Cause of Death in Chloroform Anaesthesia', *Lancet*, 21 June 1890, pp. 1366–95.

——, 'Tight Lacing', *Lancet*, 28 May 1881, p. 877.

——, 'Tight Lacing Again', *Lancet*, 10 January 1880, p. 75.

——, 'The Treatment of Prolapsus Uteri without Mechanical Means', *Practitioner: A Monthly Journal of Therapeutics*, vol. ix, July to December, 1872, pp. 305–6.

Archer, J., 'Chastity Belts', in *Man's Magazine*, vol.8, no. 7, July, 1960, pp. 94–5,

Bacchi, C., 'Feminism and the "Eroticisation" of the Middle-Class woman: The Intersection of Class and Gender Attitudes', *Women's Studies International Forum*, vol. 11, no. 1, 1988, pp. 43–53.

Barnes, R., MD, 'Observations: Introduction to Clinical Detection on the Diseases of Women', *Lancet*, 3 January 1880, p. 6.

Benfield-Barker, B., 'Sexual Surgery in Late Nineteenth Century America', *International Journal of Health Services*, vol. 5, no. 2, 1975, pp. 279–99.

Braxton Hicks, J., MD, 'On a Cause of Uterine Displacement, Not Hitherto Mentioned, Contra-indicating the Use of Pessaries', *Lancet*, 20 March 1886, pp. 537–8.

Breward, C., 'Femininity and the Problem of the Late Nineteenth-Century Fashion Journal', *Journal of Design History*, vol. 7, no. 2, 1994, pp. 71–89.

Bullough, V. and M. Voight, 'Women, Menstruation and Nineteenth-Century Medicine' in *Bulletin of the History of Medicine*, no. 47, 1973, pp. 66–83.

Cannaday, C., MD, 'The Relation of Tight Lacing to Uterine Development and Pelvic Disease', *American Gynaecological and Obstetrical Journal*, vol. 5, 1895, pp. 632–40.

Clarke, J., 'The Female Nude: The Objectification of Women in Art', *Ormond Papers: A Journal of Arts and Sciences*, vol. 11, 1994, pp. 97–111.

Cole, B., MD, 'Spring Pessaries', *Transactions of Obstetrics Society*, London, vol. xxx111, 1881, pp. 238–9.

Coleman, E., 'Boston's Athenaeum for Fashions', *Dress: Journal of the Costume Society of America*, no. 5, 1979, pp. 25–32.

Collins W.J., MD, 'The Effect of Tight Lacing Upon the Secretion of Bile', *Lancet*, 17 March 1888, p. 548.

Cooper, R., 'Victorian Discourses on Women and Beauty: The Alexander Walker Texts', *Gender and History*, vol. 5, no. 1, Spring 1993, pp. 34–55.

Cott, N.F., 'Passionlessness: An Interpretation of Victorian Sexual Ideology, 1790-1850', *Signs*, no. 4, 1978, pp. 219–23.

Cunningham, A. R., 'The "New Woman Fiction" of the 1890s', *Victorian Studies*, vol. xviii, no. 2, December 1973, pp. 177–87.

Davies, M., 'Corsets and Conception: Fashion and Demographic Trends in the Nineteenth Century', *Journal of Comparative Studies in Sociology and History*, vol. 24, 1982, pp. 611–41.

Degler, C., 'What Ought to Be and What Was: Female Sexuality in the Nineteenth Century', *American Historical Review*, vol. 79, no. 5, December 1974, pp. 1467–90.

Dickinson, R.L., MD, 'The Corset, Questions of Pressure and Displacement', *New York Medical Journal*, 46, 1887, pp. 507–16.

Doran, A., 'Deficient Development of the Uterus-Atresia of the Externum-Atrophy of the Ovaries-Insanity', *Obstetrical Journal of Great Britain and Ireland including Midwifery and the Diseases of Women and Children*, no. lxxxi, December 1897, pp. 578–9.

Duffy, J., MD, 'Masturbation and Clitoridectomy', *Journal of the American Medical Association*, vol. 8, 1863, pp. 186–246.

Edmonds, E.M., 'Female Clothing Preferences Related to Male Sexual Interest', *Bulletin of the Psychonomic Society,* vol. 22, no. 3, 1984, pp. 171–3.

Evans, G.E., 'Dress and the Rural Historian', *Costume*, no. 8, 1974, pp. 38–40.

Eyer, A., MD, 'Clitoridectomy as Cure for Masturbation in Young Women', *International Medical Magazine*, Philadelphia, vol. 3, 1894–5, pp. 259–62.

Fishman, S., 'The History of Childhood Sexuality', *Journal of Contemporary History*, vol. 17, 1982, pp. 269–83.

Fowler, O.S., 'Intemperance and Tight Lacing: Founded on the Physical Laws As Developed by Phrenology and Physiology', in *Medical Tracts, 1896–98*, London, 1892.

——, 'Tight Lacing or the Evils of Compressing the Organs of Animal Life', *Medical Tracts: 1896–1898*, London, 1898, pp. 33–6.

Frederick, C.C., MD, 'Neurasthenia Accompanying and Stimulating Pelvic Disease', *Transactions of the American Association of Obstetricians and Gynaecologists*, vol. viii, 1895, pp. 351–5.

Fuss, D., 'Fashion and the Homospectatorial Look', *Critical Inquiry*, no. 18, Summer 1992, pp. 713–37.

Galabin, W., MD, 'Fistule Caused by Zwanke's Pessary', *International Transactions of the Obstetrical Society*, London, vol. xx, 1878, p. 169.

Garrison, D., 'Immoral Fiction in the Late-Victorian Library', *American Quarterly*, Spring 1976, pp. 71–89.

Gaskell, C.M., 'Women of Today', *Nineteenth Century*, November 1889, pp. 776–84.

Gorham, D., 'The "Maiden Tribute to Babylon": Re-examined: Child Prostitution and the Idea of Childhood in Late Victorian England', *Victorian Studies*, vol. 21, no. 3, Spring 1978, pp. 353–81.

Gosling, F., 'Neurasthenia in Pennsylvania: A Perspective on the Origins of American Psychoanalysis, 1870–1910', *Journal of the History of Medicine and Allied Science*, vol. 40, no. 2, April 1985, pp. 188–206.

Graily-Hewitt, W., MD, 'Sixty Seven Cases of Uterine Distortion Or Displacement Treated During Seven Years', *Medical Press and Circular: A Weekly Journal of Medicine and Medical Affairs*, January–June 1880, pp. 519–20.

Grosz, E., 'Notes Towards a Corporeal Feminism', *Australian Feminist Studies*, no. 5, Summer 1987, pp. 1–17.

Gull, Sir W.B., Article 36, 'Hysterical Anorexia', *Half Yearly Abstract of the Medical Sciences: Being a Digest of British and Continental Medicine and of the Progress of Medicine and the Collateral Sciences*, vol. lviii, July–December 1873, pp. 43–5.

——, 'Anorexia Nervosa', *Lancet*, 17 March, 1888, pp. 516–17.

Habernas, T., 'The Psychiatric History of Anorexia Nervosa and Bulimia Nervosa: Weight Concerns and Bulimic Symptoms in Early Case Reports', *International Journal of Eating Disorders*, vol. 8, no. 3, 1989, pp. 259–73.

Haller, J.S., 'Neurasthenia* The medical profession and the "new woman" of the late nineteenth century', *New York State Journal of Medicine*, February 1971, pp. 473–82.

Hare, E.H., 'Masturbatory Insanity: The History of an Idea', *Journal of Mental Science*, vol. 108, no. 452, January 1962, pp. 2–25.

Harris, Ruth, 'Melodrama, Hysteria and Feminine Crimes of Passion in the *Fin-de-Siècle*', *History Workshop: A Journal of Socialist History*, issue 25, Spring 1988, pp. 31–64.

Harrison, B., 'Underneath The Victorians', *Victorian Studies*, vol. 10, no. 3, March 1967, pp. 239–63.

Hartman, M.S., 'Child-Abuse and Self-Abuse: Two Victorian Cases', *History of Childhood Quarterly*, no. 2, 1974, pp. 221–48.

Helverston, S., 'Popular Advice for the Well Dressed Woman in the Nineteenth Century', *Dress: Journal of the Costume Society of America*, no. 6, 1980, pp. 30–4.

Higginbotham, A.R., '"Sin of the Age": Infanticide and Illigitimacy in Victoriana London', *Victorian Studies*, vol. 32, no. 3, Spring 1989, pp. 319–38.

Hudson, R.P., 'The Biography of Disease: Lessons From Chlorosis', *Bulletin of the History of Medicine*, no. 51, 1977, pp. 448–63.

Kett, J.F., 'Adolescence and Youth in Nineteenth-Century America', *Journal of Interdisciplinery Studies*, vol. 11, no. 2, 1971, pp. 283–98.

Knight, P., 'Women and Abortion in Victorian and Edwardian England', *History Workshop: A Journal of Socialist History*, issue 4, Autumn 1977, pp. 57–70.

Kunzle, D., 'Dress Reform as Antifeminism: A Response to Helene E. Roberts's "The Exquisite Slave: The Role of Clothes in the Making of the Victorian Woman"', *Signs*, vol. 2, no. 3, 1977, pp. 570–9.

Lane, A., FRCS, 'Civilisation in Relation To the Abdominal Viscera, With Remarks On the Corset', *Lancet*, vol. 2, 13 November 1909, pp. 1416–17.

La Sorte, M.A., 'Nineteenth-Century Family Planning Practices', *Journal of Psychohistory*, vol. 4, no. 2, Fall 1976, pp. 163–83.

Mactaggart, P. & Mactaggart, A., 'Ease Convenience and Stays, 1750–1850', *Costume*, no. 13, 1979, pp. 41–51.

Mansfield, A., 'Dress of the English School Child', *Costume*, no. 8, 1974, pp. 46–50.

Masters, A., 'The Doll As Delegate and Disguise', *Journal of Psychohistory*, vol. 13, no. 3, Winter 1986, pp. 293–308.

May, M., 'Innocence and Experience: The Evolution of the Concept of Juvenile Delinquency in the Mid-Nineteenth Century', *Victorian Studies*,

Mclaren, A., 'Abortion in England 1890–1914', *Victorian Studies*, vol. 20, no. 4, Summer 1977, pp. 379–400.

Mercer, C. and Wangensteen, S., '"Consumption, heart disease, or whatever": Chlorosis, a Heroine's Illness in *The Wings of the Dove*', *Journal of the History of Medicine and Allied Sciences*, vol. 40, 1985, pp. 259–85.

Montague, K., 'The Aesthetics of Hygiene: Aesthetic Dress, Modernity, and the Body as Sign', *Journal of Design History*, vol. 7, no. 2, 1994, pp. 91–112.

Morris, R., MD, 'Is Evolution Trying to Do Away With the Clitoris?', *Transactions of the American Association of Obstetricians and Gynaecologists*, vol. v, 1892, pp. 288–303.

Negrin, L., 'The Meaning of Dress', *Arena Journal*, Series, no. 7, 1996, pp. 131–46.

Ormond, L., 'Female Costume in Aesthetic Movement of the 1870s and 1880s', *Costume: Journal of Costume and Society*, no. 2, pp. 47–52.

Paget, W., 'Common Sense in Dress and Fashion', *Nineteenth Century*, March 1883, pp. 458–64.

Parkes Weber, F., MD, 'Two Diseases Due To Fashion in Clothing: Chlorosis and Chronic Erythema of the Legs', *British Medical Journal*, 23 May 1925, pp. 960–62.

Peters, D., 'The British Medical Response to Opiate Addiction of the Nineteenth Century', *Journal of the History of Medicine*, October, 1981, pp. 455–89.

Peterson, M.J., 'Dr. Acton's Enemy: Medicine, Sexuality and Society in Victorian England' in *Victorian Studies*, vol. 29, no. 4, Summer 1986, pp. 570–90.

Playfair, W.S., MD, 'Systematic Treatment of Nerve Prostration and Hysteria Connected with Uterine Disease', *Lancet*, 28 May 1881, p. 50.

——, untitled notes regarding pessaries, *Transactions of the Obstetrical Society of London*, vol. xxi, 1879, pp. 49–51.

Porter, R., 'Is Foucault Useful for Understanding Eighteenth and Nineteenth-Century Sexuality?', *Contention*, 1, 1991, pp. 61–82.

Richardson, B.W., 'Dress in Relation to Health', *Popular Science Monthly*, vol. xvii, 1880, pp. 182–99.

——, 'Woman as Sanitary Reformer', *Fraser's Magazine*, vol. xxii, 1880, pp. 667–83.

Riegel, R.E., 'Women's Clothes and Women's Rights', *American Quarterly*, vol. 15, 1963, pp. 390–401.

Riley, R.C., 'The Industries of Portsmouth in the Nineteenth Century', *The Portsmouth Papers*, no. 25, July 1976, pp. 1–24.

Roberts, H., 'The Exquisite Slave: The Role of Clothes in the Making of the Victorian Woman', *Signs*, vol. 2, no. 3, Spring 1977, pp. 555–69.

Rohe, G.H., MD, 'The Relation of Pelvic Diseases and Psychical Disturbances in Woman', *Transactions of the American Association of Obstetricians and Gynaecologists*, vol. 5, 1892, pp. 322–27.

Routh, C.H.F., 'On the Aetiology and Diagnosis of Nymphomania and False Charges [incest]', *British Gynaecological Journal*, vol. 2, 1887, p. 490.

Russell, P., 'Old Ladies and New Women', *Australian Cultural History*, no. 13, 1994, pp. 21–52.

Savage, T., MD, 'On Oophorectomy', *Obstetrical Journal of Great Britain and Ireland*, no. lxxxvii, 15 May 1880, pp. 257–67.

Schindler, W., 'Biographical Sketch: William Stekel (1868–1940)', *International Journal of Sexology Marriage and Hygiene*, September 1970, pp. 144–61.

Schwarz, G., MD, 'Society, Physicians, and the Corset', *Bulletin of the New York Academy of Medicine*, vol. 55, no. 6, June 1979, pp. 551–90.

Sicherman, B., 'The Uses of Diagnosis: Doctors, Patients and Neurasthenia', *Journal of the History of Medicine and Allied Sciences*, vol. 32, no. 1, January 1977, pp. 33–55.

Smith-Rosenberg, C., 'The Female World of Love and Ritual', *Signs*, no. 1, 1975, pp. 1–30.

Sorge, L., '18th Century Stays: Their Origin and Creators', *Costume*, no. 32, 1998, pp. 18–32.

St Vertue, H., 'Chlorosis and Stenosis', *Guy's Hospital Report*, no. 104, 1955, pp. 329–48,

Stannard, U., 'Clothing and Sexuality', *Sexual Behaviour*, May 1977, pp. 25–33.

Steele, V., 'Le Corset: A Material Culture Analysis of a Deluxe French Book', *The Yale Journal of Criticism*, vol. 11, no. 1, 1998, pp. 29–38, at http://muse.jhu.edu/journals/yale_journal_of_criticism/v011/11.1steele.html

Stember, C. (moderator), 'Roundtable: Sex and Clothing', *Medical Aspects of Human Sexuality*, September 1970, pp. 144–161.

Strong, B., 'Toward a History of the Experiential Family: Sex and Incest in the Nineteenth-Century Family', *Journal of Marriage and the Family*, August, 1973, pp. 457–65.

Tandberg, G., 'Towards Freedom in Dress for Nineteenth-Century Women', *Dress: Journal of the Costume Society of America*, no. 11, 1985, pp. 11–30.

Tarrant, N., 'A Maternity Dress of about 1845', *Costume*, no. 14, 1980, pp. 117–20.

Taylor, J., FRCS, 'Women, (Diseases of, in relation to Dress)' (sic), *Medical Annual*, 1889, pp. 509–18.

Taylor, K.J., 'Venereal Disease in Nineteenth-Century Children', *Journal of Psychohistory*, vol. 12, no. 4, Spring 1985, pp. 432–63.

Theriot, N.M., 'Women's Voices in Nineteenth-Century Medical Discourse: A Step toward Deconstructing Science', *Signs*, vol. 19, no. 1, Autumn 1993, pp. 1–31.

Treves, F.R., 'The Dress of the Period', *Medical Tracts*, Dublin, 1851, pp. 15–16.

Van deth, R. and Vandereychen, W., 'Was Nervous Consumption a Precursor to Anorexia Nervosa?' in the *Journal of the History of Medicine and Allied Sciences*, vol. 46, no. 1, January 1991, pp. 3–20.

Valverde, M., 'The Love of Finery: Fashion and the Fallen Woman in the Nineteenth-Century Social Discourse', *Victorian Studies*, Winter 1989, pp. 169–89.

Van Der Warker, E., MD, 'A New Self Retaining Intra-uterine Stem', *New York Medical Journal*, vol. xviii, no. 4, October 1873, pp. 361–2.

Walkerwitz, J.R., 'Male Vice and Feminist Virtue: Feminism and the Politics of Prostitution in Nineteenth-Century Britain', *History Workshop*, Issue 13, Spring 1982, pp. 77–94.

Warner, D., 'Fashion, Emancipation, Reform, and the Rational Undergarment', *Dress: Journal of the Costume Society of America*, no. 4, 1978, pp. 24–9.

Williams, W., 'Ovarian Dysmenorrhoea, With Retroversion of the Uterus', *Lancet*, 25 December 1880, p. 1021.

Wolfe, B.W., 'The Riddle of Homosexuality', *Modern Thinker*, April 1932, n.p.

Books

Adburgham, A., *Shops and Shopping: 1800–1914, Where and in What Manner the Well Dressed English Woman Bought Her Clothes*, George Allen & Unwin Ltd, London, 1964.

Adler, K. and Pointon, M. (eds), *The Body Imaged: The Human Form and Visual Culture Since the Renaissance*, Cambridge University Press, Cambridge, 1993.

Aldrich, R. and Tipton, F.B., *An Economic and Social History of Europe: 1890–1939*, Macmillan Education Ltd., London, 1987.

Apter E. and Pietz, W. (eds), *Fetishism as Cultural Discourse*, Cornell University Press, Ithaca, 1993.

Ardener, S. (ed.), *Defining Females: The Nature of Women in Society*, Croom Helm, London, 1978.

Aries, P., *The Hour of Our Death*, Penguin, London, 1981.

Armstrong, I., Bristow, J. and Sharrock, C. (eds), *Nineteenth-Century Women Poets: An Oxford Anthology*, Clarendon Press, Oxford, 1996.

Arney, W.R., *Power of the Profession of Obstetrics*, University of Chicago Press, Chicago, 1982.

Ash, J. and Wright, L., *Components of Dress: Design, Manufacture and Image Making in the Fashion Industry*, Routledge, London, 1988.

Auerbach, N., *Private Theatricals: The Lives of the Victorians*, Harvard University Press, Cambridge, Mass., 1990.

Baines, B., *Fashion Revivals from the Elizabethan Age to the Present Day*, B.T. Batsford Ltd, London, 1981.

Banks, J.A. and Banks, O., *Feminism and Family Planning in Victorian England,* Schocken Books, New York, 1964.

Banner, L., *American Beauty*, Knopf, New York, 1983.

Barnes, R. and Eicher, J.B. (eds), *Dress and Gender: Making and Meaning in Cultural Contexts*, Berg Publishers, Providence, 1992.

Barnhart, J., *Working Women: Prostitution in San Francisco from Goldmining to 1900*, University of California Press, Berkeley, 1977.

Barreca, R. (ed.), *Sex and Death in Victorian Literature*, Macmillan, London, 1990.

Barret-Ducrocq, F., *Love in the Time of Victoria: Sexuality and Desire Among Working-Class Men and Women in Nineteenth-Century London*, Penguin, New York, 1992.

Bartky S.L., *Feminity and Domination: Studies in the Phenomenology of Oppression*, Routledge, New York, 1990.

Barwick, S., *A Century of Style*, George Allen & Unwin, London, 1984.

Beetham, M., *A Magazine of Her Own? Domesticity and Desire in the Woman's Magazine, 1800–1914*, Routledge, London, 1996.

Bell, Q., *On Human Finery*, The Hogarth Press, London, 1947.

Benstock, S. and Ferris, S., *On Fashion*, Rutgers University Press, New Jersey, 1994.

Berger, J., *Ways of Seeing*, British Broadcasting Corporation and Penguin Books, London, 1972.

Bergler, E., MD, *Fashion and the Unconscious*, International Universities Press Inc., Madison, 1987, reprint of 1954 edn.

Betterton, R., *Looking On: Images of Femininity in the Visual Arts and Media*, Pandora, London, 1987.

Bleier, R., *Science and Gender: A Critique of Biology and its Theories on Women*, Pergamon Press, New York, 1984.

Blum, S. (ed.), *Paris Fashion of the 1890s*, Dover Publications, New York, 1984.

——, *Victorian Fashions and Costume from Harper's Bazaar 1867–1898*, Dover Publications, New York, 1974.

Bordo, S. and Jaggar, A., *Gender, Body, Knowledge: Feminist Reconstructions of Being and Knowing*, Rutgers University Press, London, 1989.

Bradfield, M., *Costume in Detail: 1730–1930*, Harrap, London, 1968.

Branca, P., *Silent Sisterhood: Middle Class Women in the Victorian Home*, Croom Helm, London, 1975.

Brandt, A., *No Magic Bullet: A Social History of Venereal Disease in the United States Since 1880*, Oxford University Press, Oxford, 1985.

Broby-Johansen, R., *Body and Clothes: An Illustrated History of Costume*, Faber & Faber, London, 1968.

Bronfen, E., *Over Her Dead Body: Death, Femininity and the Aesthetic*, Manchester University Press, Manchester, 1992.

Bronfen, E. and Goodwin, S. (eds), *Death and Representation*, Johns Hopkins University Press, Baltimore, 1993.

Brooks, P., *Body Work: Objects of Desire in Modern Narrative*, Harvard University Press, Cambridge, Mass., 1993.

Broude, N. and Garrard, M.D., *Feminism and Art History: Questioning the Litany*, Harper and Row, New York, 1982.

Brown, A., *The Eighteenth Century Feminist Mind*, Harvester Press, Sussex, 1987.

Browne, R.B., *Objects of Special Devotion: Fetishes and Fetishism in Popular Culture*, Bowling Green University Press, Ohio, 1992.

——, *Rituals and Ceremonies in Popular Culture*, Bowling Green University Press, Ohio, 1980.

Brownmiller, S., *Against Our Will: Men, Women and Rape*, Simon & Schuster, New York, 1975.

——, *Femininity*, Simon & Schuster, London, 1986.

Brumberg, J.J., *Fasting Girls: The Emergence of Anorexia Nervosa as a Modern Disease*, Harvard University Press, Cambridge, Mass., 1988.

Buck, A., *Victorian Costume and Costume Accessories*, Ruth Bean, Bedford, 1984.

Burroughs, C. and Ehrenreich, J. (eds), *Reading the Social Body*, University of Iowa Press, Iowa City, 1993.

Burston, P. and Richardson, C. (eds), *A Queer Romance: Lesbians, Gay Men and Popular Culture*, Routledge, London, 1995.

Burton, C., *Subordination, Feminism and Social Theory*, George Allen & Unwin, Sydney, 1985.

Byatt, A.S., *Angels and Insects*, Chatto & Windus, London, 1992.

Bynum, W.F.,Porter, R. and Shepherd, M. (eds), *The Anatomy of Madness: Essays in the History of Madness, Volume I, People and Ideas*, Tavistock, London, 1985.

——, *The Anatomy of Madness: Essays in the History of Madness, Volume III, The Asylum and its Psychiatry*, Tavistock, London, 1988.

Byrde, P., *Nineteenth-Century Fashion*, B.T. Batsford Ltd, London, 1992.

Cahn, S.K., *Coming on Strong: Gender and Sexuality in Twentieth-Century Women's Sport*, The Free Press, New York, 1994.

Caine, B., *Victorian Feminists*, Oxford University Press, Oxford, 1992.

Caine, B., Grosz, E. and de Lepervanche, M. (eds), *Crossing Boundaries: Feminisms and the Critique of Knowledges*, Allen & Unwin, Sydney, 1988.

Caldwell, D., *And All Will Be Revealed: Ladies Underwear 1907–1980*, St Martin's Press, New York, 1981.

Carey, J., *The Intellectuals and the Masses: Pride and Prejudice among the Literary Intelligentsia, 1880–1939*, Faber & Faber, London, 1992.

Carter, Alison, *Underwear: The Fashion History*, B.T. Batsford, London, 1992.

Carter, Angela, *The Sadeian Woman: An Exercise in Cultural History*, Virago, London, 1982.

Celebonovic, A., *The Heyday of Salon Painting: Masterpieces of Bourgeois Realism*, Thames and Hudson, London, 1974.

Chapkis, W., *Beauty Secrets: Women and the Politics of Appearance*, South End Press, London, 1986.

Clark, K., *The Nude: A Study of Ideal Art*, Penguin Books, London, 1956.

Clayson H., *Painted Love: Prostitutes in French Art of the Impressionist Era*, Yale University Press, New Haven, 1991.

Colmer, M., *Whalebone to See-Through: A History of Body Packaging*, Cassell Australia Ltd, Stanmore, 1979.

Comfort, A., *The Anxiety Makers: Some Curious Preoccupations of the Medical Profession*, Thomas Nelson and Sons, London, 1967.

Conley, C.A., *The Unwritten Law: Criminal Justice in Victorian Kent*, Oxford University Press, Oxford, 1991.

Cooper, W., *Hair: Sex, Society and Symbolism*, Stein and Day, New York, 1971.

Cordwell, J. and Schwarz, R. (eds), *The Fabrics of Culture: The Anthology of Clothing and Adornment*, Mouton Publishers, The Hague, 1979.

Corson, R., *Fashions in Make-up: From the Ancient to Modern Times*, Owen, London, 1972.

Coveny, L., Jackson, M. and Jeffreys, S. (eds), *The Sexuality Papers: Male Sexuality and the Social Control of Women*, Hutchinson, in association with The Explorations in Feminism Collective, London, 1984.

Crawford, M. and Guernsey, E., *The History of Corsets*, Fairchild, New York, 1951.

Creed, B., *The Monstrous Feminine: Film, Feminism and Psychoanalysis*, Routledge, London, 1993.

Csordas, T. (ed.), *Embodiment and Experience: The Existential Ground of Culture and Self*, Cambridge University Press, Cambridge, 1994.

Cunningham, P.A. and Vosolab, S. (eds), *Dress and Popular Culture*, Bowling Green University Press, Ohio, 1991.

Cunnington, P and Buck, A., *Children's Costume in England: From the Fourteenth to the End of the Nineteenth Century*, Adam and Charles Black, London, 1965.

Cunnington, P. and Lucas, C., *Occupational Costume in England From the 11th Century to 1914*, Adam and Charles Black, London, 1967.

Curtin, M., *Propriety and Position: A Study of Victorian Manners*, Garland Publishing, New York, 1987.

Daley, M., *Gyn/Ecology: The Meta Ethics of Radical Feminism*, The Women's Press, London, 1991.

Damon-Moore, H., *Magazines For The Millions: Gender And Commerce In The Ladies Home Journal And The Saturday Evening Post, 1880–1910*, State University of New York Press, Albany, 1994.

Davidoff, L., *The Best Circles: Society Etiquette And The Season*, Croom Helm, London, 1973.

Davidoff, L. and Hall, C., *Family Fortunes: Men and Women of the English Middle Class, 1780–1850*, University of Chicago Press, Chicago, 1987.

Davis, F., *Fashion, Culture, and Identity*, University of Chicago Press, Chicago, 1992.

Davis, L. (ed.), *Virginal Sexuality and Textuality in Victorian Literature*, State University of New York Press, Albany, 1993.

Delamont, S. and Duffin, L., *The Nineteenth-Century Woman: Her Cultural and Physical World*, Croom Helm, London, 1978.

D'Emilio, J. and Freedman, E., *Intimate Matters: A History of Sexuality in America*, Harper and Row, New York, 1988.

de Vries, L., *American Advertisements 1856–1900*, John Murray and Sons, London, 1973.

——, *The Wonderful World of Victorian Advertisements*, John Murray and Sons, London, 1968.

Diamond, I. and Quinby, L., *Feminism and Foucault: Reflections on Resistance*, Northeastern University Press, Boston, 1988.

Dick, D., *Yesterday's Babies: A History of Babycare*, Bodley Head, London, 1987.

Dijkstra, B., *Idols of Perversity: Fantasies of Feminine Evil in Fin-de-Siècle Culture*, Oxford University Press, Oxford, 1986.

Diprose, R., *The Bodies of Women: Ethics, Embodiment and Sexual Difference*, Routledge, London, 1994.

Doane, M.A., *Femmes Fatales: Feminism, Film Theory, Psychoanalysis*, Routledge, New York, 1991.

Doctor Death: Medicine at the End of Life, exhibition catalogue published by the Wellcome Institute Museum, London, 1997.

Donnelly, M.C., *The American Woman: The Myth and the Reality*, Greenwood Press, New York, 1986.

Douglas, M., *Purity and Danger: An Analysis of Concepts of Pollution and Taboo*, Routledge & Kegan Paul, London, 1966.

Doy, G., *Seeing and Consciousness*: Women, Class and Representation, Berg, Oxford, 1995.

Duberman, M., Vicinus, M. and Chauncey, G., Jr. (eds), *Hidden From History: Reclaiming the Gay and Lesbian Past*, Penguin, New York, 1989.

Duby, G. and Aries, P., *A History of Private Life*, Belknap, Cambridge, Mass., 1987–92.

Duden, B., *Disembodying Women: Perspectives on Pregnancy and the Unborn*, Harvard University Press, Cambridge, Mass., 1993.

Dworkin, A., *Pornography: Men Possessing Women*, The Women's Press, London, 1981.

Dwyer, W., *What Everyone Needs To Know about Sex: Explained in the Words of Orson Squires and Other Victorian Moralists*, The Pyne Press, Princeton, 1972.

Eagle Russet, C., *Sex, Science and the Victorian Construction of Womanhood*, Harvard University Press, Cambridge, Mass., 1989.

Ehrenriech, B. and English, D., *Complaints and Disorders: The Sexual Politics of Sickness*, Writers and Readers Publishing Cooperative, London, 1976.

——, *For Her Own Good: 150 Years of the Experts' Advice To Women*, Anchor Books, New York, 1978.

Eisenstein, H., *Contemporary Feminist Thought*, Unwin Paperbacks, London, 1984.

Epstein, J. and Straub, K. (eds), *Body Guards: The Cultural Politics of Gender Ambiguity*, Routledge, New York, 1991.

Evans, H. and Evans, M., *The Party that Lasted 100 Days, The Late Victorian Season: A Social Study*, Macdonalds and Janes, London, 1976.

Ewen, S. and Ewen, E., *Channels of Desire: Mass Images and the Shaping of American Consciousness*, McGraw-Hill, New York, 1982.

Ewing, E., *Dress and Undress: A History of Women's Underwear*, B.T. Batsford, London, 1978.

——, *Everyday Dress 1650–1900*, B.T. Batsford, London, 1984.

——, *Fashion in Underwear*, B.T. Batsford, London, 1971.

——, *History of Children's Costume*, Charles Scribner's Sons, New York, 1977.

——, *History of Twentieth-Century Fashion*, Batsford, London, 1974.

Faderman, L., *Surpassing the Love of Men: Romantic Friendship and Love Between Women from the Renaissance to the Present*, The Women's Press, London, 1985.

Farner, P. (ed.), *In Female Disguise: An Anthology of English and American Short Stories and Literary Passages*, Karn Publications, Liverpool, 1992.

Finkelstein, J., *After a* Fashion, Polity, Cambridge, 1996.

——, The *Fashioned Self*, Polity Press in Association with Basil Blackwell, Cambridge, 1991.

Fiske, J., *Television Culture*, Routledge, London, 1989.

Fiske, J. and Hartley, J., *Reading Television*, Routledge, London, 1989.

Flandrin, J.-L., *Families in Former Times: Kinship, Household and Sexuality*, Cambridge University Press, Cambridge, 1979.

Fletcher, P. and Walker, K., *Sex and Society*, Pelican Books, London, 1969.

Fontanel, B., *Support and Seduction: a History of Corsets and Bras*, Harry N. Abrams, Inc., 1997.

Forster, M., *Significant Sisters*, Secker and Warburg, London, 1984.

Foucault, M., *Discipline and Punish: The Birth of the Prison*, Pantheon Books, New York, 1977.

——, *The History of Sexuality*, Penguin Books, London, 1976.

Fout, J. (ed.), *Forbidden History: The State, Society and the Regulation of Sexuality in Modern Europe*, University of Chicago Press, Chicago, 1990.

Fox Keller, E., Jacobus, M. and Shuttleworth, S. (eds), *Body/Politics: Women and the Discourses of Science*, Routledge, New York, 1990.

Fraisse, G. and Perrot, M. (eds), *A History of Women in the West*, vol. IV, *Emerging Feminism from Revolution to World War*, Harvard University Press, Cambridge, Mass., 1993.

Fraser, F., *The English Gentlewoman*, Barrie Jenkins, London, 1987.

French, M., *The War Against Women*, Hamish Hamilton, London, 1992.

Gaines, J. and Herzog, C., *Fabrications: Costume and the Female Body*, Routledge, New York, 1990.

Gallagher, C. and Laqueur, T. (eds), *The Making of the Modern Body: Sexuality and Society in the Nineteenth Century*, University of California Press, Berkeley, 1987.

Gamble, A., *An Introduction into Modern Social and Political Thought*, Macmillan, London, 1982.

Gannan, L. and Marshment, M. (eds), *The Female Gaze: Women As Viewers of Popular Culture*, The Women's Press, London, 1988.

Garber, M., *Vested Interests: Cross Dressing and Cultural Anxiety*, Routledge, New York, 1992.

Gardiner, J. (ed.), *The New Woman: Women's Voices 1880–1918*, Collins and Brown, London, 1993.

Garrigan, K. (ed.), *Victorian Scandals: Representations of Gender and Class*, Ohio University Press, Athens, Ohio, 1992.

Gay, P., *The Cultivation of Hatred: the Bourgeois Experience from Victoria to Freud*, HarperCollins, London, 1993.

Gernsheim, A., *Fashion and Reality 1840–1914*, Faber & Faber, London, 1963.

——, *Victorian and Edwardian Fashion: A Photographic Survey*, Dover Publications, New York, 1963.

Gibbs-Smith, C., *The Fashionable Lady in the Nineteenth Century*, Victoria and Albert Museum Publication, London, 1960.

Gill, M., *Image of the Body: Aspects of the Nude*, Doubleday, New York, 1989.

Gilman, S.L., *Sexuality; An Illustrated History*, John Wiley and Sons, New York, 1989.

Ginsberg, M., *Victorian Dress in Photographs*, Holmes and Meir, New York, 1982.

Glynn, P., *Skin to Skin: Eroticism in Dress*, George Allen & Unwin, London, 1982.

Goodwin, M. (ed.), *Nineteenth-Century Opinion: An Anthology of Extracts From The First Fifty Volumes Of The Nineteenth Century 1877–1901*, Penguin, Harmondsworth, 1951.

Gordon, M. (ed.), *The American Family in Social-Historical Perspective*, 2nd edn, St Martin's Press, New York, 1978.

Goreham, D., *The Victorian Girl and The Feminine Ideal*, Croom Helm, London, 1982.

Gould, S., *The Mismeasure of Man*, Pelican Books, Harmondsworth, 1982.

Grosz, E., *Volatile Bodies: Toward a Corporeal Feminism*, Allen & Unwin, Sydney, 1994.

Gubar, S. and Hoff, J., *For Adult Users Only: The Dilemma of Violent Pornography*, Indiana University Press, Bloomington, 1989.

Haley, B., *The Healthy Body and Victorian Culture*, Harvard University Press, Cambridge, Mass., 1978.

Hall, R. (ed.), *Dear Dr Stopes: Sex In The 1920s*, Penguin, Harmondsworth, 1978.

Haller, J. and Haller, R., *The Physician and Sexuality in Victorian America*, University of Illinois Press, Urbana, 1974.

Halttunen, K., *Confidence Men and Painted Women: A Study of Middle-Class Culture in America, 1830–1870*, Yale University Press, New York, 1982.

Hammerton, A.J., *Cruelty and Companionship: Conflict in Nineteenth-Century Married Life*, Routledge, London, 1992.

Hamner, J. and Maynard, M. (eds), *Women, Violence and Social Control*, Macmillan, Hampshire, 1987.

Harman, B.L. and Meyer, S. (eds), *The New Nineteenth Century: Feminist Readings of Underread Victorian Fiction*, Garland Publishing Inc., New York, 1996.

Harrison, F., *The Dark Angel: Aspects of Victorian Sexuality*, Sheldon Press, London, 1977.

Hartman, M. and Banner, L. (eds), *Clio's Consciousness Raised: New Perspectives on the History of Women*, Harper and Row, New York, 1974.

Haugh, F., *Female Sexualisation: A Collective Work of Memory*, Verso, London, 1983.

Hausman, C.R., *Metaphor and Art: Interactionism and Reference in the Verbal and Nonverbal Arts*, Cambridge University Press, Cambridge, 1989.

Hearder H., *Europe in the Nineteenth Century: 1830–1880*, Longman, New York, 1966.

Herndl, D.P., *Invalid Women: Figuring Feminine Illness in American Fiction and Culture, 1840-1940*, University of North Carolina Press, Chapel Hill, 1993.

Hess, T.B. and Baker, E. (eds), *Art and Sexual Politics: Why Have There Been No Great Women Artists?* Collier Books, New York, 1971.

Hess, T.B. and Nochlin, L. (eds), *Women as Sex Object: Studies in Erotic Art, 1730–1970*, Allen Lane, London, 1973.

Hickok, K., *Representations of Women: Nineteenth-Century British Women's Poetry*, Greenwood Press, Westport, 1984.

Hindley, D. and Hindley, G., *Advertising in Victorian England 1837–1901*, Wayland Publishers, London, 1972.

Hobsbawm, E.J., *The Age of Empire: 1875–1914*, Weidenfeld & Nicolson, London, 1987.

Holbrook, D., *Sex and Dehumanisation: In Art, Thought and Life in Our Time*, Pitman Publishing, London, 1972.

Hollander, A., *Seeing Through Clothes*, The Viking Press, New York, 1978.

——, *Sex and Suits*, Alfred A. Knopf, New York, 1994.

Howells, K. (ed.), *The Psychology of Sexual Diversity*, Basil Blackwell, Oxford, 1984.

Hower, R., *History of Macey's of New York, 1858–1919, Chapters in the Evolution of the Department Store*, Harvard University Press, Cambridge, Mass., 1946.

Hubbard, R., *The Politics of Female Biology*, Rutgers University Press, London, 1990.

Hudson, L., *Bodies of Knowledge: The Psychological Significance of the Nude in Art*, Weidenfeld & Nicolson, London, 1982.

Hyde, M.H., *A History of Pornography*, William Heinemann, London, 1964.

Irwin, M., *Picturing: Description and Illusion in the Nineteenth Century Novel*, George Allen & Unwin, London, 1979.

Jachimowicz, E., *Eight Chicago Women and Their Fashions 1866–1929*, Chicago Historical Society Publication, Chicago, 1978.

Jackson, M., *The Real Facts of Life: Feminism and the Politics of Sexuality 1850–1940*, Taylor & Francis, London, 1994.

Jackson, S. (ed.), *Women's Studies, A Reader*, Harvester Wheatsheaf, New York, 1993.

Jalland, P., *Death in the Victorian Family*, Oxford University Press, Oxford, 1996.

Jeffreys, S., *Anticlimax*, The Women's Press, London, 1990.

——, *The Spinster and Her Enemies*, Pandora Press, London, 1985.

Jenkyns, R., *The Victorians and Ancient Greece*, Basil Blackwell, Oxford, 1980.

Johnson, M., *The Body in the Mind: The Bodily Basis of Meaning, Imagination, and Reason*, The University of Chicago Press, Chicago, 1987.

Jones, G., *Social Darwinism and English Thought: the Interaction between Biological and Social Theory*, Harvester, Sussex, 1980.

Jordanova, L., *Sexual Visions: Images of Gender in Science and Medicine between the Eighteenth and Twentieth Centuries*, Harvester Wheatsheaf, New York, 1989.

Jubb, M., *Cocoa and Corsets: A Selection of Victorian and Edwardian Posters and Showcards*, Her Majesty's Stationers Office, London, 1984.

Kaplan, L., *Female Perversions*, Penguin Books, London, 1991.

Katz, J., *The Invention of Heterosexuality*, Dutton Books, Penguin, New York, 1995.

Kauffman, R.W., *Sexual Liberation and Religion in Nineteenth Century Europe*, Croom Helm, London, 1977.

Kennedy, D., *Sexy Dressing Etc.*, Harvard University Press, Cambridge Mass., 1993.

Kent, S.K., *Sex Suffrage in Britain*, 1860–1914, Princeton University Press, Princeton, 1987.

Kern, S., *The Cult of Love: Victoria to the Moderns*, Harvard University Press, Cambridge, Mass., 1992.

Klein, V., *The Feminine Character: History Of An Ideology*, Routledge & Kegan Paul, 1946.

Koehler, C., *A History of Costume*, G. Harrap and Company, London, 1979.

Konig, R., *The Restless Image: A Sociology of Fashion*, George Allen & Unwin, London, 1973.

Kramarae, C. and Russo, A., *The Radical Women's Press of the 1850s*, Routledge Chapman and Hall Inc., New York, 1991.

Kristeva, J., *Powers of Horror: An Essay on Abjection*, Columbia University Press, New York, 1982.

Kroller, E.M., Smith, A., Mostow, J. and Kramer, R. (eds), *Pacific Encounters: The Production of the Self and Others*, University of British Columbia, Vancouver, 1997.

Kuhn, A., *The Power of the Image: Essays on Representation and Sexuality*, Routledge & Kegan Paul, London, 1985.

Kuntz, M. and Kuntz, P. (eds), *Jacob's Ladder and the Tree of Life: Concepts of Hierarchy and the Great Chain of Being*, Peter Lang, New York, 1987.

Kunzle, D., *Fashion and Fetishism: A Social History of Corsets, Tight Lacing and Other Forms of Body Sculpture in the West*, Rowman and Littlefield, New Jersey, 1982.

Langevin, R. (ed.), *Erotic Preference, Gender Identity, And Aggression In Men: New Research Studies*, New Jersey, 1985.

Langner, L., *The Importance of Wearing Clothes*, Elysium Growth Press, Los Angeles, 1991.

Laqueur, T., *Making Sex: Body and Gender from the Greeks to Freud*, Harvard University Press, London, 1990.

Laver, J., *Children's Fashions in the Nineteenth Century*, B.T. Batsford, London, 1951.

——, *Clothes*, Burke Publishing, London, 1952.

——, *Costume and Fashion, A Concise History*, Thames and Hudson, London, 1969; reprinted 1992.

——, *English Costume of the Nineteenth Century*, A.C. Black Ltd., London, 1929.

——, *Modesty in Dress: An Inquiry into the Fundamentals of Fashion*, Houghton Mifflin and Co., Boston, 1969.

——, *Taste and Fashion from the French Revolution to the Present Day*, George Harrap and Company Ltd., London, 1945.

——, *Victoriana*, Ward Lock and Co., Ltd., London, 1966.

Laws, S., *Issues of Blood: The Politics of Menstruation*, Macmillan, 1990.

Leach, W., *True Love and Perfect Union: The Feminist Reform of Sex and Society*, Basic Books, Inc., New York, 1980.

Leidholt, D. and Raymond, J. (eds), *The Sexual Liberals and the Attack on Feminism*, Pergamon Press, New York, 1990.

Lerner, G. (ed.), *The Female Experience: An American Documentary*, Bobbs-Merrill, Indianapolis, 1977.

Lester, D., *Unusual Sexual Behaviour: The Standard Deviations*, Charles Thomas Publisher, Illinois, 1975.

Levitt, S., *Victorians Unbuttoned: Registered Designs For Clothing, their Makers and Wearers, 1839–1900*, Allen and Unwin, London, 1986.

Levitt, S., in association with the National Portrait Gallery, *Fashion in Photographs, 1880–1900*, Batsford, London, 1991.

Lewis, J. (ed.), *Labour and Love: Women's Experience of Home and Family, 1850–1940*, Basil Blackwell, Oxford, 1986.

Licata, S. and Peterson, R. (eds), *Historical Perspectives on Homo-sexuality*, co-published by Hawthorn Press and Stein and Day Publishers, New York, 1981.

Linden, R., Pagano, D., Russell, D. and Star, S.L. (eds), *Against Sado-masochism: A Radical Feminist Analysis*, Frog in the Well, California, 1982.

Lipman-Blumen, J., *Gender Roles and Power*, Prentice Hall Inc., New Jersey, 1984.

London Feminist History Group, *The Sexual Dynamics of History*, Pluto Press, London, 1983.

Long Laws, J. and Schwartz, P. *Sexual Scripts: The Social Construction of Female Sexuality*, University Press of America, Washington, 1981.

Lurie, A., *The Language of Clothes*, Random House, New York, 1981.

Macleod, A.S., 'The Caddy Woodlawn Syndrome', *A Century of Childhood: 1820–1920*, New York, 1984, pp. 65–96.

MaHood, J. and Wenberg, K. (eds), *The Mosher Survey: Sexual Attitutudes of Forty Five Victorian Women*. The original author of survey was Clelia Duel Mosher who interviewed/collected data from forty-five women between 1892 and 1920. The survey was eventually published by Arno Press, New York, 1980.

Mancini, J.G., *Prostitutes and Their Parasites*, Elek Books, London, 1962.

Mangan, J.A. and Park, R.J. (eds), *From Fair Sex To Feminism: Sport and the Socialisation of Women in the Industrial and Post Industrial Eras*, Frank Cass, London, 1987.

Marcus, S., *The Other Victorians: A Study of Sexuality and Pornography in Mid-Nineteenth Century England*, Weidenfeld & Nicolson, London, 1966.

Marsh, J., *The Illuminated Language of Flowers*, Balance House, New York, 1978.

Martin, E., *The Woman in the Body*: *A Cultural Analysis of Reproduction*, Beacon Press, Boston, 1989.

Marwick, A., *Beauty in History: Society, Politics and Personal Appearance c.1500 to the Present*, Thames and Hudson, London, 1988.

Mason, M., *The Making of Victorian Sexual Attitudes*, Oxford University Press, Oxford, 1994.

Masserman, J.H. (ed.), *Dynamics of Deviant Sexuality: Science and Psychoanalysis*, vol. xv, Grune and Statton, New York, 1969.

Maynard, J., *Victorian Discourses on Sexuality and Religion*, Cambridge University Press, Cambridge, 1993.

McClintock, A., *Imperial Leather: Race, Gender and Sexuality in the Colonial Contest*, University of Indiana Press, Bloomington, 1995.

McCrone, K.E., *Playing the Game: Sport and the Physical Emancipation of English Women, 1870-1914*, The University Press of Kentucky, Lexington, 1988.

McMillan, P., *Men, Sex and Other Secrets*, Text Publishing Company, Melbourne, 1992.

Meech-Pekarik, J., *The World of the Meiji Print: Impressions of a New Civilisation*, Weatherill, New York, 1986.

Mendus, S. and Rendall, J. (eds), *Sexuality and Subordination: Interdisciplinary Studies of Gender in the Nineteenth Century*, Routledge, London, 1989.

Michie, H., *The Flesh Made Word: Female Figures and Women's Bodies*, Oxford University Press, Oxford, 1987.

Miles, R., *The Rites of Man: Love, Sex and Death in the Making of the Male*, Paladin, London, 1992.

Millet, K., *Sexual Politics*, Sphere Books, London, 1971.

Millum, T., *Images of Woman: Advertising in Women's Magazines*, Chatto & Windus, London, 1975.

MIT List Visual Arts Center, *Corporal Politics*, Beacon Press, Boston, 1992.

Mitford, J., *The American Way of Birth*, Victor Gollancz, London, 1992.

Modleski, T. (ed.) *Studies in Entertainment: Critical Approaches to Mass Culture* Indiana University Press, Bloomington, 1986.

Moore, D.L., *Fashion Through Fashion Plates 1771–1920*, Ward Lock, London, 1971.

Morgan, M., *Manner, Morals and Class in England, 1774–1858*, Macmillan Press, London, 1994.

Moscucci, O., *The Science of Woman: Gynaecology and Gender in England, 1880–1929*, Cambridge University Press, Cambridge, 1990.

Muldoon, P., *The Essential Byron*, Ecco Press, New York, 1989.

Mulvey, L., *Fetishism and Curiosity*, Indiana University Press, Bloomington, 1996.

——, *Visual and Other Pleasures*, Indiana University Press, Bloomington, 1989.

Nadoff R., Tazi, N. and Feyer, M. (eds), *Fragments For a History of the Human Body*, Cambridge, New York, 1989.

Nathanson, C., *Dangerous Passage: The Social Construction of Sexuality in Female Adolescence*, Temple University Press, Philadelphia, 1991.

Nead, L., *Myths of Sexuality: Representations of Women in Victorian Britain*, Basil Blackwell, Oxford, 1988.

Nevett, T.R., *Advertising in Britain: A History*, Heinemann, London, 1982.

Newton, S.M., *Health, Art and Reason: Dress Reformers of the Nineteenth Century*, John Murray, London, 1974.

Nochlin, L., *The Politics of Vision: Essays on Nineteenth-Century Art and Society*, Harper and Row, New York, 1989.

——, *Women, Art, and Power and Other Essays*, Thames and Hudson, London, 1989.

Oakley, A., *The Captured Womb: A History of The Medical Care of Pregnant Women*, Basil Blackwell, New York, 1984.

Oppenheimer, J., '*Shattered Nerves': Doctors, Patients, and Depression in Victorian England*, Oxford University Press, Oxford, 1991.

Oriel, J.D., *The Scars of Venus: A History of Venerology*, Springer-Verlag, London, 1994.

Ortner, S.B. and Whitehead, H., *Sexual Meanings: The Cultural Construction of Gender and Sexuality*, Cambridge University Press, Cambridge, 1981.

Page, C., *Foundations of Fashion: The Symington Collection 1856 to the Present Day*, Leicestershire Museums Publication, London, 1981.

Parry, L., *The Victoria and Albert Museum's Textile Collection: British Textiles from 1850-1900*, Victoria and Albert Museum publication, London, 1993.

Pearl, C., *The Girl With the Swansdown Seat*, Frederick Muller Ltd, London, 1955.

Pearsal, Ronald, *Public Purity, Private Shame: Victorian Sexual Hypocrisy Exposed*, Weidenfeld and Nicolson, London, 1976.

——, *Tell Me, Pretty Maiden: The Victorian and Edwardian Nude*, Grange Books, London, 1992.

——, *The Worm in the Bud: The World of Victorian Sexuality*, Random House, London, 1969.

Peiss, K. and Simmons, C., *Passion and Power: Sexuality in History*, Temple University Press, Philadelphia, 1989.

Perkin, J., *Victorian Women*, John Murray Publishing, London, 1993.

——, *Women and Marriage in Nineteenth-Century England*, Routledge, London, 1989.

Perrot, M. (ed.), *A History of Private Life: Vol. 4 From the Fires of Revolution to the Great War*, Harvard University Press, Harvard, 1990.

Perrot, P., *Fashioning the Bourgeoisie: A History of Clothing in the Nineteenth Century*, Princeton University Press, Princeton, 1994.

Petrie, G., *A Singular Iniquity: the Campaigns of Josephine Butler*, The Viking Press, New York, 1971.

Pick, D., *Faces of Degeneration: A European Disorder, c.1848–c.1918*, Cambridge University Press, Cambridge, 1989.

Pike, M. and Armstrong, G., *A Time to Mourn: Expressions of Grief in Nineteenth-Century America*, Museums at Stony Brook, Stony Brook, New York, 1981.

Pivar, D., *Purity Crusade: Sexual Morality and Social Control, 1868–1900*, Greenwood Press, Westport, 1973.

Polhemus, T., *Body Styles*, Lennard Publishing, London, 1988.

Pollock, G., *Vision and Difference: Femininity, Feminism and the Histories of Art*, Routledge, London, 1988.

Pool, D., *What Jane Austin Ate and What Charles Dickens Knew: From Fox Hunting to Whist – The Facts of Daily Life in Nineteenth-Century England*, Simon & Schuster, New York, 1993.

Porter, R., *A Social History of Madness: The World through the Eyes of the Insane*, Tavistock Publications, New York, 1989.

Porter, R. and Teich, M. (eds), *Sexual Knowledge, Sexual Science: The History of Attitudes to Sexuality*, Cambridge University Press, Cambridge, 1994.

Praz, M., *The Romantic Agony*, Oxford University Press, Oxford, 1970.

Presbrey, F., *The History and Development of Advertising*, Greenwood Press, New York, 1968.

Probert, C., *Lingerie in Vogue Since 1910*, Thames and Hudson, London, 1982.

Prost, A. and Vincent, G. (eds), *A History of Private Life: Riddles of Identity in Modern Times*, Harvard University Press, Cambridge, Mass, 1991.

Pykett, L., *The 'Improper' Feminine: The Women's Sensation Novel and the New Woman*, Routledge, London, 1992.

Pykett, L. (ed.), *Reading Fin de Siècle Fictions*, Longmans, London, 1996.

Radford, J. and Russell, D., *Femicide: The Politics of Woman Killing*, Open University Press, Buckingham, 1992.

Reed, J., *Decadent Style*, Ohio University Press, Athens, Ohio, 1985.

Reekie, G., *Temptations: Sex Selling and the Department Store*, Allen & Unwin, Sydney, 1993.

Reinhardt, J., *Sex Perversions and Sex Crimes*, Charles Thomas Publisher, Illinois, 1957.

Richards, T., *The Commodity Culture of Victorian England: Advertising and Spectacle, 1851–1914*, Stanford University Press, Stanford, 1990.

Riddle, J.M., *Eve's Herbs: A History of Contraception and Abortion in the West*, Harvard University Press, Cambridge, Mass., 1997.

Robinson, J., *Body Packaging: A Guide to Human Sexual Display*, Macmillan, Melbourne, 1988.

Robinson, P., *The Modernisation of Sex: Havelock Ellis, Alfred Kinsey, William Masters and Virginia Johnson*, Harper Row Publishers, New York, 1976.

——, *The Sexual Radicals*, Paladin, London, 1972.

Rogers, K., *Feminism in Eighteenth Century England*, University of Illinois Press, Urbana, 1976.

Root, J., *Pictures of Women: Sexuality*, Pandora Press, London, 1984.

Rose, L., *The Massacre of the Innocents: Infanticide in Britain 1800–1939*, Routledge & Kegan Paul, London, 1986.

Rosenberg, C. and Vogel, M., *The Therapeutic Revolution: Essays in the Social History of American Medicine*, University of Pennsylvania Press, Philadelphia, 1979.

Ross, E., *Love and Toil: Motherhood in Outcast London 1870–1918*, Oxford University Press, Oxford, 1993.

Rover, C., *Love, Morals and the Feminists*, Routledge & Kegan Paul, London, 1970.

Rowbotham, S., *Hidden From History*, Penguin, London, 1975.

——, *Woman's Consciousness, Man's World*, Penguin, Middlesex, 1973.

Ruby, Jay, *Secure the Shadow: Death and Photography in America*, The MIT Press, Cambridge, Mass., 1995.

Ruby, Jennifer, *Costume In Context: The Edwardians After The First World War*, B.T. Batsford, London, 1988.

Rudofsy, B., *The Unfashionable Human Body*, Rupert Hart-Davis, London, 1972.

Rugoff, M., *Prudery and Passion: Sexuality in Victorian America*, Rupert Hart-Davis, London, 1971.

Russell, D. (ed.), *Making Violence Sexy: Feminist Views On Pornography*, Open University Press, Buckingham, 1993.

Russett, C., *Sexual Science: The Victorian Construction of Womanhood*, Harvard University Press, London, 1989.

St George, A., *The Descent Of Manners: Etiquette, Rules and the Victorians*, Chatto & Windus, London, 1993.

Saint Laurent, C., *The Great Book of Lingerie*, The Vendome Press, New York, 1986.

——, *The History of Ladies' Underwear*, Michael Joseph, London, 1966.

Schefer, J.L., *The Enigmatic Body: Essays on the Arts by Jean Louis Schefer*, Cambridge University Press, Cambridge, 1995.

Scull, A. (ed.), *Madhouses, Mad Doctors, and Mad Men: The Social History of Psychiatry in the Victorian Era*, University of Pennsylvania Press, Philadelphia, 1981.

Seeley, M. and Seeley, C., *Doll Collecting for Fun and Profit*, H.P. Books, Tucson, 1983.

Shevelow, K., *Women and Print Culture: The Construction of Femininity in the Early Periodical*, Routledge, London, 1989.

Shorter, E., *A History of Women's Bodies*, Penguin, Middlesex, 1982.

Showalter, E., *Sexual Anarchy: Gender and Culture at the Fin de Siècle*, Virago Press, 1992.

——, *The Female Malady, Women, Madness and English Culture, 1830–1980*, Pantheon Books, New York, 1985.

Smart, C. (ed.), *Regulating Womanhood: Historical Essays on Marriage, Motherhood and Sexuality*, Routledge, New York, 1992.

Smith, F.B., *The People's Health 1830–1910*, Croom Helm, London, 1979.

Smith-Rosenberg, C., *Disorderly Conduct: Visions of Gender in Victorian America*, Oxford University Press, Oxford, 1985.

Sontag, S., *Illness as Metaphor*, Farrar Straus and Giroux, New York, 1977.

Spector Person, E. and Stimpson, C. (eds), *Women, Sex and Sexuality*, University of Chicago Press, Chicago, 1980.

Spender, D., *Women of Ideas and What Men Have Done to Them*, Pandora, London, 1982.

——, (ed.), *The Penguin Anthology of Australian Women's Writing*, Victoria, 1988.

Stage, S., *Female Complaints: Lydia Pinkham and the Business of Women's Medicine*, W.W. Norton & Company, New York, 1979.

Staniland, K., *Fashion in Miniature*, museum costume booklet, Platt Hall, Manchester, nd.

Stanko, E., *Everyday Violence: How Women and Men Experience Sexual and Physical Danger*, Pandora Press, London, 1990.

Stanley L. and Wise, S., *Breaking Out Again: Feminist Ontology and Epistemology* (new edn), Routledge, London, 1993.

Steele, V., *Fashion and Eroticism: Ideals of Feminine Beauty from the Victorian Era to the Jazz Age*, Oxford University Press, Oxford, 1985.

——, *Fetish: Fashion, Sexuality and Power*, Oxford University Press, Oxford, 1996.

Stocktay, G.G., *America's Erotic Past, 1868–1940*, Greenleaf Classics, California, 1973.

Stone, L., *The Family, Sex and Marriage In England 1500–1800*, Harper and Row, New York, 1977.

Storm, P., *Functions of Dress: Tool Of Culture and the Individual*, Prentice Hall, New Jersey, 1987.

Stott, R., *The Fabrication of the Late Victorian Femme Fatale: The Kiss of Death*, Macmillan, London, 1992.

Suleiman, S.R. (ed.), *The Female Body in Western Culture: Contemporary Perspectives*, Harvard University Press, Cambridge, Mass., 1986.

Synnott, A., *The Body Social: Symbolism, Self and Society*, Routledge, London, 1993.

Szasz, T., *Sex by Prescription*, Anchor Press/Doubleday, New York, 1980.

——, *Sex: Facts, Frauds and Follies*, Basil Blackwell, Oxford, 1980.

Szirom, T., *Teaching Gender? Sex Education and Sexual Stereotypes*, Allen & Unwin, Sydney, 1988.

Taylor, L., *Mourning Dress: A Costume History*, George Allen & Unwin, London, 1983.

Theriot, N., *The Biosocial Construction of Femininity: Mothers and Daughters in Nineteenth Century America*, Greenwood Press, New York, 1988.

Tinling, T., *The Story Of Women's Tennis Fashion*, The Wimbledon Lawn Tennis Museum, London, 1977.

Tolchin, L., *Mourning, Gender, and Creativity in the Art of Herman Melville*, Yale University Press, New Haven, 1988.

Tong, R., *Feminist Thought*, Unwin Hyman, London, 1989.

Trudgill, E., *Madonnas and Magdalens: The Origins and Development of Victorian Sexual Attitudes*, Holmes and Meier, New York, 1976.

Turner, B., *The Body and Society: Explorations in Social Theory*, Basil Blackwell, Oxford, 1984.

Turner, G., *British Cultural Studies*, Routledge, London, 1990.

Tyrrell, I., *Women's World, Women's Empire: The Woman's Christian Temperance Union in International Perspective, 1880–1930*, University of North Carolina Press, Chapel Hill, 1991.

Ussher, J.M., *Women's Madness: Misogyny or Mental Illness?* Harvester Wheatsheaf, New York, 1991.

Vance, C. (ed.), *Pleasure and Danger, Exploring Female Sexuality*, Routledge & Kegan Paul, New York, 1984.

Vicinus, M. (ed.), *A Widening Sphere: Changing Roles of Victorian Women*, Indiana University Press, Bloomington, 1977.

——, *Suffer and Be Still: Women in the Victorian Age*, Indiana University Press, Bloomington, 1972.

Vrettos, A., *Somatic Fictions: Imagining Illness in Victorian Culture*, Stanford University Press, Stanford, 1995.

Wald, C., *Myth America, Picturing Women 1865–1945*, Random House, New York, 1975.

Walkley, C., *The Way to Wear 'em: 150 Years of Punch on Fashion*, Peter Owen, London, 1985.

Walkley C. and Foster, V., *Crinolines and Crimping Irons, Victorian Clothes: How They Were Cleaned And Cared For*, Peter Owen, London, 1988.

Walkowitz, J., *City of Dreadful Delight: Narratives of Sexual Danger in Late Victorian London*, Virago, London, 1992.

Walters, R. (ed.), *Primers For Prudery: Sexual Advice to Victorian America*, Prentice Hall Inc., New Jersey, 1974.

Walvin, J., *Victorian Values*, André Deutsch, London, 1987.

Warner, M., *Monuments and Maidens: The Allegory of the Female Form*, Picador, London, 1987.

Waugh, N., *Corsets and Crinolines*, B.T. Batsford, London, 1954.

Waugh, T., *Hard to Imagine: Gay Male Eroticism in Photography and Film from their Beginning to Stonewall*, Columbia University Press, New York, 1996.

Weeks, J., *Sex Politics and Society: The Regulation of Sexuality Since 1800*, Longman Inc., New York, 1981.

White, C., *Women's Magazines 1693–1968*, Joseph, London, 1970.

Whitelaw, L., *The Life and Rebellious Times of Cecily Hamilton: Actress, Writer, Suffragist*, The Women's Press, London, 1990.

Willett, C. and Cunnington, P., *English Women's Clothing in the Nineteenth Century*, William Heinemann Limited, London, 1937.

——, *The History of Underclothes*, Faber & Faber, London, 1951.

——, *Why Women Wear Clothes*, Faber & Faber, London, 1952.

Wills, G. and Midgely, D., *Fashion Marketing: An Anthology of Various Practices and Perspectives*, George Allen & Unwin, London, 1973.

Wilson, E., *Adorned in Dreams: Fashion and Modernity*, Virago Press, London, 1987.

——, *The Sphinx in the City: Urban Life, The Control of Disorder, and Women*, Virago Press, London, 1991.

Wilson, E. and Taylor, L., *Through the Looking Glass: A History of Dress from 1860 to the Present Day*, BBC Books, London, 1989.

Winship, J., *Inside Women's Magazines*, Pandora Press, London, 1987.

Wohl, A.S. (ed.), *The Victorian Family: Structure and Stresses*, Croom Helm, London, 1978.

Worrell, E., *Children's Costume in America 1607–1910*, Charles Scribner's Sons, New York, 1980.

Yeazell, R.B., *Fictions of Modesty: Women and Courtship in the English Novel*, University of Chicago Press, Chicago, 1991.

Young Atherton, J. (ed.), *Across the Years: Jane Bardsley's Outback Letterbook*, Angus and Robertson, Sydney, 1987.

Unpublished Theses

Fischer, G. 'Who Wears the Pants? Women, Dress Reform and Power in Mid-Nineteenth Century United States', unpublished doctoral thesis, Indiana University, 1995.

Gould, T., 'The Shifting Erogenous Zone in Twentieth Century American Women's Daytime Fashion', Master's Thesis, Indiana University, 1987.

Index